The Intellectual Property of Food and Hospitality: From Sybaris' Banquets to NASA's Deep Space Food Challenge

The Intellectual Property of Food and Hospitality: From Sybaris' Banquets to NASA's Deep Space Food Challenge

A Sourcebook

Nuno Pires de Carvalho

Wolters Kluwer

Published by:
Kluwer Law International B.V.
PO Box 316
2400 AH Alphen aan den Rijn
The Netherlands
E-mail: lrs-sales@wolterskluwer.com
Website: www.wolterskluwer.com/en/solutions/kluwerlawinternational

Sold and distributed by:
Wolters Kluwer Legal & Regulatory U.S.
920 Links Avenue
Landisville, PA 17538
United States of America
E-mail: customer.service@wolterskluwer.com

ISBN 978-94-035-1137-5

e-Book: ISBN 978-94-035-1147-4
web-PDF: ISBN 978-94-035-1157-3

for Ana (for ever)
For André, Hugo, and Carolina
For Theo, Felipe, Pedro, Sofia, and Mateo

Table of Contents

List of Figures

Preamble

This book may be seen as a companion to other books that I prepared recently, which speak of the evolution of Intellectual Property as applied to different fields of human trade.[1] Those books include a few discussions on the meaning and functions of intellectual property, but they consist essentially of sources, which show how intellectual property has evolved through the Ages in respect of different subject matters. This book follows the same organization: each paragraph is generally preceded by an introductory note that aims at placing the corresponding text(s) in perspective, with the eventual assistance of illustration(s). This book starts with a chapter on Appropriation of Knowledge, followed by a chapter on Business Identifiers. The reason for giving precedence to the various intellectual property mechanisms for the appropriation of knowledge in the fields of food and hospitality is due to the need to solve a sort of an enigma. Indeed, even if the industry of food has the figure of the cook as its main actor, one does not see many patents issued in their favor to ensure the exclusivity of inventive recipes and dishes. One can see some trade secrets and, more abundantly, copyright claims in association with chefs and their techniques. But no patents.

And yet, a sort of patent, with the permission for some conceptual distortion, is what we see at the very beginning of Chapter 1. In Sybaris, in the sixth century BC, cooks who presented to public banquets new dishes of quality received laurels and were granted one year of exclusivity to sell them to whoever wished to buy them. This particular benefit, which contrasted greatly with the discredit that was at that time accorded to manual professions in general, was due to the fact that the Greeks and the Romans saw cooks as a kind of artists, in the same line as sculptors, poets, and playwrights. The latter had their works examined in public competitions, often produced directly on the stage, when not only the jury but also the public would vote for the best plays. Their authors would be rewarded by the city or by a private patron and would receive permission to have the plays performed publicly on stages.

1. *See* Nuno Pires de Carvalho, From Antiquity to the COVID-19 Pandemic: The Intellectual Property of Medicines and Access to Health—A Sourcebook (Wolters Kluwer, 2021), and The Intellectual Property of Textiles and Fashion: From the Medieval Loom to the New York Fashion Week—A Sourcebook (Wolters Kluwer, 2021).

But this book will show that cooks have understood that the patent system is not designed for entrepreneurs who sell goods or provide services to individual customers. That is why we see patents being granted to manufacturers and sellers of foodstuffs for ass consumption. This has become a reality after the Industrial Revolution, with the emergence of a vast middle class able and eager to consume.

Actually, intellectual property is the result of social change, not in the sense of the change of general beliefs and ways of living, but in the sense of deep changes in the way of doing business. Intellectual property protects the differentiating intangible assets of entrepreneurs, who resort to them to individualize their products and services, as well as themselves, vis-à-vis competitors, in the face of present and prospective clients. Intellectual property changes when the relation of intellectual property holders with their clients and with their rivals changes. Importantly, intellectual property changes as its holders perceive the need to change the ways they capture their knowledge and reputation.

We have seen that in the previous sourcebooks mentioned above. We will see that again in the context of food and hospitality. The first business identifiers appeared when merchants started doing business at a distance and needed to submit themselves to contract liability. Their stamps and signatures were the proof of such liability. This continued through Antiquity but stopped at the nebulous period that followed the fall of the Roman Empire when trade was interrupted, roads fell into decay, and Europe saw itself encircled by the Vikings in the north and the Muslims in the south. During a long period, industry and commerce were confined to the boundaries of the monasteries. Intellectual property was not needed due to the proximity of sellers and buyers and the disappearance of commercial rivalry.

This situation changed profoundly with the Commercial Revolution between the eleventh and the fourteenth centuries. It changed again with the Renaissance and the profound social fractures caused by the expansion of trade into other continents, the introduction of new articles of commerce, such as spices, and the deeply innovative trend introduced by the curious and scientific spirit of Renaissance intellectuals and artists. This association between the evolution of intellectual property and social change may be explored in another book. But what matters now is to call attention to the fact that the evolution of intellectual property as applied to food and hospitality also responds to those deep social changes, namely:

- in the course of the Commercial Revolution, the first rules on trademarks for cooks and other food and hospitality-related professions appeared; in the same period, the first rules on unfair competition were also introduced; and, albeit hesitantly, the growth of cities led to the granting of industrial privileges to lure foreign skilled artisans, who were invited to bring their expertise to the granting city and teach it in exchange for the privilege (the privilege basically consisting of the permission for those artisans to exercise their profession even if they were not enrolled in the local guild);
- with the Renaissance, several phenomena impacted the intellectual property of food and hospitality (as well as the intellectual property for all human businesses); first, the reinvention of the press led to the birth of the industry of

books, which inventive cooks would later use to monetize their knowledge; in the absence of a specific regime to protect such industry, governments resorted to the system with which they had already some experience: industrial privileges; second, increase in trade led to the growth in the use of distinctive signs of various sorts, and increasingly outside the domain of guilds—in other words, trademarks ceased to be mere signs of certification, and became true business identifiers; as European economies grew and trade intensified, we also see in the end of this period (sixteenth and seventeenth centuries) more regulations requiring the central registration of artisans' trademarks, in an effort to ensure publicity and the examination of distinctiveness; and, third, the scientific spirit of the Renaissance promoted continued invention, which led to the increase in the grant of privileges;

- the Industrial Revolution led to the emergence of a vast middle class eager to consume the growing output of industries; in parallel, production surpluses had to find new markets abroad, which led to a tension on the purely territorial protection of intellectual property; these two movements led to modern intellectual property, as we have it today: a branch of law that is based on the growing rivalry between merchants located in different countries, which has given origin to a movement toward international harmonization; the need for such harmonization originated in the international exhibitions of the nineteenth century and the consequent exposure of articles of industry and commerce to the direct contact with competing articles from other parts of the world; and the setting of mechanisms for the granting of global titles of industrial property (trademarks, designs, geographical indications).

Food and hospitality have, however, some particularities that lead to some different dimensions of intellectual property as compared to other areas of business. Hospitality, for example, is basically a matter of services (although, as it will be shown, in the Middle Ages, there was some proximity between cooks and innkeepers, which generated some conflicts regarding the protection of exclusivity in the making and trading of food). Because hospitality is a matter of service, the area of intellectual property applies to it more significantly is that of business identifiers (although, a bit surprisingly, we will see today's patents being granted for some kinds of hospitality services).

Food, however, calls for every variant of IP because of the multiple nature of the human activities that are behind it. We could name designs for cooking devices and shapes given to some dishes, namely pastries, trademarks, trade names, slogans, patents and trade secrets, copyrights for cooking books, and database protection for organized compilations of recipes.

In this book, we will see examples of unfair competition between chefs and their restaurants. To a large extent, as the Secretariat of WIPO has said (*see* §1.18), chefs, as regards their knowledge of the techniques of cooking, are in a situation that is similar to that of doctors and surgeons, who invent new methods of medical treatment and surgery. However, unfair competition between medical doctors is somewhat scandalous, and that is why United States society reacted so strongly when a certain Dr. Pallin, who had invented a surgical method for eye treatment and patented it, threatened colleagues with patent infringement lawsuits.[2]

If you enter a large bookstore, such as Barnes and Noble, on 5th Avenue, in Manhattan, New York, or Hodges Figgis, on Dawson Street, Dublin, Ireland, you will certainly not miss noticing the large number of shelves dedicated to cooking books, of all kinds, tastes, and origins, some authored by famous chefs whose faces you will recognize from TV shows. Very probably, the first efforts of Human creativity have started with determining ways of finding food and how to prepare it. The huge number of books dedicated to that field of technology (and, to a great extent, of art) that you find in those two bookstores speaks to that. But it speaks to more than that. Actually, it also speaks to the initiatives by food creators and enthusiasts of capturing from readers—i.e., from consumers, from the market—the rewards for useful their work.

However, in stark contrast, patent databases do not show as many titles granted for exercise of inventiveness in the field of cooking as those thousands of culinary books. A quick visit to the European Patent Organization (EPO) statistical database confirms this elementary—and yet shocking to some extent—reality. Considering that the act of cooking attends to one of the most basic necessities of human beings, one could expect that the constant exercise of inventiveness in that crucially important field would correspond to a proportionally high number of patent applications. Under the International Patent Classification (IPC), which is administered by WIPO, the preparation of food falls under classes A21 to A23 in the sector that corresponds to Human Necessities. The simple name of that Section could lead us to believe that patent offices are overwhelmed with patent applications concerning new and inventive soups, sauces, flavor enhancers, and recipes in general. And yet, that is not true. The analysis provided by the EPO concerning patent applications filed with the Office in all technical fields does not even show food preparations as an independent field of technology. It simply refers to *food chemistry*, which goes much beyond the traditional area of chefs' and cooks' exercise of their creativity. Announcing a series of lectures on food technology, the EPO website says:

> Patents play an important role in many technical fields, and food technology is no exception. Some of the foundation stones of biochemistry were laid by bakers and brewers. Today, research into more sustainable production and processing, meat substitutes, foods with lower sugar and salt, and foods with better nutritional value or greater longevity, is booming. This advanced lecture series will provide participants with insights into the innovations shaping the food industry of the future, and reveal how IP strategy can lead to success.[3]

But even this field does not seem to lure a great number of inventors. In 2022, out of a total of 193,460 patent applications filed with the EPO on all fields, only 1,985 applications corresponded to food chemistry—i.e., 1,02 %.[4] Compared to the number

2. *See* Nuno Pires de Carvalho, From Antiquity to the COVID-19 Pandemic, *supra* note 1, at 300 et seq.
3. *See* legacy.epo.org/app/service/ipcal/i_event.php?id = 14032&isPopup = 1&id = 14032&isPopup = 1.
4. *See* report-archive.epo.org/about-us/annual-reports-statistics/statistics/2022/statistics/patent-applications.html#tab3.

of applications filed in the fields of digital communication (16,705), computer technology (15,193), or medical technology (15,683), the number of patent applications for food chemistry is quite dismal. And yet, this figure, as dismal as it may be, is obviously inflated because, as noted above, most of the applications that appear in that category cover inventions made by the chemical industry and for the chemical industry, not by chefs or cooks to be directly used in restaurants.

It is worth noticing that almost all the privileges (109) granted by the Republic of Venice between 1475 and 1550 concerned mechanical inventions, mills and devices to dig canals appearing as the most frequent. Only one covered a method of preparing food.[5] In the same token, no patent concerning the preparation of food appears in a list of patents granted in Germany between 1531 and 1700 (a total of 111 patents).[6]

Actually, when it comes to cooking methods (i.e., the special methods created by skilled, inventive cooks), we need to distinguish between those methods that lead to the making of mass-consumption foodstuffs, such as those commercialized by companies likeHeinz, Nestlé and Unilever, and those that consist of preparing meals for a few persons, such as in a restaurant. The last situation refers to something that is inherently dependent on the individual skills of the chef in question. In that regard, as WIPO has said in a document (*see* §1.47), there is similarity between chefs who prepare meals and medical doctors who administer medical and surgical methods: neither need patents to extract revenue. But, of course, there is also a conceptual difference between the two sorts of creations: while nobody would be shocked if a chef filed for and obtained a patent concerning a particular method of cooking, many people have great reluctance, on moral grounds, to the patenting of medical and surgical methods. This is the reason that the TRIPS Agreement permits WTO Members to exclude those methods from patentability.

Generally, society does not pay to IP as applied to food in spite of its vital importance for human living and health, the same attention it pays to IP as applied to health. Nevertheless, in this book, some examples of a certain discomfort with IP in the area of food will be shown. For example, there have been ethical concerns with the use given to the patent rights on the method of increasing the contents of vitamin D in certain foodstuffs (*see* §1.44), and there are restrictions on the misleading use of distinctive signs for certain formulae for babies (§2.22). For a certain period, coinciding with the time when a significant number of countries excluded medicines from patentability, a number of countries also excluded foodstuffs from patentability (§1.45). More recently, this initiative was reintroduced in countries like India and Brazil, but it was abandoned subsequently.

To conclude this Preamble, I would like to emphasize the association between food and fashion. About this connection, Braudel wrote:

5. Giulio Mandich, *Venetian Patents (1450-1550)*, 30 Journal of the Patent Office Society 166, 219 (March 1948).
6. *See* Hansjoerg Pohlmann, *The Inventor's Right in Early German Law—Materials of the time from 1531 to 1700*, 43 JPOS 121 (1961).

> In fact, fashion governs cooking like clothing. Famous sauces fall into disrepute one day and after that elicit nothing but condescending smiles.[7]

The very term "Restaurant," for example, is a product of fashion, as a French historian explains:

> Boulanger, a maître d'hôtel who thrived around 1766 and who was not a fool (there are hardly any in the profession), imagined, to attract the attention of onlookers, to write on his signboard, in distorting for its benefit a verse from the Bible: "Come to me, all you who hunger, and I will restore you. *Venite ad me, omnes qui stomacho laboratis, et ego restaurabo vos.*" It was a way like any other to accommodate the remains of the Gospel. His play on words was first successful, then his cooking. Sometimes little is enough, in Paris, to create fashion. Those caterers who, contrary to the old custom, kept open tables at their establishments, like Boulanger, seized the title of restaurateur that was given to him. The modern restaurant was founded.[8]

Fashion, as it corresponds to current trends in the consumption of goods, dictates the preferences of consumers as regards food. But for cooks and chefs, fashion may dictate their success or failure. Recently, fashion houses in the area of clothing have also joined the crowded business world of restaurants and hotels. A question, thus, follows: will the way that IP applies to food and hospitality be impacted by the intervention of art and fashion, given that these two fields have their own peculiarities as to the protection of the respective intangible differentiating assets?

At this point, with the reader's indulgence, I borrow the last paragraphs of the Preamble I prepared for the sourcebook THE INTELLECTUAL PROPERTY OF FOOD AND FASHION,[9] with a few changes.

Before I give a voice to those who have made (and continue making) the intellectual property of food and hospitality, three preliminary editorial notes are in order.

First, the sources are particularly focused on France, the United Kingdom (indifferently designated in the book as Britain or Great Britain, even if that is not correct) and the United States. The reason is the same as indicated in the Preamble to FROM BABYLON TO THE SILICON VALLEY:[10] the first two countries were the greatest European powers for many centuries and were also the first to foster a legal environment that supported competition and rivalry in trade and industry (although, for a long period, framed by the corporatist regime), and thus molded and influenced the way intellectual property developed. The United States took the same role after the nineteenth century, when, moved by its people's innate entrepreneurial spirit and respect for private property, it redesigned intellectual property—and especially patent

7. Fernand Braudel, THE STRUCTURES OF EVERYDAY LIFE—THE LIMITS OF THE POSSIBLE, CIVILIZATION AND CAPITALISM 15TH-18TH CENTURY, at 189 (Univ. of Cal. Press, 1992).
8. Jules Forni, *Origines et Histoire de la Corporation des Restaurateurs et Limonadiers de Paris, Discours prononcé au banquet du 20 avril 1886*, at 11 (Librairie des Bibliophiles, 1886). *Source*: gallica.bnf.fr.
9. *See supra* note 1, at xxiv-xxxv.
10. From BABYLON TO THE SILICON VALLEY: THE ORIGINS AND EVOLUTION OF INTELLECTUAL PROPERTY—A SOURCEBOOK (Wolters Kluwer, 2020).

law—and fitted it to serve its industrial development. Another country will be cited several times in this book: Brazil. Brazil does not have the economic and political dimension that could make it a *maker* of intellectual property policies—instead, it is and has been a *taker* of intellectual property policies. Nevertheless, Brazil, at the beginning of its life as an independent country, was a pioneer in the field of patents, and thus, it has some interesting stories to tell about the intellectual property of food.

Second, many of the sources in this book have been translated. When the translations are not mine, translators' names are provided in the Credits section. But because a majority of those are indeed mine (with, in some cases, the assistance of Google Translation—an increasingly superb tool), a word of caution is appropriate: given that translation is (re)creation, eventual inaccuracies in those translations are entirely my fault. I only hope there are not too many.

Finally, the selection of sources is exactly that: a selection. The criteria for choosing one special document and not another were exclusively dictated by my belief that the former could be more illustrative of the way intellectual property has developed in association with food and hospitality than the latter. Moreover, as a selection, the collection of sources is not, nor is it intended to be, exhaustive. My choice focused on those sources that appeared to me as being of more relevance, as stones in a road's pavement. I did not include all the stones, but just those that, as I view them, are sufficient to permit one's walk the road without having to jump over deep gaps. This book has been structured in accordance with the same design as the previous sourcebooks mentioned above.

In the last years, the belief that many of the current debates on intellectual property are mere repetitions of discussions maintained by the generations that preceded ours has grown in me, along with the idea that it might be useful to learn how arguments and counterarguments have been absorbed or discarded by the laws. This puts things in perspective, which is always useful. More importantly, as already said, intellectual property evolves in coordination or in conformity with those social changes that have an impact on the way society engages in business activities. Another line of research and thought that has grown within me is related to the intellectual property of the humble—the intellectual property of individual creators, and entrepreneurs, the artisans. In this book, as in the previous ones, several moments in which the humble appear as holders and users of intellectual property are reflected, which increases the significance of this branch of law in our daily lives.

This book includes a few pictures and drawings that illustrate some aspects of the peculiarities of intellectual property as applied to food and hospitality. The reason for that is easy to explain: a picture is worth one thousand words, as the saying goes. Well, frequently, it is worth more than one thousand words.

To me—and, I hope, to the reader too—these texts are not just literary expressions of frequently conflicting interests in the trade of food and hospitality but also, and mainly, expressions of human beings trying to make a living from their work. It is true that not all those human beings have pursued their interests in an honest manner, but that is life—and that makes the analysis from an intellectual property perspective even more appropriate because imposing honesty in trade is, after all, the ultimate goal of this branch of law.

I cannot close the presentation of this book without thanking my wife, Ana, for her care and her almost infinite patience while I went (again) through a lot of reading, searching, browsing, and looking for expressions of intellectual property in association with food and hospitality. Through this journey, Ana has been by my side, always interested in listening to the fascinating stories I found in some of the selected sources. Ana is a fantastic cook, and inventor and improver of some dishes, like her cod with cream, which she has prepared and served in Christmas suppers to the family (to us two, first, then to us and the children, and then to us, to the children, and to the grandchildren) for almost 50 years—recipe and technique which, incidentally, she has never kept secret, but instead has shared with her relatives and friends. This book is a tribute to her cooking art and technique. But more than her knowledge, patience, care, and suggestions, this book has greatly benefited from her companionship and love.

Dublin, Ireland, December 13, 2023

CHAPTER 1

Appropriation of Knowledge

§1.1 IN ANCIENT GREECE AND ROME, COOKS WERE THE BENEFICIARIES OF THE FIRST INCENTIVES TO INVENT AS WELL AS OF ATTEMPTS TO ENSURE THE PRIVATE APPROPRIATION OF KNOWLEDGE—SIXTH CENTURY BC ONWARD

Athenaeus of Naucratis (end of the second, beginning of the third century AD), in his BANQUET OF THE LEARNED, *quoting from Phylarcus, a Greek historian of the third century BC, puts in the mouth of a banquet participant a description of the luxurious habits of the Sybarites and implies the great prestige that cooks who catered to public banquets had in that city. Sybaris was a Greek colony located in the Gulf of Taranto, south of Italy. It was founded in 720 BC and destroyed by a neighboring city, Kroton, around three centuries later. Sybaris was a very wealthy colony due to its productive agriculture and strategic geographic location. A great part of its revenue came from tolls the city charged on merchant ships that navigated through the safer waters across. The statute of Sybaris mentioned by Athenaeus had a very specific purpose of promoting the creation of new and especially tasty dishes in the context of public banquets, which played a very important role in culture and religion.*

The fact that the first known rule concerning the private appropriation of knowledge concerned cooks rather than other artisans was not casual. In both Classical Greece and Rome, cooks were compared to artists, such as poets and playwrights, who would gain the right to have their works performed publicly in public contests.[11] *Such parallel would not disappear even in Rome, when most cooks would be slaves imported*

11. Athenaeus of Naucratis, the same historian where we find the source for the Sybaris law granting the one-year exclusive right for certain cooks to produce and sell dishes of their invention, quoted a playwright making that same comparison: "Thus spoke the king to the admiring guests: / 'A cook is quite as useful as a poet, / And quite as wise, and these anchovies show it.'" Athenaeus, THE DEIPNOSOPHISTS OR BANQUET OF THE LEARNED, translated by C.D. Yonge, vol. 1, at 11 (Henry G. Bohn, 1854). *Source*: archive.org.

from Greece. By contrast with cooks, other artisans were seen with social disdain in spite of their utility.

According to Athenaeus of Naucratis, a Greek rhetorician and grammarian (second-third centuries AD), cooks were also held either as philosophers or as heralds, and in some Greek cities, they were in charge of offering sacrifices—a sort of religious profession. Another playwright quoted by Athenaeus, Sosipater, puts in the mouth of a cook from Syracuse the information that cooks used to learn about astronomy and architecture.[12]

Writing about banquets held in the wealthy Greek colony of Sybaris, Athenaeus affirmed that during those banquets, competitions for cooks were held. The prizes granted to those cooks who invented new and tasty recipes, besides the same laurel crowns that were accorded to winning artists and athletes, consisted of granting them the right of exclusively making and selling those dishes for one year. Thus, as far as Sybarite cooks were concerned, public banquets had the same function as stages for poets and playwrights, where they competed for the right of having their works performed. Athenaeus implied that each dish presented by cooks at the banquets was submitted to some sort of examination as to its peculiarity (i.e., novelty and inventiveness) and excellency (which we could grosso modo *associate with utility).*

Rewarding inventive cooks became, it seems, a common practice in Classical Antiquity. But, the importance of Sybaris precedent as an intellectual property statute should not be underestimated. In fact, Sybaris statute, instead of according to inventive cooks some specific prize, gave them an exclusive right, which empowered them to go to the market to look for the reward. The market, i.e., the sum of the purchasers of those cook's products, was therefore in charge of rewarding—or not—the inventors for the quality of their work. In another passage of his book, Athenaeus quotes from Clearchus the Solensian, who wrote that the kings of the Medes (an ancient Iranian people, later conquered by the Persians) used to reward those cooks who came up with new and delicious recipes, but, unlike the Sybarites, they would keep the consumption of those recipes for them exclusively. This means that, by contrast with Sybaris, the inventors were rewarded by the kings, not by consumers.

In Rome, cooks, by contrast with other manual workers, were also treated with great consideration, like artists. Livy (Titus Livius, 59 BC—17 AD), a Roman historian, in his History of Rome, said the following about cooks:

> *Indeed, it was the army of Asia which introduced into Rome the taste for oriental luxury; it was its leaders who were the first to bring beds decorated with bronze, precious carpets, veils and other loose fabrics, and, what was considered at the time as the complement of magnificent furniture, dining tables with a single foot and sideboards. Soon the musicians, the harpists, the games of the jugglers came to add to the luxury of the feasts; and the meals themselves required more research, and involved more expense. Soon the cook, formerly the vilest slave, of the lowest value and least utility, became of great value; and, what was at first just a profession, was considered an art. However, these sumptuous things, which we saw then, were hardly the germ of the luxury to come.*

12. The same association between cookery and architecture would be proposed some twenty centuries later by Marie-Antoine Carême, the famous nineteenth century French chef. *See infra* §1.26.

Another Roman writer, Pliny the Elder, reported on a proposal by Marcus Gavius Apicius, well-known gourmet and author of a famous cooking book—De Re Coquinaria—on the establishment of a prize for those who invented new manners of preparing the garum, *a sauce made of the liver of rougets (a fish from the Mediterranean). Apicius lived in the first century AD during the reign of Tiberius.*

In another passage of his Natural History, Pliny wrote about a great inventor, Sergius Orata, who became rich by selling one of his inventions, the suspended bath. According to Pliny, Orata also proposed the organization of a competition for the invention of a new sauce.

§1.1.1 Athenaeus of Naucratis Mentions the Prizes Granted in Sybaris to Inventive Cooks Who Serve New and Most Exquisite Dishes at Public Banquets: Crowns and One-Year Exclusive Rights for Making and Selling the Dishes They Have Invented

[The Sybarites] also celebrate in public numbers of feasts; and they honour those who display great magnificence on such occasions with golden crowns, and they proclaim their names at the public sacrifices and games; announcing not only their general goodwill towards the city, but also the great magnificence which they had displayed in the feasts. And on these occasions they even crown those cooks who have served up the most exquisite dishes... .

And if any confectioner or cook invented any peculiar and excellent dish, no other artist was allowed to make this for a year; but he alone who invented it was entitled to all the profit to be derived from the manufacture of it for that time; in order that others might be induced to labour at excelling in such pursuits... .

§1.1.2 Athenaeus Mentions the Honors Granted by the King of the Medes to His Inventive Cooks

9. But Clearchus the Sonsian, in the fourth book of his Lives, ... having previously spoken about the luxury of the Medes ... a little further on says—"And accordingly. while he gave to all those who could invent him any new kind of food, a prize for their invention, he did not, while loading them with honours, allow the food which they had invented to be set before them, but enjoyed it all by himself, and thought this was the greatest wisdom. For this, I imagine, is what is called the brains of Jupiter and of a king at the same time."

§1.1.3 Chiromenes Wins a Competition in Athens for His Recipe of Truffles—470 BC

Around the year 470 BC, the bigwigs of finance, those who lived with exuberance, and renowned gourmands of the capital of Attica formed a Society for the encouragement and development of the culinary industry. The statutes provided, among other norms, that a prize of several hundred drachmas was established in order to reward the tastiest method for cooking quails, grasshopper and cockchafer bellies, green lizard linings and squirrel ears.

An incalculable number of candidates entered the competition. The commission appointed for this purpose had the competitors working before their eyes in front of furnaces installed in the public square; they only distributed prizes and rewards after tasting the materials prepared in front of them on site.

But the great gastronomic question debated among the Athenians was that of truffles. It was decided that there was no better way to reward the inventor of a good method for cooking this succulent tuber than by granting him the right of citizenship.

A certain Chiromenes won the prize. His method consisted of this: "to involve the truffles coated with pork bacon from Thessaly, with garlic, dry spices, honey and dry raisins, in a short crust pastry pie; sprinkle everything with Corinthian white wine, and stew it for a good hour."

We believe that gourmets today would hardly be in favor of such a method, but would our fine Parisian forks combine their fortunes to found a prize intended to remunerate the inventor of a new culinary preparation of truffles?

§1.1.4 Pliny the Elder (First Century AD) Refers to Several Proposals on Prizes for Inventive Cooks and Refers to Their Monetary Value (as Slaves)

Book IX Chapter XXX (The various kinds of mullets, and the sargus that attends them).

M. Apicius, a man who displayed a remarkable degree of ingenuity in everything related to luxury, was of opinion that it was a most excellent plan to let the mullet die in the pickle—known as the 'garum of the allies'—for we find that even this has found a surname—and he proposed a prize for anyone who should invent a new sauce, made of the liver of this fish. I find it much easier to relate this fact, than to state how it was that gained the prize.

Chapter XXXI (The enormous prices of some fish)

Asinius Celar, a man of consular rank, and remarkable for his prodigious expenditure on this fish, bought one at Rome, during the reign of Caius, at the price of eight thousand sesterces. A reflection upon such a fact as this [the very high price of a fish] will at once lead us to turn our thoughts to those who, making loud complaints against luxury, have lamented that a single cook costs more money to buy than a horse; while at the present day, a cook is only to be obtained for the same sum that a triumph would cost, and a fish is only to be purchased at what was formerly the price for a cook! Indeed, there is hardly any living being held in higher esteem than the man who understands how, in the most scientific fashion, to get rid of his master's property.

Chapter LXXIX (The first person that formed oyster-beds).

The first person who formed artificial oyster-beds was Sergius Orata, who established them at Baiae, in the time of L. Crassus, the orator, just before the Marsic War. This was done by him, not for the gratification of gluttony, but of avarice, as he contrived to make a large income by this exercise of his ingenuity. He was the first, too, to invent hanging baths, and after buying villas and trimming them up, he would every now and then sell them again.

Book X Chapter 27 (Who first taught to use the liver of the goose for food)

Our people [the Romans], however, are wiser; for they only esteem the goose for the goodness of its liver. When they are crammed, this grows to a very large size, and on being taken from the animal, is made still larger by being soaked in honeyed milk. And, indeed, it is not without good reason that it is matter of debate who it was that first discovered so great a delicacy; whether, in fact, it was Scipio Metellus, a man of consular dignity, or M. Seius, a contemporary of his, and a Roman of equestrian rank. However, a thing about which there is no dispute, it was Messalinus Cotta, the son of the orator Messala, who first discovered the art of roasting the webbed feet of the goose, and of cooking them in a ragout with cocks' combs: for I shall faithfully award each culinary palm to such as I shall find deserving of it.

Figure 1.1 A banquet in Ancient Greece, as depicted in part of the fourth frieze, which surmounts the cella of the Nereid Monument, a tomb found at Xanthos (Lycia, Southwestern Turkey), about 380 BC, on display at the British Museum.

§1.2 THE BY-LAWS OF THE CORPORATION OF COOKS OF PARIS INCLUDED TWO RULES AGAINST UNFAIR COMPETITION—1270-1300

*The notion of fairness in competition is inherent to intellectual property, and one of its earliest expressions can be found in the by-laws of the first corporations organized in France, whose texts were collected and published by Étienne Boileau (*Le Livre des Métiers de Paris*), provost of Paris under King Louis XI (thirteenth century). The by-laws of the guild of cooks (*cuisiniers*) of Paris included three clauses against unfair trade practices.*

The first two clauses concerned what today we could designate as unlawful (or tortious) interference in contracts. Those two clauses were repeated in subsequent by-laws (we will see an example dated of 1509[13]*), and that one that specifically dealt with* débauchage *(the prohibition against hiring an employee or apprentice who is at the service of a competitor) is still found in today's labor and IP laws. The purpose of that*

13. *See infra* §1.5.

rule was not only to avoid disturbing the work of a competitor's shop but also to prevent the employee or apprentice from delivering confidential information acquired in the previous job to the new employer. As said somewhere else, the Code of Hammurabi, in the chapter dealing with family law, had a similar provision[14]*—eventually, the first written norm on IP ever adopted.*

*The third clause, against the misleading disparagement of a competitor's goods, appears in the second proviso of paragraph 3 of Article 10*bis *of the Paris Convention, and as such, it is a mandatory rule in its 179 Contracting Parties.*

TITLE LXIX.

Of Cooks.

These are the by-laws of the trade of the roasters of the city of Paris. Firstly, that all those who want to have a table or window to sell food, know how to prepare all manner of meats common and profitable to the people to whom they sell it... .

Item, that if a master has hired an assistant [apprentice], that another master shall not extract, receive, or hire [that assistant] from him until he has served his term, and unless it be with the consent of him to whom he was hired, on penalty of x. s., namely vi. s. to the King, and iiii s. to the masters.

Item, that if any person is in front of a cook's table or window for selling or buying from the mentioned cooks, that if any of the other cooks calls such person before [he or she] leaves the table or window of his own free will, that he be fined in v s., iii s. to the King and ii the said masters.

Item, that no one blames the meat of the other, if it is good, on penalty of a fine of v s.

§1.3 A CONTRACT OF APPRENTICESHIP CONTAINING A SECRECY CLAUSE, ENGLAND—APRIL 1, 1459

Very rarely, the by-laws of medieval guilds contained clauses on the mandatory protection of the secrets of the trade. The probable reason was that those by-laws were mainly addressed to the masters, who did not need to be reminded of the importance of keeping the secrets to themselves. However, when hiring the services of apprentices, some masters would be careful in including a clause requiring the apprentices to keep the secrets they would receive in the course of their training. The text that follows is an example of one of such clauses adopted in the context of food.

This indenture made between John Gibbs of Penzance in the county of Cornwall of the one part and John Goffe, Spaniard, of the other part, witnesses that the aforesaid John Goffe has put himself to the aforesaid John Gibbs to learn the craft of fishing, and to stay with him as apprentice and to serve from the feast of Philip and James next to come after the date of these presents until the end of eight years then next ensuing and fully complete; throughout which term the aforesaid John Goffe shall well and

14. *See infra* note 22.

faithfully serve the aforesaid John Gibbs and Agnes his wife as his masters and lords, shall keep their secrets, shall everywhere willingly do their lawful and honourable commands, shall do his masters no injury nor see injury done to them by others, but prevent the same as far as he can, shall not waste his master's goods nor lend them to any man without his special command. And the aforesaid John Gibbs and Agnes his wife shall teach, train and inform or cause the aforesaid John Goffe, their apprentice, to be informed in the craft of fishing in the best way they know, chastising him duly and finding for the same John, their apprentice, food, clothing linen and woollen, and shoes, sufficiently, as befits such an apprentice to be found, during the term aforesaid. And at the end of the term aforesaid the aforesaid John Goffe shall have of the aforesaid John Gibbs and Agnes his wife 20s. sterling without any fraud. In witness whereof the parties aforesaid have interchangeably set their seals to the parts of this indenture. These witnesses: Richard Bascawen, Robert Martyn and Robert Cosyn and many others. Given at Penzance, 1 April in the 37th year of the reign of King Henry the Sixth after the Conquest of England.

§1.4 PRIVILEGE GRANTED BY ISABEL OF SPAIN, IN 1478, TO HER PHYSICIAN, PEDRO AZLOR—FEBRUARY 24, 1478

As explained in the Preamble, the examples of private appropriation of knowledge by inventive cooks are not abundant, even if such an appropriation, in a form that evoked current patents, appears as one of the first expressions of intellectual property in Sybaris in the sixth century BC. By contrast, examples of privileges concerning machinery and devices for the production and cooking of food, such as furnaces and mills, were relatively abundant. This has to do, as explained, with the specific nature of the inventions in question and the ways available to inventors to extract revenue from their commercialization. Naturally, patents for mills and furnaces are much more effective for obtaining rents than for cookeries and specific dishes that, in early times, would not be commercialized to the masses.

With the practice of industrial privileges consolidated and spread throughout Europe, in the fifteenth century, each country would add its own idiosyncrasies and specificities to the mechanism. This privilege granted by Queen Isabel of Spain to her physician acknowledges that the invention to be protected did not exist yet—it was just a promise. Eventually, the technique to be used by the grantee did not concern a genuine invention in strict terms but rather a known technique with some improvements.

That the privilege was granted to someone who belonged to the inner circle of the Queen's relations might be an expression (found in many other industrial privileges) of explicit favoritism.

Lady Isabel, by the grace of God, Queen of Castilla, of León, of Toledo, of Sicily, of Portugal, of Galicia, of Sevilla, of Córdova, of Murcia, of Jahen, of the Algarves, of Algeziras, of Gibraltar, princess of Aragón and Lady of Viscaya and of Molina.

To the infants, dukes, marquises, counts, elected, masters of the orders, priors, commanders and sub-commanders, mayors of the castles and strong and flat houses and rich men and to the councils and councilors, assistants, mayors, magistrates, civil servants, twenty-fours,[15] squires and officers and good men of the very loyal city of Seville, as well as of the other cities, villages and places of my Realms and Ladyships and to any other of my vassals and subjects and to each and any of you to whom this letter of mine or its transcription signed by a public notary will be shown.

Health and grace: Know that Dr. Pedro Azlor, my physician, has informed me that he wanted to invent and make in my Realms and Ladyships new buildings of mills and grinds for grinding bread, which he says will result in great benefit and utility of the public affairs of my Realms and Ladyships, and that he fears and dreads that, after having invented and shown the said grindings, some people seeing his industry and care that he in them has, soon will want to make the same things in the manner that he had done them, being the first that to these Realms of mine brought and created them. And having spent many costs of maravedís in this and in its working and inventing, trusting to take advantage of his knowledge, and that if another person were to take his invention, he would lose all his work and could not extract from it the costs that he would put in it. Who, if it so happened, says he would receive great injury and damage, because he has worked and spent his time in building and will incur in expenses in it, for which cause he begged me and asked for mercy on him, provided him with the order that within a certain period no one would dare to make or build grinds according to the new manner he had built it about the said grinds for grinding bread, of water as of men, or the force of beasts or of the wind, in the new manner that he had invented it, and begged me that I granted him in respect of it. And I have agreed, thus I command you that since the day that said Pedro Azlor builds or shows the shape of the said grinds of his new manner, during the next first twenty years, do not consent nor permit that any people dare to make or make grinds or mills in such a manner that the said Pedro Azlor makes. And allow and consent that he makes and builds in any proper place of my Realms and Ladyships any mills and grinds that he wants to make, provided that it does not cause harm or damage to any other. And during this period, that [in respect of the above-mentioned invention] or part of it do not impose nor consent to impose obstacles or any difficulty. And if other people want to make it, that you, judges, do not only refuse your consent or approval, but also destroy it. And the twenty thousand maravedís for the said doctor, it will be levied in such a manner that no cost remains from it during the said term of twenty years as from the day the said doctor Pedro Azlor starts discovering the art of the buildings of the said grinds or erecting them in a way that he can use the said devices for twenty years, as it is said. And do not prevaricate, under penalty of my grace and of thirty thousand maravedís for the city hall.

Given in the very noble and loyal city of Sevilla on the twenty-fourth day of February, year of the birth of our Lord Savior Jesus Christ of one thousand four hundred and seventy-eight years. I, the Queen, had made it written by order ... (Signed).

15. Twenty-four was the name given to certain civil servants in a number of Spanish municipalities.

§1.5 TWO UNFAIR COMPETITION-RELATED RULES INCLUDED IN THE BY-LAWS OF THE GUILD OF MASTER COOKS OF PARIS—MARCH 1509

As already noted (see §1.2), the provisions of the thirteenth-century by-laws of the guild of cooks of Paris concerning unfair competition would resist the passage of time. Three centuries later, similar rules were repeated in a similar statute.

[Patent] Letters on the statutes of the master roasters of Paris. Paris, March 1509.

(13) *Item.* If any person is in front of the workshop and window of the said master roasters, for the sale or the purchase of the said meat, that no other master may call [such person], before he has left the said workshop and window of his own free will, and this on the penalty of five sols parisis, three sols to the king, and two sols parisis to the said master jurors.

(14) *Item.* That no one should blame the meat on each other if it is fair and good, on the penalty of a fine of five Parisian sols.

§1.6 PATENTS COVERING METHODS OF PREPARING FOOD UNDER THE STATUTE OF VENICE OF 1474

The two historians—Giulio Mandich and Roberto Berviglieri—who have examined in detail the privileges granted both to national and foreign inventors under the Statute of Venice of 1474 could find only two privileges that directly concerned the preparation of food and its ingredients. As it happened in other countries, the Senate of Venice granted several privileges on mills and other devices but only two on foodstuffs. This contrast confirms that inventive cooks have never been enthusiastic about using the patent system to ensure the extraction of revenue from their dishes.

Interestingly, the privilege reported by Berviglieri did not grant exclusivity in the making and selling of the foodstuff but a monetary reward. The reason was that the inventor refused to disclose his alleged invention—and for that same reason, the privilege may have been canceled. In Berviglieri's view, the inventor's reluctance in disclosing his invention was due to the abundance of the matter used in preparing the foodstuff whose invention he claimed, which might have been chestnut flour—a fruit available throughout the State of Venice during the Autumn and Winter seasons. But no more details have been found in the Archive of the Senate.

§1.6.1 A Privilege of 1540 Concerning the Preparation of Dough for Bread

1540, July 20 (S[enato] T[erra] r[eg]. 31 p. 36 r.) Giovanni Antonio Bianchini, called the clockmaker, wants a 50-year patent for his "new mode of kneading dough for bread." Granted by the Senate for 30 years.

§1.6.2 Privilege Granted to Filippo Ruher, a German Citizen, on September 20, 1606, and Renewed on April 7, 1607, for a Secret Foodstuff

The German citizen Filippo Ruher, on July 30, 1606 addressed a petition to the Doge, informing him that he had invented a sort of foodstuff made with some substance that was very abundant in the State of Venice. His invention was very nutritious and easily preserved for long periods (for 15, 20, 30 and more years, as he alleged) and could be used to feed the army with savings of at least one third (as compared to common bread). The inventor, who resided in Venice with his wife and two sons, asked for the payment by the State of 30 ducats per month for his and his two children's lives.

Based on favorable reports by various bodies of the government, issued on the condition that the inventor's claims as to the utility of his invention were truthful, and that the (unknown) substance "was not made of rice, pumpkin or any other similar sort of matter," the Senate granted to Phillip Ruher a privilege for his and his children's lives of twenty ducats a month for his and his children's lives. The privilege was granted on the condition that the inventor disclosed his invention within eight days after the grant.

But it seems that Ruher has failed to comply and that, consequently, the privilege has been canceled. Several months later, in March of 1607, the inventor submitted a request for a new privilege for the protection of his "very unique secret." One month later the Senate renewed the privilege to Ruher, but on the same condition of, within fifteen days from the grant, disclosing "his secret about the material which will be found in abundance throughout the State, healthy to eat and which will cost half the price of the wheat and with which it will be possible to feed vast quantities of people with savings of at least one third of public money."

§1.7 A SPANISH INVENTOR OBTAINS A PATENT FOR THE SECRET INVENTION OF PRESERVING SNOW—NOVEMBER 2, 1549

This invention is described by the Spanish historian Nicolás García Tapía in his remarkable book PATENTES DE INVENCIÓN ESPAÑOLAS EN EL SIGLO DE ORO. *The use of ice with the purpose not only of refreshing beverages but also of preserving food has been known since Antiquity. One of the most common methods for avoiding the melting of ice was to keep the snow collected during winter in wells, the walls of which were carefully coated with insulating materials, such as cork. The invention mentioned by Tapía has not been described, and thus, its manner of operating is unknown. Tapía suggests that the invention might consist of keeping the snow where it fell without the need to move it to wells. The text that follows is a citation of Tapía's text.*

The system for conserving the snow that had fallen in winter, in order to be available for use in summer, was to leave it in some deep wells dug in the ground, for which a simple construction was built, topped with a slate or a tile. It was what was called the "snow well," which some villages or in particular important convents or palaces used to share. With this same purpose of conserving the snow, Jerónimo Ruiz, from the village of Auñon, obtained a patent on November 2, 1549, for a "a certain secret to preserve the snow where and in the parts where it falls when it snows, so that it can serve and be useful in summer." [note omitted] This means that, apparently, it was no longer necessary to move the snow to the well, but rather it was kept in the proper place where it fell. We have no news of the system or if this curious invention has been put into practice. The patent was granted in Cigales (Valladolid), by the then Regent Maximilian of Austria.

§1.8 QUEENS MARY I AND ELIZABETH I OF ENGLAND GRANT TWO PATENTS FOR DEVICES USED FOR MAKING BEER AND MILLING CORN—1557 AND 1559

The first of the following privileges was granted to a German inventor and consisted of a five-year exclusivity. The main utility that was claimed was the saving of firewood, which was an advantage often invoked by inventors of new furnaces in an era in which firewood was one of the main sources of energy employed in domestic and industrial appliances.

The second privilege concerned an imported mill for grinding corn that was imported into the UK. The patent letters reflect the claim that the inventor had spent significant efforts in inventing the device. So, this was not a privilege for simply importing but an acknowledgment of the invention.

These privileges were granted seven decades before the Statute of Monopolies was introduced in 1623.

§1.8.1 Privilege to John Herdegen for His Invention of Furnaces for Seething Vessels in Pans or Kettles Used in the Making of Beer and Other Substances (Soaps, Dyes, Etc.)—November 26, 1557

Whereas John Herdegen, Almain, citizen of Norrenberghe, has by his great travail attained unto such knowledge of a new fashion of making all sorts of furnaces meet for seething vessels in pans or kettles of beer brewers, ale brewers, dyers, soap makers, salt seethers and other like, not heretofore used in the realm, as may serve for the well-doing of the premises with much less firewood than is presently expended:

> In consideration of the favour that should be given to the first finders of anything profitable for the commonwealth and of the commodity that may grow to those using the said crafts in the great scarcity of firewood.

Protection to Herdegen and grant that he, his servants, factors, etc., English and strangers, and no others for 5 years from the present date make or cause to be made within the realm of England or Ireland all sorts of new kinds or fashions for seething vessels, kettles, pans, leads or coppers for the purposes aforesaid and to sell and distribute the same; and no other person shall make furnaces for seething vessels of the new fashion under pain of imprisonment; offenders are to remain in ward without bail until they have made fine to the crown for their contempt and reasonable recompense to Herdegen.

§1.8.2 Privilege to William de Berger for Importing the Corn Mills He Invented—October 26, 1559

Licence for seven years for William de Berger, stranger, born in Utright [Utrecht] beyond the seas, to make and sell a form of corn mill brought into the realm by him; no others without authority from the licensee to make or import such mills, on pain of forfeiture of the mills and 20*l.* for each offence (one half to go to the Crown and the other to the licensee); interpretation of such offences reserved to the queen and Council. The invention of the mill has cost him much money and study during the past seven or eight years.

§1.9 AN ITALIAN ENGINEER REQUESTS A MONETARY REWARD FROM QUEEN ELIZABETH I IN EXCHANGE FOR HIS REVEALING THE SECRET OF A NEW PORTABLE MILL—1559

The following text is a letter from Sir Thomas Challoner, a member of Elizabeth's court, to his friend, William Cecil, chief advisor to the Queen. The letter conveys the request by an Italian inventor, John Baptista Ficuffino, of a monetary reward in return for his disclosing an invention of a small mill "very pretty, all of iron and no bigger than his fist, which in half an hour grinds meal to feed ten mouths a day." The applicant sends his request from France and asks for an urgent response, given that he will not stay long in England. The result of the request is unknown.

November 23, 1559

Challoner to Cecil

Of late he received a letter from Throckmorton in commendation of one John Baptista Ficuffino, an Italian engineer, who, coming forth of France, delivered the same to him [Challoner]. He proponed the overture of certain of his inventions (very rare and strange if he can perform the same) to the Queen, if she could bestow on him his demanded warrant, the articles whereof were partly before exhibited to Sir Nicholas, and certain new additions are enclosed. By his talk it seems he is a practiser in alchemy. Considering his late coming out of France, Challoner knows not what to judge of his errand, having being told by one who knew him six years past that he can speak a little broken English, and was among the merchants at Antwerp then suspected to be a spy. This perchance is untrue; but sure, his inventions are strange and worth a reward, if he can perform his word, as he demands no trifling sums. The writer moved him to go into England to procure for himself, which he is willing to do if the Queen pleases; and he wishes to know her pleasure before the 8th of next month, for longer he tarries not in these parts. Begs to have the Queen's answer speedily. The invention of his mill is very pretty, all of iron and no bigger than his fist, which in half an hour grinds meal to feed ten mouths a day. Saw by chance the inward secret thereof, and with aid of a workman could make the like for 10s.

§1.10 BARTOLOMEO SCAPPI, COOK TO POPE PIUS V, CAPTURES THE REWARD FOR HIS INVENTIVE DISHES THROUGH PRINTING PRIVILEGES—1570

Throughout history, cooks may not have been keen to capture the rewards for their inventions from the market through patents, which would accord them exclusivity in the making of their dishes, but since early times, they have resorted to the indirect method of appropriating their writings about culinary, and in that manner being paid for their skills and knowledge. Cooking books did not contain newly invented recipes only. Authors on gastronomy might include them, but they also included other recipes they were familiar with, as well as advice on utensils they used and the manners of arranging and decorating a table.

Such method of appropriating expressions of knowledge (culinary or other) has been created in Europe as a consequence of the dissemination of Gutenberg's reinvention of the movable-type printing press. In the absence of a legal system directed to protect authors, European States, in the course of the fifteenth and sixteenth centuries—Venice being the first country to do it—adopted the already consolidated practice of granting industrial privileges to inventors and importers of new techniques.

It should be noted that these early cooking books were addressed to the wealthy, who could afford to buy foodstuffs out of the ordinary. As Fernand Braudel explained, "there was no real luxury or sophistication of eating habits in Europe before the fifteenth or sixteenth centuries." Actually, "the diet of the peasants, that is the vast majority of the population, had nothing in common with the cookery books written for the rich."[16]

*One of the cooks to benefit from such a legal mechanism was Bartolomeo Scappi, cook to Pope Pius V, who authored one of the first culinary books published in Europe—*DEL MODO DI CUCINARE*. The book contains not only instructions on how to cook but also suggestions on how to organize a reception and prepare a table. The book also contains several engravings illustrating the manners of preparing food and the respective devices. Scappi's book was protected under no less than three privileges—one was granted in Rome by the Pope; another was granted in Venice by the Senate; and the third privilege was granted in Florence by Cosimo I Medicis.*

The first of the two printing privileges that follow was accorded to the brothers Franciscus and Michaele Tramezinus, initially for ten years (but extended to twenty years soon afterward). The brothers were printers and booksellers (Michaele's shop was based in Rome, and Franciscus's, in Venice).

The second privilege, granted by the Senate of Venice, had the author as a direct beneficiary. The reason was that Venice, anticipating what would become the rule after the British Statute of 1710, which inaugurated modern copyright, adopted a statute in 1554 determining that printing privileges would be granted to the authors.

16. Braudel, *supra* note 7, at 187-188.

§1.10.1 Privilege Granted by Pope Pius V to the Printers of Bartolomeo Scappi's Book—April 3, 1570

Pope Pius V. It is my wish, etc. Whereas the beloved sons Franciscus and Michael Tramczinus [Michele Tramezzino], Venetian booksellers, have recently explained to us that they have jointly, on their own, paid the expenses concerning the printing of a book on culinary and receptions as well as on healthy food; whereas all those things are illustrated by their figures, and also they are the work of my dearest servant, the most skilled Master Bartholomeo Scappi, who works in my private kitchen; which has hitherto not been printed in the City of Venice; and to avoid that works of this kind be afterwards printed by others without their permission, which would tend to their greatest prejudice. We are therefore willing to protect them from harm.

In the same token, and considering that the same Franciscus and Michael have ensured that the aforesaid work had not been printed until now and was to be printed by them, if or after it had been approved upon investigation by the office of the Inquisition of the said State, for a hundred years after the first printing of the same work; We grant and hold that it may not be printed without their permission, and only by them, and sold by them, or kept in their stores, or in their warehouses, or offered for sale without the consent of Franciscus and Michael, or to be kept printed, or to be printed.

We prohibit all, and each one and every believer of Christ both in Italy and outside Italy, and in particular all booksellers and printers of books, upon the sentence of ex-communication in the lands that, directly or indirectly, are under the obeyance of S.R.E., and, in addition, the payment of 200 ducats of gold to the Chamber, and in addition to the penalty of the loss of all the books, if it is found that the said work has been printed for a whole decade since the first printing of the said work, and therefore I grant Franciscus and Michaelus that during the said ten years they may print either by themselves, or by others besides Francis and Michael, or to sell the print, and to have it for sale at a price, or to offer it for sale for a price that they may fix.

We command all the venerable brothers of the Archbishopric and their Vicars in the spiritual, general, and in the temporal state of S.R.E. also the Legates and Vice-Legates of the Apostolic See, and the governors of the same state, that whenever Franciscus and Michaelus request them, or it is requested on their behalf, that they assist them in the enforcement of the effective prohibitions, and protect the said Franciscus and Michaelus against counterfeiters through Ecclesiastical interdictions, which may be aggravated, and by other remedies of law they are enforced by Apostolic authority.

I also invoke for this the help of the secular arm, as needed, and, because it would be very difficult to carry the present Order in all places, I also authorize that it may be copied by Apostolic authority and signed by some Notary Public, and with the seal of some Court, or in person, as established by the ecclesiastical dignity of the plenipotentiary, and that the copy has the same faith as it is attributed to the present original, and that the signature alone suffices [to validate it]. It is hereby ordered that anything whatever that happens otherwise is void, and null, and attempts at the foregoing apostolic rules and ordinances, as well as the rest; to those who do the contrary, notwithstanding whatever, &c.

This is my wish because it pleases me.

Given at Rome at St. Peter's, on the third day of April in the fifth year.

§1.10.2 The Senate of Venice Grants Bartolomeo Scappi a Privilege for the Printing of His Culinary Book—March 22, 1570

That it be granted to our faithful Michiel Tramezino, that Others than he, or [other than] those who will succeed him, cannot print in our domain, or elsewhere with the purpose of selling in our domain, for the period of the next XX years, in a book entitled Epulario, or De Re Coquinaria, by Bartolomeo Scappi, under penalty of losing the works, & paying three hundred ducats, to be divided—one third to the accuser, one third to our house of the Arsenal, and the other third to the Magistrate, who will carry out the execution. Being obliged to observe the provisions of our laws regarding printing.[17]

Figure 1.2 Cover of the 1570 edition of Scappi's book, which contains the two privileges translated above.

OPERA DI M.
BARTOLOMEO
SCAPPI, CVOCO SECRETO
DI PAPA PIO QVINTO,
DIVISA IN SEI LIBRI.
Nel primo si contiene il ragionamento che fa l'Autore con Gio. suo discepolo.
Nel secondo si tratta di diuerse uiuande di carne, sì di quadrupedi, come di uolatili.
Nel terzo si parla della statura, e stagione de pesci.
Nel quarto si mostrano le liste del presentar le uiuande in tauola, così di grasso come di magro.
Nel quinto si contiene l'ordine di far diuerse sorti di paste, & altri lauori.
Nel sesto, & vltimo libro si ragiona de' conualescenti, & molte altre sorti di viuande per gli infermi.
Con il discorso funerale che fu fatto nelle essequie di Papa Paulo III.
Con le figure che fanno bisogno nella cucina, & alli Reuerendissimi nel Conclaue.

Col priuilegio del sommo Pontefice Papa Pio V. & dell'Illustriss. Senato Veneto per anni XX.

17. The Senate here refers the statute of 1559.

§1.11 CLAUSES REGULATING COMPETITION AMONG COOKS IN THE BY-LAWS OF THE GUILD OF COOKS OF PARIS—MARCH 1599

We have seen above (§§ 1.2 and 1.5) that, like other professions, cooks gathered in guilds needed to obey strict anticompetitive rules (or, rather, rules that restricted competition). Those rules, in particular those dealing with tortious interference in contracts—which today also belong in the field of unfair trade practices, depending on the level of market power acquired through those practices—have remained and are part of the current scenarios involving antitrust and unfair competition.

The main change that we can see in these latter rules was that, in the sixteenth century, the corporation of cooks was under the administrative supervision of the Châtelet, which means that, like all other corporations, it had lost a great deal of the autonomy it enjoyed in the Middle Ages.

In the second chapter, we will see that these same by-laws also provided for a rule on trademarks.

Articles, Statutes, Ordinances and Regulations by the Jurors, former Bachelors, Master Cooks [Queux, Porte-Chappes] & Caterers of the City, outskirts, Suburbs, Prévôté & Viscounty of Paris.

Extracted from the By-laws accorded to them by the late King Henry the Great according to the Letters Patent of the month of March 1599, registered before the Provost of Paris, or his Civil Lieutenant, on the Conclusions of His Majesty's Attorney at the Châtelet, on the 29th of the said month, confirmed by the late King Louis XIII, of glorious memory, in the month of December 1612, & by His Majesty now reigning [Louis XIV], in June 1645.

XL. They are also forbidden to undertake on each other for Wedding Markets, Feasts, Banquets and other things dependent on their Art, under similar penalties. [deprivation of the honors of the said Community, fine of two hundred pounds, half applicable in favor of the Community, & the surplus to the said Brotherhood, & of all costs, damages & interests]

XLI. Similarly, they shall not engage any Companions unless they obtain the consent of the Masters under whom they have stayed, and that the latter are satisfied with [such engagement], on pain of being blamed in their General Assembly, which the said Jurors will convene for this purpose, by permission, which they will take in the usual manner, from His Majesty's Attorney at the Chatelêt.

§1.12 A SUMPTUARY LAW IMPOSES RESTRICTIONS ON THE NUMBER OF PLATES SERVED IN CERTAIN FESTIVITIES AND FIXES MAXIMUM PRICES

In the context of textiles, sumptuary laws have had a particular impact on the development of the use of intellectual property by fashion designers.[18] *In effect, the*

18. *See* Nuno Pires de Carvalho, The Intellectual Property of Textiles and Fashion, *supra* note 1.

restrictions on the use of certain fabrics and designs imposed contention on the development of new designs and fashions. Only in 1779, Louis XVI, King of France, through a statute, acknowledged the irresistible progress of society toward affirming individual tastes through new fashion designs and admitted the protection of trademarks designating the new fabrics made outside the constraints of the corporative regime.[19] *In the field of food, sumptuary laws were also enacted, but their impact on the development of a special intellectual property regime was not the same. Indeed, as we will see below, the protection of differentiating intangible assets in the field of cooking has demanded certain special uses of intellectual property but not the setting of new rights (as it happened with fashion, which, at some point in the sixteenth century, imposed the development of new rules on industrial designs, and in the nineteenth century, required the extension of copyright).*

Ordinance (Code Michaud) on the complaints of the states assembled in Paris in 1614 and of the assembly of notables in Rouen and Paris in 1617 and 1626.

(134) We prohibit all persons of whatever quality and condition, from using in the service of their table, for whatever pretext and motivation whatsoever, even at wedding and engagement feasts, more than three services in all, and of a single row of dishes, of more than three services added one to the other: and there may not have more than six pieces on the dish, either boiled or roasted, of any kind of small poultry or whatever game, either in their houses, or in public houses and venues, where it is customary to serve, on pain of confiscation of the tables, crockery, whether they are their property, borrowed or rented, and upholstery of the venues and rooms where the said feasts will be held. We also forbid all banquets and feasts under the motivation of entrance, welcoming, receptions and masterships, admissions to brotherhoods, rendering of accounts, communities, elections, taking of oaths, in any charge whatsoever, on the penalty of a fine of three hundred, payable without deduction against those who will convene the said feasts, masters of the said brotherhoods, jurors of the said communities, and others as need be.

(155) And because we are informed that those who hold offices, under the pretexts of the assemblies which they make with their friends to dispute against them, and to prepare for the examination of their reception, have introduced an abusive custom of feasts of insupportable expense, of whose vanity they often care more than of their own ability; we expressly forbid the said feasts, and the customary meals for the reception of their friends shall not exceed forty or fifty pounds at the most, under penalty of [their] being rejected and not received at the exam, and a fine of five hundred pounds.

(156) All those who carry out the profession of catering to and holding feasts for weddings or engagements, for any person whatsoever, at a fixed price or at a certain sum per head, shall not hereafter cater for, take or receive a price higher than one crown per head; and in proportion to this, if it is at fixed price, or a certain amount per dish, of a penalty of a fine of fifteen hundred pounds, of reimbursement against them

19. *Id.*, at 99.

by the fathers and custodians of those who will have held the said feasts, or by the administrators of the hospital, of the sums that they will have received, and of confiscation of all the crockery and pieces of furniture which will have been used for the aforesaid feasts, and in the venues and rooms where they will be held. We forbid them, on the penalty of imprisonment and fine of three thousand pounds, to receive in their houses and to organize feasts for our officers and the children of families, except for weddings and engagements, for the remuneration reason.

§1.13 BRITISH PATENTS UNDER THE STATUTE OF MONOPOLIES FOR CULINARY RECIPES AND FOODSTUFFS—1635 ONWARD

Soon after the Statute of Monopolies was enacted, in 1624, patents for inventions related to the preparation of food were granted, but, as before, they had to do more with machinery and utensils than with recipes. The first patents for cooking recipes appeared significantly later, during the Industrial Revolution, and had as subject matter those foodstuffs that could be sold in massive quantities, such as the patent granted in 1859 to Edward Thomas Hughes for biscuits (this patent having been granted under the Patent Act Amendment of 1852).

§1.13.1 July 23, 1635 AD—Halse, Sir Nicholas[20]

Certain necessary kilns, principally for the sweet and speedy drying of mault and hopes by the use of sea coale, turf, broome, furres, brakes, hearth, or any other fewell, and that without touch of smoake, and very usefull likewise for bakeing, boyling, roasting, starching, and of callavances, fine wheat flour, salt and water. Thirty pounds of callavances are to be boiled in thirty gallons of water. They are to be sprinkled with flour, covered with bay leaves, and left for six days spread out on a table. Forty pounds of common salt are to be boiled in water, and the callavances put to stand for five months in the water. At the end of that time the liquid is to be strained off.

[No Drawings]

§1.13.2 October 7, 1691 AD—Porter, Thomas, and White, John

A grant unto them of the sole use, exercise, and benefit of their new invention of keeping and preserving by liquors or otherwise all sorts of flesh, fowle, and fish, and many other things, either in pieces or in whole bodyes, at a cheaper rate, for many years in pieces in all clymates, without changing the nature, quality, taste, smell, or colour thereof, as good, palatable, and wholesome, to be eaten and made use for any

20. This patent has given rise to some controversy. It seems that Sir Halse had a competitor, Nichola's Page, who claimed inventorship and also received a patent. The dispute led to an action. The Hampton Court ordered that Sir Halse was the legitimate owner of the patent and vacated Page's patent. *See* Robert Edward Anderson, DICTIONARY OF NATIONAL BIOGRAPHY, 1885-1900/Halse, Nicholas, at en.wikisource.org (accessed on June 26, 2023).

intent and purpose whatsoever, as when first killed or put into such liquor; to hold and enjoy the same for 14 yrs according to the statute.

[No Specification of this invention has been enrolled].

§1.13.3 July 29, 1763 AD—Cockburn, Alexander

"Curing salmon with spices," by boiling them in a given time with water to which has been added in certain proportions, the following ingredients; namely, cloves, mace, common pepper, vinegar, and salt. Water, to which has been added, in certain proportions, vinegar, salt, cloves, mace, and common pepper, and the whole boiled for a given time and allowed to cool, "is put upon the salmon," when boiled and cold.

§1.13.4 July 5, 1780 AD—Levy, Jacob

"The art of making from wheat, the growth of this kingdom, semolina, from which vermicelli and macaroni are manufactured."

The wheat is ground in a power mill, and the flour separated from the midlins; the said midlins are dressed in a boulting mill in four different sorts, and then sifted through parchment sieves till all the bran and pollard is separated from it.

[No Drawings]

§1.13.5 October 30, 1787 AD—Blunt, Richard Tillyer

"New-invented composition to be used as yeast."

"To make a yeast gallon of the above composition, to be used as yeast, such as yeast gallon containing and to contain eight beer quarts: Boil in common water eight pounds of potatoes as for eating, bruise them perfectly smooth, and mix with them whilst warm two ounces of honey, or any other sweet, and one beer quart (being the eighth part of a gallon of yeast) of common yeast; and for making bread, mix three beer pints of the above composition with a bushell of flower, using warm water in the making of the bread. The water to be warmer in winter than in summer, and the composition to be ujsed a few houres after it is made; and as soon as the spunge (the mixture of the composition with the flower) begins to fall the first time, the bread should be made and put into the oven."

[No Drawings]

§1.13.6 February 8, 1791 AD—Jayne, William

Preserving eggs "for the space of two years at the least," by keeping them in a mixture of that consistence "that it will cause an egg put into to swim with its top just above the liquid," and composed of the following substances, in certain proportions; namely, quicklime, salt, cream of tartar with water.

§1.13.7 April 24, 1830 AD—McInnes, John

"The manufacture or preparation of certain substances which I denominate 'the British tapioca,'[21] and the cakes and the flour to be made from the same."

The tapioca is to be made from potatoes, parsnips, beet or other tuberous roots. The roots are mashed to a pulp with water. The "mucilage or farine" is separated by sieves, washed and dried. It is then gradually put through a common sieve into a broad "cast-iron pan placed on the fire." When it becomes "dry and gritty," the manufacture is complete. To make cakes, "a wooden frame of the size or shape the cakes are wished, is placed on the pan before-mentioned, filled up with farine, taking care that the pan is not too hot." The cakes last for years. The flour may be mixed with wheat flour, and used for general purposes.

[No Drawings]

§1.13.8 May 3, 1836 AD—Whiting, John

"Improvements in preparing certain farinaceous foods."

The improvement relates to the lighter sorts of bread, biscuits, etc., and consists in the employment of muriatic acid and carbonate of soda. For every seven pounds of flour, 350 to 500 grains of carbonate of soda, and sufficient of the acid to neutralize the carbonate of soda are used (from 420 to 560 grs. of acid for every 350 grs. of alkali). The carbonate of soda is mixed with 2¾ pints of water, the muriatic acid with ¾ pint. The flour is divided into two equal portions. One portion is kneaded into dough with the soda solution; the remainder is thrown in and the acid solution poured in while the whole is kneaded. Salt may be added for flavouring. Other methods of mixing may be employed.

[No Drawings]

§1.13.9 January 27, 1859—Hughes, Edward Thomas (A Communication from Messrs. Pascal and Sirben)

"Manufacture of biscuits."

Gluten or wheaten flour "or other farinaceous vegetable" are mixed with oil, butter "or similar nutritious matters."

Proportions: 1 kilogramme gluten, 800 grammes flour, 40 grammes oil, etc. The dough is kneaded in any suitable way.

[No Drawings]

21. The term "British Tapioca" was not coined by the inventor. It was an expression widely used meaning potato-flour in grains. *See, e.g.*, Margaret Dodds, The Cook and Housewife's Manual, at 353, "To use the British Tapioca" (Oliver and Boyd, 1825).

§1.14 GEORGE MANBY OBTAINS A PATENT FOR A FURNACE, UPON THE OPPOSITION OF THOUSANDS OF SALT WORKERS—1650

As we saw in the previous paragraph, the Statute of Monopolies has given rise to a regular flow of patent applications, including devices and machinery used in in the field of food making. The following texts show a curious example of one of those patents. George Manby applied to the House of Commons for a patent for his invention of a furnace, which he presented as an "invention for the saving of much fuel in making salt, brewing, etc." The application had the opposition of thousands of salt workers, who feared that Manby was seeking exclusivity in making salt. The patent was granted, but with the caveat that it would not prejudice the rights of those who were in the business of making salt. Interestingly, the title of the patent, as granted, omitted any reference to the making of salt, even if that was eventually the main objective of Manby's invention, given the high prices charged upon that precious ingredient for flavoring and preserving food.

§1.14.1 The House Receives Manby's Patent Application

Monday, February 4, 1649.

Prayers.

Manby's Invention.

Sir Arthur Heslerigge reports from the Council of State, the Petition of George Manby, concerning his Invention for the saving of much Fewel in making Salt, Brewing, &c.: Which Petition was read.

An Act, prohibiting all Persons, for Fourteen Years, to make use of the Invention found out by George Manby for the Saving of much Fewel in making Salt, Brewing, & c. was this Day read the First time; and ordered to be read the Second time on this-day-seven nights.

§1.14.2 The House Receives the Opposition to Manby's Patent Application and Submits the Matter to the Committee of the Navy for Consideration

Saturday, March 30, 1650

Prayers

An Act, That George Manby, for Fourteen Years, shall have the Use and Benefit of his new Invention for Making of Salt, and Saving and Preserving of Fuel, in this Nation, was this Day read for the Second time; and, upon the Question, committed to the Committee of the Navy: and that Sir Arthur Hesilrig, Sir John Darroers, Colonel

Thompson, Colonel Jones, Sir Wm. Armyn, Mr. Garland, Colonel Wauton, Sir John Hippesley, Sir Richard Lucy, Mr. Bond, Mr. Leman, Mr. Richard Darley, be added to the Committee of the Navy, as to this Business: And all that come to have Voices, as to this Purpose: And to sit where the Committee of the Navy sit, this Afternoon at Tow of the Clock: And Mr. Garland is to have the care of it.

The humble Petition of many Thousands interested, and whose Livelihoods consist in the Salt-works, and Making of Salt in the North, was this Day read.

Ordered, that the Confederation of the said Petition be referred to the same Committee to whom the Act touching the new Invention of *George Manby*, touching Salt, is committed; to consider thereof; and to hear the Parties concerned on both Sides; and report their Opinion to the House.

§1.14.3 The House Reads a Draft Act Granting Manby's Patent

November 27, 1650: An Act for George Manby to prohibit any to make use of his Invention for the boiling of all sorts of Liquors for fourteen years.

George Manby to enjoy the sole use of his invention in boiling liquors, for fourteen years.

Whereas George Manby hath in long continuance of time, and by his great cost, charges and labor, found out a New Invention to prevent the great consumption of Cole and Wood, and also of Iron, Lead and Copper, used for the Boiling of all sort of Liquors in Brewhouses, Salt-works, and other works of that kind; whereby sufficient Quantities of Salt will be made within a short time to serve this Nation, without the help of Foreigners, at much cheaper Rates then heretofore have been; Be it Enacted by this present Parliament, and by Authority thereof, That the said George Manby, his Executors, Administrators and Assigns, shall have and enjoy the sole Use of his Invention, in the making of Salt, and in Brewing and Boiling any Quantities of Liquor, for and during the term of Fourteen years, from the First day of September, *Anno Dom.* one thousand six hundred and fifty: And that no person or persons, Bodies Politique or Corporate, shall make use of his said Inventions within the Commonwealth of England or Ireland, in any Occupation or Manufacture, during the said time. Provided, That all and every person and persons may use such ways and works as they have used to do, or otherwise, so as they make no use of the said Invention. And provided, That it shall be lawful to and for every such person and persons, their Executors, Administrators and Assigns only, whom the said George Manby and George Gray the elder Esq; their Executors and Administrators, shall hereafter jointly allow of, and appoint in writing under Hand and Seal, to make use of such New Inventions in any Occupation or Manufacture, according to the tenor of such Allowance and Appointment, and for none else nor otherwise.

The forfeiture for making use of the said invention.

And be it further Enacted by the Authority aforesaid, That if any person or persons shall make use of the said Invention, in the making of Salt, Brewing or Boiling of Liquor, or any other Occupation, and proof be thereof made by the Oath of two or more witnesses, to be taken before two or more Justices of the Peace within the County, City, Borough, Town Corporate, or Privilege place within the Commonwealth of England or Ireland, where the Fact shall be done; which said Justices of the Peace have hereby power, and are upon complaint required to administer, That then such Vessels and Works shall be broken and pulled down by Warrant of such Justices of the Peace: And the said George Manby, his Executors, Administrators and Assigns, shall and may bring his or their action of Debt against any person or persons, Bodies Politique or Corporate, offending herein, within any Court of Record, for the penalty of ten pounds lawful English Money for setting up of such Works, and twenty shillings for every day using or continuing any Vessel or Work by the said George Manby invented as aforesaid, and to him, his Executors, Administrators and Assigns, hereby granted to be solely used for the term aforesaid; In which Action shall be no Essoin, Wager of Law, Privilege, or other Delay whatsoever allowed or permitted; And wherein the said George Manby, his Executors, Administrators and Assigns, shall also recover his Costs of Suit and Damages sustained.

Indemnity to Justices and other officers.

And be it further Enacted by the Authority aforesaid, That if any action shall be brought against any Justice, Justices of Peace, or other Officer or person concerning what they shall do in execution of the premises, every such person shall have benefit of the Statutes made in that behalf, as in other cases wherein they act as Justices of the Peace, and under their command.

§1.14.4 The House of Commons Confirms Manby's Patent

November 28, 1650

Manby's Invention. The House this Day resumed the Debate upon the Act for *George Manby*, to prohibit any to make use of his Invention for the Boiling of all Sorts of Liquors.

And the said Act, upon the Question, passed; and ordered to be forthwith printed and published.

§1.15 ANOTHER FAMOUS COOK, LA VARENNE, OPTS TO OBTAIN THE REWARD FOR HIS INVENTIVE COOKING THROUGH THE PUBLICATION OF A BOOK—1651

The cooking book authored by François Pierre La Varenne, which justified a privilege granted in 1651 to its bookseller, is of exceptional importance. For the first time, a cook revealed recipes and ways of cooking that dispensed with the spices and other ingredients that were so frequently used at the tables of the wealthy during the Middle Ages. Indeed, the greatest merit of Le Cuisinier François *lies in the use of local ingredients and seasonings. In practical terms, this book has given birth to modern French cooking. This new approach to the culinary art is explained by the bookseller in an introductory text addressed to the reader as having two great advantages: first, the recipes proposed by La Varenne, out of his experience as the Chief Cook for more than ten years, for Louis Chalon du Blé, Marquis of Uxelles and Counsel to the King of France (Louis XIV), were significantly healthier than those previously used, in particular those that concerned the preservation and consumption of meat. Consequently, the recipes described by La Varenne also had the advantage of saving money that was spent by those who would rely on old and unhealthy methods of cooking in buying "an enormous quantity of drugs, herbs, medicines and other troublesome remedies to recover [their health]."*

La Varenne, in his long career as a cook, certainly introduced new recipes and new methods of using local ingredients. However, following the practice initiated long before him, and that is maintained up to today, he did not apply for industrial privileges—which he would certainly have obtained given his high ranking among the servants of a powerful nobleman—and preferred instead to obtain his reward not by selling the food he prepared but by having his book sold and thereby reaping the reputation and prestige that derived from the publication.

La Varenne's book was a commercial success. Not only had several editions in France but it was also translated and published in other languages.

Extract from the King's Privilege.

By Grace & Privilege of the King, Pierre David, Merchant Bookseller in Paris, is authorized to print or have printed the Book entitled, *Le Cuisinier François*, elaborated by Sieur de la Varenne, Ecuyer de Cuisine of Monsieur le Marquis d'Uxelles, during the time & space of ten years, from the day it will be printed, with prohibition to all others to print it or have it printed under the penalties imposed by those Letters. Given at Paris on the seventeenth day of July one hundred and fifty-one.

Signed Guitonneau.

Figure 1.3 Cover of the book Le Cuisinier François, authored by La Varenne, and published in Paris in 1651.

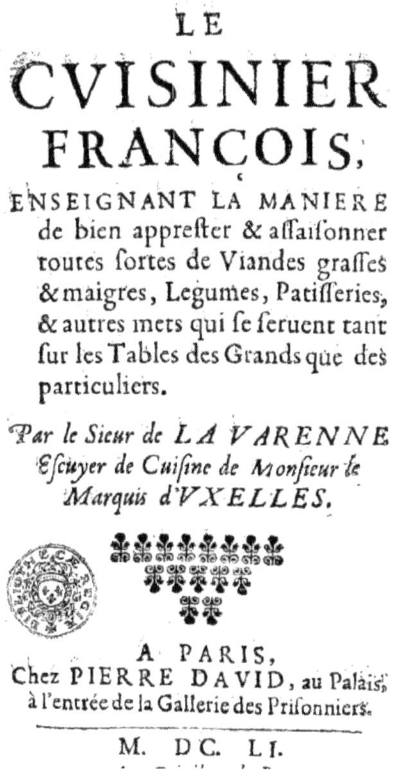

LE
CVISINIER
FRANCOIS,
ENSEIGNANT LA MANIERE
de bien apprefter & affaifonner
toutes fortes de Viandes graffes
& maigres, Legumes, Patifferies,
& autres mets qui fe feruent tant
fur les Tables des Grands que des
particuliers.

Par le Sieur de LA VARENNE
Efcuyer de Cuifine de Monfieur le
Marquis d'VXELLES.

A PARIS,
Chez PIERRE DAVID, au Palais,
à l'entrée de la Gallerie des Prifonniers.

M. DC. LI.

§1.16 LOUIS XIV GRANTS DAVID CHALIOU A PRIVILEGE FOR THE MAKING AND SELLING OF CHOCOLATE IN FRANCE—MAY 28, 1659

As Europe extended its influence over the world new foodstuffs would become known and coveted by consumers. The introducers of those new materials would naturally apply for—and sometimes obtain—commercial privileges that, for a number of years, would shield them against competing importers. But the privilege that follows, which also concerns the introduction in France of a foodstuff then scarcely known—the chocolate—has more than a merely commercial nature: it also refers to the acquisition by the grantee, David Chaliou, of the secrets involved in its preparation. In this privilege, there is, thus, an element of appropriation of knowledge that makes it an aspect of industrial property and not only an element of commercial and administrative law. Strictly speaking, David Chaliou was not the first person to bring chocolate to France, but he was responsible for the dissemination of the habit of consuming it, even if, at first, chocolate was seen as a medicine rather than as a foodstuff and tidbit.

The patent letters, granted in 1659, mention a period of twenty nine years, but when they were registered in the Parliament seven years later, the privilege was reduced to fifteen years from the date of registry, which means that Chaliou enjoyed a period of twenty-two years of exclusivity.

The patent letter says that one of the reasons that led Louis XIV to grant the privilege was the plea of one of his "most special assistants." Given that David Chaliou was a member of the queen's court, it is not impossible that such a "most special assistant" was the queen herself.

Louis [XIV], etc.

Our dear and beloved David Chaliou has very humbly shown us that he would have made various trips to Spain, Poland and other places in Europe, during which he dedicated himself to the search for secrets that can be useful to the human body, [and that] he has among other things acquired the knowledge of a certain composition which is called chocolate, the use of which being very healthy, he would like to share it with the public if it would please us to grant him permission to commercialize it alone, and thereupon grant him our necessary letters.

For these reasons, desiring to treat the said supplicant favorably, both in consideration of the plea that has been made to us in his favor by one of our most special assistants, and to give him the means of compensating himself for the expenses he has incurred in learning the perfect composition of this liquor, we have ... permitted him and permit to make, to cause to be sold and commercialized, in all towns and other places of this kingdom that he sees fit, the said chocolate, whether in liqueur or pastilles or in boxes, or in such manner as he pleases, and import from foreign countries for such purpose the things necessary for the composition of the said chocolate, without anyone being able to prevent it.

And this, during the space of twenty-nine whole and consecutive years, during which time we impose very express inhibitions and prohibitions against all persons of whatever quality and condition against their making, or selling or commercializing the aforesaid chocolate, under any pretext or whatever new name ...

Registered... to be executed and enjoyed by the applicant of the effect and content thereof during the space of fifteen years, following today's order. In Paris in Parliament, on the ninth day of February, one thousand six hundred and sixty-six. Conferred with its original,

Du Tillet.

§1.17 JEAN-BAPTISTE COLBERT'S CORRESPONDENCE REFLECTS THE ATTENTION GIVEN TO THE TECHNIQUE SKILLS OF MAKING SALT—1672

The techniques involved in the extraction and preparation of salt have always been a matter of great interest to governments. Salt's relevance resulted not only from the fact

that it served (and still serves) as a simple and immediate source of seasoning food but also from its role in preserving foodstuffs. Those countries that dominated the techniques for extracting salt from the sea were, therefore, very keen to maintain the commercial advantages that stemmed from such knowledge (associated with their geographical location). Any measures deemed necessary for that purpose would be taken, sometimes of an extreme nature, as we will see below.

The following extracts from two letters sent by Jean-Baptiste Colbert, the Minister of Finance of Louis XIV, to the French Ambassador in Denmark reflect the importance given by the government of France to the knowledge involved in extracting salt. The first letter shows Colbert's first reaction to the news that Denmark had granted a privilege to a French citizen for his extraction of salt in that country. In Colbert's view, there were no reasons for concern with possible competition in the industry because the climate of Denmark would not allow any success for such undertaking. But in the second letter, Colbert is more direct: he still believes that the Danish privilege has no practical interest but, in any event, he recommends the Ambassador to try to persuade the French citizen to return to France. Colbert also informs that, in the meantime, he had taken measures to prevent the débauchage *(the diversion) of skilled workers from the region of La Rochelle, where salt of the highest quality (*la fleur de sel*) had been extracted for centuries.*

Colbert to the Knight of Terlon, envoyed of France in Denmark

November 4

I have great difficulty in believing that the privilege granted to a certain Desbordes, to make salt alone in Denmark can be of any use to him, considering that it is impossible that the climate of that kingdom could permit it. You know that in Normandy, Picardy, Holland and England we have never been able to make it, because the heat of the sun is not great enough there, having in France only the coast of Poitou, then of Aunix and that of the south of Bretagne where it is made. Therefore, I do not think that there is much diligence to be done to prevent the execution of the projects of the said Desbordes, who will end up being a visionary, and who will not care to carry out what he promises, provided that he obtains some money to subsist.

December 2

I received the copy of the privilege which was granted to Sieur Desbordes, to make salt in Denmark; although I consider it impossible to succeed in Jutland, if you find a way to send this man back to France, by giving him something, it will certainly be good to do so. However, I have given the necessary orders to La Rochelle to prevent the diversion of those who dedicate themselves to the making of salt ...

§1.18 CLAUSE OF THE BY-LAWS OF THE GUILD OF THE MERCHANTS OF LEMONADE OF PARIS PROHIBITING THE *DÉBAUCHAGE* OF THE MASTERS' COMPANIONS—1676

This clause against the débauchage *of skilled workers has been present in laws and regulations concerning labor relations since ancient times—actually, since Babylon—and continues being a valid rule, as footnote 10 to the TRIPS Agreement shows.*[22] *Another example of such a clause follows, this time as an element of the by-laws that were approved by Louis XIV for the merchants of lemonade of Paris, who had engaged in a dispute involving the payment (or, rather, the lack of it) of a tax imposed by Colbert.*

First statute of the sellers of lemonade

January 28, 1676

X. All masters may have one apprentice only at any given time. They may nevertheless have several companions, in regard of whom they will be required to choose those who have completed their apprenticeship, excluding the foreigners. And the masters shall not divert the companions hired by the other masters, nor have them working or receive them in their service, without having first asked permission to the master with whom the said companion was engaged.

§1.19 IN A DECISION INVOLVING AN INDUSTRIAL PRIVILEGE FOR THE MAKING OF FOODSTUFFS (PANCAKES), COLBERT ESTABLISHES A FUNDAMENTAL RULE OF TODAY'S PATENT LAW: PRIVILEGES ARE ONLY TO BE GRANTED FOR INVENTIONS THAT ARE GENUINELY NEW—FEBRUARY 17, 1679

In this letter, Jean-Baptiste Colbert states his (hence, the King's) policy concerning industrial privileges: they would not be granted unless the matter to be protected was new technology. Possibly, it was this idea that led Colbert to support and sponsor the Academy of Sciences and its role of examining patent applications as to their novelty and utility.[23]

To Mr. Dalliez, Director of the Compagnie du Levant.

Saint-Germain, February 17, 1679

I will examine the proposals you make to me concerning the manufacture of pancakes; but as it has been some time since I have its current situation examined, I am almost persuaded that it will be maintained by allowing to the public the freedom to work in it, and by revoking the privilege of Mr. Dupuy. You must be assured that whenever I find either a greater advantage, or an equal advantage, I do not hesitate to take away all privileges, especially since you see that that of Mr. Dupuy has not been successful.

---

22. A discussion on Law 189 of the Code of Hammurabi, of *circa* 1750 BC, and its similarity with footnote 10 to the TRIPS Agreement can be found in Nuno Pires de Carvalho, From Babylon to the Silicon Valley, *supra* note 10, at 157.
23. *Id.*, at 29.

§1.20 THE INVENTION OF ONE OF THE MOST FUNDAMENTAL COOKING DEVICES—THE PRESSURE COOKER—AND THE MISERY OF HIS INVENTOR, DENIS PAPIN—1681

An article published several years ago described the invention of the happiness machine and the resulting unhappiness of its inventor.[24] *The article identified a paradox that affects the inventors of inventions with a very high social value, such as those related to medicines, due to the reluctance of society to pay the value that their inventors would, theoretically, be allowed to privately capture. The article proposes a theorem, which has the impact of a paradox: the higher the invention's social value is, the lower is, in proportion, the private value the inventor is able to capture. The article, besides its humoristic approach, was based on the observation of reality. However, through history, we find cases in which the unhappiness of inventors was caused by themselves, either because of their incompetence in managing their intellectual property assets (as was the case of Gutenberg and his lack of acumen in handling his trade secret, which he ended up losing to his partner), or because of their reluctance in resorting to the appropriation of their knowledge. This last case was the situation in which Denis Papin (1647-1713), the inventor of the pressure cooker and pioneer of the steam engine, put himself.*

As one of the texts below shows, Papin not only failed to apply for an industrial privilege for his invention, in spite of his belief that it could generate great profits but also did not spare efforts in publicizing it. At this point, it is worth noticing that when he made the invention, he was residing in London and working for the Royal Society of Arts. At the end of the seventeenth century in England, there was already a spread of awareness of the patent system and its advantages. So, when Papin deliberately gave up the possibility of filing for and obtaining a patent, he knew what he was doing. Eventually, Papin hoped that Charles II would accord him his patronage, but his request in that regard was unsuccessful due to a movement in the Court that ridiculed his invention. It seems that the refusal by Charles II of Papin's request was due to a practical joke: someone had attached to the neck of the king's hunting dogs a petition on the dogs' behalf that Papin's invention (which had the initial purpose of transforming bones into gelatine) be rejected because it would destroy the dogs' exclusive privilege to eat bones. Eventually, such petition was inspired by a letter Gottfried Wilhelm Leibniz (the famous German scientist and, at some point, Papin's correspondent) had sent to the Duke of Hannover, where Papin lived and worked for a period. The letter, purportedly (and jokingly) written on behalf of the dogs, complained that Papin's invention would destroy their privilege to the crushing of bones with their teeth.[25]

Papin has made other inventions, including a boat with paddle wheels. Having obtained permission to test his invention in Germany, Papin built one boat and tried to cross a river in Essen. The local boatmen, worried that Papin's invention might destroy

24. Nuno Pires de Carvalho, *A invenção da máquina da felicidade e a infelicidade do seu inventor—o paradoxo do sistema de patentes* [*The invention of the happiness machine and the unhappiness of its inventor—the paradox of the patent system*], Revista da ABPI no. 177, Mar-Apr 2022, at 7 et seqs.
25. Leibniz's letter to the Duke of Hannover, under the title of "Request of the Dogs," in French and in English, can be found at www.jehsmith.com (accessed on October 9, 2023).

their business, seized the boat and destroyed it. Like Barthelemy Thimmonier, another creator of a seminal and disruptive invention—the sewing machine—Papin died in dire poverty. As one author puts it, it is not an exaggeration to say that Papin died of starvation.

§1.20.1 Papin Describes His Invention of the Pressure Cooker (Excerpt)

To use this Engine with conveniency and ease, it ought to be fitted in a Furnace built on purpose for it, and should go in as far as the Appendices CC: so the fire being underneath, and the Screws FF well fastened, you may boil your meat as long as you please, without danger of wasting it by the exhalation of the volatile parts.

It is to be noted, that such a long and slender shape is better than any other for such an Engine, because it may be kept shut with less strength: for it is well known, that the wider an aperture is, the more strength is required to keep the cover from being lifted up by the inward pressure.

It is to be noted also that the cover BB must have some depth, that being filled with water, it may always keep some moisture in a circular piece of paper, which is to be put in the joint II: for the two Cylinders can never be ground to one another so exactly as to keep in Liquors when highly compress, unless there be some paper put between them, and that paper cannot stop it exactly neither, unless it be wet: yet the depth of the said cover BB ought to be but little, that the Engine being almost all closed in the Furnace, it may the better receive and keep the heat.

This Engine is, without doubt, simple enough, and easy enough to be kept in order, but the mischief is, that it is much more troublesome to look into it than into ordinary pots: and because it doth more or less effect, according as the included water is more or less compress, and according as the heat also is greater or less; it may sometimes happen, that you will draw your meat before it is ready enough; and sometimes too you may burn it: It was therefore necessary to find out some way how to know both the quantity of the inward pressure, and the degree of heat. …

§1.20.2 Papin Discusses the Costs and Profits Involved in the Use of His Invention and Asserts That He Has Never Had the Intention of Obtaining a Patent for It

CHAPTER IX.

A Calculation of the price that a good big Engine may come to, and of the profit it may afford.

Because people are loath to meddle with new Inventions, less the expense should be greater than the profit to be got by them, I will subjoin here a calculation of the price which a good Engine may come to, and of the profit that may be got by it.

I have been at an Iron-mongers house, and there I caused a cast Iron Pipe to be weighed: This being six inches in Diameter and two feet long, and, without doubt, strong enough to endure an inward pressure twenty times stronger than the ordinary pressure of the Air; This Pipe, I say, did weigh but 57 pounds: so that such another Pipe 12 inches in Diameter, and as strong proportionably to its bigness, will weigh but about 228 pounds: But let a covered Vessel weigh 250, yet it will not come to 48 shillings, seeing the Merchants can with good profit afford such Metal at two pence half penny a pound.

Now if the cover and the Vessel were ground to one another, and that in a Country where Workmen are cheap, the grinding will scarce come to two shillings.

Then the Iron pieces DD with four Screws (lest two should not do enough) and the Iron rod LM may be afforded much under five shillings, especially if made in the Country and in numbers.

Five shillings would also be a great deal too much for setting the Pipe HH, and fitting a Valve to it.

The inward Pot GG of cast Iron, or glass, or stone-pot might also be got under 20 shillings strong enough and big enough to hold 80 pounds of water: I confess it would be a hard matter to make a Glass so big; but instead of one they may make three or four to be set in the same Frame one above the other: So that we may be sure that a Merchant may with good profit afford such Engines ready in good condition at 4 *l.* sterling apiece.

Now such an Engine is able to make above 50 pounds of the Jelly at a time, and may do the same quantity at least twice in 24 hours, (for I have tried that my great Engine, which is 6 inches in diameter, may in less than an hours' time be heated enough to make Gelly of Bones) therefore one may make 100 pounds of Gelly every day.

Now in *Paris* where people constantly keep Jelly ready to sell, the price of it is 20 pence a pound; but in London, where they make none, unless it be bespoken, Apothecaries use to sell it at 2 shillings a pound; therefore, it would be a very good thing for the Public, if any one would sell Jellies for a groat a pound: yet at that price the aforesaid Engine would make Gelly for above 33 shillings every day.

The fire will not come to six pence, and the bones with some Harts-horn might be got cheap enough too, since it is not necessary to have them for this Engine, and a little Sugar serves for Jellies: yet let the expense come to 13 shillings a day, there will be still 20 shillings profit for the Owner of the Engine, and so in four days' time he will be fully requited for his first expense, and one man alone may at the same time keep five or six such Engines at work for several uses, whereof some perhaps will prove more profitable than the making of Jellies: Therefore we must not question but those that will set upon such things, may make their own profit very well, and at the same time do a great service to the Public. I have not therefore thought it right, in a thing of so general use, that a man by virtue of a Patent should hinder other people from working that may perhaps have more skill in doing things good and cheap; and I have instructed Mr. Mayor, a Founder, in *Old Bedlam* how to make these Engines of cast Brass, so that anybody may see them and buy them of him.

§1.20.3 Papin Seeks the Patronage of Charles II (to No Avail)

Denys Papin was the first to have the idea of extracting gelatine from bones using the digester that bears his name (1681). He proposed to the King of England, Charles II, to manufacture in 24 hours, with 11 pounds of coal, 150 pounds of jelly for use in poor houses and hospitals; jokers attached to the neck of the king's pack [of hunting dogs] a request to the effect of preserving for the dogs the privilege of eating bones, and Papin's idea was rejected; ...

Figure 1.4 Denis Papin's pressure cooker (1681).

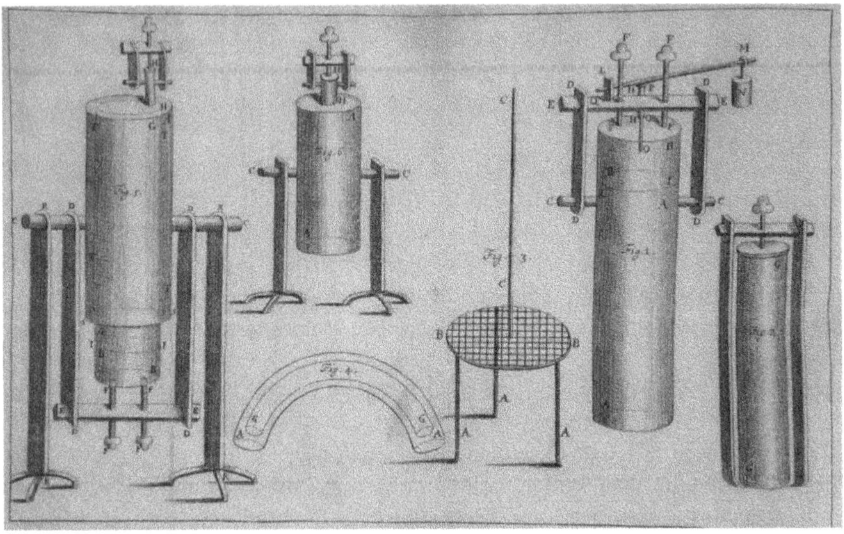

§1.21 THE KING OF PORTUGAL IMPOSES THE DEATH PENALTY AND CONFISCATION OF GOODS TO THOSE SKILLED PORTUGUESE EMPLOYEES WHO LEFT THE MANUFACTURE OF SALT OF CASTRO MARIM AND MOVED ABROAD—FEBRUARY 15, 1695

It was said above that sometimes governments would take extreme measures to avoid that the competitive advantages of their countries in extracting salt be lost to foreign countries. The text that follows is a good example of that sort of measures.

The Manufacture of Marines and Working of the Salt that the Portuguese statute refers to was located in Castro Marim, a town in Algarve, south of Portugal. Historical records show that Phoenician merchants traveled to Castro Marim to trade for its salt, which was used, among other utilities, to prepare the garum, *a sauce made of the guts of certain species of fish that was very popular in Roman cooking. The salt ponds of Castro Marim are still in use today.*

Law of King Dom Pedro II by which He prohibits, with the death penalty, that none of the Officers who manufacture Salt go to Foreign Kingdoms to teach how to manufacture it.

Dom Pedro, by the grace of God, King of Portugal and the Algarves, on both sides of the Sea, in Africa, Lord of Guinea and the Conquest, Navigation, Trade of Ethiopia, Arabia,

Persia, and India, etc. I make known to those who see this Law of Mine, that, having been informed that the Officers of the Factory of Salt Ponds and Work of the Salt, native of these Kingdoms, moved by the slight interest of some increase of Salary, which they are given in Foreign Kingdoms, go to teach them the said Factory and work in the culture of salt, and because it is convenient to avoid the serious damage that could result from this both to My Vassals and to My Treasury,

I decide and it pleases me that no Officer of the said Factory of Salt Ponds and Salt shall move to any foreign Kingdom to teach how to make Salt Ponds or to work in the Culture of Salt under penalty of death and confiscation of goods and that those who are outside the Kingdom engaged in this activity within the term of three months after the publication of this Law of mine withdraw to the Kingdom, and failing to do so will incur the same death penalty, and confiscation of goods, since having everyone work to occupy themselves and earn their daily allowances in the Salt Ponds of this Kingdom, should not, to the great damage of the common good, go introduce this Factory abroad, and it [the Law] shall be inviolably kept as it provides, and ignorance shall not be alleged.

I order Doctor João de Rozas e Azevedo, from my Council, and My Head-Chancellor of this Kingdom to publish it in my Chancellery and send a Copy of it to all the Ministers of the Heads of their Municipalities and to all the Places of the Kingdom where there are Salt Ponds, in which Edicts shall also be placed under My Seal, with a sign for them to have it executed, and it will be registered in the Books of Chancellery of the Palace, House of Pleas, Court of Appeals of Porto, where similar Laws are usually registered. Manoel da Silva Collaço made it in Lisbon, on the fifteenth of February, one thousand six hundred and ninety-five. Francisco Galvão had it written.

The King.

§1.22 ANOTHER EXAMPLE OF A CLAUSE PROHIBITING UNFAIR TRADE PRACTICES IN THE COOKING PROFESSION—JUNE 1744

The following text repeats a clause prohibiting unfair competition that was present in early by-laws of the guilds that gathered cooks.[26] *But this specific clause seems to go further than previous rules because it prohibits the guilty professional from selling his merchandise on preferable terms to the competitor whose goods are being inspected by the customer. Today, this sort of rule would lead to the prohibition of certain practices that are generally accepted, such as comparative advertisement and the offer of rebates when the customer finds in another merchant's shop the same merchandise at a lower price.*

Statutes, Ordinances and Regulations of the Community of Master Roasters of the City, Suburbs and Outskirts of Paris

Article XXXII.

No Master or other of the said trade may call the Bourgeois near the shop of a Roaster in order to sell preferably & to his prejudice, on the penalty of a fine of

26. *See* §§ 2 and 5, above.

50 pounds, for the benefit of the plaintiff, in accordance with Articles XIII & XIV of the said old Statutes of 1509.

§1.23 THE COURT OF KING'S BENCH HOLDS THAT A PATENT ON A BREWING DEVICE IS NOT GOOD FOR A MERE EFFECT—1803

As already exemplified above, discussions on the appropriation of knowledge related to the preparation of food have sometimes led to important decisions that have had an impact on the formulation of long-standing rules and principles of industrial property law. The example that follows is an Opinion that decided that the effect of an invention, intended or not, is not a sufficiently differentiating feature to justify novelty. This is a topic that continues haunting today's patent owners when they claim that the merit of inventions does not lie specifically on new features and operations introduced in previously known devices or substances, but on new effects or results the inventors have found in those old devices or substances.

The plaintiff and the defendants in this legal dispute were partners in a famous London brewery.

Hare v. Harford and Taylor

In the Court of King's Bench, July 14, 1803

A patent was taken out by a Mr. Hare for an apparatus used in brewing beer whereby the essential oil of hops, obtained from the steam of the worts, was preserved and used for heating the water for brewing. By a previous invention the water had been boiled by a similar method, which accessorily preserved the oil, although not intended to do so. Held that the patent of Mr. Hare was not new, and a verdict was therefore given for the defendant. The action was brought on a bond conditioned for the payment of money the consideration for the purchase of the patent.

The cause was tried at the Guildhall of the City of London, before Lord Alvanley and a special jury. The plaintiff was Mr. Hare, a gentleman of Bath, who was previously the owner of an extensive brewery at Limehouse, and the defendants were Messrs. Harford and Taylor, his successors in the concern. The action was brought on a bond conditioned for the payment of an annuity to Mr. Hare during the existence of a patent granted to him in September 1792, in consideration of his licensing the defendants to use the invention for which it was obtained. The defendants pleaded that one Sutton Thomas Wood had, before the date of the patent, practiced the same thing; that the plaintiff's invention was therefore not new, and the patent consequently void: the question before the Court therefore was, respecting the similarity or dissimilarity of the two inventions of Mr. Hare and Mr. Wood. Mr. Hare's patent had been granted for "An apparatus whereby the essential oil of hops, which was before lost and dissipated in the air during the operation of boiling worts for beer, is preserved and applied to use, and the water for brewing at the same time heated to a sufficient degree of heat without any application of fire to the vessel containing it." Mr. Wood had previously, in 1785, obtained a patent for "Certain new discoveries in the application of steam, and also certain methods of using the water produced from condensed steam, and for applying the water from the coppers or boilers of steam engines to other purposes than that of working the steam-engine, and also various methods of heating and applying water for the several purposes of breweries and distilleries, and for forwarding the process of brewing, and also certain methods of constructing and adapting coopers, boilers, tubes, and other hollow bodies, and of rendering such coppers, boilers, tubes, and other hollow bodies, as are employed in the breweries and distilleries, steam and air-tight," in the specification of which he had said nothing respecting the preserving the essential oil of the hop. It was argued that Mr. Wood's patent could not be used when acting with brewers' worts without producing the same effect as the plaintiff's.

The plaintiff's witnesses described Mr. Hare's invention by a model which was produced in Court, consisting of a concave vessel, placed over the dome or head of the copper, in which concave vessel the liquor for the succeeding mashes was to be contained. From the center of the dome proceeded a large perpendicular trunk, provided with safety valves on the top, from which trunk issued a horizontal tube having three smaller tubes suspended from it, whose extremities were immersed in the water in the concave vessel, so that all the steam which issued from the copper during the process of boiling worts, must necessarily (except in the event of its acquiring sufficient elasticity to open the safety-valves) pass into the liquor in the concave vessel, and could only rise into the atmosphere by bubbling up through that liquor. The steam thus combining with the water heated it very rapidly, and at the same time impregnated it strongly with the aroma of the hop... .

Mr. Wood's invention was described by the witnesses to consist of a somewhat similar vessel to Mr. Hare's, but the difference was, that instead of the steam from his copper being mixed or brought into contact with the water in the concave vessel, it was carried off by a trunk, and applied to work a steam-engine during the boiling of the worts.

It was contended, on the part of the plaintiff, that this contrivance was totally different from his, inasmuch as it was not part of Mr. Wood's object to preserve the aroma or essential oil of the hop, which was the primary object of Mr. Hare's patent, and that even with respect to the heating the water, which was only performed in Mr. Wood's basin by the heat transmitted by the dome from the steam below it, was by no means accomplished in the same degree for the purpose of brewing.

A number of scientific persons were called on the part of the plaintiff, who stated their opinions as to the dissimilarity in principle and effect between the two inventions, and their reasons for conceiving that the objects of the plaintiff's patent could not be attained by Mr. Wood's apparatus.

On the part of the defendant, several scientific gentlemen were called and gave a contrary opinion; and Mr. Wood was also called on the part of the defendants to explain the nature and effect of his invention, and that it was antecedent to Mr. Hare's. He stated that he had once entertained an idea of preserving the essential oil of the hop, but that the experiment had failed, and he did not think it worth repeating.

The jury, on the Lord Chief Justice's proceeding to sum up the evidence, appearing previously to have made up their opinions, and inclining through the whole course of the trial to the side of the defendant, pronounced their verdict without any hesitation for the defendant.

Figure 1.5 The brewery founded by Hare & Salmon in 1730 in Limehouse, London, UK, and sold to the defendants, Harford and Taylor, in 1796.

§1.24 NICOLAS APPERT'S GROUNDBREAKING INVENTION ON A MANNER OF PRESERVING FOOD AND HIS SOLUTION TO THE DIFFICULTIES IN COLLECTING GAINS FROM ITS USE: A GOVERNMENTAL AWARD—1810

Once an inventor finishes his/her invention, he/she has to consider which of the three possible manners to monetize such invention he/she is going to choose: to file for and obtain a patent and to exploit it by putting the invention to use or by licensing or selling the patent; or to keep the invention as a secret and exploit it while the secret is preserved and/or no competitor reinvents it; or to extract a monetary award from a patron—generally the government, but not necessarily. The two first methods imply the operation of the market. Consumers will reward the inventor or not by acquiring the products or services resulting from his/her invention. The third method is not market-oriented and depends very much on the particular inclinations (political, social, and others) of the patron concerned.

We have seen that the earliest solutions for the monetization of inventions in the area of food were of the third kind: inspired by the systems of acknowledgment of the merits of artists, poets, and playwrights, in Greece and Rome, inventive cooks were recognized through awards (even if the very first method known, which was adopted in Sybaris, in the sixth century BC, had some similarities with today's patents). But patents, in spite of their medieval origins, in the form of industrial privileges, are a construction of the Industrial Revolution and are based essentially on concepts associated with capitalism and free market-oriented economies. So, increasingly, the inventors in the field of food—except the cooks or chefs, as it will be shown—after the eighteenth century, relied on the patent system to secure exclusivity in their inventions, and thus the possibility of seeking in the market the ways to monetize them.

And yet, there are exceptions. Sometimes, the invention in question may be too revolutionary, and the inventor be afraid that it will take a long time for the market to respond positively. Other times, the invention responds to a very specific demand, which converts the prospective market into a very narrow avenue of commercial opportunities. In both cases, inventors may tend to seek solutions for monetization outside the patent system. The law of trade secrets can be a good solution when the inventor still believes that one day, the market will give him/her the positive response he/she seeks. But more frequently, the inventor will divert his/her attention to luring the favor and the protection from a patron.

An example of the use of this third path comes from Nicolas Appert, the French cook and confectioner who, in 1810, invented a method for preserving food. After several years of experiments and failures, Appert invented a method that consisted of hermetically sealing foodstuffs within a jar and sterilizing them by putting the jar in boiling water. Appert did not know how his invention worked, i.e., he was unaware of the scientific principles that led to the killing of bacteria and the prevention of their proliferation in foodstuffs kept in sealed containers. He only knew his invention worked.

Appert could have obtained a patent for his invention, which was indeed genuinely new. Instead, he opted to apply for a monetary reward from the French government, as shown by the first text that follows.

Although Appert did not file for a patent for his method of preserving food, he did not abandon completely other possible mechanisms to capture some financial gains from his invention. As shown by the second text, one mechanism was copyright in the booklet he published, in compliance with the condition imposed by the Minister for granting him a monetary award. A third text shows that Appert also resorted to advertisements to ensure that customers would buy his conserves from his factory.

Appert's invention was improved (or was it copied, or has it served as inspiration?) by two British inventors, Peter Durand and Augustus de Heine. Both inventors obtained patents in the UK in 1810. Durand's invention consists basically of replacing the glass jars used by Appert with tin-coated iron cans. Heine has claimed a more complex method of eliminating air from the vessels containing the food to be preserved. Heine's method was oriented toward an industrial use of food preservation. In the specifications, Heine refers to other processes of eliminating the air from the containers (such as with common air pumps and with steam) as being known. Importantly, Heine claims that the food can be preserved in "The vessels which I call the preserving vessels, may be made of iron, glass, or any other metal, or of earthenware of any shape and size required, strong enough to withstand the pressure of the atmosphere when exhausted." The fifth and sixth texts are extracts of these two patents.

Appert was a prolific inventor and made other inventions (for which he did apply for patents), such as a type of gelatine to be employed as an ingredient for the purification of wine. His authorship of this particular invention has been bitterly contested by a certain Lainé, who claimed that his wife was the true inventor of such substance, but in a way that was much more effective. According to Lainé, Appert's gelatine, instead of improving the wine, destroyed it.

The exchange of accusations between Appert and Lainé can be found in two booklets. One is a work by Appert, titled Notice sur la Dépuration de la Gélatine Extraite des Os, et Rendue Propre à la Clarification des Vins, Eaux-de-Vie, Liqueurs, Etc., *the second edition of which was published in Paris in 1827. An extract of the preamble to this second edition of Appert's booklet follows:*

> *When in 1826, M. Appert published the first edition of this notice, he hoped to stop the torrent of insults and calumnies with which the Lainé couple were pursuing him. He believed that by stating the facts with simplicity, he would silence his opponents. That event has particularly disappointed him.*
>
> *The more moderation he had brought to his reply, the more the facts presented in their true light became indisputable, the more Madame Laine's fury redoubled. Her feminine pride was irritated to the point of losing her reason; and, from that moment, no longer considering any convenience, listening only to her blind anger, there is no assertion, however absurd, that she has not dared to print in her libels. . . .*
>
> *Here is another kindness of this lady that we will treat with less indulgence: she affirms, because this is her favorite proposition, that M. Appert's gelatin is made with tablets of bad meat and vegetable juices. This is a bit strong, and Madame Lainé seems to us to be strangely abusing the privilege of talking nonsense: she hopes to persuade the public that M. Appert is mad enough to make wine glue with carrots, onions, garlic, coles, etc., etc.! Nobody will want to believe her, or, better said, nobody can imagine that Madame Laine, the wife of a druggist, herself very familiar with all that is a drug, has printed such nonsense. . . .*

In response, the husband Lainé, in 1828, published an open letter to Appert, whose heading dispenses with any quotes from its text: "To Mr. Appert, Artist in Calumny, Maker of Bad Stews that are thrown into the water, and of Gelatin that spoils the wines."[27]

§1.24.1 Appert Is Granted an Award of 12,000 Francs by the Minister of the Interior of France, Count Montalvé, on the Condition That He Publicizes His Invention on the Method for Preserving Food—1810

The Minister of the Interior, Count of the Empire, to Mr. Appert

Paris, 30th January 1810.

Second Division.

Board of Arts and Manufactures

My Board of Arts and Manufactures has reported to me, Sir, the examination it has made of your process for the preservation of fruits, vegetables, meat, soup, milk, &c. and from that report no doubt can be entertained of the success of such process. As the preservation of animal and vegetable substances may be of the utmost utility in Sea voyages, in hospitals and domestic economy, I deem your discovery worthy of a special

27. Appert's booklet and Lainé's open letter are available at gallica.bnf.fr.

mark of the goodwill of the government. I have in consequence acceded to the recommendation made me by my council to grant you a recompense of 12,000 francs. In so doing I had in view the assigning you the reward due to the inventors of useful processes, and also the indemnifying you for the expenses you have been obliged to incur, either in the forming your establishment or in the experiments necessary to establish the success of your process. You shall be immediately informed when you may repair to the public treasury and receive the 12,000 francs.

It appears to me of importance, Sir, that you should spread the knowledge of your preserving process. I desire, therefore, that agreeably to your own proposal, you will digest a detailed and exact description of your process. This description, which you will remit to my Board of Arts and Manufactures, shall be printed at your expense, after it shall have been examined. You will then transmit me 200 copies. The transmission of these copies being the only condition I impose on you for the payment of the 12,000 francs, I doubt not you will hasten to fulfil it. I desire, Sir, you will acknowledge the receipt of my letter.

Accept assurances, &c.

§1.24.2 Appert Asserts His Copyright in the Booklet Describing His Invention on the Method of Preserving Food

The author has complied with everything required by law to secure his ownership; he therefore warns that he will prosecute counterfeiters and sellers of counterfeit copies, and that any copy that does not bear his signature will be deemed *counterfeit.* [A sample of Appert's signature follows].

Figure 1.6 Facsimile of Appert's claim of his copyrights and sample of his signature.

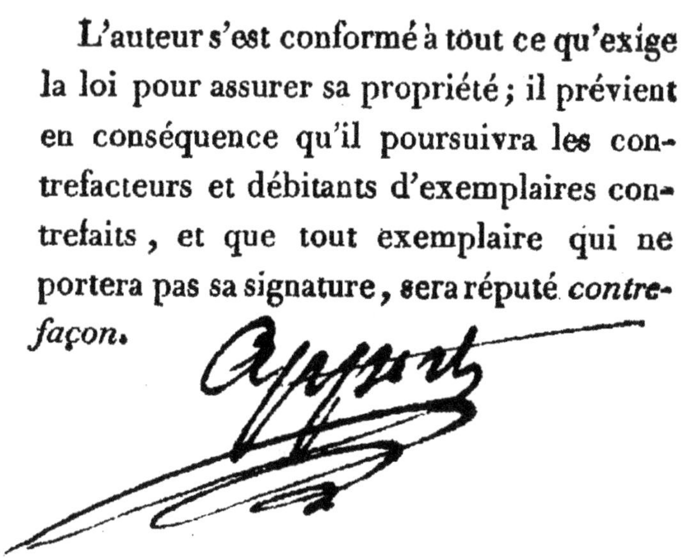
L'auteur s'est conformé à tout ce qu'exige la loi pour assurer sa propriété; il prévient en conséquence qu'il poursuivra les contrefacteurs et débitants d'exemplaires contrefaits, et que tout exemplaire qui ne portera pas sa signature, sera réputé *contrefaçon.*

§1.24.3 Appert's Publisher Advertises Where Legitimate Products Can Be Found

Editor's Notice

To avoid the counterfeits which could take place in the manufacture of preserved substances which could be announced as from the Massy factory, we have just made arrangements with Mr. Appert that allow us to announce to the public, that they will find in our stores, at the Napoléon quai, at the corner of rue de la Colombe, no. 4, in the City, in Paris, an assortment of edibles preserved from the Massy factory, at moderate prices, and which will be inserted in a catalog that we will publish shortly through the newspapers.

N.B. Because certain are not prepared in large numbers, MM. the Admirals in command of fleets, and the Chiefs of staff who would like to stock up for long-distance voyages, are asked to make their requests in advance.

§1.24.4 In the English Version of the 2nd Edition of His Book, Appert Acknowledges That His Invention Has Been Patented by Another Person (Peter Durand? or Augustus de Heine?) but Claims That, Because He Sells His Products in Small Quantities, There Is No Infringement

Advertisement

... From the public papers we learn that a patent has been taken out for preserving provisions according to the process described in this book. We do not pretend to determine how far this patent may interfere with the adoption by other persons of this same process as a manufactory and trade; but, it is certain, that on the small scale on which provisions would be preserved for single families, every person will be at liberty to avail himself of the instructions he may meet with in this volume... .

§1.24.5 The Specifications of Peter Durand's Patent Issued in England in 1810

August 25, 1810 AD—Durand, Peter

"First, preserving animal food, vegetable food, and other perishable articles a long time from perishing and becoming useless," by excluding "all communication with the external air." The food or articles are enclosed "in bottles or other vessels of glass, pottery, tin, or other metals or fit materials," and they are closed by "the usual means of corking, airing, luting or cementing." When large vessels are employed, corks are used "formed of pieces glued together," so that "the pores of that substance shall be in a cross direction with regard to the aperture into which such corks are to be driven." Making use of vessels with "stoppers fitted, or ground with emery, or screw caps with or without a ring of leather or other soft substance between the faces of closure, and also of corks or cross plugs or covers of leather, cloth, parchment, bladder, and the like."

Second, Immersing the vessels which "have been thus charged or well closed" completely in cold water, gradually heating to boiling, and continuing the boiling "for a certain time." "Vegetable substances are to be put into the vessels in the raw or crude state, and animal substances partly or half cooked, although these may be put in raw." The vessels are opened when their contents shall be wanted for consumption.

Lastly, Although the application of the water bath as described is preferred, "an oven, or a stove, or a steam bath, or any other fit situation for gradually & uniformly raising the temperature of the same, and suffering them to cool again," may be employed; and also, the "aperture of the vessel, or a small portion thereof," may be left open, and is closed when "the effect of the heat has taken place."

§1.24.6 The Specification of Augustus de Heine's Patent Issued in 1810

AD 1810—Preserving Animal and Vegetable Food

To all whom these presents shall come, I, Augustus de Heine, of Burr Street, East Smithfield, in the County of Middlesex, Gentleman, send greeting.

Whereas His most Excellent Majesty King George the Third did, by His Letters Patent under the Great Seal of the United Kingdom of Great Britain and Ireland, bearing date at Westminster, the Twenty-sixth day of February, in the fiftieth year of His reign, give and grant unto me, the said Augustus de Heine, my executors, administrators, and assigns, His especial license, full power, sole privilege and authority, that I, the said Augustus de Heine, my executors, administrators, and assigns, during the term of years therein mentioned, should and lawfully might make, use, exercise, and vend, within England, Wales, and the Town of Berwick-upon-Tweed, my Invention of "Certain Apparatus by the Application of known Principles to Preserve Animal Food, Vegetable Food, and other Perishable Articles a long- Time from Perishing or becoming Useless;" ...

My Invention consists in the construction of the vessels wherein the substances are to be preserved, and in the manner of exhausting the same vessels by an apparatus to be described. The vessels which I call the preserving vessels, may be made of iron, glass, or any other metal, or of earthenware of any shape and size required, strong enough to withstand the pressure of the atmosphere when exhausted; the opening must be made as small as the introduction of the substances to be preserved will allow, the cover must be made of iron, glass, or any other metal or hard air-tight substance well fitted in the vessel. On this cover is a box or protuberance wherein a valve is fitted that will let the air escape out of the vessel, but not suffer it to come in... .

Figure 1.7 The drawings that accompanied Augustus de Heine's patent specifications, 1810.

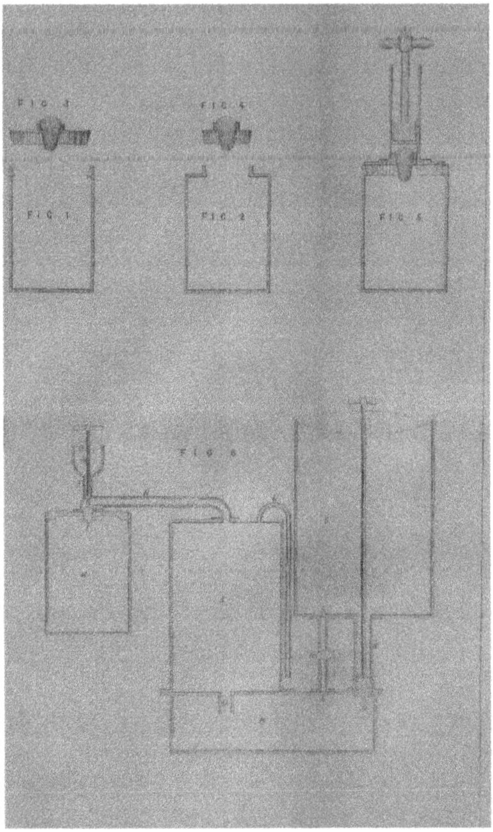

§1.25 BRITISH PATENTS COVERING COOKING RECIPES—1830 ONWARD

It has already been said that through the history of patents the appropriation of cooking recipes is not common. Instead, what we have seen thus far is that the protection of patents has been sought for the devices and equipment necessary for obtaining food ingredients. Foodstuffs and ingredients have also been the subject matter of patenting, but only when they were destined to be mass produced. The Industrial Revolution and the acquired awareness of entrepreneurs of the importance of patents have been instrumental in the growth of the granting of private property rights in those two fields. But cooking recipes have been left outside the patent system to a large extent, for the reason discussed in the Preamble: inventive cooks have other ways, more user-friendly, to get hold of the eventual gains that may result from the exploitation of their inventions.

We will see this in abundance in Chapter 2 when we will be looking at the identification of food and hospitality-related businesses.

However, there are exceptions. Next, some examples of patents granted in the UK for cooking recipes—i.e., not for ingredients that are necessarily mass produced—that have been granted under the Statute of Monopolies. It is not casual that the first patent of that sort that we could find was issued in 1830, i.e., more than two centuries after the Statute was enacted. The reason for such a delay is that in the nineteenth century, every British entrepreneur was under the spell of the patent system as if it provided a secure recipe formula for business success.

§1.25.1 April 24, 1830 AD—McInnes, John

"The manufacture or preparation of certain substances which I denominate 'the British tapioca' and the cakes and the flour to be made from the same."

The tapioca is to be made from potatoes, parsnips, beet or other tuberous roots. The roots are mashed to a pulp with water. The "mucilage or farine" is separated by sieves, washed and dried. It is then "gradually put through a common sieve into a broad cast-iron pan placed on the fire." When it becomes "dry and gritty," the manufacture is complete. To make cakes, "a wooden frame of the size or shape the cakes are wished, is placed on the pan before-mentioned, filled up with farine, taking care that the pan is not too hot." The cakes last for years. The flour may be mixed with wheat-flour, and used for general purposes.

[No drawings].

§1.25.2 May 3, 1836—Whiting, John

"Improvements in preparing certain farinaceous foods."

The improvement related to the lighter sorts of bread, biscuits, etc., and consists in the employment of muriatic acid and carbonate of soda. For every seven pounds of flour, 350 to 500 grains of carbonate of soda, and sufficient of the acid to neutralize the carbonate of soda are used (from 420 to 560 grs. of acid for every 350 grs. of alkali). The carbonate of soda is mixed with 2³⁄₄ pints of water, the muriatic with ³⁄₄ pint. The flour is divided into two equal portions. One portion is kneaded into dough with the soda solution; the remainder is thrown in and the acid solution poured in while the whole is kneaded. Salt may be added for flavoring. Other methods of mixing may be employed.

[No drawings].

§1.25.3 September 11, 1858 AD—Baker, William (Provisional Protection Only)

"Preparing food."

"This invention consists in combining the following ingredients:—Indian meal, locust beans, oatmeal, rice, carbonate of soda, turmeric, caraways, ginger. These ingredients are finely powdered and mixed together, being all first kiln dried; the composition is then packed in packages, and is fit for immediate use. The composition may be made into bread or cakes, or may be made into puddings in the same manner that rice is now used."

[No Drawings].

§1.25.4 January 27, 1859 AD—Hughes, Edward Thomas (A Communication from Messrs. Pascal and Sirben)

"Manufacture of biscuits."

Gluten or wheaten flour "or other farinaceous vegetable" are mixed with oil, butter or "similar nutritious matters."

Proportions: 1 kilogramme gluten, 800 grammes flour, 40 grammes oil, etc. The dough is kneaded in any suitable way.

[No Drawings].

§1.26 MARIE-ANTOINE CARÊME, KNOWN AS THE FIRST FRENCH CHEF, RESORTS TO COPYRIGHT TO APPROPRIATE (IN PART) HIS CREATIVE GENIUS—1833

Marie-Antoine Carême, French pâtissier and cook (1783-1833), was the first professional to designate himself as a "Chef." An extremely inventive professional, he considered his work closely related to that of architects, and accordingly, he developed recipes and complex designs for the pastries he prepared and sold in Paris. In parallel with his successful business as owner of a pastry shop in Paris, Carême also served high-ranking politicians and noble persons, such as Talleyrand in France, George VI, king of England, and Alexander I, czar of Russia.

As it was the common practice of master cooks, Carême did not seek direct protection for his numerous creations, either for his recipes (mainly in the field of pastry but also in general cooking) or for the models of his pastries. Carême was also the author of a number of books on culinary art (and science and technique). In one of his best-known books, L'Art de la Cuisine Française au dix-neuvième siècle *(published in Paris in 1833, in the author's own edition), Carême did not fail to invoke the exclusivity that he obtained from copyright law. Of course, such exclusivity falls on the text itself, not on the ideas and formulae eventually described in the book. Nevertheless, although incomplete, that was the sort of IP protection that creative chefs—along with other intellectual property avenues that speak directly to the protection of personal prestige and reputation—have chosen.*

The following Carême's copyright claim has been extracted from the first volume, the first edition, of his book.

THE ART OF FRENCH CUISINE will consist of 4 volumes, in-8, appearing in two deliveries. The first delivery will be decorated with 13 boards.

Having complied with the formalities required by law, and this work being my property, I declare that I will prosecute those publishers of cookbooks who take, partly or in whole, articles in my book; and also any copy that will not bear my signature.

Figure 1.8 Facsimile of Carême's copyright claim in his book L'ART DE LA CUISINE FRANÇAISE (1833).

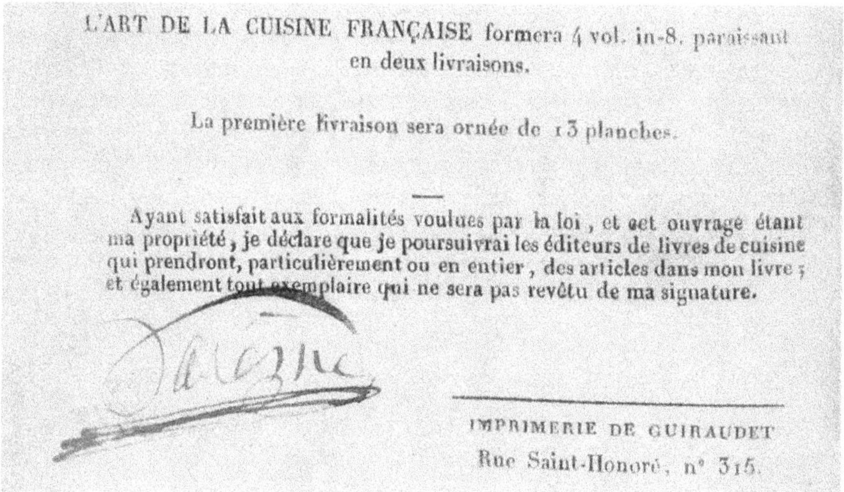

L'ART DE LA CUISINE FRANÇAISE formera 4 vol. in-8, paraissant en deux livraisons.

La première livraison sera ornée de 13 planches.

—

Ayant satisfait aux formalités voulues par la loi, et cet ouvrage étant ma propriété, je déclare que je poursuivrai les éditeurs de livres de cuisine qui prendront, particulièrement ou en entier, des articles dans mon livre; et également tout exemplaire qui ne sera pas revêtu de ma signature.

IMPRIMERIE DE GUIRAUDET
Rue Saint-Honoré, n° 315.

Figure 1.9 On the left, "Hermitage at Sion, in Switzerland." Illustration inserted in Carême's book Le Patissier National Parisien ou Traité Élémentaire et Pratique de la Patisserie Ancienne et Moderne, Suivi d'Observations Utiles au Progrès de cet Art, *vol. 2, at 154 (2nd ed., Garnier Frères, w/d) The illustration refers to the following instructions: "You execute this dessert with almond paste, while the roofs and frames will be in chocolate-colored paste. The body of the pine will be pale green, and the branches of the tree, spring green. You can add small groups of foam after the hermitage, and on the roofs, here and there, you place (see Figure 76) small irregular squares of almond paste marbled with chocolate and pale green. These small squares have the purpose of imitating the stones that the Swiss are in the habit of placing on their houses, in order to protect the roofs from the impetuous gusts that come from the mountains. The three tiers are also made of white almond paste and striped with chocolate-colored paste. The three toppings consist of small croque-en-bouche glazed with caramel, dauphinois cakes with coarse sugar and pistachios, and almond paste crusts colored in the oven and then decorated with pistachio-colored threads; they should be topped with chocolate whipped cream." (id. 153-154). On the right, portrait of M.A. Carême, inserted in the first volume, 2nd edition, of* Le Pâtissier National.

Fig. 76. — Ermitage de Sion en Suisse.

M. A. CARÊME

§1.27 EARLY BRAZILIAN PATENTS ON FOOD RECIPES—1833 ONWARD

Brazil was part of the Portuguese maritime empire until 1822. On April 28, 1809, the king of Portugal, who had fled Lisbon, under the escort of a British fleet, to escape from

Napoleon's army and had set residence in Rio de Janeiro, passed a statute dealing with incentives for the establishment of the national industry. Among various measures, such as tax incentives for the imports of raw materials and favored treatment for the acquisition of nationally produced uniforms for the army, the statute adopted a provision that, in its language and in its spirit, was very similar to the section of the Statute of Monopolies, of 1624, which excepted patents for new manufactures from the general prohibition against monopolies. The adoption of such provision was part of the results of the negotiations between Portugal and England in return for the protection granted by the latter to the Portuguese royal family against France's expansionist efforts. As a result, the British provided an escort for the Portuguese fleet that left Lisbon for Bahia and, later, to Rio de Janeiro and brought the Portuguese heir to the throne (D. João VI) and his family, as well as his entourage. The British fleet remained anchored in Guanabara Bay, in front of Rio de Janeiro, for several years. On its part, Portugal promised (and delivered) the negotiation of a free navigation and trade agreement between the two countries and, in addition, the setting of a patent system that might benefit English inventors. The reason that England could be interested that Brazil had adopted such a system was that Napoleon's blockade of the navigation in the Atlantic Ocean had created concerns for the British economy, then already fully immersed in an Industrial Revolution and producing large surpluses, which needed to be exported.[28]

Section VI of the 1809 Alvará, manifestly inspired in Section VI of the Statute of Monopolies, promised that "the inventors and introducers of any new machine and invention shall enjoy the exclusive privilege ... and all persons in that situation shall present the plan of their new invention to the Royal Board of Commerce; and that the latter, acknowledging the truth and foundation [of such plan], grant them the exclusive privilege for fourteen years, ..."

In the end, English inventors did not need to use the Brazilian patent system as leverage for exporting their surpluses because the war with France ended soon afterward. Moreover, the Brazilian economy suffered from an absolute shortage of skilled human labor, given that its economy was largely based on extractive activities, grounded on slavery. Nevertheless, the patent system was still used by a few Brazilian inventors and importers of new machinery.

The Alvará of 1809 remained in force until 1824 when Brazil (which became an independent country in 1822) adopted a Constitution. A new law on patents was adopted by the Brazilian Parliament in 1830. The patents granted under both statutes were essentially addressed to inventions in the mechanical area, in particular to inventions concerning machinery and transportation. As far as foodstuffs were concerned, patents would cover inventions concerning agricultural staples, such as sugar, coffee, and manioc. Nevertheless, a few patents were granted during that period that respected ways of preparing, cooking and preserving food.

28. For an explanation of the 1809 Alvará and a description of how it was implemented in practice, *see* Nuno Pires de Carvalho, 200 ANOS DO SISTEMA BRASILEIRO DE PATENTS—O ALVARÁ DE 28 DE ABRIL DE 1809—COMÉRCIO, TÉCNICA E VIDA (Lumen Juris, 2009).

The first of the following texts seems to concern a purely commercial privilege, but the fact that the Decree refers to the law of August 28, 1830, which dealt exclusively with the "discovery, invention, or improvement of a useful industry," might imply that the two grantees were importing the machinery and the technology necessary for making and distributing ice. However, that was not the case. Indeed, the privilege was canceled on February 22, 1836, "because such a grant should not have taken place, given that it was not in accordance with the Law of August 28, one thousand eight hundred and thirty, which, making effective the promise of paragraph twenty-six of article one hundred seventy-nine of the Constitution, defined and expressly fixed by articles first and second the cases and conditions under which similar patents must be granted, within which it is not possible to include the privilege granted to the grantees, who not even could take advantage of an extension of the third article of the aforementioned Law, which orders to reward the introducers of foreign industries, because the import of ice cannot be considered as such ...".[29]

The second text refers to the payment of monetary compensation to the inventor of a process of obtaining pekoe tea, which is black tea obtained from the second leaf of the bud. It seems that the inventor was using a different variety of tea, adapted to Brazil (or native of Brazil?) because the Decree mentions that the product resulting from the claimed process needed to become equal to or similar to Chinese tea. Anyway, the remuneration was split into two installments, the payment of the second one depending on Borges' improving his method and eliminating the "herbaceous taste" that his tea left in the mouth. Actually, this remuneration did not correspond exactly to the provisions of the Decree because, under the Decree, the remuneration was to be paid in the case the government decided to acquire the invention and disclose it.[30] *Borges, however, besides obtaining the remuneration, was authorized to keep the ownership of the invention through the grant of an exclusive privilege, as the third text shows.*

The fourth and fifth texts concern the establishment of a factory of paste in the suburbs of Rio de Janeiro by an Italian citizen, Archangelo Fiorito. The examination of his application for a privilege was carried out by the Sociedade Auxiliadora da Indústria Nacional *[...], the foundation of which was inspired by the establishment in France, in 1801, of the* Société d'Encouragement pour l'Industrie Nationale. *For several decades, the* Sociedade Auxiliadora *served as a sort of patent office (in addition to other attributions, such as accompanying and reporting on important technological developments both in Brazil and abroad), with the difference that the competence for granting patents remained with the Emperor. Fiorito's privilege, however, did not correspond to the mere introduction of a foreign industry but to a real improvement, according to the text of the grant.*

---

29. Collecção das Leis do Império do Brazil, 1836, Part 2, at 9 (Typographia Nacional, 1861).
30. The reason for this provision was that, unlike the Alvará of 1809, which was of British inspiration, as said above, the law of 1830 was influenced by the French law of 1791, which allowed inventors to keep their inventions secret until the expiry of the patent.

§1.27.1 Privilege Granted to Giacomo Alessi and Manoel Peman—1833

Imperial Letter of August 3, 1833

Grants to Giacomo Alessi and Manoel Peman exclusive privilege for 15 years to trade ice in the Empire.

The Regency, on behalf of Emperor D. Pedro II, Lets those who see this Letter know that, given what Giacomo Alessi and Manoel Peman pleaded about the privilege they need, for the exclusive trade of ice in this Empire, is pleased, having heard the Attorney of the Crown, Sovereignty and National Treasury, Grant to the aforementioned Giacomo Alessi, and Manoel Peman, for a period of 15 years, the exclusive privilege they require, for the said trade; remaining in the enjoyment of the guarantees, and subject to the clauses, and conditions expressed in the Law of August 28, 1830. And for the assurance of everything that has been said, It has ordered that this Letter be given, signed by the same Regency, with the seal of the coat of arms of the Empire.

Given at the Palace of Rio de Janeiro, on the third day of August, one thousand eight hundred and thirty-three, the twelfth year of independence and of the Empire.

§1.27.2 Financial Award Granted to Manoel Rodrigues Borges for His Disclosure of the Process of Making Pekoe Tea That He Invented—1852

Decree no. 921 of February 28, 1852

Grants to Manoel Rodrigues Borges the sum of ten thousand *reis*, as a prize for the disclosure of the process, which he discovered, to manufacture pekoe tea, or black [tea] with a white tip.

In response to what Manoel Rodrigues Borges has pleaded to Me, asking for a pecuniary remuneration for the disclosure of the process, which he discovered, to manufacture pekoe tea or black tea with a white tip; and having been competently recognized that the tea manufactured by the Applicant is the true pekoe or black [tea] with a white tip, since it still has a slight herbaceous taste, which after some time will disappear, as presumed by the people knowledgeable in this matter, who have been consulted: I am pleased, by virtue of Art. 3 of the Law of August 28, 1830, and in accordance with the opinion of the Empire Business Section of the State Council, issued in the Consultation of August 19, 1851, to grant to the aforementioned Manoel Rodrigues Borges, as a prize for the disclosure of that process, the amount of ten thousand *reis*, which will be paid in two installments, one of four thousand *reis*, as soon as the consignment of the necessary means for this purpose is obtained from the Legislative Body obtains and another of six thousand *reis*, which will only be paid if, after a reasonable period, the herbaceous taste, which is still noticeable in the tea manufactured, disappears completely, according to the process in question, so that it becomes identical to the analogous tea of Chinese production; otherwise, the product of the aforementioned second installment will remain in reserve to be given as a prize to whoever improves the said process, perfecting it to the point of obtaining pekoe tea, or black tea with a white tip, free of the strange flavor mentioned above. That Viscount of Mont'Alegre, Councilor of State, President of the Council of Ministers, Minister and Secretary of State for Empire Affairs, takes knowledge of it, and have it executed.

Palace of Rio de Janeiro on the twenty-eighth of February, one thousand eight hundred and fifty-two, the thirty-first day of independence and of the Empire.

With the initials of His Majesty the Emperor.

Viscount of Mont'Alegre.

§1.27.3 Manoel Rodrigues Borges Obtains a Patent for His Method of Making Pekoe Tea—1857

Decree no. 1,863 of January 3, 1857

Grants to Manoel Rodrigues Borges the privilege for 10 years to manufacture pekoe tea, or black tea with a white tip, according to the process of his invention.

In response to what Manoel Rodrigues Borges has requested of Me, and in accordance with My immediate Resolution of December 31 of last year, grounded on the opinion of the Empire Business Section of the Council of State, issued in Consultation on the fourteenth of last November: I am pleased to grant to him an exclusive privilege for ten years for the manufacture of pekoe tea, or black with a white tip, according to the process that he claims to have invented, and in accordance with the Law of August 28, 1830, the corresponding letter will be issued to him, upon his complying the provisions of §§ 1 and 2 of Article 4 of said Law. That Luiz Pedreira do Couto Ferraz, of My Council, Minister and Secretary of State for Empire affairs, takes knowledge of it, and have it executed. Palace of Rio de Janeiro on January 3, 1857, the thirty-sixth day of Independence and of the Empire.

With the initials of His Majesty the Emperor.

Luiz Pedreira do Couto Ferraz.

§1.27.4 Report of the Examination by *Sociedade Auxiliadora da Indústria Nacional* of the Application for an Exclusive Privilege Filed by Archangelo Fiorito for a New Process of Making Pasta and for the Establishment of a Factory in the Suburbs of Rio de Janeiro—1854

Mr. Faust, Perpetual Secretary, reporting on pending matters, presents and reads the following notices from the Ministry of the Empire:

> Accompanying the request of Archangelo Fiorito, in which he asks for an exclusive privilege for 10 years to establish a pasta factory in the suburbs of this city, so that the Society states its decision. —It is referred to the manufacturing and artistic industry commission... .

About the claim of Archangelo Fiorito, which is as follows:

The Commission for the Manufacturing and Artistic Industry, to which with Archangelo Fiorito's application has been submitted, in which he asks for a ten-year privilege to establish a large-scale pasta factory, respectfully comes today to present its opinion.

The Commission, after having demanded a description of the processes, and some samples of the product that the said Fiorito is intended to manufacture, has visited his small factory and saw him working. The process employed is good, and the product, if not equal to the best we import, is perhaps because it lacks the indispensable means to do so, such as raw material of first quality, skilled workers and good machines. The Commission considers that the claimant's request must be favorably granted; and to persuade the council, its they have the honor of offering it the samples given to them; and on which its judgment largely rests.

Session room, May 31, 1854.—José Albano Cordeiro.—Caetano da Rocha Pacova.—Manoel da Cunha Galvão.

§1.27.5 Archangelo Fiorito Obtains a Patent for a New Process of Making Pasta and for the Establishment of a Factory in the Suburbs of Rio de Janeiro—1855

Decree no. 1,533 January 22, 1855

Grants to Archangelo Fiorito an exclusive privilege for five years to manufacture pasta.

In response to what Archangelo Fiorito informed Me, and in accordance with My Immediate Resolution of the second of the current month, based on the opinion of the Empire Business Section of the Council of State issued in consultation of last November 23: I am pleased to grant to the petitioner exclusive privilege for five years for the manufacture of pasta through a process improved by him, and using flours from the Country, according to the description and drawings submitted and which duly filed.

That Luiz Pedreira do Couto Ferraz, of My Council, Minister and Secretary of State for Empire Affairs, takes knowledge of it, and have it executed. Palace of Rio de Janeiro on the twenty-second of January, one thousand eight hundred and fifty-five, the thirty-fourth of the Independence and of the Empire.

With the initials of His Majesty the Emperor.

Luiz Pedreira do Couto Ferraz

§1.27.6 José Antonio Gomes Obtains a Patent for His Invention of a Wine Made of Barley—1864

Decree no. 3,278 of June 6, 1864

Grants to José Antonio Gomes the privilege for 10 years to prepare and sell in the Empire wine made of barley of his invention.

In response to what José Antonio Gomes has informed Me, and having heard the Counselor Attorney of the Crown, Sovereignty and National Treasury, I am pleased to grant him the privilege for a period of ten years to prepare and sell in the Empire wine made of barley of his invention.

That Domiciano Leite Ribeiro, of My Council, Minister and Secretary of State for Agriculture, Commerce and Public Works, takes knowledge of it, and have it executed. Palace of Rio de Janeiro on June 6, 1864, forty-third of the Independence and of the Empire.

With the initials of His Majesty the Emperor.

Domiciano Leite Ribeiro

§1.28 AN IMPORTANT (AND EARLY) BRITISH COURT OPINION INVOLVING A MATTER OF TYING-IN IN RELATION TO A PATENT FOR A METHOD OF MANUFACTURING SUGAR—1835

The following text refers to an interesting case involving a patent on the manufacturing of sugar. The process of making sugar was at that time covered by several patents, and its consumption had increased with the economic growth and the increase of wealth of the middle class that resulted from the spreading and intensification of the Industrial Revolution. This opinion is important because it involves a matter that today we would call "tie-in:" if the specification of the patent could be read as indicating that one of the ingredients used in the invention—bituminous schistus—was specific and could not be obtained in England but only in France, then the conclusion was that the patent owner, a French entrepreneur, would automatically acquire a monopoly for supplying that substance to any English user.[31] *Consequently, the patent would be void. But if that ingredient was a current one and could be obtained in England by any of the users of the invention, then the patent was valid. The jury found in the latter direction, and the plaintiff was accorded an injunction.*

Derosne v. Fairrie and Others

In the Court of Exchequer, Westminster, before the Lord Chief Baron (Lord Abinger), and a special jury.—February 14, 1835

This was an action for the infringement of a patent granted to the plaintiff, on the 29th of September, 1830, for "Certain improvements in extracting sugar, or syrup, from cane-juice and other substances…".

The Lord Chief Baron then proceeded to sum up the case.—Gentlemen of the jury, this case has occupied a very considerable time; it involves a question of great importance to the plaintiff, and of some importance to the plaintiff. The plaintiff complains of an infringement of his patent, which he took for a new invention of improving the process of manufacturing sugar. I do not think it necessary to trouble you with any objections that arise on the face of the patent and the specification,

31. Similar debates have arisen in relation to patents recently obtained for the unmodified genome sequences of genetic resources that are only found in certain areas in developing countries, such as maca. The patents, if valid, would grant their owners a monopoly in the trade of those resources.

because as they are matters of construction, and therefore matters of law, they cannot in any way be assisted by your verdict, unless, indeed, terms of art are explained by evidence, and then it would be for you to consider whether the evidence produced satisfies you that the terms of art were used in the sense put upon them... .

But the great question turns upon the third and fourth issues. The third issue puts it upon the plaintiff to show, that he has enrolled a specification "setting forth a particular description, and ascertaining the nature of his said invention, and in what manner the same might be performed, in manner and form hereinafter mentioned." The fourth issue is much to the same purpose, except with respect to the question of time, which has been disposed of. So that the question you have to try is this, whether upon the evidence in the case you feel satisfied that certain parts of the specification to which your attention has been called by the counsel who last addressed you, appear to you to be supported by evidence, in such a manner as to satisfy you, that the plaintiff has given in a full and clear account, sufficiently clear for the purpose of practice, of the invention for which his patent is taken out.

Now I will not trouble you with any observations arising from a comparison of one part of the specification with another: it must be admitted that it is obscure... .

But the specific points called to your attention, and which I thought was the only important point worthy of your consideration, is this, is the bituminous schistus, which forms part of the mode of filtration, in your judgment, according to the evidence you have heard, sufficient to satisfy you that the plaintiff meant fairly to communicate, and has fairly communicated, satisfactorily to the world engaged in this sort of trade, which his object was? For you see, that the law requires, that a man, as the price of the monopoly which he obtains for fourteen years for any invention, shall enable the public, after that monopoly has ceased, to have a full and distinct account of the whole of that invention, that the public may have the benefit of it; you are paying to genius a price for the discovery that his genius makes—that price being fourteen years monopoly. But if the genius does not in return tell you what it is, he has fourteen years given him for nothing. It has been established by law, that in the specification he must give in, a full and true disclosure of the nature of his said invention, so that the rest of mankind be able to profit by it when the monopoly ceases, and if he leaves any part of his invention in a state of obscurity, if he leaves any uncertainty about it, and does not give good definite directions how to perform it, he loses the advantages of his patent. Now, it is perfectly true, that in setting forth his specification, he has thought fit to say, that his "invention consists in a means of discoloring syrups of every description, by means of charcoal produced by the distillation of bituminous schistus alone, or mixed with animal charcoal, or even animal charcoal alone." ... Then, gentlemen, you certainly have upon the evidence these facts:—that the bituminous schistus, from which he says the charcoal was to be made by distillation (he means by calcination no doubt) is of various substances, containing various degrees of sulphuret of iron. Plaintiff says the sulphuret of iron ought to be expelled; he does not state which of the various bituminous schistus he makes use of; he may make use of any one of them. He does not state any process of expelling the sulphuret of iron... .

On the other hand, if you should find it in evidence, that there is no bituminous schistus that is proved to be used, except that which plaintiff himself supplies; and if you should think from that, that it was not improbable he contemplated the use of his own, that might be a reason for his being so general, that no party could find in England the sort which would answer the purpose, he might apply to the plaintiff who manufactures it abroad to get it from him. But if such was his intention, that would destroy the patent... .

Now this is the evidence you have to consider on the part of the plaintiff, which it does strike me is the only part which it is necessary for me to read to you; because if on this part of the case you are satisfied that the plaintiff has made out a case, which, in your judgment sets up the specification, I then think the rest of the case is with the plaintiff. But this part I think is doubtful; not on the face of the specification alone—I wish to be well understood—the doubt does not arise on reading the specification. I presume you would suppose that any chemist would know what bituminous schistus meant; that it was some substance which when distilled, would produce charcoal; therefore, on the face of the specification there is no objection so far as that goes. But when you consider the evidence, when you find by the evidence that there are various sorts of bituminous schistuses, and that there is none of them known, at least as far as appears by the plaintiff's case, in England, capable of producing it without the sulphuret of iron, by any process known to experienced chemists (it may be known in France, there may be various substances there capable of producing it by calcination), then certainly in that case my opinion is that you ought to find a verdict for the defendant. Now, on the evidence, there is nothing to show that bituminous schistus has been discovered of this sort. If the plaintiff has it in France, it is very likely he might suppose that it might be found anywhere capable of performing the object: it is his misfortune that he has not inquired whether this country produces the same: in that case he might have stated that such schistus might be imported from France, that would have made the patent good; but he made that no part of his specification. It is for you to say upon the evidence you have heard from the plaintiff, combined with any knowledge you may have upon the subject yourselves. Supposing you are of the opinion that there are various bituminous schistuses, which might not equally answer the purpose, and that those not being set forth in the specification, it is probable that any person using the specification would be obliged to have recourse to the plaintiff to procure it; if you are of that opinion on the evidence, then I think the defendants are entitled to your verdict. If you are also of opinion upon the evidence that bituminous schistus will not do—one witness says that he disapproves of it, and another found it not to answer; the difficulty of the case is to ascertain whether they have not used the bituminous schistus found here, or whether they have not got it from a different part... .

The jury retired for about fifty minutes, and brought in a verdict for the plaintiff.

The Lord Chief Baron (to the jury).—Are you satisfied upon the evidence that the bituminous schistus obtained in England might be properly adopted?

Foreman of the Jury.—That seems to be the opinion of the jury.

§1.29 SOME PATENTS AND DISPUTES INVOLVING ONE OF THE MOST IMPORTANT FOOD-RELATED INVENTIONS OF ALL TIMES: THE REAPING MACHINE—1831-1857

Mechanization in agriculture has been a human endeavor for a long time, and the invention of the reaping machine has enormously contributed to it. The reaping machine permitted a significant increase in the surfaces of lands to be sowed and in the productivity of farming and food production. The success of agriculture through its intensive mechanization explains the economic growth of the United States in the nineteenth century and its reaching worldwide economic and technological leadership, along with the UK.

The reaping machine was not the product of a single invention, but it was rather the result of the gradual improvement of a very old concept, which started emerging in Antiquity. Sickles and scythes are mentioned in the Bible and were used in Ancient Egypt. Pliny the Elder has described a mechanical reaper that was used in Gaule. Of course, Humankind had to wait for the expansion of scientific and mechanical knowledge that emerged from the Renaissance and the subsequent Scientific Revolution to invent machines of great effectiveness. But once inventors were in hold of sufficient expertise, the invention of the modern reaping machine started.[32]

The history of the invention of the reaping machine has been summarized by Holland Thomson as follows:

> *The first attempts to build a machine to cut grain were made in England and Scotland, several of them in the eighteenth century; and in 1822 Henry Ogle, a schoolmaster in Rennington, made a mechanical reaper, but the opposition of the laborers of the vicinity, who feared loss of employment, prevented further development. In 1826, Patrick Bell, a young Scotch student, afterward a Presbyterian minister, who had been moved by the fatigue of the harvesters upon his father's farm in Argyllshire, made an attempt to lighten their labor. His reaper was pushed by horses; a reel brought the grain against blades which opened and closed like scissors, and a traveling canvas apron deposited the grain at one side. The inventor received a prize from the Highland and Agricultural Society of Edinburgh, and pictures and full descriptions of his invention were published. Several models of this reaper were built in Great Britain, and it is said that four came to the United States; however, this may be, Bell's machine was never generally adopted.*
>
> *Soon afterward three men patented reapers in the United States: William Manning, Plainfield, New Jersey, 1831; Obed Hussey, Cincinnati, Ohio, 1833; and Cyrus Hall McCormick, Staunton, Virginia, 1834. Just how much they owed to Patrick Bell cannot be known, but it is probable that all had heard of his design if they had not seen his drawings or the machine itself.*

32. An account of the progressive invention of the reaping machine since Antiquity can be found in Bennett Woodcroft, APPENDIX TO THE SPECIFICATIONS OF ENGLISH PATENTS FOR REAPING MACHINES (George Edward Eyre and William Spottiswoode, 1853).

§1.29.1 William Manning's Patent of 1831

Specification of a patent for an improved Machine for Cutting Grass and Grain. Granted to William Manning, Plainfield, Essex county, May 3, 1831.

I provide an axle tree with two wheels, of the common construction. To this axle tree I attach shafts, by which a horse is to draw the machine. From the axle tree extend two arms in the direction of the shafts; these arms are morticed into, or otherwise attached to the axle tree; they are of greater length than the shafts, extending beyond them a sufficient distance for the cutting apparatus to be entirely clear of the horse. The two arms are united together by a cross bar at their extreme ends; which cross bar, when the machine is in action, rests, and slides forward on the ground; teeth of six or eight inches in length, more or less, are set like rake teeth, standing forward on the cross bars. These are made slender, and are for the purpose of holding the grass or grain to be cut.

The cutters stand immediately above the teeth; and receive a traversing motion in a way to be presently described... .

What I claim as my invention, and for which I ask letters patent, is the combined action of the teeth and cutters, whether the cutters are moved in a traversing or a revolving direction.

§1.29.2 Obed Hussey's Patent—1833

United States Patent Office

Obed Hussey of Cincinnati, Ohio

Improvement in Machines for Reaping and Cutting Grain

Specification forming part of Letters Patent dated December 31, 1833

To all whom it may concern:

> Be it known that I, Obed Hussey, of Cincinnati, in the county of Hamilton and State of Ohio, have made an improvement in the useful arts, being a machine for reaping or cutting all kinds of small grain and grasses, which is described as follows, reference being had to the annexed drawings... .

In this machine the following points are claimed as new and original:

1. The straight horizontal saw with the teeth sharp on their two sides for cutting grain.
2. The guards forming double bearers above and below the saw, whereby the cutting is made sure, whether with a sharp or a dull edge, the guards at the same time protecting the saw from rocks or stones or other large substances it may meet with.

3. The peculiar construction that the saw teeth may run free, whereby the necessary pressure and consequent friction of two corresponding edges cutting together as on the principle of scissors are entirely avoided.
4. The peculiar arrangement by which the horses are made to go before the machine, being more natural and greatly facilitating the use of the machine, and the general arrangement of the parts, as above described.
5. In cutting grass the platform is reduced in width and the grass falls on the ground as it is cut.

§1.29.3 Criticism of Hussey's Patent—1831

For a Machine for reaping Grain; Obed Hussey, Cincinnati, Hamilton county, Ohio, December 1831.

The mowing machine here described is to run upon wheels attached to the frame or carriage, in front of which the horses draw... .

On the 3rd of May, 1831, W. Manning, of New Jersey, obtained a patent for a machine for cutting grass and grain, see vol. viii. p. 195, essentially like that now patented, The comb, it is true, is not double, in that machine, but this is not a point of importance; the cutters are perfectly similar, and are made to vibrate upon the comb. The first claim, therefore, in the present patent necessarily falls to the ground, and with it the whole superstructure. The claim in the first patent is to "the combined action of the teeth and cutters." We are not quite sure that the double teeth are an improvement, as there will be much danger of stubble insinuating itself within, and obstructing them.

§1.29.4 McCormick's First Patent—1834

United States Patent Office

Cyrus H. McCormick, of Rockbridge County, Virginia

Improvement in Machines for Reaping Small Grain

Specification forming part of Letters Patent dated June 21, 1834

To all whom it may concern:

> Be it known that I, Cyrus H. McCormick, of Rockbridge county and State of Virginia, have invented a new and useful Improvement in Reaping all Kinds of Small Grain; and I do hereby declare that the following is a full and exact description of the construction and operation of the said machine as invented or improved by me.
>
> ...

My claim is for the arrangement of the several parts so as to constitute the above-described machine, and I particularly claim the method of cutting by means of a vibrating blade operated by a crank having the edge either smooth or with teeth, either with stationary wires or pieces above and below, and of securing them.

I also claim the method of gathering and bringing the grain back to the cutter and delivering it on the apron or platform by means of a reel, as described above, movable to any height required to suit the grain, and the platform to hold the grain until a sufficient quantity shall have been collected for a sheaf, more or less.

...

§1.29.5 Another Patent of Cyrus McCormick, Issued in 1847 and Reissued in 1853

United States Patent Office

Cyrus H. McCormick, of Chicago, Illinois

Improvement in Reaping-Machines

Specification forming part of Letters Patent No. 5,335, dated October 23, 1847; Reissue No. 239, dated May 21, 1853

To all whom it may concern:

> Be it known that I, Cyrus H. McCormick, of Chicago, Illinois, have invented new and useful improvements in the reaping-machine formerly patented by me; and I do hereby declare that the following is a full, clear, and exact description thereof, reference being had to the accompanying drawings, making part of this specification, in which—
>
> ...

What I claim as my invention, and desire to secure by Letters Patent, as improvements on the reaping machine secured to me by Letters Patent bearing date the June 21, 1834, and the January 31, 1845, is—

(1) Placing the gearing and crank forward of the driving-wheel farther back than heretofore, and sufficiently so as to balance the rear part of the frame and the raker thereon when this position of the parts is combined with the sickle back of the axis of motion of the driving-wheel by means of the vibrating lever, substantially as herein described.

(2) The combination of the reel for gathering the grain to the cutting apparatus and depositing it on the platform with the seat or position for the raker arranged and located as described, or the equivalent thereof, to enable the raker to rake the grain from the platform and deliver and lay it on the ground at the side of the machine, as described.

§1.29.6 Notice on Hussey's and McCormick's Reaping Machines at the London Great Exhibition of 1851; McCormick's Invention Is Recognized with a Council Medal

UNITED STATES.

65. Hussey, Obed, Baltimore, Maryland— Inventor, Patentee, and Manufacturer. Reaping and mowing machine.—Plate, p. 1437.

"We have then two good American reaping machines. Their respective merits time will discover. At present we only know that Mr. McCormick's machine is best for barley and oats, when not intended to be bound up in the sheaf; Mr. Hussey's for corn laid by the weather, or standing upon steep ridges. Mr. Hussey's can cut rushes, as was shown in Windsor Park. Mr. McCormick's has received a prize this autumn in the United States for cutting prairie grass, competing with three others."—Juries' Reports.

73. McCormick, C. H., Chicago, Illinois—Inventor. Virginia grain reaper.—Plate, p. 1437.

This machine is worked by four horses throughout the day, and is attended by a man or boy to drive the team, and a man to take the grain from it into parcels of suitable size for binding. Six to eight men are required to bind and shock the grain. This is the estimated labor of harvesting wheat that stands up and yields from 20 to 30 bushels per acre. If the wheat be heavier and fallen, the operation will be more difficult, and the speed retarded.

...

[Though by no means the first to originate the construction of a reaping machine, it would seem that America has been the first to all but realize the most perfect machine of the kind, had not evidence to the contrary been in existence.]

...

McCormick's, or that for which the Council Medal was granted in the Great Exhibition of 1851, is distinguished by the great simplicity of its cutting part, and resembles a straight saw vibrating rapidly from right to left; the teeth inclining alternately in each direction, so that at every vibration, half of them are inclined in the direction of the motion. The Jury in their award point out that some amendment is required to fit them for cutting the additional number of straws in a given space. "The yield in England nearly doubles that of America," they must therefore be adapted to the superior farming they will have to encounter.

...

Juries' reports.

§1.29.7 McCormick (Unsuccessfully) Sues the Successor of Manning on the Allegation That the Latter's Patent Infringes His Own—1857

U.S. Supreme Court

***McCormick v. Talcott [successor of Manning]*, 61 U.S. 20 How. 402 (1857)**

Syllabus

The reaping machines made by Manny do not infringe McCormick's patent, either as to the divider, the manner in which the reel is supported, or the combination of the reel with a seat for the raker.

McCormick not being the original inventor of the machine called a divider, but the patentee of only an improvement for a combination of mechanical devices, could not hold as an infringer one who used only a part of the combination.

...

Mr. Justice Grier delivered the opinion of the Court.

The bill charges the defendants with infringing two several patents granted to complainant, for improvements in the machine known as McCormick's Reaper. One of these patents bears date the 31st of January, 1845; the other on the 24th of May, 1853, being the reissue of a previous one, dated 23rd of October, 1847. The defendants are charged with infringing the fourth and fifth claims of the patent of 1845 and the second claim of the reissued patent of 1853.

I. The first infringement charged is that of the divider, or that part of the reaping machine which is defined "as an arrangement or apparatus for separating the grain to be cut from that which is to be left standing."

...

The arrangement, combination, and location of the raker's seat by defendants has been patented to Manny as an independent contrivance and distinct invention. The place for the raker is obtained by a change in the shape of the platform, different from any before employed. It differs from the complainant's device in principle as well as in form and combination. The raker's seat is on a different part of the machine, where he may stand without destroying the balance of the machine or tilting it up. It requires no modification of the reel. It requires no such combination or modification of parts of the machine in order to find a place for the raker, which is an essential part of complainant's claim.

It is substantially different, both in form and in combination, from that claimed by the complainant, and is consequently no infringement of his patent.

Concurring, as we do, in the opinion and decision of the court below on these several points, the decree is.

Affirmed with costs.

Figure 1.10 Hussey's (left) and McCormick's (right) reaping machines, as exhibited in London at the 1851 World Fair.

§1.30 IN THE FIRST HALF OF THE NINETEENTH CENTURY, COMMON LAW HAD ALREADY CONSOLIDATED THE NOTION OF TRADE SECRETS AS PROPRIETARY BUSINESS ASSETS

The text that follows consists of excerpts from an opinion of the British Court of Common Pleas that settled a dispute involving the licensing and communication of a secret process that transformed British brandy into an imitation (in taste and in color) of (French) cognac, which "should be fully equal, if not superior, to the patent French distilled brandy." The importance of this opinion—from an intellectual property perspective—lies in the several clauses of the agreements between the parties dealing with the communication of the secret, its use, the preservation of its confidentiality, and the technical assistance provided by the owner to the licensees. It results from the description of the facts that the secret was not fully in the hands of the plaintiff—a certain Johann Gottfried Stumpf having been called to supply some additional secrets and to provide technical management of the process of rectifying the British brandy and giving it the same color and taste of the French drink. Interestingly, the several agreements involved periods that were multiples of seven years (including the engagement of Stumpf), exactly like the fourteen-year term of patents, which, as explained elsewhere, has a Biblical connotation.[33] *In addition to that aspect, which could be seen*

---

33. *See* Nuno Pires de Carvalho, A ESTRUTURA DOS SISTEMAS DE PATENTES E DE MARCAS—PASSADO, PRESENTE E FUTURO [THE STRUCTURE OF THE PATENT AND TRADEMARK SYSTEMS—PAST, PRESENT, AND FUTURE], at 233 (Lumen Juris, 2009):

> Lambert has provided an interesting explanation of the adoption of the seven-year period for apprenticeship. According to him, seven years was the time that old English law established as necessary for a farm servant to become free: at the end of seven years of work, that servant became free. [J. Malet Lambert, TWO THOUSAND YEARS OF GILD LIFE—OR AN OUTLINE OF THE HISTORY AND DEVELOPMENT OF THE GILD SYSTEM FROM EARLY TIMES, WITH SPECIAL REFERENCE TO ITS APPLICATION TO TRADE AND INDUSTRY, TOGETHER WITH A FULL ACCOUNT OF THE GILDS AND TRADING COMPANIES OF KINGSTON-UPON-HULL, FROM THE 14TH TO THE 18TH CENTURY, at 195 (A. Brown & Sons, Hull, 1891)]. The parallel was that, during the period of apprenticeship, the apprentice was dependent on his master. After this period, the apprentice was freed. The seven years necessary for

as outdated, the agreements reveal that in the first half of the nineteenth century, in the UK, common law had already reached a clear understanding of the legal value of trade secrets, not very different from what we have today.

The dispute was caused by the divergence between the parties concerning the sums of money to be paid by the licensees to the licensor. In the end, the plaintiff won the case. For the sake of brevity, most of the details of the financial arrangements between the parties have been omitted.

Home v. Booth Bart., and Grimble

January 31, 1842

Assumpsit. The first count stated-that before and at the time of the making of the articles of agreement, and of the making of the defendants' promise, thereinafter respectively mentioned, certain persons trading under the style and firm of Betts and Co., sold a certain liquor, to wit, British brandy, at Smithfield Bars in London, whereof the defendants then had notice; that afterwards and before the making of the said promise, to wit on the 27th of July 1835, by certain articles of agreement bearing date, &e., made between the plaintiff of the first part, the defendant Grimble of the second part, and the defendant Booth of the third part, the plaintiff; in consideration of the emoluments to arise as thereinafter mentioned, covenanted with the defendants respectively to communicate to them, their executors and administrators, and to communicate to them only, and to use all the knowledge he possessed connected with a certain process for the rectification and effectual purification of grain-spirit, and communicating to it the flavor of Cognac brandy, without the admixture of any imported brandy, and without any infraction or evasion of the then existing excise laws, the plaintiff, in consideration of certain emoluments, agreed with the defendants respectively, to communicate to them only, all the knowledge he possessed, connected with that matter, and to develop to them the whole process for conducting the same, and to convey to them all necessary information as to materials, &e., so that they might be able to prosecute the same independently of the plaintiff. And by the said articles it was agreed that the plaintiff should, within twenty-one days of the date thereof, make out and deliver to the defendants, or one of them, a written statement of the whole of the inventions and discoveries connected with his improved process for the rectification of spirit and preparing of brandy, and the art of giving the same the true coloring in imitation of the most approved Cognac brandy, setting forth also his theoretical and practical views applicable to the rectification of spirit, &e. &e. And by the said articles the plaintiff declared that he had not divulged, and would not divulge, any of those processes to any other person or persons whatsoever during the existence of that

---

the farm servant to free himself from dependence on his master were taken as a paradigm. It was certainly not based on any concrete analysis of the market and the technology, as few industries would require such a long learning period. It is worth noticing that the English legal tradition had biblical origins (Genesis, 29, 20), which Camões reflected in his famous sonnet that begins with these verses: "For seven years as a shepherd Jacob served/ Laban, father of Rachel, beautiful mountain woman./ But he didn't serve her father, he served her/ and he only wanted her as a reward."

contract, and that he would answer all inquiries from the defendant Booth or the defendant Grimble touching those matters, and render his best aid and assistance at all reasonable hours in forwarding the progress of that undertaking, and that he would give his personal attention and superintendence to the rectification and the flavoring and coloring of the spirit, &e. &e., and act and do in all things in respect of that matter to the best of his power and ability, and as a faithful party to the interests of the defendants, and should and would be true and faithful to the defendants in all things, and keep true and just and complete accounts of all dealings, orders, and transactions made and entered into, by the plaintiff for and on behalf of the defendants in, or connected with, the said undertaking, and make out and deliver to the defendant Grimble or the defendant Booth all or any of such accounts whenever thereunto required by the defendant Grimble or the defendant Booth, or their respective executors or administrators, he, the plaintiff, having all necessary assistance for those purposes; and further that he, the plaintiff, should not at any time during that contract, instruct any other person or persons in those matters, nor engage in any other business or employment whatsoever, or enter into any liabilities as a partner or surety, and should not hold himself out as a partner with the defendants, or either of them, in that undertaking, &e. And it was in the said articles stipulated that the plaintiff should give his attendance to direct and as superintending only, and as might be necessary to forward the usual proceedings of the manufacturing establishment; and that his presence and attention were to be given for that purpose only, and no further, notwithstanding any thing previously contained; and that if any other superintendent should be appointed to interfere in those proceedings, the plaintiff should no longer be required to give his personal attendance. And the plaintiff thereby further engaged that the articles produced by him on his being supplied with such suitable spirit and materials as might be specified in the statement to be made out by the plaintiff, should be fully equal, if not superior, to the patent French distilled brandy (meaning thereby the said Betts and Co.'s, of Smithfield Bars, British brandy then selling in London). And in consideration of the premises the defendants did, for themselves and each of them, their and each of their heirs, executors, and administrators, jointly and severally, undertake that the defendant Grimble should, within twelve months from the date thereof, carry into operation the said discovery or improved process, agreeably to the directions contained iii the written statement to be given in by the plaintiff, and provide a suitable capital and plant, and all proper utensils and apparatus to carry on the same; and that the defendant Grimble, his executors and administrators, should pay unto the plaintiff annually, for a term of twenty-one years, determinable as thereinafter mentioned, to commence from the 19th of July then instant, the sum of 1501., and the further payment of 6d. per gallon on all spirit sold, sent out, or used rectified by the said process, and on all brandy sold and sent out, but not drunk on the premises, or bona fide given away as samples... . And it was thereby agreed that the plaintiff should be empowered to select and purchase the articles used in that new process of rectification, or used for flavoring and coloring the produce, rendering at all times just and true accounts and the original invoices and memoranda of all purchases made by him—and which should not exceed the sum of 1001. for materials on hand—which the defendants thereby agreed to provide for payment of. And to prevent all dispute between the parties, it was thereby agreed that at the same time that the plaintiff delivered his written process to the defendant Grimble or the defendant Booth, as aforesaid, a written statement should be given in by them, or one of them, to the plaintiff of the exact process then used and employed by them, stating and setting forth, &e.; and if no such written statement should be at that time given in, or if such process should be different from that communicated, by the plaintiff, that it should be considered that his process was a new and distinct process, and should be taken as such accordingly, and that no improvement or alteration or modification of the plaintiffs process thereafter should annul or alter the said engagements in the said articles of agreement contained... . And it was thereby further agreed that it should not be lawful for the defendant Grimble or the defendant Booth, to use or apply, or in any manner to aid in carrying on, the said processes, or any part thereof, except such as were then already used or carried on by the defendant Grimble or the defendant Booth, as set forth by their statement, in any other establishment, during the existence of that contract, than such premises as were then taken for those purposes, and situated, &e., without the plaintiff's consent and participation. And it was thereby agreed, that if, at the expiration of the first seven or fourteen years of the said term of twenty-one years, the defendants should desire to relinquish and abandon the said processes and that undertaking entirely, then it should be lawful for them so to do on giving to the plaintiff six calendar months' previous notice in writing, and thereupon that agreement should be at an end, except as to the enforcement, up to that time, of the stipulations therein contained. And it was thereby covenanted between the parties thereto, that the receipts falling due to the plaintiff annually, should, after the lapse of two years from the date of the said articles of agreement, amount to 4001. annually; and that should they fall short in any one year, and not be made up to that amount, the plaintiff should not be obliged to confine his attention or his secrets to the defendant Grimble or the defendant Booth. And the said parties thereby agreed that a penalty of 10,0001. should be recoverable in any court of law, as liquidated damages, if either party should, during the continuance of the said term, divulge to any other person or persons whatsoever any of the processes, secrets, or knowledge touching the said matters, whereby the purification, &e. should or might be imitated; or if the defendants, or either of them, should, after the determination of the said term, by notice as thereinafter mentioned, divulge such process, secrets, or knowledge to any other person or persons whatsoever; or make, rectify, or otherwise use the same processes for any purpose whatsoever; ...

That afterwards and before the commencement of the suit, to wit, on the 23rd of August 1836, by an agreement then made between one Johann Gottfried Stumpf, the defendants, and the plaintiff—under which the plaintiff was to have the benefit of Stumpf's services, and of certain secrets possessed by him, in the prosecution of the process or manufacture—it was agreed that Stumpf should deposit with the plaintiff a written description of the modus operandi, and a recipe of the ingredients to be used; that Stumpf should, with the consent of the plaintiff, be engaged by the defendants for a term of seven years from the 1st of August 1836—the agreement to be absolute, and binding on all parties, for a further term of seven years, provided the house, after the expiration of the first seven years, should, with the consent of the plaintiff previously obtained in writing, continue to use the flavoring or the processes of Stumpf, or should fail to give Stumpf six months' previous notice of the intended relinquishment; that should the attendance of Stumpf be requested in England, the annual sum of 300l. should be allowed him for the same, or such proportional part as might accord with the period of his required occupation, as well as all reasonable travelling expenses, in addition to his other allowances; ... and the defendants thereby agreed to sell the brandy made at the works at Albany Street, at fair usual mercantile prices; and it was thereby agreed that the parties thereto should not divulge those processes or secrets, or the knowledge contained in the statement, or the recipe of Stumpf; and that the defendants would not otherwise use or apply the same than at the said works at Albany Street, (then followed a clause for referring disputes to arbitration); ...

§1.31 THE KING'S BENCH DIVISION ENDORSES A NON-COMPETING CLAUSE IN AN AGREEMENT INVOLVING THE TRANSFER OF A BUSINESS AND A SECRET RECIPE FOR THE MAKING OF GINGER BEER—1847

Because their success is dictated by prestige, and because such prestige is often associated with location, restaurant owners tend to be very aware of the geographical proximity of competitors. That is the reason that explains why it is frequent that agreements involving the transfer of the premises in which the services of restoration are provided, along with the business identifiers and secret recipes, involve a clause of non-competing within certain geographical boundaries. This case of 1847 confirms this. Even though the first judge (not identified in this report) believed that the agreement not to compete was illegal because of its undetermined duration, the majority decided otherwise, in the sense that the geographical boundaries were defined (and, actually, narrow). Anyway, the first judge used the term that presides over this discussion: the non-competing clause must be proportional to the interests protected.

King's Bench Division

Pemberton v. Vaughan

Tuesday, February 9, 1847

An agreement to give up a house and goodwill of a business for 7l., and not to open a shop in the same line of business within one mile of the said house under a forfeiture of 20l., is not illegal on the ground that the restraint of trade is unlimited in point of time and may continue though the purchaser ceases to carry on the business... .

Assumpsit. The declaration stated that, before the agreement thereinafter mentioned, defendant was possessed of a house in which he carried on the trade of a maker and seller of ginger beer, and was also possessed of a certain recipe for making ginger beer. That it was agreed by plaintiff and defendant that, in consideration of 7l. to be paid to defendant by plaintiff, defendant should give up possession to plaintiff of the house, together with the goodwill of the said trade, and the recipe for making ginger beer; and that the defendant, for the consideration aforesaid, further agreed not to open any shop in the same line of business within one mile of the house aforesaid, under a forfeiture of 20l. Averment of mutual promises, and that plaintiff paid the 7l. to defendant, and took possession of the house, recipe and goodwill. Breach, that defendant had opened a shop as maker and seller of ginger beer within the prohibited distance, and had thereby forfeited 20l., which he had not paid.

...

The agreement is illegal; for the defendant is restrained in his business for life, and even though the plaintiff should use the house for purposes of some other business. The restraint on the defendant is disproportionated to the protection required by the plaintiff. The agreement is in effect a protection of the house.

Lord Denman C.J.... As to the other point, there is no case which decides that an agreement in restraint of trade is illegal because it is for life. It does not follow that the plaintiff will not require the protection of the agreement because he may not himself continue the business: he may sell the business, and sell it on better terms on account of the protection secured by the agreement.

Paterson J. I am of the same opinion. Even if the cases cited did establish the point, which they do not, that the jury were bound to give 20l. as damages in this case, yet that 20l. is not subject matter of the agreement. With respect to the other point, the agreement is perfectly legal; the restraint of trade is limited as to distance, although it is not as to time.

Coleridge and Wightman Js. concurred.

Rule discharged.

§1.32 NANCY M. JOHNSON OBTAINS A PATENT FOR A FREEZER AND GIVES BIRTH TO THE ICE CREAM INDUSTRY—1843

As seen above, the search for obtaining and preserving ice for culinary purposes—either for cooking or for preserving foodstuffs—has been a long endeavor in History, with not always successful results. A major breakthrough came with Nancy Maria Johnson's invention of a freezer, which enormously facilitated the task of preparing ice cream. It can be said that this invention is the starting point of today's global, huge industry of ice cream.

United States Patent Office

Nancy M. Johnson, of Philadelphia, Pennsylvania.

Artificial freezer.

Specification of Letters Patent No. 3,254, dated September 9, 1843; Antedated July 29, 1843

To all whom it may concern:

> Be it known that I, Nancy M. Johnson, of the city of Philadelphia and State of Pennsylvania, have invented a new and useful Improvement in the Art of Producing Artificial Ices, and that the following is a full and exact description of the machinery for carrying into effect the said improvement:

...

I do not confine myself to any particular material in the construction of the freezer or beater for lemon, orange and other juices containing acid which might react slightly upon tinned iron, I prefer glass cylinders for freezers and hard wood or ivory for the wings of my beater, for cream and other substances which are not acid in their properties, the thickest of tinned iron is the most suitable material of which to form the beater.

When the substance to be frozen is placed in a freezer formed of two concentric cylinders and having ice and salt in a central cylinder the beaters may be attached to horizontal arms on the main vertical axis and go down on opposite sides of the central refrigerating cylinder.

...

What I claim as new in this my invention and for which I desire to obtain Letters Patent is—

The above-described revolving curved beater with its vertical axis, in combination with a freezing apparatus as above described and adapted to the purpose herein set forth.

Figure 1.11 Left: Illustration of Nancy Jonhson's invention, part of her patent specifications. Right: Portrait of Nancy M. Johnson.

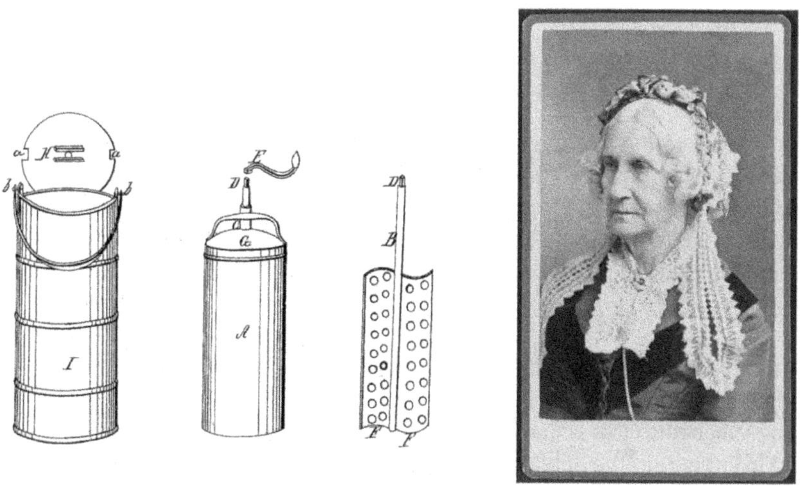

§1.33 TWO FRENCH INVENTORS OBTAIN A PATENT FOR GINGERBREAD COOKIES WITH THE SHAPES OF THE LETTERS OF THE ALPHABET—1851

In the nineteenth century, creative manufacturers of foodstuffs had already understood the economic value of patents and had started using the system as a business practice.

This happened, as noted above, in regard of those foodstuffs apt to be mass-consumed. Chefs learned very soon that, in their case the patent system is replaced with great advantages by trade secret protection and the capture of prestige through business identifiers. In the universe of foodstuff-related patents, one nineteenth-century title stands out: a patent for cookies made in the shape of alphabet characters, with the purpose of luring children to the voluntary, if not enthusiastic, learning of reading. The invention was received with irony from the press and criticism from the industrial word, as the following texts show; nevertheless, the manufacturers of the alphabet cookies did not waste efforts in advertising their product.

§1.33.1 Decree Granting a Patent to Victor Claude and Antoine Léopold Chéradame for Their Invention of "Hygienic Alphabets"—1851

Patent for invention

without Government guarantee.

The Minister of Agriculture and Trade,

Considering the Law of July 5, 1844;

Considering the file constituted on July 1, 1851, at 10:30 a.m., at the General Secretariat of the Prefecture of the Seine department and noting the filing made by Messrs. Claude and Chéradame of a fifteen-year patent application for hygienic alphabets.

Considering the regularity of the request, Orders the following:

Article One.

It is granted to Messrs. Claude (Victor), merchant, & Chéradame (Antoine Léopold), expert in paintings, in Paris, rue du Sentier 32, at their own risk, without prior examination, and without guarantee, either of the reality, of novelty or merit of the invention, either of the fidelity or accuracy of the description, a fifteen-year patent of invention, which began to count on July 1, 1851, for hygienic alphabets.

Article two.

This decree, which establishes the patent of invention, is granted to Messrs. Claude & Chéradame to serve as their title.

Attached to this order will be the certified copy of the description and drawing filed in support of the application, the conformity of which with the original filing has been duly recognized.

Paris, September fifteenth, one thousand eight hundred and fifty-one.

The Minister of Agriculture and Trade.

By the Minister and by Delegation:

The Secretary General.

§1.33.2 A Journalist Makes Ironic Comments on the Patent for "Hygienic Alphabets"—1865

Public nutrition.—An inventor, full of ingenuity, found a way to make the first steps taken in the study of the mother tongue enjoyable for children.

He has invented the *Hygienic Gingerbread Alphabet*!

The letters being represented by pieces of cake, the child, it is hoped, will henceforth develop a taste for instruction—and it is expected that this appetizer will raise the level of literacy.

In any case, we can truly say that the French feed on literature.

But, at this moment in the epidemic, perhaps it would be imprudent to push the study of the alphabet and gingerbread too far.

Despite everything, we can already clearly see the advantage that can be gained from the new invention.

Thanks to gingerbread, most works will become easily digestible—and Mr. de Rémusat[34] will have *readers*.

I only fear that this innovation will suddenly cause a certain disturbance in the world of letters.

Since long works are frightening, novelists will find themselves forced to fit their epics into a few tablets for the use of feeble stomachs.

And what dedication it will take to read the *Adventures of Rocambole*[35] in the future!

§1.33.3 The Editorial of a Technical and Scientific Review Criticizes the Patent for the Cookies with Alphabetic Shapes—1865

Certain patents for inventions. While numerous and tireless researchers are looking for a smoke eraser that meets the required conditions, others are creating a new engine, others a new more economical and more solid fabric, we see emerging from certain brains the strangest, the most singular devices. We are far from wanting to blame the inventor, for example, of the *hygienic gingerbread alphabet*. We are convinced that his alphabet is destined to develop in many of our babies a budding taste for study; we believe it to be very hygienic, but in our eyes it is a bizarre anomaly to see this patent alongside a patent for a blower in foundry ovens, for example. And this is not an isolated example; we cannot imagine the number of bizarre patents that germinate each year in the heads of our compatriots. Our readers will perhaps ask us what consequences we can extract from such facts, they would be numerous; but the purely scientific and industrial character of this publication, on the one hand, and our incomplete knowledge of industrial jurisprudence, on the other, do not allow us to

34. This reference probably concerns Charles de Rémusat (1797-1865), a French controversial politician and writer on political and philosophical matters.
35. Les *Aventures de Rocambole* is the title of a novel authored by Ponson du Terrail, published in a series of chapters between 1857 and 1870 in a French newspaper, La Patrie.

draw conclusions from these oddities. We can only note this and submit them to the reader who may wish to analyze them.

*Figure 1.12 Advertisement, 1864. The letterhead reads: "Hygienic Alphabets in gingerbread & crunchy spices from Munier & Cie. (patented S.G.D.G. [*sans garantie du gouvernement, *with no government guaranty]), Manufacture rue de Reully, 59, in Paris." On the left: "Come! Come! Come! Unwise little children who cry or make faces when you have to learn to read! Come, Mothers who are obliged to replace this gracious smile which suits your charming faces so well, with big eyes that are as wicked as possible! Come, Dads who regretfully scold the unruly student." On the right: "Everyone come! Now, all this is going to change: Moms will smile again; Dads will recover their good humor, and little children will find these first lessons, until now so dry and painful, too short, attracted by the pleasure of sinking their teeth into the letter that they will have named well, which will be for them a treat as healthy as it is pleasant." In the bottom: "They can be found: At all confectioners, grocers, bakers & children's toy sellers."*

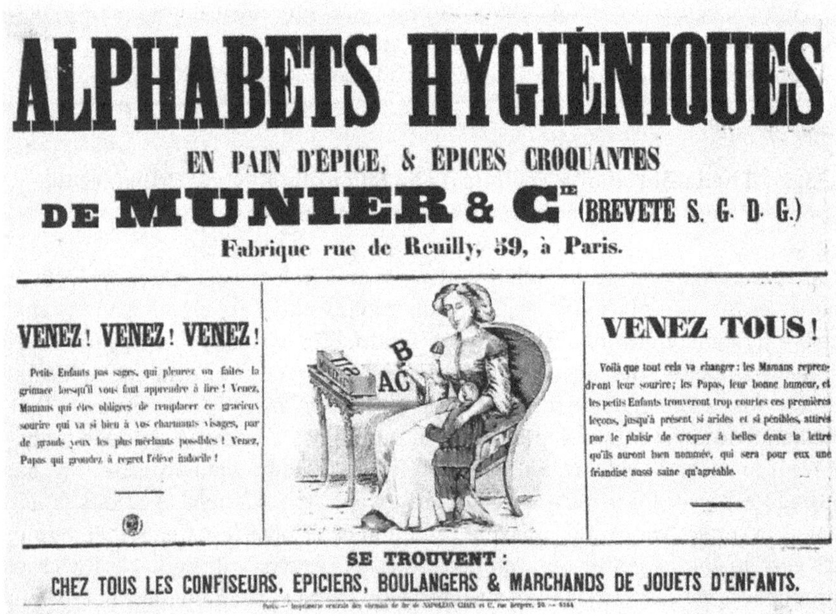

§1.34 SOME COUNTRIES EXCLUDE FOOD-RELATED INVENTIONS FROM PATENTABILITY—1852 ONWARD

As it happened earlier with medicine-related inventions, whose patentability was banned in France in 1844, some European countries, guided by the same concerns of scarcity and high prices that patentability could give cause to, started modifying their patent laws so as to exclude food-related inventions from patentability. Ultimately, as some of the statutes mention, the objective was to prohibit patents in the field of chemistry, an industry that was at that time expanding vigorously based on copying and espionage and which some governments feared could be harmed by the introduction of patents. An additional reason was the association of food with medicines. Indeed, as we shall see, in the nineteenth century, patents would be applied for certain foodstuffs claiming their therapeutic effects. But those concerns have, in the meantime, been put aside, and the exclusion did not last for long. The exceptions are perhaps India and Brazil, which, moved by a protectionist rationale, in their laws passed in the early 1970s, imposed restrictions on the patentability of food-related inventions. Later, we will come back to this (see §1.45, infra*). The following are examples of those statutes that, in the nineteenth century, provided in that sense.*

§1.34.1 The Law of Austria-Hungary Bans Patents for Food—1852

Law of August 15, 1852.

We, Francis Joseph the First, by the grace of God Emperor of Austria, King of Hungary and Bohemia, King of Lombardy and Venice, of Dalmatia, &c., &c.,

Being desirous of granting proper protection to the inventive genius even in those provinces of our empire which hitherto have been deprived of patent laws, and considering that the experience earned since the promulgation of the law of March 31, 1832, has shown that many reforms and enlargements are necessary, at the advice of our ministers and of our Imperial Council we have decreed the following rules for the whole extent of our empire: —

Section I

On the Subject of an Exclusive Privilege.

§1. Exclusive privileges may be granted under the restrictions stated in §§ 2, 3, 4 and 5, for every new discovery, invention, or improvement having for its object—

a. A new product of industry; or,
b. A new means of production; or,
c. A new method of production;

whether such privileges be demanded by an Austrian subject or by a foreigner, unless the invention be not patentable according to §§ 2-5.

...

§ 2. No privileges can be granted for preparations of food, beverages, and medicines, nor for discoveries, inventions, or improvements which cannot be worked for reasons of public health, morals, or safety, or as being contrary to that general interest of the state, according to the existing regulations.

§1.34.2 Portugal Prohibits the Grant of Patents for Food—1852

Decree of December 30, 1852

It being convenient to guarantee the property rights of new inventions and their introduction, and to regulate this important matter in such a way that the general interest is not prejudiced by the exercise of a private right; and experience having shown that the Decree of January 16, 1837 is deficient, and that it was very convenient to replace it with other provisions more in line with those adopted in this regard in other nations; and Having heard the Manufactures Section of the General Council for Commerce, Agriculture and Manufactures, with the opinion of which I have been Served to conform: I am pleased to Decree the following:

Of the privileges of invention, or the introduction of new inventions

Title I

Of privileges

Article 1. It is guaranteed under the terms of this Decree, and within the period of time established by it, the exclusive right of ownership for new discoveries and new inventions, or for their introduction in the mainland of the kingdom and adjacent islands, when referring to:

1st The invention of new industrial products;
2nd The invention of new processes, or their application, to obtain a product or a result with reference to the industry;

...

Art. 4. Patents of invention and introduction shall not be granted concerning:

I. Foodstuffs;
II. Medicines;

...

§1.34.3 Germany Also Excludes Food-Related Inventions from Patentability—1877

Law of July 1, 1877

First Section

Patent Rights

§1. Patents are granted for new inventions which can be turned to account in trade. The following are excepted: —

1. Inventions the use of which would be incompatible with the law or public morals.

2. Inventions of articles of food (for nourishment or luxuries), of medicines and of substances produced by chemical process, so far as the invention does not relate to a definite method of producing such articles.

...

§1.34.4 Luxembourg Bans Patents for Food-Related Products but Not for the Processes of Their Making—1881

Law of June 30, 1881

We, William the 3rd, by the grace of God, King of the Low Countries, Prince of Orange, Nassau, Grand Duke of Luxembourg, &c.

Our Council of State heard, &c., &c., have ordered and do order:

Chapter I

General dispositions

Article 1. Patents for new inventions susceptible of being worked industrially shall be granted, with the following exceptions:

First. Inventions the working of which would be contrary to the law or good morals.

Second. Those inventions which have for their object food or other objects of consumption, pharmaceutical products, or substances obtained by chemical means. Nevertheless, this exception does not apply to any special process for manufacturing these objects.

...

§1.34.5 Patentability of Food Products Is Excluded in Norway and Sweden but Not on Processes and Devices Used in Their Manufacture—1885

Law of June 16, 1885

We, Oscar, by the Grace of God, King of Norway and Sweden, the Goths, and the Vends, make known that there has been laid before us the resolution of the now assembled honorable Storting, on the 8th of June this year, as follows:

1. Patents shall be granted for new inventions which are useful in industry, excepting, however,
   (a) inventions which, if brought out, would be contrary to the law, morality, or public order;
   (b) inventions the subject-matter of which is beverage, food, or medicine.

Nevertheless, in relation to these, patents will be granted for processes or apparatus specially described for their manufacture... .

§1.35 ALEX SOYER'S INVENTION OF THE OSMAZOME—1853

Alexis Soyer (1809-1958) was a French chef who acquired a vast reputation and became influential in London. Soyer was also the inventor of many cooking preparations and devices and author of several successful cooking books. Soyer has also engaged in social activities of assistance to the poor and afflicted by war. One of his inventions was an extract of meat that he called "Soyer's Osmazome Food," for which he applied for a patent and obtained provisional protection under the British Patent Act of 1852. However, because Soyer had failed to give notice of his intention to proceed with the application in accordance with section XII of the Act, the provisional protection was canceled. Eventually, Soyer was aware that he would not be able to obtain the patent because of lack of novelty, given that two years earlier, he and his business partner, George Warriner, had exhibited that same extract in the South Gallery of the Great Exhibition of London, under Class III (Substances used as Food), for which they received a Mention of Honor. The texts that follow are the report of the Honourable Mention granted to Soyer's business partner and the notice of voidance of his patent application. Figure 13 confirms that Soyer was not only a chef and an intellectual but also a smart entrepreneur who used advertising as a tool for success. The illustrations have been obtained from one of Soyer's most influential books, THE MODERN HOUSEWIFE OR MÉNAGÈRE, but they circulated intensively within daily newspapers.

§1.35.1 The Osmazome Is Recognized at the 1851 Exhibition with an Honorable Mention

The osmazome of G. Warriner (Cl. III, 21, p. 202) is the nutritious matter or juice of meat which is set free during the operation of boiling down fat for tallow in Australia. This is afterwards concentrated and preserved in the form of sausages. A great amount of nutriment is thus obtained in a portable form, and when boiled with gelatine, it forms a palatable diet. The price is very moderate, 1s. per lb., and it hence commands a market, and is much used to form a gravy to meat. The exhibitors declare that one pound weight is the equivalent of the nutriment of 30 lbs. of fibrine, which argues a high economic value. Chemical examination gives 2.1 per cent of nitrogen, or 13.65 per cent of flesh-forming principle. Honourable Mention was awarded.

§1.35.2 Soyer Applies for a Patent for His Osmazome—1853

SOYER, March 2, 1853

Alexis Soyer, of 59, Fenchurch Street, in the City of London, Restaurateur, for an invention for—"Improvements in preparing and preserving soups, which he denominates 'Soyer's Osmazome Food.'"

Provisional protection only.

§1.35.3 Soyer Abandons His Patent Application for an Extract of Meat—1853

March 2, 1853 AD

Soyer, Alexis. This invention is void by reason of notice to proceed not having been given within the time prescribed by the Act. The Provisional Specification states it to be "Improvements in preparing and preserving soups." The result is denominated "Soyer's osmazome food." As a basis for several soups, a substance is prepared, which is named "osmazome,—but it may also be eaten separately,"—by stewing "together for hours leg of beef, knuckle of veal, ham, and calves' feet, adding onions, butter and water in proportion;" the fibrous part is separated "from the gravy, which is reduced by boiling, and afterwards deposited in bottles or other proper receptacles, which are subjected to heat, and sealed, and in which it will keep till required." The soups, &c. "may be prepared with and kept as 'osmazome,' or prepared with 'osmazome' when required."

Figure 1.13 Alexis Soyer was not only a very well-known French chef but also a cunning entrepreneur. The figure shows two pieces of advertisement included in his book THE MODERN HOUSEWIFE OR MÉNAGÈRE*, published in 1849.*

§1.36 FRENCH PATENTS FOR FOOD RECIPES AND PREPARATIONS—1862 ONWARD

We have already seen that, by contrast with machinery and devices for use in agriculture and in cooking, patents for food recipes have not been taken abundantly, including those that were supposed to be produced industrially and used by a large quantity of consumers. But here and there, exceptions have appeared. As far as food-related inventions are concerned, the adoption of the 1791 Patent Act only originated a few patents on mills and other machinery. There was the need to wait for the 1844 Patent Act, when the Industrial Revolution was in full swing in France, and the trust in the patent system had increased significantly for the first French patents for food preparations to be granted. We saw above (§1.33) a patent granted in 1851 for cookies with the shapes of alphabet letters, which invention had the purpose of facilitating the alphabetization of children. The following are a few examples of other patents for food recipes and preparations and related devices.

Bulletin of Laws No. 1201

No. 12,258—Imperial Decree that proclaims 1,379 Patents of Invention and Certificates of Addition

Napoleon, by the grace of God and the national will, Emperor of the French, to all present and future, greetings.

On the report of our Minister Secretary of State at the Department of Agriculture, Commerce and Public Works:

> Having regard to article 14 of the law of July 5, 1844,
>
> We have decreed and decree the following:
>
> Art. 1. [The following] Are proclaimed:
>
> ...

520th The fifteen-year patent for invention, the application for which was filed on September 20, 1862, at the secretariat of the prefecture of the Seine department, by Messrs. Pierquin (Jean-Baptiste) and Tuot (Jean-Baptiste), electing domicile at the [address of the] first, in Paris, rue Rousselet, no. 11, for the composition of a cheese known as *perfumed cheese of Paris or petit-Paris.*

...

695th The fifteen-year patent for invention, the application for which was filed on October 7, 1862, at the secretariat of the prefecture of the Seine department, by Messrs. Fillette (Joseph-Adolphe) and Martin (Jules-Stéphane), electing domicile at the [address of the] first, in Paris, rue Chemin-Vert, no. 32, for a device intended for serving oysters known as *table oyster bench.*

...

716th The fifteen-year patent for invention, the application for which was filed on October 9, 1862, at the secretariat of the prefecture of the Seine department, by Mr. Wiss (Rémi), represented by Mr. Reluze, in Paris, rue Baillet, no. 3, for the process of manufacturing a so-called *honey fly gingerbread.*

...

805th The fifteen-year patent of invention, the application for which was filed on October 28, 1862, at the secretariat of the prefecture of the Nord department, by Mr. Mirland and company, manufacturer of apple pastes, in Bavay, for *rhubarb pulp preserve.*

...

1202nd The certificate of addition for which the request was submitted on August 30, 1862, to the secretariat of the prefecture of the Seine department, by Mr. Demeurat (Louis), electing domicile in Paris, Faubourg-Saint-Honoré, no. 124, and attached to the fifteen-year patent of invention taken out on April 7, 1862, for *preserved food.*

...

Art. 2. Our Minister Secretary of State at the Department of Agriculture, Commerce and Public Works is responsible for the execution of this decree, which will be inserted in the Bulletin of Laws.

Done at the Tuileries Palace, January 27, 1864.

§1.37 A FRENCH JOURNALIST AFFIRMS AN ESSENTIAL TRUTH: IN CONTRAST WITH OTHER INVENTORS, CHEFS AND COOKS HAVE NEVER BEEN THE TARGETS OF OFFICIAL AWARDING PROGRAMS—1868

The almost absolute absence of patents issued for food recipes invented by individual chefs may not only be the result of an entrepreneurial strategy of those chefs, who have historically preferred to monetize their reputation directly and their inventions indirectly, eventually through the rules of trade secrets and copyright. Such absence may also be the product of a deliberate policy of disregarding the importance of such inventions by the authorities that are in charge of promoting invention and innovation (except, of course, as seen above, in Greece and Rome). This fact was noted in the nineteenth century by Paul Lacroix Méry (1806-1884), a well-known French journalist and author, in a letter addressed to another journalist, Léon Brisse, known as Baron Brisse, who was about to launch a weekly newspaper dedicated to gastronomy and the food industry in general. The newspaper was LA SALLE À MANGER, REVUE DE LA TABLE ET DE L'OFFICE, *and was published between 1864 and 1866. Méry's letter was included in the introduction to the book* LES 366 MENUS DU BARON BRISSE, AVEC 1200 RECETTES, *published in Paris in 1868. Léon Brisse has become known as one of the first gastronomic journalists ever.*

My dear Brisse,

In these times of controversy in which we live, one can challenge the usefulness of all newspapers, but I make an exception for the newspaper that you are going to found. You ask me for my opinion, here it is: put this question on the carpet, that is to say on the tablecloth, and all men who know how to live will rally to my opinion. I do not want to consider the usefulness of your journal from the exclusive point of view of gastronomic progress, although this material side should not be neglected, but I am delighted to see that you will dedicate the best part of your publication to the services that it can provide to the domestic economy. Given that the Academy of Sciences has never offered a prize to the inventor of a new dish, it is undoubtedly good that a special newspaper fills this academic gap and strives to add a few articles to the old repertoire of our classic cuisine; but what is necessary above all is to come to the help of families, by neutralizing the dangers of clandestine spoliation, and by eliminating the ruinous intermediaries who stand between the producer and the consumer. If there is no law against market hoarders, a newspaper must affirm its own authority and watch over the interests of households. Where will the increases of prices stop in terms of edibles? God knows; but we already guess that life will be very difficult to carry on, when Paris, with its innumerable streets of palaces, will have given itself an extra million eaters, and when by the force of attraction, the work in the countryside will be abandoned for the work in the cities. We must therefore hasten, in the present, to resolve this great question of the future! Let's not force our nephews to be millionaires under the death penalty.

Your devoted friend,
Mery

§1.38 THE INVENTION OF BAKING POWDER BY E.N. HORSFORD AND THE STRUGGLE TO KEEP THE PATENT—1856 ONWARD

One of the most fundamental and pervasive ingredients used in the preparation of modern food, in particular bread, is baking powder. The inventor was Prof. Eben Norton Horsford (1818-1893). In addition to being a prolific inventor and owner of several patents in the US and the UK, he was a historian, author of culinary books, and academic (for a number of years, he was Professor of Chemistry at Harvard University). Prof. Norsford founded the Rumford Chemical Works, Rhode Island, where his main invention was manufactured. The invention of baking powder was thus described in the Proceedings of the American Academy of Arts and Sciences (1892-1893):

> *Another of these important inventions was the phosphatic yeast powder, the object of which was to return to the bread the phosphates lost in bolting the flour, and which, as is well known, form such an essential constituent of the food of animals. In 1856 he undertook the manufacture of this yeast-powder, founding the Rumford Chemical Works for this purpose, and after he had secured his rights by a lawsuit which dragged along during seven wearisome years, and overcome the great difficulties inseparable from the establishment of a new process on a commercial scale, he made it a great success, which was enhanced later by the use of the acid portion of the yeast-powder as a medicine and beverage under the name of acid phosphate. It is pleasant to see that this work, which was undertaken primarily for the good of mankind by improving the quality of our principal food, should have brought him such a substantial reward. The demands of this business, however, became so great, that, in 1863, he was obliged to resign the Rumford Professorship to devote himself entirely to its management.*

Along the process of inventing and improving baking powder, Prof. Horsford obtained several patents covering various aspects of the ingredient and its making. The basic patent was granted to him on April 22, 1856. As it happens with very successful inventors, whose contrivances are well received by the market, Prof. Horsford had to defend (with mixed results) his patents against several challenges as to their validity, as well as against generalized infringement. The following texts are excerpts from two court opinions settling lawsuits initiated by the inventor against infringers. In the first case, Rumford Chemical Works v. John E. Lauer, *the court voided the first claim, which concerned the product itself. But that same claim was invoked in subsequent cases, such as* Rumford Chemical Works v. Hecker, *and eventually led to the sentencing of some defendants. In 1909, in* Rumford Chem. Works v. Hygienic Chem. Co., *215 U.S. 156, the United States Supreme Court denied* certiorari *of an opinion of the Second Circuit that had decided against the infringement of the product, not of the process.*

§1.38.1 The Claims of Horsford's Patent on the Making and the Composition of Baking Powder—April 22, 1856

United States Patent Office.

The Rumford Chemical Works, of Providence, R.I., Assignees, by Mesne Assignments of Eben Norton Horsford.

Improvement in pulverulent acid for use in the preparation of soda-powders, farinaceous food and for other purposes.

Specification forming part of Letters Patent No. 14,722, dated April 22, 1856; Reissue No. 2,597, dated May 7, 1867; Reissue No. 2,979, dated June 9, 1868

To all whom it may concern:

> Be it known that Eben Norton Horsford, of Cambridge, in the county of Middlesex and State of Massachusetts, has invented a new Pulverulent Acid for Use in the Preparation of Soda-Powders, Farinaceous Food, and for other Purposes; and it is hereby declared that the following is a full and exact description thereof, and of the mode of its preparation.
>
> ...
>
> 1. I claim, as a new manufacture, the above described pulverulent phosphoric acid.
> 2. I claim the manufacture of the above-described pulverulent phosphoric acid, so that it may be applied in the manner and for the purposes above described.
> 3. I claim the mixing, in the preparation of farinaceous food, with flour, of a powder or powders, such as described, consisting of ingredients of which phosphoric acid, or acid phosphates and alkaline carbonates, are the active agents for the purpose of liberating carbonic acid, as described, when subjected to moisture or heat, or both.
> 4. The use of acid phosphates, when employed with alkaline carbonates, as a substitute for ferment or leaven in the preparation of farinaceous food.

In testimony whereof I, EBEN N. Horsford, President of the Rumford Chemical Works, have hereunto affixed my signature in presence of two witnesses.

§1.38.2 Horsford Sues (Unsuccessfully) an Alleged Infringer in the South District of New York—1869

Pulverulent Acid

U. S. Circuit Court, Southern District of New York. In equity.

The Rumford Chemical Works v. John E. Lauer

Opinion of the Court. July 13, 1869.

Blatchford, Judge.

In this case the original patent was granted to Prof. Eben N. Horsford, April 22, 1856, and was reissued to the plaintiffs, who are assignees, May 7, 1867, and reissued to them a second time, June 9, 1868. The infringement alleged in the bill is the making and selling by the defendant, of pulverulent acid, in infringement of the said reissued patent of 1868.

The specification of the plaintiff's patent states the invention to be "a new pulverulent acid for use in the preparation of soda powders, farinaceous food, and for other purposes."

...

The defenses set up are, that Horsford was not the original and first inventor of anything which has been made and sold by the defendant, and that the defendant has not infringed the patent.

...

That the pulverulent phosphoric acid, as a chemical substance, claimed in the first claim of the plaintiff's patent, existed prior to the invention of it by Horsford, is established by the evidence in this case. The first claim is, therefore, void, for want of novelty.

As to the second claim, if it be regarded as a claim to the process described in the patent for making the acid, the defendant has not infringed it, for his process is as different from that of the plaintiff's is different from that described by Berzelius or Gmelin.

...

As already remarked, the third and fourth claims of the plaintiffs are not involved in the case.

...

It may be that there are claims which Horsford could make and hold in reference to certain constituents and qualities of the pulverulent acid that is made by this process, but the broad claim made to the acid described, is not tenable.

The bill must be dismissed with costs.

§1.38.3 A Manufacturer of Baking Powder Is Found to Infringe Horsford's Exclusive Process—1876

Rumford Chemical Works v. Hecker

2. Bann. & Ard. 351

Nixon, 1876

"The use of phosphoric acid or acid phosphates, when employed with alkaline carbonates, as a substitute for ferment or leaven in the preparation of farinaceous food." Defendant manufactured and sold a self-raising flour; the materials mixed with the flour were the bicarbonate of soda and acid phosphate. Defendant advertised and sold this self-raising flour, and claimed in his advertisements that his self-raising flour was an invaluable article for producing in a few minutes, by the addition of cold water only, without yeast or heat, the most nutritious and wholesome bread. It was held that on the evidence defendant was an infringer, or at least the burden was upon him of showing that the self-raising flour prepared by him was in fact not used for bread-making.

Figure 1.14 Left: Advertisement of Dr. Horsford's invention, "the best in the world," with therapeutic effects, and strongly recommended by customers, as it appeared in GOOD HOUSEKEEPING, For the Homes of the World, *a semi-monthly magazine published in New York, NY, on May 30, 1885. Right: The buildings of Rumford Chemical Works in Providence, Rhode Island, in 1891.*

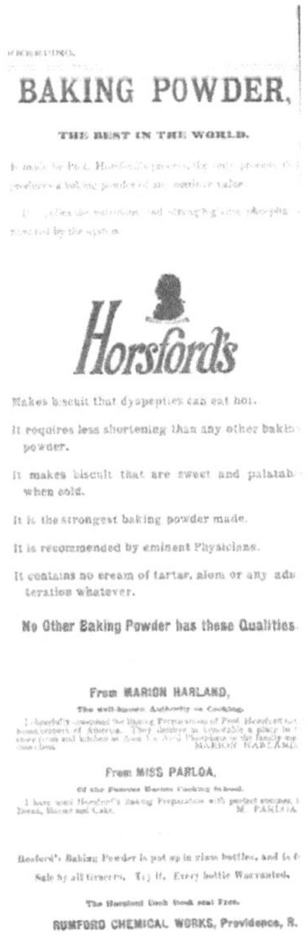

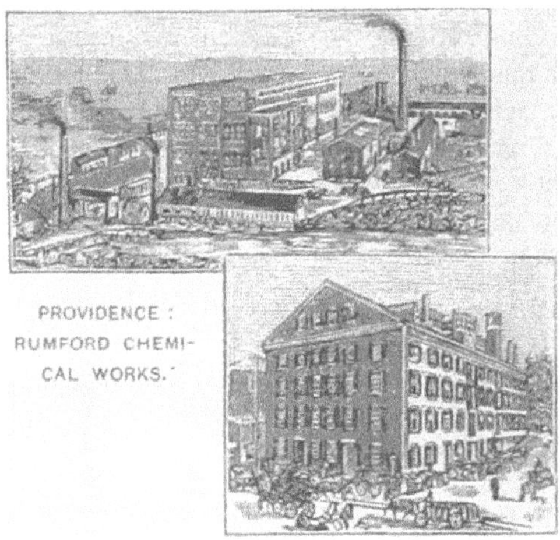

§1.39 *ANOTHER FOOD-RELATED BREAKING-THROUGH INVENTION AND PATENT: THE MAGGI SOUP—1891*

One of the most pervasive foods and one of the most notorious brands all over the world is the "Maggi Bouillon." Its recipe and manner of preparation were invented at the end of the nineteenth century by a Swiss entrepreneur, Julius Maggi (1842-1912). His motivation, as the website of Nestlé (the company that today owns Maggi trademarks and proprietary recipes) says, was to create a sort of food of universal acceptance and to be sold at low prices. The result was the famous bouillon Maggi, but the brand immediately afterward expanded to other varieties of foodstuffs, such as sauces and dry soups. Julius Maggi was a believer in the patent system. He not only obtained a patent for his bouillon but also applied for and obtained patents for some of his other inventions. The enormous success of the venture, however, has brought problems:

during World War I, for example, the company was accused of serving the interests of Germany rather than those of Western Europe. The text that follows reproduces the claims of Julius Maggi's patent on his bouillon as filed in Canada's patent office (patent nr. CA 3658 A, 04.05.1891).

Specification

Julius Maggi of Hemptthal in Switzerland, manufacturer

Improvements in the making up of food or substances in rations or definite quantities in readiness for use in the preparation of beverages, soups or otherwise.

...

Claims:

I claim as of my invention:

(1) Extracts of meat, extracts of vegetables or any other alimentary substances (including those for preparing beverages) in sufficiently condensed or solid form, which, in suitable mixture, and eventually in single layers, are put into tubes (for instance of gelatine) being dissolvable in water with the contents thereof.

(2) The production of concentrated alimentary substances according to claim 1 for the production of alimentary substances, which are to be consumed in liquid or pulpy form.

Signed in the presence of ...

Emil Blum, Zurich

This is the specification referred to in the affidavit of Julius Maggi hereto annexed, sworn before me the 14th of January 1890, at the British Consulate in Zurich.

Figure 1.15 Left: Facsimile of Maggi's patent application as certified by the British Consulate in Zurich, Switzerland, and filed with the Canadian Patent Office in 1890. Right: Maggi arrived in the United States in 1942, as advertised in the CULINARY REVIEW.

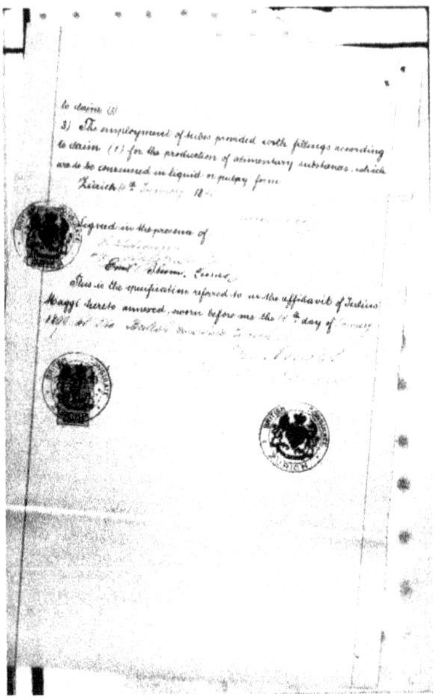

§1.40 JOHN HARVEY KELLOGG INVENTS AND OBTAINS A PATENT FOR CORNFLAKES; LATER, HE FIGHTS HIS BROTHER (AND COMPETITOR) FOR THE RIGHT TO USE HIS FAMILY NAME AS A TRADEMARK—1896

John Harvey Kellogg (1852-1943), a medical doctor, in 1895 applied for a patent for cornflakes. There are doubts about Dr. Kellogg's having been the only inventor. It seems that at least one of his brothers, Will, who worked with him for several years, was a co-inventor. The patent specifications describe the cereals not only as tasteful foodstuff but also as contributing to human health. The patent was issued in 1896. A few years later, his brother, Will, with the aim of increasing sales, proposed to add a coat of sugar to the flakes, an idea that John rejected. Consequently, Will created his own company—Battle Creek Toasted Corn Flake Company, which later would be renamed Kellogg Company. The two brothers maintained during several years a dispute over the right to the use of their family name as a trade name and as a trademark, which was (and still is today) on display in the package as a facsimile of a hand signature—a dispute that was brought to the Supreme Court of Michigan and that Will won. This dispute did not involve business identifiers only but also the use of secret formulae of food recipes developed by Dr. Kellogg and the processes to manufacture them. The text of the agreement was included in the Opinion of the Supreme Court of Michigan that recognized Will Kellogg as the legitimate owner of the trade name and trademarks, as well as of the trade secrets.

§1.40.1 Claims of John Kellogg's Patent on Cornflakes—1896

John Harvey Kellogg, of Battle Creek, Michigan

Flaked Cereals and Process of Preparing the Same

Specification forming part of Letters Patent No. 558,393, dated April 14, 1896

Application filed May 31, 1895. Serial No. 551,192. (No specimens.)

To all whom it may concern:

Be it known that I, John Harvey Kellogg, of Battle Creek, in the County of Calhoun and State of Michigan, have invented a certain new and useful Alimentary Product and Process of Making the Same, of which the following is a full, clear, and exact description.

...

My invention relates to an improved alimentary product and to the process of making it; and the object of the improvement is to provide food which is in a proper condition to be readily digested without any preliminary cooking or heating operation, and which is highly nutritive and of an agreeable taste, thus affording a food product particularly well adapted for sick and convalescent persons.

To this end my invention consists in the new process and the new article of manufacture hereinafter described and claimed.

...

Having thus described my invention, I claim as new and desire to secure by Letters Patent—

1. The process hereinbefore described for the manufacture of an improved alimentary product, which consists, first, in soaking the grain in water for some hours, whereby it is subjected to a preliminary digestion with its contained cerealin, and at temperature which prevents actual fermentation; second, subjecting the previously-soaked grain to heat for a time sufficient to completely cook the starch; third, drying the grain; fourth rolling the grain between cold rollers; and fifth, baking the flakes until thoroughly dry and crisp, as specified.
2. The improved cooked alimentary product, from grain such as wheat, hereinbefore described, which exists in the form of large, attenuated, baked, crisp and slightly brown flakes of practically uniform thickness, the same being readily soluble and containing dextrin, as specified.

§1.40.2 Agreement (Excerpt) Between John Harvey Kellogg and His Brother Will of 1911, Assigning the Latter Some Secret Processes and Formulae and Imposing the Obligation Not to Disclose Them

Memorandum of Agreement made this fifteenth day of February, 1911, between John Harvey Kellogg, The Kellogg Food Company, and the Kellogg Toasted Rice Flake and Biscuit Company, all of Battle Creek, Michigan, of the first part, and the Kellogg Toasted Corn Flake Company, of the same place, of the second part.

...

Fourth

The first parties and each of them hereby covenant and agree not to divulge to others any formula for the manufacture of flaked cereal foods, except:

(a) As the same is divulged to their own employees, with an agreement with the employees not to divulge the same, or—
(b) As the same is divulged in connection with the actual sale of the good-will of the business of manufacturing some specific food other than corn flakes, and then only on the express agreement with the vendee, that such formula shall be used only in the manufacture of such specified food.

§1.40.3 Will Kellogg's Company Recognized the Right to the Use of the Trade Name, Trademark and Trade Secrets Concerning the Manufacture and Sale of Kellogg's Products

John Harvey Kellogg, et al. v. Kellogg Toasted Corn Flake Co., et al.

Supreme Court of Michigan

December 21, 1920

(Syllabus)

1. Unfair Competition—Use of Family Name—Acquiescence—Estoppel.

Where plaintiff, engaged in the manufacture of certain cereal products with his brother, the defendant, as managing partner, acquiesced for several years in the use of the latter's facsimile signature on the package, and later sold to the defendant his interest in the business and engaged in a similar business, without reserving any right to the use of his name therein, he is thereby estopped from any claim to the exclusive use of the said name or from claiming any damages resulting from its use by defendant.

2. Unfair Competition—Trade-name—Contractual Rights In-Bearing of Decision in Opposition Proceedings.

In the case at issue, where plaintiff has by contract, conveyed to defendant the right to the use of their common name as a trade-name, reserving to himself only a restricted right therein, he forfeits all claim to its exclusive use. The fact that plaintiff opposed the registration by defendant of the name "Kellogg's" in the Patent Office, and the opposition was sustained by the Court of Appeals, but without final judgment on its merits, has no bearing on the case at issue.

3. Unfair Competition—Trade-Mark—Right to Use Assignment—Meaning and Effect of Contract.

The Granting by defendant to plaintiff by contract of the right to use the trade-name "Kellogg Food Company" and other trade-names, containing the surname Kellogg, does not convey any right to use the trade-mark "Kellogg's," registered by the former, nor license him to trail his products under such mark; and, such license, if granted, would have been unlawful.

Figure 1.16 Kellogg's Corn Flakes, an advertisement with Will Keith Kellogg's portrait and signature. Rock Island Argus newspaper (Rock Island, Ill., May 2, 1907). The signature whose facsimile appears is Will's, not John's. This fact could have reinforced Will's claims to the right to use the trademark. The strategy of using the manufacturer's signature as proof of product authenticity was often used in the eighteenth and nineteenth centuries in the context of medicines.[36]

36. *See* Nuno Pires de Carvalho, *supra* note 1.

§1.41 AN INVENTION THAT WOULD ORIGINATE ANOTHER UBIQUITOUS INGREDIENT IN WORLD CUISINE: THE PORTABLE MILL FOR MAKING PEANUT BUTTER—1903

Ambrose W. Straub, inventor of several grinding mills, created the machine that enormously facilitated the making of peanut butter, a foodstuff that, at the end of the nineteenth century, was already known in the United States but not of general use. The impact of Straub's machine was due to its portability. Consequently, small businesses could use it and manufacture peanut butter without the need for large facilities and heavy fixed costs. The success story of peanut butter started a few years later, at the St. Louis World Fair of 1904, where C.H. Sumner, using one of Ambrose Straub's machines, made and sold peanut butter to visitors.

United States Patent Office

Ambrose W. Straub, of Philadelphia, Pennsylvania

Mill for Grinding Peanuts for Butter

Specification forming part of Letters Patent No. 721,651, dated February 24, 1903.

Application filed February 20, 1901. Serial No. 48,104. (No model.)

To all whom it may concern:

Be it known that I, Ambrose W. Straub, a citizen of United States, residing at Philadelphia, in the county of Philadelphia and State of Pennsylvania, have invented certain new and useful Improvements in Mills for Grinding Peanuts for Butter; and I de hereby declare the following to be a full, clear, and exact description of the invention, such as will enable others skilled in the art to which appertains to make and use the same.

This invention relates to improvements in portable mills adapted for grinding peanuts, used in the manufacturing of peanut-butter, and all kinds of hard, friable, tough, and moist substances; and the objects of my improvements are, first, to provide a casing, a detachable yoke, a crushing roll or cylinder, one end of which is journaled in the casing and the opposite end thereof in a yoke, a stationary grinding-disk, and a rotary disk, the rotary disk and cylinder having means for interlocking the two together, devices for adjusting the crushing roll or cylinder and for clamping the antifriction devices in place, and, second, to construct a casing and supporting-standard having a base provided with a lip and a hinged clamp for securing the casing and standard to support... .

Figure 1.17 The invention that permitted the popularization of peanut butter in the United States: the portable grinding mill for peanuts.

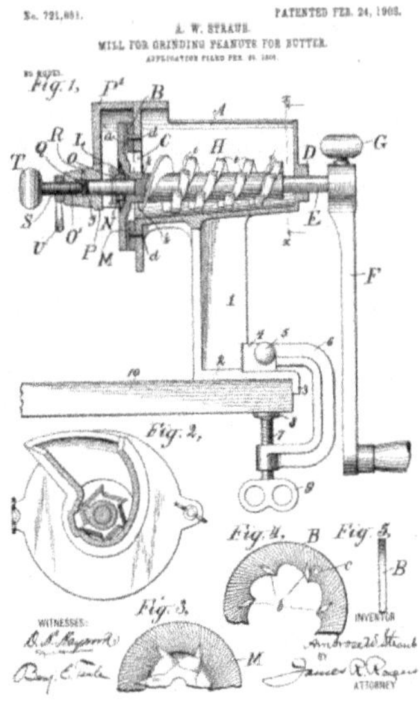

§1.42 CULINARY SECRETS BECOME PART OF THE POPULAR IMAGINATION: A FRENCH COMIC ABOUT A FAMOUS SECRET RECIPE FOR A PASTRY—1926

It has already been said more than once in this first chapter: individual chefs are not keen to appropriate their inventions by direct means, i.e., through patents. The main reason is that the period of protection of a patented invention is short as compared to the life span of a secret recipe, if the secret is well kept. Moreover, chefs generally carry on their business in small firms, which tend not to afford the costs of patent procurement and, subsequently, of litigation involving the validity and the infringement of rights. And, exactly because of the nature of the business of chefs, who prepare their recipes in conveniently isolated places—restaurants' kitchens—under conditions that are easy to supervise, and, moreover, because, once ready, the dishes are directly and individually served to customers, the risk of culinary secrets to evade control is very small as compared to trade secrets in other professions. This is what explains why certain culinary secrets resist the passage of time and are preserved for decades. In Chapter 2 (see §2.25), we will look at one of those secrets and the trade dress that a small and prestigious chain of restaurants (Le Relais de l'Entrecôte) has built around it. But now we will see an example of how some famous secret recipes can become part of popular imagination. The texts and images that follow have been extracted from a comic published in Paris in 1926 in Les Belles Images, *a French weekly comic magazine that targeted young readers. The comic strips are about an adventure of political intrigue, greed, heroism, and treason, all this evolving around an imaginary famous and valuable recipe for a pastry.*

Story of Assoub, the Pastry Chef, by Asy

[First panel] There was once in Baghdad, a pastry chef called Assoub, who was a very honest man and an artist in pastry. He had invented an inimitable tart, which included a mysterious ingredient that he kept secret, and all the pastry chefs of Baghdad had turned pale... (or rather blushed!) in front of their oven for months trying to counterfeit the famous tart, but in vain. Caliph Schemmar, who was gourmand and feared that the secret ingredient would run out one day, so Assoub ...

[Second panel] ... sold pies, summoned him in and proposed him to be his official pastry chef, with very large profits, in return for which the highly prized tart would only be made for him and his court; the people would serve themselves with ordinary pastries... Assoub agreed and swore never to sell or give away his secret, so that no one else could boast of tasting something as good as Schemmar. However, several weeks later, a poor fellow called Hazoum, who had not eaten for two days, fell from weakness ...

[Third panel] ... in front of Assoub's house. The latter had him to be lifted by his servants and served him a good meal; after which, Hazoum, shedding tears, threw himself at the feet of the pastry chef, begging him to keep him as a servant, to do the shopping, or heat the oven, or carry the wood. Touched with pity, Assoub kept him. However, this Hazoum was the cook of a rich and powerful sheik of Arabia, who, extremely gourmand, had heard of the secret of Assoub, and had sent Hazoum to steal it from him. We saw how the latter ...

[Fourth panel] ... had entered Assoub's house, whose good heart he had heard praised. But he noticed that Assoub made the caliph's tarts himself and locked himself in a small special room at night. Despite his cunning and vigilance, the sheikh's slave was never able to enter that room. He then resolved to resort to drastic measures. The secret of the pastry chef was worth a fortune, Hazoum did not intend to report it to his master, but he thought of settling in some foreign country, and enrich himself with the famous tart. He decided to force Assoub to speak, but ...

Figure 1.18 The first 6 (out of a total of 24) panels of the comic Story of Assoub

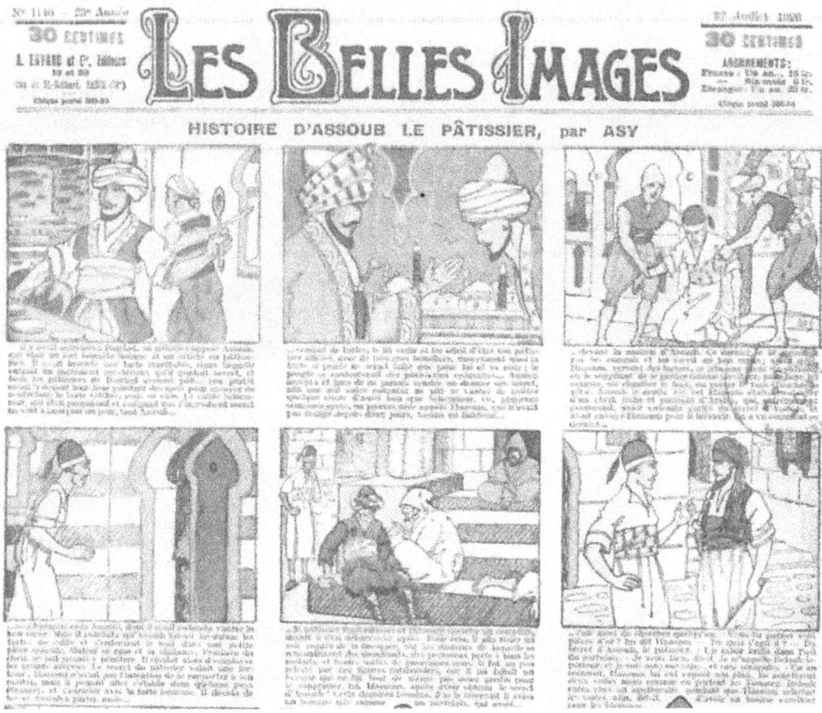

§1.43 IN THE FIRST HALF OF THE TWENTIETH CENTURY, ADVANCES IN PLANT BREEDING AND THE INCREASE IN RIVALRY BETWEEN COMMERCIAL NURSERIES LED TO THE EMERGENCE OF PLANT PATENTS, FIRST, FOLLOWED BY THE EMERGENCE OF A SUI GENERIS REGIME FOR NEW PLANT VARIETIES—1921 ONWARD

Thus far, we have seen instances of appropriation of knowledge concerning foodstuffs and the devices for obtaining or making them. But we have not seen the appropriation of knowledge of the raw materials of food, this meaning plant varieties that have been modified by human ingenuity in pursuit of increased productivity, resistance to hostile weather conditions, or other useful characteristics. The knowledge concerning new plant varieties can be preserved through three legal regimes: patents, a sui generis *system, and trade secrets. These three regimes are not incompatible in the sense that the breeder may opt for any one of them, except in those countries that, having adopted the* sui generis *system, exclude plant varieties from patentability.*

Social pressure to accept the idea of granting breeders the same rights as inventors in mechanical fields has taken a long time to bear fruit. The resistance to such an idea was caused by the perception that the patent system, since 1624, had the purpose of acknowledging inventions that concerned new manufactures, *a term that was explained by Lord Kenyon, Chief Justice of the Court of the King's Bench, in* Hornblower and Maberley v. Boulton and Watt, in error *(1799), as meaning "something made by the hands of man."*[37] *However, the technical success of breeders such as Luther Burbank (1849-1926), who passed away without being able to obtain a single patent for one of his hundreds of inventions, persuaded Congress of the need to amend the Patent Act so as to accommodate plants. Plant patents were (and still are) reserved for asexually reproduced plants. Other sorts of plants and propagating materials and techniques could be patented as utility patents if the corresponding requirements were met. Later, in 1970, the United States bowed to the growing international practice of according new plant varieties, including those sexually reproduced, a* sui generis *sort of protection.*

A U.S. scholar, Bill Kriss, has offered an explanation of the circumstances that led to the introduction in the United States in 1930 of patent protection for plants:

> *During World War I, a number of countries, including the U.S., had greatly expanded agricultural production; as Europe recovered from the war and its agriculture production reached earlier levels, production worldwide exceeded consumption and prices fell around the world. Farmers had gone into debt during the boom times, investing in new equipment and land, and were hard hit when prices fell.*[38]

These circumstances have naturally put additional pressure on farmers and nurseries who invested time and resources in obtaining new varieties, which would naturally lead them to exercise pressure on their representatives to make the patent system available to them as a way of recouping those investments. In this token, one can say that it was overproduction, not low production, of plants that was partly behind the US Plant Patent Act of 1930.

The first and third of the following texts show the first legal attempts at protecting plant varieties— not yet through the appropriation of knowledge corresponding to their new or modified characteristics (and respective commercial use), but through the appropriation of the denominations attributed to them. Those were indirect mechanisms, but they did not lack some efficacy to the extent that the denomination was reserved for new varieties. In other words, the recognition and protection of the denominations were dependent on a prior examination of novelty and stability. Those two initiatives took place in Czechoslovakia in 1921 and in France in 1923.

The second text illustrates the eagerness of French plant breeders for some mechanism that protected invention in the field of plant varieties. In 1921, an association of French breeders proposed to set a self-regulated regime under the supervision of a private organization called "National Horticultural Property Office," which would be in charge of securing exclusive rights in new varieties and registering the respective

37. *See* Nuno Pires de Carvalho, From Babylon to the Silicon Valley, *supra* note 10, at 42-43.
38. *See* Bill Krist, *Did the Smoot-Hawley Tariff Cause the Great Depression?*, June 16, 2014, available at www.wita.org.

denominations as trademarks. In the same year, as the records of the French Parliament show, a bill was introduced aiming at transforming that idea into a statute.[39] *But it produced no result.*

The fourth text describes the practical (and not much significant) results of the implementation of the "National Horticultural Property Office" in Lyon. In two years, i.e., between 1921 and 1923, in only two instances, French breeders resorted to such self-regulated mechanism.

The sui generis *plant variety protection regime was introduced in 1961 through a Convention that also created the UPOV (*Union pour la Protection des Obtentions Végétales, *or the International Union for the Protection of New Varieties of Plants). The 1961 Convention was revised in 1978 and 1991. The two first versions of the Convention prohibited Contracting Parties from adopting double protection "for one and the same botanical genus or species." In 1991, that clause was eliminated so as to permit a country to make both systems available to breeders, such as the United States. The TRIPS Agreement, in Article 31.3(b), provides that "Members shall provide for the protection of plant varieties either by patents or by an effective* sui generis *system or by any combination thereof." Given the ambiguity of these words, a Member may choose to have one of the systems or a system that combines that of patents with that of the* sui generis *regime (*sui generis *meaning the UPOV system, even if the TRIPS Agreement is silent about that*[40]*), or, as said, simply having both systems in coexistence.*

The fifth text reproduces an article published by the League of Nations applauding the US initiative of establishing the patentability of some new plants.

The sixth text reproduces the letter of invitation sent by the Government of France to the first session of the Diplomatic Conference that later approved the 1961 Convention. That session took place in 1957. That letter is important to the extent that it reveals the combination of factors that led to the adoption of a special regime designed for the protection of plant varieties. The first (and main) factor was of a commercial nature: the dramatic growth in the market of seeds that took place at the beginning of the second half of the twentieth century. The second factor was the robust progress in biotechnology that permitted the creation of new seeds. The third factor was less decisive, but it still had some relevance: the discomfort that several European countries had with the inadequacy of the traditional patent system to address the specificities of inventions in the agricultural field and the growing trade of seeds.

The seventh text is an excerpt from a document presented to the U.S. Senate during the debates that led to the adoption of the Plant Variety Protection Act of 1970. That document is of interest because it gives a brief overview of how the law on the protection of plant varieties has evolved in the U.S.

---

39. *See* Journal Officiel de la Republique Française, Documents Parlementaires—Chambre des Deputes, annexes aux proces-verbaux des seances, June 26, 1921, Session of June 21, 1921, annex no. 2835, at 2525-2527 (available at gallica,bnf.fr).
40. The silence of the TRIPS Agreement in that respect was imposed by India during the GATT negotiations. India was very unhappy with the limitations to the exceptions of breeders' rights established by the 1991 version of the UPOV Convention. At that time, small farmers paraded on the streets of some Indian cities, protesting against the possibility of the TRIPS Agreement making adherence to the rules of the 1991 UPOV Convention mandatory.

Texts from eighth to tenth illustrate specific and current questions of law relating to the acquisition and enforcement of rights concerning new varieties through the three mechanisms above-mentioned: patents, sui generis *plant variety protection, and trade secrets. Those cases correspond to the opinions of U.S. courts. Naturally, the availability of two different (and yet similar) regimes for the same sort of inventions has given rise to questions about their reciprocal compatibility.*

The patent and the sui generis *regimes are similar, but a number of significant differences make them distinct, such as the* sui generis *protection requirements (novelty [of a purely commercial nature], distinctness, uniformity, and stability). In general, patents are more difficult to obtain than plant variety certificates, and, besides novelty not being so strictly imposed, that is due to the natural difficulty in describing certain characteristics that one can find in plants, such as color, taste, and scent, but not in mechanics or chemistry. For that reason, in applying for a new variety certificate (or for a plant patent, for that matter), the breeder is not required to provide a description in the same terms as a utility patent applicant. On the other hand, two additional elements make the protection of plant varieties stronger: one is the limitations imposed on compulsory licenses—they can be granted on grounds of public interest only (which means that they cannot be granted based on lack of exploitation, unless the absence of exploitation becomes a matter of public interest, and, moreover, only anticompetitive acts with a general impact can be sanctioned); the other element is the territorial scope of exhaustion, which the UPOV Convention of 1991 sets as being purely national (with the possibility of extension to the territories of countries that are Members of the same intergovernmental organization).*[41] *On the other hand, the 1991 Convention introduced the so-called "farmers' exemption," according to which "each Contracting Party may, within reasonable limits and subject to the safeguarding of the legitimate interests of the breeder, restrict the breeder's right in relation to any variety in order to permit farmers to use for propagating purposes, on their own holdings, the product of the harvest which they have obtained by planting, on their own holdings, the protected variety" or an essentially derived variety. As regards this provision, concerns have been raised that it imposes unacceptable limitations on the customary practice of saving and exchanging seeds by traditional, small farmers. For that reason, several UPOV Members who introduced this exception in their laws have associated it with the (small) size of the farms benefiting from it.*

Before we move to the texts, one additional observation should be added. In the majority of countries, animals and their parts are not patentable subject matter. The reason for that is, in general, one of ethics. If parliaments admitted the patentability of animals, they might be a step too close to also admitting the patentability of human beings or their parts, which could lead to an implication of the encouragement of the

41. The text of the Convention does not include a definition of the intergovernmental organizations concerned. That was an unfortunate omission. Initially, the idea behind the language adopted was to attend a concern of the (then designated as) European Communities. However, the language adopted is so broad that a UPOV Member could very well extend the exhaustion effects to the lawful transfer of title in the plant variety to the entire Membership of the United Nations. A correct language should have limited the territorial extension of exhaustion to the Members of regional trade agreements within which customs are eliminated. That would attend the European Communities and, at the same time, would acknowledge the commercial nature of the provision.

*genetic engineering of humans. The Supreme Court of Canada, in 2002 [*Harvard College v. Canada, 2002 SCC 76]*, took a more neutral stance and held that higher living forms (such as a genetically modified mouse) were not patentable subject matter because they were not a "manufacture" or "composition of matter" within the meaning of "invention." The Court decided that would be a matter for Parliament to decide, given the various serious implications that a different holding might lead to:*

> *Since patenting higher life forms would involve a radical departure from the traditional patent regime, and since the patentability of such life forms is a highly contentious matter that raises a number of extremely complex issues, clear and unequivocal legislation is required for higher life forms to be patentable.*[42]

Most plant variety certificates are granted to ornamental plants.[43] *The Report issued by the USPTO concerning plant patents issued between 1996 and 2020 shows that the five companies that obtained more patents are all in the field of ornamental crops (Yoder Brothers, Terra-Nova Nurseries, Ball Horticultural Company, Klemm + Sohn GMBH, and Poulsen Roser). The company that is primarily dedicated to food plants (Syngenta Crop Protection) appears in the ninth place. By contrast, the companies that seek utility patent protection for plants and their parts are biotech giants, such as Monsanto and Pioneer Hi-Bred, which are primarily (although not exclusively) concerned with supplying seeds to farmers around the world.*[44]

§1.43.1 Czechoslovakia Adopts a Statute Providing for the Protection of Denominations of New Plant Varieties—1921

Law concerning the Recognition of the Originality of Types, Seeds and Plants, and the Examination of Horticultural Subject Matter

Law No. 128, of March 17, 1921

The National Assembly of the Czecho-Slovak Republic has adopted the following law:

> § 1—In order to promote the development of horticulture, this law establishes the conditions under which the following can be done:
> 1st recognize the originality of horticultural subjects;
> 2nd recognize the seeds and plants of the types obtained;
> 3rd examine horticultural subjects.
>
> The authorization to use the designation "original subject", or "recognized seed", or "recognized plants", or "registered subject" is governed by the provisions of this law.
>
> § 2.—Recognition is made, at the request of horticulturists, by the legitimation commissions established within agricultural corporations that the Ministry of

42. The opinions of the Supreme Court of Canada are available at scc-csc.lexum.com.
43. This may be the reason, conscious or not, that the figurative logo used by UPOV for designating its database search engine, named "Genie," shows a genius of the lamp holding flowers in his hands. *See* www.upov.int/genie/ (December 28, 2023).
44. Data are available at www.uspto.gov.

Agriculture has charged with organizing the recognition by people in the trade. The costs of the legitimation procedure are borne by the applicant.

...

§ 5.—For recognized seeds and plants, the commission issues a certificate of legitimation. Recognized seeds and plants are listed by category in the lists drawn up by agricultural corporations. The registration of seeds and plants of an original subject matter can only take place when the subject matter has been expressly recognized as original.

...

§ 8.—The authorization to designate a subject matter as an original subject matter is published in the "Véstnik ministerstvazemědelstvi" (Bulletin of the Ministry of Agriculture). The recognition of seeds and plants is published in the "Vestnik" by the Legitimization Commission.

§ 9.—Original subject matter whose quality is recognized following comparative tests carried out over several years by stations and public establishments in certain parts of the territory of the Czecho-Slovak Republic are registered, by the Ministry of Agriculture, after the decision of the Central Legitimization Commission, in the register of tested subject matter. The entry in the register will be published in the "Véstnik".

§ 10.—Registration in the register of original subject matter, or on the lists of seeds and plants, or in the register of proven subject matter authorizes registered horticulturists and producers to put their articles on the market, but only with the indications that appear in the registration made; other owners of seeds and plants can obtain the same authorization from the Legitimization Commission.

§ 11.—The use of trademarks in accordance with the law of January 6, 1890, amended by those of July 30, 1895, March 17, 1913 and July 24, 1919, is only permitted, for seeds and plants, to individuals or to establishments producing original subject matter.

...

§ 13.—The right to use the mark for an original subject matter expires at the same time as the authorization to designate the subject matter as original; but the registration remains valid for six months following the moment when the original character of the subject ceased to be recognized. If, during this period, the trademark is not renewed, it expires.

§ 14.—Infringements of trademarks registered under this law are prosecuted in accordance with the provisions of the law of January 6, 1890.

§1.43.2 The National Society of Horticulture of France Proposes a Private, Self-Regulated System for the Protection of New Plant Varieties—1921

The intensification of plant breeding in the context of a significant increase in the production of plants and seeds in the period that followed World War I has given rise to discomfort with breeders. As early as 1921, French breeders, in the absence of a legal regime that provided them with exclusivity in the results of their inventions and discoveries, proposed the adoption of a private, self-regulated system, which the following text describes. This solution reminds us of a note made by Plato in the Republic, who proposed that some elements of commerce should be self-regulated, creating a sort of courtesy of trade:

> *[Socrates] And again: in Heaven's name, as to these transactions relating to contracts which men of different classes make with one another in the market-place, or, if you please, the contracts of builders, or insults, unprovoked assaults, the bringing of lawsuits, the impaneling of jurors, the exactions or payments of customs that may be necessary either in the markets or in the harbors, and, in general, whatever concerns the market, the city or the port, or the like, shall we venture to legislate about any of them?*
>
> *[Adeimantus] There is no need to impose laws about these matters on good and noble men; for they will easily discover themselves whatever legislation is necessary.*[45]

The Protection of horticultural novelties

This important problem, which has been under study for a long time, has not until now received any precise solution. A breeder who obtained a new plant most often derived only an insignificant profit from it, especially when it was a plant that could multiply easily and quickly; the first year after it was put on the market, the new plant, very widespread, no longer brought in anything for the breeder since buyers could obtain it directly from their usual supplier. On the other hand, no law allows a patent to be taken for a new plant, as one is taken for an invention. Very recently, Mr. Jules Grec, the distinguished director of the *Petite Revue Agricole et Horticole d'Antibes*, reported a case of court dispute between two breeders over a new variety sold by one to the detriment of the other, who claimed to be the breeder. The judges were forced to recognize that the current law did not make it possible to satisfy the plaintiff, the case not being provided for.[46]

The National Horticultural Society of France, after having studied the question at length, has just, in agreement with several other horticultural groups, decided to create a National Office for Horticultural Property. La *Revue Horticole* recently published the measures taken by this Office to achieve its intended goal.

We will try to summarize them below, in order to bring our readers up to speed on this important issue.

The Office will operate under the auspices of the Natural History Museum and the following Societies: Federation of Horticultural Societies of France, Federation of Horticultural Unions of France, National Horticultural Society of France, Pomological Society of France, Society of French Rose Breeders, French Society of Chrysanthemum Breeders. The Office will have its headquarters in Paris, 84, rue de Grenelle. It will be administered by an office that will meet at least once a month.

Article 2 of the Statutes of this new organization defines the objectives pursued as follows:

> Its goal is to centralize all provisional registrations of qualified Companies on a single register and to issue the definitive certificate of first presentation.

45. Alexander Kerr (transl.), The Republic of Plato—Book IV, at 14 (Charles H. Kerr & Co., 1904). *Source*: archive.org.
46. Today, if plant variety protection were not available, the offended party could invoke the theories of unfair competition and unjust enrichment.

> It must, by all means, encourage the planters and guide the technical societies in their operation; take all measures to safeguard the rights of breeders, while awaiting the vote of a law which it must engage itself to obtain.
>
> The date of registration with regard to the right of ownership is that of the declaration to the technical company concerned and not that of the delivery of the definitive certificate.

The societies qualified to examine the new plants are: the National Horticultural Society of France, the Pomological Society of France, the Society of French Rose Breeders, and the French Society of Chrysanthemum Breeders. Each of these four organizations will provide all useful information regarding the conditions in which the plants must be presented to them; they will also provide a model of the declaration to be filled-in. These societies will issue breeders with a provisional registration certificate and interested parties will subsequently receive a definitive certificate established by the National Horticultural Property Office.

The duration of protection will vary from 5 to 25 years, depending on the wishes of the breeder. The latter will have to pay, for each new variety put on the market by him, and for which he has requested protection, a fixed sum of 20 francs, plus a fee of 50 francs for each period of five years of protection.

The Office will publish every month the list of new varieties registered and their description, as well as the names of the breeders who have acquired the right to sell them. This list will be sent to the corresponding entities.

A breeder who has obtained a new variety may either multiply it and sell it himself, or transfer all his rights to another person for the total or partial duration of the protection, or transfer the right of sale on condition that each unit will be accompanied by a mark of origin purchased from the breeder.

Until a law has sanctioned these various provisions, horticultural companies will have to appeal to the honesty and good faith of breeders so that they are respected. There is no doubt that these entities will exercise all the necessary supervision and that, for their part, breeders will strictly comply with the rules set by the National Horticultural Property Office.

§1.43.3 France Passes a Decree Granting Exclusive Rights in the Denominations of New Plant Varieties—1922

The interesting aspect of this Decree, which followed the same approach as that of the Czechoslovakian law of 1921, is the reference to the possible secrecy of the method of production of the concerned plant.

Decree Establishing a Register of Selected Plants and Establishing a Seed Control Committee

(of December 5, 1922.)

Article 1.—Any person who has obtained, invented, discovered a new and specific species or variety of plant, may request the registration of this variety or this new species in the "Register of selected plants", held at the Ministry of Agriculture (Office agricultural information);

...

Art. 3.—Anyone wishing to keep a particular production process secret must mention it on their request. In this case, the investigation will be continued by delegates from the Administration, who may, on a confidential basis, request any useful information.

ART. 4.—To be entered in the register of selected plants, the variety must possess not only the character of novelty, but also present indisputable merits, merits confirmed by the cultural trials provided for in Article 5.

...

ART. 8.—As soon as he is in possession of the acknowledgment of receipt of the application for registration, the applicant may claim the exclusive use of the name given to the new variety, but, in the trade of this variety, he shall not submit his registration request before the delivery of the final certificate. Reproduction and trade in seeds of a registered variety are authorized unless expressly prohibited by the inventor. As far as the trade of seeds is concerned, the inventor alone has the right to reserve to himself the term "Seeds entered in the Register of Selected Plants".

§1.43.4 The Industrial Property Journal Describes Two Voluntary Initiatives of Compliance with the Self-Regulated Mechanism of Plant Variety Protection Proposed in 1921 by the National Horticultural Society of France—1923

FRANCE

COPYRIGHT IN HORTICULTURE

The *Revue horticole* of April 16 last contains an article by M. L. Chasset, secretary general of the *Société pomologique de France*, concerning the protection of horticultural property, which we allow ourselves to reproduce as is, in view of the interest it offers for the question which was the subject of the general study published in the March 31 issue of Industrial Property (at 31) under the title *On the protection of plant novelties*.

"There has been a lot of talk about copyright; an organization has resulted: the National Horticultural Property Office; there are forms, registers, a designated office, in a word, everything is ready, only the new [varieties] to be protected have not yet decided to present themselves.

However, two efforts are already to be noted in this direction, and this beginning of execution needs to be known to bring new goodwill around the people who dared to start.

In Lyon, Mr. Hautin, arborist in Villefranche-sur-Saône, presented a very deserving cherry under the name Cherry Hautin, to the permanent studies commission of the Pomological Society of France.

Having no firm idea on how to take advantage of his idea, Mr. Hautin has offered samples to his pomologist colleagues, and, on our proposal, everyone has undertaken not to sell this novelty without referring it to M. Hautin, who remains free to set the compensation to which he is entitled.

This compensation may be paid to him either by a percentage, or by the purchase, which the sellers of his new variety will make, of special guarantee seals, following the idea dear to the late Lucien Ballet, an idea that we have always recognized as being the best. The guarantee seal provides security for the breeder who no longer has to proceed with controls, and for the buyer who can have recourse, in the event of deception, against his seller.

We have grafted Cherry Hautin and one of our colleagues from Orléans having asked us for grafts, we have sent them to him, informing him of the restriction regarding the breeder.

The multiplication therefore goes its own way, it is done everywhere in silence, and shortly the tree will be launched by several houses after agreement with the breeder.

What do the undecided think?

For the new roses, two houses have just taken a step towards the goal to be achieved, one (an Orléans house), having obtained a new rose, entrusts it to a Parisian house for forcing and presentation.

The agreement between the two firms was very rapid, thanks to the confidence and broad-mindedness of the breeder, and to the great scrupulousness of the presenter; there is a collaboration there which can only be useful to all, rights being as well as respected as the obligations.

When we have policed ourselves, we can try to police our neighbors, and then police a whole world of producers with a law; setting an example is still the best way to achieve a result. This spirit of collaboration between two firms that might seem like competitors to ordinary people is a modest example of what can be done. We can do more, of course, but let us start modestly so that the long road towards national, then international, understanding is clearly illuminated by the results obtained, instead of being traveled too quickly to the top, at the risk to get lost in the many detours, or to fall into the precipices which necessarily exist on the edges of the most beautiful roads!"

§1.43.5 The League of Nations Lobbies for the Introduction of the Protection of New Plant Varieties—1929

In an article published in La Coopération Internationale, *the League of Nations applauded the introduction of a bill in the United States Congress aiming at amending the patent law and making new plant varieties patentable subject matter.*

Protection of discoveries and inventions in the field of botany

The Congress of the United States of North America is considering a bill aiming at granting patent protection to breeders who enrich humanity by the creation of new species or new varieties of plants. The Bill was presented to the Senate by Mr. Townsend, and in the House of Representatives by Mr. Turnell. The Patent Committees of the two Houses issued a favorable opinion and submitted for approval to Congress a bill amending the patent law.

According to the bill, a patent could be issued to any person who has "invented or discovered a new and distinct variety of plant that can be reproduced by means of grafts, cuts, divisions, etc.", "but not by means of seeds, except by means of tubers." The patent gives its owner "the exclusive right to create, use and sell his invention or discovery, and, in the case of a plant patent, also the exclusive right to reproduce the plant by the means mentioned above. above listed."

The Parliamentary Commissions noting, in the explanatory memorandum, that there is no logical reason not to remunerate the services rendered to society by plant breeders, "whose genius, patience, foresight have created fruits and plants of great value and utility." It is to be hoped that the talents of America's young farmers will thus be led to devote themselves to the profitable work of inventing and discovering new plants that will revolutionize agriculture, such as inventions in the field of electricity, chemistry, etc., have revolutionized them. The history of the men who produced, developed and propagated the cultivation of new plants of inestimable value to humanity and who died in poverty amply demonstrates that this type of piracy, which consists of the unfair appropriation of their life's work, must be recognized as illegal.

The project is supported by the Secretary of Agriculture, by the National Horticultural Board, by the American Nursery Association, by the American Farm Bureau Federation, by the National Grange and by numerous commissioners of the Department of Agriculture, by employees of trial stations, by individual breeders and nurserymen.

Mr. Thomas A. Edison, of whom the Commission asked the opinion, declared on this subject: "Congress can do nothing for agriculture that will be of greater importance and of more lasting action than to grant to the breeders of plants the same status as that currently possessed by inventors in mechanics and chemistry, under patent law."

§1.43.6 The French Government Invites Countries to Participate in a Diplomatic Conference Aimed at Creating a New Sui Generis Regime for the Protection of New Plant Varieties and Explains the Reasons for Such Protection—1957

Invitations to the Conference

Circular Letters of Invitation

addressed by the Ministry of Foreign Affairs of the French Republic

to the French Ambassadors accredited in the invited States[47]

Paris, February 14, 1957

During the revision in London, in 1934, of the Paris Convention for the Protection of Industrial Property, of March 20, 1883, industrial property was defined in Article 1(3)

47. Another letter has been sent to three international organizations inviting them to participate in the Conference as observers: the BIRPI (Bureaux Réunis pour la Protection de la Propriété Industrielle et de la Propriété Littéraire et Artistique, the predecessor of WIPO), the FAO (Food and Agriculture Organization), and the OEEC (Organization of European Economic Cooperation).

as being understood in the broadest sense and applying "not only to industry and commerce proper, but likewise to agricultural and extractive industries and to all manufactured or natural products, for example, wines, grain, tobacco leaf, fruit, cattle, minerals, mineral waters, beer, flowers, and flour."

The wording of this article has given rise to much controversy. Some have seen in it an affirmation of the possibility of patenting the creations of new plant varieties on an equal footing with industrial inventions. They have concluded that it was necessary to protect plants by patent to the exclusion of any other system. Others, on the contrary, have emphasized the fundamental differences that exist between the creation of a new variety of plant and the invention of an industrial nature, and have formally rejected the patent for invention [utility patent] as an institution capable of protecting creations in the vegetable domain.

The problem, poorly defined in 1934, has become increasingly acute as plant genetic science progressed.

Since its first post-war Congress, the International Association for the Protection of Industrial Property has taken up the issue. At the end of its Congresses in Vienna (1952) and Brussels (1954), it expressed wishes that the protection of new plant varieties be organized on the basis of the patent for invention or any other means.

The International Chamber of Commerce has issued several motions to this effect. The Committee of Patent Experts of the Council of Europe adopted a similar recommendation during its July 1951 session, in The Hague. The European Conference on the Development of Seed Production and Trade, held in Stockholm in July 1954, within the framework of the Organization of European Economic Cooperation, tabled similar conclusions.

Finally, agricultural professionals have formed an international organization, the International Association of Professional Breeders for the Protection of New Varieties of Plants (ASSINSEL) which, during its last Congress (Vienna-Semmering, June 1956), urged that an international convention establishes established practices and facilitates international trade in new plant varieties.

There are also legislative or regulatory provisions on this matter in various countries. In addition, some states are in the process of adopting special legislation or amending their legislation to accommodate these special agricultural needs.

It therefore appears desirable that an agreement be established between the different States willing to promote the seed trade on the principles that should govern the protection of new plant varieties and, if possible, on the appropriate institutions to ensure this protection.

Following a proposal made by the Delegate of France before the General Assembly of ASSINSEL, on June 12, 1956, and taking into account the favorable reception reserved for this proposal by the other delegates, the French Government decided to convene an international conference for this purpose.

Its main purpose could be to study the technical aspect of the problem, taking into account in particular the requirements presented by the seed trade. To the extent that this technical aspect could be defined, the participating States could discuss the usefulness of introducing into a convention the common principles that could have been established, either in the form of a convention creating a distinct international union, open to all States that might wish to participate.

I would be grateful if you would kindly invite the Government to which you are accredited to send delegates to this Conference, which will open on May 7, 1957, in Paris, and ask it to let you know the names of its representatives.

You would also like to convey to it the attached aide-memoire concerning the questions raised by the protection of plant varieties.[48]

It would be desirable for each delegation to include at least one representative from the Agricultural Administration who could be assisted by an official from the Industrial Property Administration.

Invited States:

Germany (Federal Republic of), Austria, Belgium, Denmark, Spain, Finland, Italy, Norway, The Netherlands, United Kingdom, Sweden, Switzerland.

§1.43.7 US Congress Discusses the Extension of Protection to Sexually Reproduced Plants—1967

Influenced by the success of UPOV and under pressure from U.S. breeders, discontent with the absence of protection for sexually reproduced plants, the U.S. Senate holds a hearing on the need to pass new legislation, which would be later enacted as the Plant Variety Act of 1970.

Legal Protection for New Plant Varieties Which Reproduce Sexually

(by National Council of Commercial Plant Breeders, Washington, D. C., January 1968)

...

On May 23, 1930, President Hoover signed the Townsend-Purnell Plant Patent Act (46 Stat. 376). For the first time in the history of our nation the discoverer or originator of certain plants was given an option to seek legal protection for his contribution. In 1931, Plant Patent No. 1 was granted to the discoverer of a climbing rose variety, which was named New Dawn. In the years which have passed, more than 2700 Plant Patents have been granted by the United States Patent Office.

The motivation behind the enactment of this Plant Patent legislation may be readily learned by a reading of selected quotations which follow from Senate Report No. 315, dated April 2, 1930. The Report was directed to reasons for making certain new plants eligible for patent protection and was published at the time the Plant Patent bill was before the Senate. This Report states:

48. The aide-mémoire contained a number of very detailed and precise legal/technical questions on the protection of new varieties of plants that an eventual future convention should attempt to answer. The example, the French Government asked the delegates whether plant breeders should receive a right similar to those of patentees and whether such a right should be temporary or perpetual; whether a protected variety could be used by another person as a starting point for the breeding of a new variety; whether protection should be linked to the rules dealing with the trade of seeds (such as phytosanitary regulations).

> "The purpose of the bill is to afford agriculture, so far as practicable, the same opportunity to participate in the benefits of the patent system as has been given industry, and thus assist in placing agriculture on a basis of economic equality with industry."
>
> "Today the plant breeder has no adequate financial incentive to enter upon his work. A new variety once it has left the hands of the breeder may be reproduced in unlimited quantity by all. The originator's only hope of financial reimbursement is through high prices for the comparatively few reproductions that he may dispose of during the first two or three years. After that time, depending upon the speed with which the plant may be asexually reproduced, the breeder loses all control of his discovery. Under the bill the originator will have control of his discovery during a period of 17 years, the same term as under industrial patents. If the new variety is successful, the breeder or discoverer can expect an adequate financial reward. Today plant breeding and research is dependent, in large part, upon Government funds to Governmental experiment stations, or the limited endeavors of the amateur breeder. It is hoped that the bill will afford a sound basis for investing capital in plant breeding and consequently stimulate plant development through private funds."

On September 23, 1954, President Eisenhower signed the only amendment (68 Stat. 1190) to the Plant Patent Act which provided for the patenting of certain newly found plants which had been excluded from patent protection in the past.

...

The test of time has proven the existing Plant Patent Act to be workable. More than 2700 Plant Patents have been issued by the Patent Office in the past thirty-seven years. The number of Plant Patents contested as to validity in the Federal Courts is less than a dozen, and no Plant Patent has been declared invalid as failing to meet the standard of unobviousness. Plant Patents have had a substantial impact upon the upgrading of the nursery industry, and a sound basis for investing capital in the breeding of plants which reproduce asexually has been provided. This has occurred through the development of superior new plant varieties brought about by the increased research efforts. Truly the development of new plant varieties by private industry has been stimulated by providing the originator with legal protection.

...

During the past half century plant breeding and the production of new plant varieties have become a recognized science. This development has been attributed by many to a rediscovery of Mendel's Laws of Heredity which has provided a basis for sound plant research efforts. Although the results of heredity obtained through controlled plant matings as well as other characteristics of plant reproduction have been observed for hundreds of years, man's concerted investigation of these principles and their practical application has occurred largely in the twentieth century. A vast amount of data on existing plant varieties has been assembled and cataloged which provides a starting point for the development of useful new varieties of plants. Many American colleges and universities offer students the opportunity to include courses in the science of plant breeding and related disciplines within their studies. As a result, technically trained scientists are now available who are capable of carrying out meaningful plant research.

...

The plant breeder in the United States is an innovator and creator of products of immense value to the well-being of our nation. Many new plant varieties may be reproduced or "manufactured" in the same form year after year provided the necessary procedures are followed. Conversely, innovations made in other areas of technology such as in the mechanical or chemical arts may be manufactured in great numbers. The ability of plant varieties to reproduce true to form is recognized by those skilled in the biological sciences in general, by the federal and state seed laws, by seed certification regulations, by the seed trade, by farmers, and by the consumers of farm products. Agricultural research as well as industrial research can only be financed if the efforts of the researchers are in some manner rewarded where useful results are achieved. This means that protection against the taking by others of the products of research must be provided. Today there is wide acceptance for the philosophy that public funds should not be expended where industry is capable and willing to conduct applied research. The inventor of plants which reproduce sexually (i.e., by seed) is entitled to the same consideration and encouragement as provided innovators in other areas of technology.

The originator of a new sexually reproduced variety today is provided no legal protection under the Plant Patent Act regardless of the new plant's merit. When one considers that the bulk of the economically important plants grown in this country reproduce by seeds, the inadequacies of the Plant Patent Act in its present form are apparent. No country other than the United States is known to make a distinction between plants which reproduce sexually and plants which reproduce asexually in its system for the legal protection of new plant varieties.

...

The grant of legal protection to the inventors of new varieties of plants which reproduce sexually will provide a new dimension to plant research conducted by private industry. The one missing link needed to encourage more research in this area has been the need for a reasonable assurance that research and development funds may be recovered when a valuable contribution is made. The United States Patent System is considered capable of providing the stimulus required to promote broad advances in all areas of plant breeding technology.

Plant scientists have indicated a willingness to substantially increase research efforts if provided legal protection within the framework of the Plant Patent Act for new varieties of plants which reproduce sexually. The amendment of the Plant Patent Act to eliminate its present deficiency will effectively remove the hesitancy of plant breeders to invest their time and resources in the development of new plants which, if currently introduced, may be freely reproduced to the financial gain of others without any reimbursement being paid to the plant's originator. More useful new plant varieties than ever before would be expected to be produced through increased research efforts to the substantial benefit of the consumer, and industry would be provided the possibility of recouping development costs when a contribution is made.

...

§1.43.8 The U.S. Court of Appeals for the Eighth Circuit, in an Opinion Involving the Trade of Genetically Modified Seeds, Sets a Strong Foundation for the Protection of Trade Secrets—1994

This is an important opinion to the extent it discusses to some length the (three) requirements for the enforcement of trade secret rights. Also of great relevance is the discussion on the lack of clear evidence that the defendant had practiced some unlawful or ethically blameful act for acquiring the plaintiff's trade secret. Indeed, the opinion reflects that the defendant made several unsuccessful attempts to obtain the secret either by acquiring the seeds in question (which was not possible because the plaintiff concealed its characteristics by combining the seeds containing the reserved technology with other seeds) or through reverse engineering. The opinion accepts that the secret was so well concealed that it was virtually impossible to have access to it unless the owner permitted it—or unless some unlawful act had been practiced.

Court of Appeals for the Eighth Circuit

Pioneer Hi-Bred v. Holden Foundation Seeds

Decided July 12, 1994.

John R. Gibson, Senior Circuit Judge.

This case involves a dispute between competing breeders of corn seed. The district court awarded $46,703,230.00 to Pioneer Hi-Bred International based on Holden Foundation Seeds, Inc.'s misappropriation of the genetic make-up of certain seed corn. Holden contests the district court's liability determination and damage award on numerous grounds. Pioneer cross-appeals from the district court's denial of prejudgment interest. We affirm.

The Honorable Donald E. O'Brien, United States District Judge for the Southern District of Iowa.

The bench trial in this case consumed over 37 days, spread over 14 weeks. The massive record consists of over 9,000 pages of transcript and 1,100 exhibits. Thus, our recitation of the facts is, of necessity, somewhat abbreviated.

The sale of hybrid seed corn is a multi-billion-dollar industry. Pioneer is a vertically integrated seed corn company. It conducts a breeding program, develops parent seed, and produces hybrid seed corn for the retail market. The superior performance of its products, obtained in part through millions of dollars spent annually on corn research and development, has enabled it to gain a sizeable portion of the retail seed corn market. Its marketed seed corns include Pioneer hybrids 3780 (Pioneer's leader in sales for several years) and 3541—which share a common parent, designated H3H.

Holden indirectly competes with Pioneer. Holden is a foundation seed company that develops inbred parent seed lines and sells these lines to its customers, also seed corn companies, which use them to produce hybrid seed in competition with Pioneer. During the 1980s, Holden's LH38, LH39, and LH40 ("LH38-39-40") were among its most popular parent lines.

...

Pioneer sued Holden on a number of legal theories, Claiming that Holden developed LH38-39-40 from misappropriated Pioneer H3H or H43SZ7 —protected trade secrets of Pioneer ("H3H/H43SZ7"). During discovery, the district court decided, at Pioneer's request, that the nature of this dispute required that Holden "freeze in" a particular story regarding the development of LH38-39-40. The court did so to prevent Holden from altering its story to conform to the scientific evidence eventually introduced. Holden claimed that although LH38-39-40 demonstrated some similarity to Pioneer's seed lines, Holden developed LH38-39-40 from an internal line, designated L120. The district court held that the genetic make-up of H3H/H43SZ7 is a protected trade secret of Pioneer. The court determined that although LH38-39-40 differed in some respects from Pioneer's seed, the lines had nonetheless been derived from misappropriated Pioneer material. The district court based its decision on expert testimony that LH38-39-40 derived from H3H/H43SZ7 and Holden's inability to offer adequate evidence of its "L120 story." The court also ruled in Pioneer's favor on its Lanham Act, interference with business advantage, unjust enrichment, and conversion claims. The district court awarded over 46 million dollars in damages to Pioneer. Holden appeals.

Pioneer claimed that Holden violated § 43(a) of the Lanham Act, 15 U.S.C. § 1125(a) (1988), and also brought pendent state law claims based on trade secret misappropriation, unjust enrichment, interference with business advantage, conversion, and unfair competition. The parties focused their efforts before this court on the district court's trade secret holding.

Pioneer initially asserted that Holden misappropriated Pioneer's seed known as H3H. Trial testimony showed, however, that H3H and H43SZ7, derived from H43SZ7, could have been used interchangeably to create LH38-39-40. Thus, the court permitted Pioneer to bring H43SZ7 into the litigation. For our purposes, they can be considered as a single line, "H3H/H43SZ7."

Stating that "the law of trade secrets provides a better fit for the facts of this case," the court expressed concern over pushing the frontiers of common law conversion … . Thus, the court made its ruling in favor of Pioneer on its conversion claim conditional on the ultimate failure of its trade secret claim. *Id.*

The court held in favor of Holden on Pioneer's state unfair competition claim. Pioneer does not appeal from this decision.

…

II.

Much of Holden's argument before this court focused on the district court's ruling that Holden misappropriated Pioneer's protected trade secret. According to Iowa law, a plaintiff must generally show three elements to prevail in a trade secret action: "(1) existence of a trade secret, (2) acquisition of the secret as a result of a confidential relationship, and (3) unauthorized use of a secret." …

Holden does not argue on appeal that genetic messages cannot qualify as trade secrets… . Holden instead argues that it should not be liable for misappropriating H3H/H43SZ7 because Pioneer failed: (1) to keep the genetic messages secret; (2) to prove that Holden actually possessed the protected genetic messages; and (3) to prove that Holden obtained the material by improper means. The district court rejected each of Holden's arguments.

...

A.

Holden argues that H3H/H43SZ7 are not trade secrets because Pioneer failed to maintain their secrecy. Fundamental to the existence of a trade secret is that the matter be, in fact, secret ... .

The district court found that the genetic messages of H3H and H43SZ7 were trade secrets... The district court found that the "formula" did not exist outside Pioneer's and its contractors' fields, and that Pioneer took reasonable precautions to protect the secrecy of the genetic message ... .

Pioneer takes several measures to preserve the secrecy of its inbreds. Growers operate under contracts which prohibit disclosure of the seed. Fields have no labels indicating what seed is being grown, and all seed bags are coded to avoid identification. Pioneer removes male inbred lines and commingles them with other corn, thereby frustrating those seeking to obtain the inbred seed.

By restricting the availability of its inbred lines, Pioneer prevents competitors from obtaining access to the genetic message contained therein. It is this message that we assume is protected by trade secret law ... .

Despite these steps, Holden argues that Pioneer failed to maintain adequate security in several ways. First, during the 1970s Pioneer harvested the male rows of its production fields and sold the seed to grain elevators. This grain was readily available to any purchaser. Holden also states that H3H could be present in Hybrid Pioneer 3780 or 3541 seed sold to farmers, and thus H3H plants may be found in farmers' fields. Holden further argues that Pioneer lost the requisite secrecy by selling H3H/H43SZ7 in the Soviet Union without restriction. Holden cites testimony indicating that some of this seed was "leaked out," and that Pioneer taught experts in Hungary how to produce H3H and H3H-derived hybrids.

Although there is conflicting evidence on whether Pioneer had maintained the secrecy of the genetic messages, there is sufficient evidence to support the district court's finding that Pioneer took reasonable precautions to protect the secrecy of the genetic message of H3H/H43SZ7 ... . First, Holden's claim that the message was "widely disseminated" because it could be obtained from seed elevators and farmers' seed bags is overstated. Although a Pioneer employee, Thomas Urban, acknowledged that the male corn could get into a seed bag as a contaminant, he also stated "it's almost impossible." Urban explained that Pioneer had "many, many employees who stood looking at corn ears ... [and] [t]he chances of that happening are not very great." Urban knew of no instances of the male corn being found in bags of hybrid seed. Moreover, the seed in the bags and elevators is mixed, and a grower would have no way of easily identifying the desired male seed from the many other seeds in the overall mix. "The more difficult, time consuming and costly it would be to develop the information, the less likely it is 'readily' ascertainable." ...

It is also relevant that the possible means identified by Holden of obtaining H3H/H43SZ7 were not the means by which Holden claimed it developed LH38-39-40.

Many courts have held that the fact that one "could" have obtained a trade secret lawfully is not a defense if one does not actually use proper means to acquire the information … .

Holden's argument that Pioneer abandoned its trade secret by selling H43SZ7 to the Soviet Union is similarly unpersuasive. Pioneer did sell H43SZ7 to the Soviet Union during the 1970s. This sale, however, was pursuant to an agreement which restricted use of the seed and contained a confidentiality provision … . Holden's evidence that the material was "leaked out" of the Soviet Union to other Eastern bloc countries is based only on rumor, and does not convince us that the district court clearly erred in finding that Pioneer maintained the requisite secrecy for trade secret protection of H3H/H43SZ7.

…

C.

We next consider Holden's argument that Pioneer failed to prove the second requisite element of a trade secret action. Although frequently listed as such, a "confidential relationship" is not in fact a prerequisite to a trade secret action. Holden admits that a contractual or confidential relationship is not required to maintain a trade secret action. The district court held, and the parties agree, that a plaintiff may prevail in the absence of such a relationship by showing that the secret was obtained by improper means … . Conduct which is not otherwise unlawful may nonetheless be improper… . Holden contends, however, that Pioneer failed to prove improper means. In support of its position, Holden suggests there is absolutely no evidence of misappropriation or improper means. Thus, Holden argues we must reverse because mere possession of a trade secret cannot support a trade secret award.

We do not mean to suggest that the owner of a trade secret enjoys an absolute property right in the trade secret which may be used to exclude the world from using the secret. We have found no case so holding, and believe that any attempt by state law to do so might well be preempted by the federal patent laws. Trade secret law and patent law—both aspects of the elusive concept of intellectual property—serve quite different functions. Patent protection, which is often difficult and costly to obtain, gives the patent holder the right to exclude others from using the patented device, process, etc., for a limited time period. Trade secret law, on the other hand, protects a person's right to keep certain information "secret," by providing a cause of action against anyone who misappropriates a reasonably-protected secret. Moreover, by labeling certain wrongful, if not actually otherwise illegal, acts "improper," trade secret law plays an important role in regulating commercial behavior. If the law forces businesses to take extreme measures to protect themselves against all forms of commercial espionage not otherwise unlawful, "the incentive to invest resources in discovering more efficient methods of production will be reduced and with it the amount of invention." … Our analysis is consistent with the stated purposes of trade secret protection: (1) maintaining commercial morality, and (2) encouraging innovation … .

The record displays a long history of Holden attempts to obtain Pioneer's genetic material. Roland Holden, the now-retired founder of Holden's Foundation Seeds, Inc., testified about his repeated searches for Pioneer's seed. As the court stated, "it is very clear that for a number of years, Roland Holden was doing anything he could to try to find out more about and grow Pioneer lines." ... These efforts included searching "friendly farms" for stray inbred plants (e.g., H3H)—a process by which he admitted obtaining possession of several Pioneer lines .... at 8-30. Although the court concluded that "Pioneer has not specifically shown" that these efforts were the "exact source" of L120, the testimony supports such an inference .... Holden's inadequate explanation of its faulty record-keeping and the untimely disposal of all L120 seed also give rise to an inference of misappropriation ... .

An inference of misappropriation from limited facts is especially warranted in situations such as this where the secret itself is so unique that any form of duplication would probably be improper ... . Unlike the situation where a competitor is found to have possession of a process, product or fact which is similar to plaintiff's "secret," this case involves possession of a product *derived from* the protected secret. Proof of derivation removes the possibility of independent development, further supporting the court's finding that Holden misappropriated genetic material from Pioneer.

The court did not end its analysis after determining that Pioneer met its burden as to misappropriation or improper means. Rather, the court concluded that since Pioneer "met this burden, Holden has the burden of showing that H3H and/or H43SZ7 were lawfully acquired"—a burden which the court concluded Holden did not meet. Holden construes this language as expressing the court's decision to place upon it, and not Pioneer, the burden of proof on the issue of improper means.

...

It was only after finding sufficient evidence of "misappropriation" by Holden that the court first discussed shifting the burden of proving lawful acquisition to Holden .... The court's later discussion of "burden shifting" merely expresses its appreciation of the fact that once Pioneer produced convincing evidence of misappropriation, Holden was obligated to provide persuasive evidence of lawful derivation. We reject Holden's argument that the court improperly placed the burden on it to show that it lawfully acquired H3H/H43SZ7. The court's procedure can simply be read as an allocation of the burdens of going forward with the evidence. After weighing and balancing the parties' competing evidence, the district court found Holden's L120 story less persuasive than Pioneer's misappropriation claim, hence the district court held in favor of Pioneer. In light of the evidence discussed above, and after reviewing the entire record, we cannot say the district court's finding of misappropriation was clearly erroneous.

We are not unmindful that the court said:

> The Court further finds on the record that Holden merchandised a line of seed corn that was very similar to Pioneer's and that, therefore, the burden has shifted to Holden to show that it did in fact have a corn line or something closely similar thereto which had been produced by independent breeding efforts.
>
> ...

This statement, however, came after the court's statement, discussed in the text:

> [T]his Court is persuaded that Pioneer's H3H and/or Pioneer's H43SZ7 have been used by the Defendant Holden. The Court further finds that Pioneer has met its

> burden regarding misappropriation. Since it has met this burden, Holden has the burden of showing that H3H and/or H43SZ7 were lawfully acquired.

...

While these statements could arguably suggest some ambiguity as to whether the court shifted the burden after finding mere use by Holden, or only after expressly finding Pioneer met its initial burden of showing misappropriation or improper use. The first paragraph cited above should not be interpreted without the benefit of the court's prior finding of misappropriation.

The district court faced a Herculean task in dealing with this massive case which began over a decade ago. The court's liability opinion, alone, contains over 100 pages of discussion. In light of the size and complexity of this case, the existence of some isolated ambiguity in the district court's order is not surprising since the parties focused on whether Holden possessed H3H/H43SZ7, not on how it obtained it. Holden never claimed that it lawfully acquired Pioneer's genetic material. Its entire defense effort sought to prove independent development of a different product. Thus, the court's finding of misappropriation depended in large part on inferences drawn from Pioneer's discrediting of Holden's L120 story. We are persuaded that the district court never swayed from the requirement that Pioneer prove each and every element of its case.

III.

Holden makes several additional arguments on appeal. We briefly consider these remaining claims. First, Holden argues that the district court erred in its holdings on Pioneer's Lanham Act, unjust enrichment, intentional interference with a business advantage, and conversion theories. We need not consider the merits of the alternate state law theories of recovery because we affirm the district court's trade secret award.

...

C.

Holden also argues the Plant Variety Protection Act, 7 U.S.C. § 2321-2582 preempts state trade secret law as applied to sexually reproducing plants. Holden contends the available legislative history demonstrates Congress' intent that the Act be the sole legal protection for sexually reproducing plants. If clearly expressed, congressional intent to preempt state law will be given effect ... . However, neither the plain language of the Act nor the legislative history cited by Holden demonstrates any such intent. We read the House Report as reflecting Congress' determination that no patent or patent-like protection existed for sexually reproducing plants. The language simply does not show a legislative intent to preempt all state protection of plants. Congress merely acknowledged and addressed the absence of protection for sexually reproducing plants qua plants. It did not suggest that state law could not address improper conduct that happened to involve plants or plant material. The Supreme Court has expressly held that trade secret and patent protection can "peacefully coexist." ... We have carefully considered Holden's preemption argument, and conclude it is without merit.

IV.

The district court bifurcated the liability and damage trials. After considering the various submissions of the parties in the separate damage trial, the court awarded Pioneer $46,703,230 in lost profits. The court further determined that, in the alternative, the proper damages under an unjust enrichment theory would be $21,174,913. The court also enjoined Holden from distributing or disposing of 177 inbred lines containing LH38-39-40 or their progeny, pending a determination of whether such lines should be turned over to Iowa State University.

...

Accordingly, we find no error in the court's lost profits methodology and conclude the district court did not err in awarding Pioneer $46,703,230.

We affirm the district court's judgment and order of damages.

§1.43.9 The U.S. Supreme Court Sets the Boundaries of the Farmers' Exemption under the Plant Variety Protection Act—1995

United States Supreme Court

Asgrow Seed Co. v. Winterboer

513 U.S. 179 (1995)

January 18, 1995

Justice Scalia delivered the Opinion

[Syllabus]

Petitioner Asgrow Seed Company has protected two varieties of soybean seed under the Plant Variety Protection Act of 1970 (PVPA), which extends patent-like protection to novel varieties of sexually reproduced plants (plants grown from seed). After respondent farmers planted 265 acres of Asgrow's seed and sold the entire salable crop-enough to plant 10,000 acres-to other farmers for use as seed, Asgrow filed suit, alleging infringement under, *inter alia,* 7 U. S. C. § 2541(1), for selling or offering to sell the seed, and § 2541(3), for "sexually multiply[ing] the novel varieties as a step-in marketing [them] (for growing purposes)." Respondents contended that they were entitled to a statutory exemption from liability under § 2543, which provides in relevant part that "[e]xcept to the extent that such action may constitute an infringement under [§2541(3)]," a farmer may "save seed ... and use such saved seed in the production of a crop for use on his farm, or for sale as provided in this section: *Provided,* That" such saved seed can be sold for reproductive purposes where both buyer and seller are farmers "whose primary farming occupation is the growing of crops for sale for other than reproductive purposes." In granting Asgrow summary judgment, the District Court found that the exemption allows a farmer to save and resell to other farmers only the amount of seed the seller would need to replant his own fields. The Court of Appeals reversed, holding that § 2543 permits a farmer to sell up to half of every crop he produces from PVPA-protected seed, so long as he sells the other half for food or feed.

(a) Respondents were not eligible for the § 2543 exemption if their planting and harvesting were conducted "as a step-in marketing" under § 2541(3), for the parties do not dispute that these actions constituted "sexual multiplication" of novel varieties. Since the PVPA does not define "marketing," the term should be given its ordinary meaning. Marketing ordinarily refers to the act of holding forth property for sale, together with the activities preparatory thereto, but does not require that there be extensive promotional or merchandising activities connected with the selling... .

(b) By reason of the proviso, the first sentence of § 2543 allows seed that has been preserved for reproductive purposes (saved seed) to be sold for such purposes. However, the structure of the sentence is such that this authorization does not extend to saved seed that was grown for the purpose of sale (marketing) for replanting, because that would violate § 2541(3). As a practical matter, this means that only seed that has been saved by the farmer to replant his own acreage can be sold. Thus, a farmer who saves seeds to replant his acreage, but changes his plans, may sell the seeds for replanting under the proviso's terms. The statute's language stands in the way of the limitation the Court of Appeals found in the amount of seed that can be sold... .

§1.43.10 The U.S. Supreme Court Holds That Sui Generis and Patent Protection for Sexually Reproduced Plants Are Not Incompatible—2001

United States Supreme Court

J. E. M. Ag Supply, Inc. v. Pioneer Hi-Bred International, Inc.

534 U.S. 124 (2001)

December 10, 2001

Justice Thomas delivered the Opinion

[Syllabus]

Respondent Pioneer Hi-Bred International, Inc. (Pioneer), holds 17 utility patents issued under 35 U. S. C. §101 that cover the manufacture, use, sale, and offer for sale of its inbred and hybrid corn seed products. Pioneer sells its patented hybrid seeds under a limited label license that allows only the production of grain and/or forage, and prohibits using such seed for propagation or seed multiplication or for the production or development of a hybrid or different seed variety. Petitioner J. E. M. Ag Supply, Inc., doing business as Farm Advantage, Inc., bought patented seeds from Pioneer in bags bearing the license agreement and then resold the bags. Pioneer filed this patent infringement suit against Farm Advantage and distributors and customers of Farm Advantage (collectively Farm Advantage or petitioners). Farm Advantage filed a patent invalidity counterclaim, arguing that sexually reproducing plants, such as Pioneer's corn plants, are not patentable subject matter within §101. Farm Advantage maintained that the Plant Patent Act of 1930 (PPA) and the Plant Variety Protection Act (PVPA) set forth the exclusive statutory means for protecting plant life because these statutes are more specific than §101, and thus each carves out subject matter from §101 for special treatment. The District Court granted Pioneer summary judgment. Relying on this Court's broad construction of §101 in *Diamond v. Chakrabarty*, 447 U. S. 303, the District Court held that §101 clearly covers plant life. It also held that in enacting the PPA and the PVPA, Congress neither expressly nor implicitly removed plants from §WI's subject matter. In particular, the District Court noted that Congress did not implicitly repeal §101 by passing the more specific PVPA because there was no irreconcilable conflict between the two statutes. The Federal Circuit affirmed.

Held: Newly developed plant breeds fall within the subject matter of §101, and neither the PPA nor the PVPA limits the scope of §WI's coverage... .

(a) In approaching the question presented here, this Court is mindful that it has already recognized that §101's language is extremely broad and has concluded that living things are patentable under that provision, *Chakrabarty, supra*, at 308, 313, 315. Since 1985, the Patent and Trademark Office (PTO) has had an unbroken practice of conferring utility patents for plants. Nonetheless, petitioners argue that the PPA and the PVPA are the exclusive means of protecting new varieties of plants, and so awarding utility patents for plants upsets the scheme contemplated by Congress ...

(b) Neither the PPA's original nor its recodified text indicates that its protection for asexually reproduced plants was intended to be exclusive. The 1930 PPA amended the general patent provision to protect only the asexual reproduction of a plant. And Congress' 1952 revision, which placed plant patents into a separate chapter 15, was only a housekeeping measure that did not change the substantive rights or the relaxed requirements for such patents. Plant patents under the PPA thus continue to have very limited coverage and less stringent requirements than §101 utility patents. Importantly, chapter 15 nowhere states that plant patents are the exclusive means of granting intellectual property protection to plants. The arguments that petitioners advance for why the PPA should preclude assigning utility patents for plants are unpersuasive because petitioners fail to take account of the forward-looking perspective of the utility patent statute and the reality of plant breeding in 1930... .

(c) That the PVPA specifically authorizes limited patent-like protection for certain sexually reproduced plants does not evidence Congress' intent to deny broader §101 utility patent protection for such plants. While the PVPA creates a comprehensive statutory scheme with respect to its particular protections and subject matter, giving limited protection to plant varieties that are new, distinct, uniform, and stable, nowhere does it restrict the scope of patentable subject matter under §101. The PVPA contains no statement of exclusivity. Furthermore, at the time the PVPA was enacted, the PTO had already issued numerous utility patents for hybrid plant processes, which reaffirms that such material was within §WI's scope. Petitioners also err in arguing that the PVPA altered §101's subject-matter coverage by implication. Repeal by implication requires that the earlier and later statutes be irreconcilable, ... The differences in the requirements for, and coverage of, utility patents and PVPA plant variety certificates, however, do not present irreconcilable conflicts because the requirements for a §101 utility patent are more stringent than those for a PVP certificate, and the protections afforded by a utility patent are greater than those afforded by a PVP certificate. Petitioners' suggestion that dual protection cannot exist when statutes overlap and purport to protect the same commercially valuable attribute or thing is rejected as well. This Court has given effect to two overlapping statutes, so long as each reaches some distinct cases, ..., and it has allowed dual protection in other intellectual property cases, ... In this case, many plant varieties that are unable to satisfy §101's stringent requirements might still qualify for the PVPA's lesser protections... .

(d) The PTO has assigned utility patents for plants for at least 16 years, and there has been no indication from either Congress or agencies with expertise that such coverage is inconsistent with the PVPA or the PPA. Congress has not only failed to pass legislation indicating that it disagrees with the PTO's interpretation of §101; it has even recognized the availability of utility patents for plants... .

§1.44 A CASE OF ABUSE OF PATENT RIGHTS IN DAIRY INDUSTRY-RELATED INVENTIONS WITH MEDICINAL VALUE; ITS MAJOR IMPACT ON THE HEALTH OF POOR CHILDREN; AND THE STRONG CONDEMNATION BY THE COURT OF APPEALS FOR THE NINTH CIRCUIT—1944

In the 1920s, Dr. Harry Steenbock, professor of biochemistry at the University of Wisconsin, invented a method of irradiating several food substances with ultraviolet rays by using a quartz mercury vapor lamp, with the resulting production of provitamin D in those substances. The invention was of great relevance to health, in particular to children's children, because of its effect of increasing the body's bone metabolism through the consumption of vitamin D-enriched products, thereby avoiding rachitis. Dr. Steenbock filed for and obtained several patents and continuations around his invention in the United States and other countries (such as Canada, the UK, and France). However, understanding the complexities of managing patent rights in a business-efficient manner, Dr. Steenbock transferred his rights over the patents to an entity created by the University of Wisconsin (the Wisconsin Alumni Research Foundation) with the single purpose of licensing the patents, collecting the ensuing royalties, and reinvesting them in University's research programs. But there was a problem: the University of Wisconsin is owned by the State, and the State of Wisconsin was (and is) a major producer of dairy products. However, poor families could not afford butter and other dairies, especially in times of war (when even middle-class families struggled to buy butter). Instead, those families purchased and consumed oleomargarine. This situation has created a serious conflict of interests with an obvious ethical dimension: the Foundation would license the patent with an important use restriction: the invention could not be used to enrich non-dairy substances. Therefore, the poor and the blue-collar working classes lost access to a cheap, functional, and effective means of preventing rachitis. In the end, as one of the following texts shows, one licensee would breach the restriction-of-use clause and would use the invention to enrich non-dairy products. The Foundation sued for breach of contract and patent infringement and won at the District level. But the Court of Appeals for the Ninth Circuit, with indignation and repulse, agreed with the unclean hands defense raised by the alleged infringer. However, instead of decreeing what we could designate as a compulsory license (the permission for the defendant to continue using the invention in return for the payment of royalties—which is the normal solution for cases that involve the unclean hands' doctrine), the Court preferred to invalidate the patents. In the Court's view, the specifications had failed to specifically clarify how Dr. Steenbock's method was applied so as to obtain the antirachitic effect. Apparently, the mere identification of the use of a vapor lamp was not sufficient. However, such an invalidation was utterly inappropriate and can only be explained by the feeling of repulse for the sort of patent misuse that the opinion of the judges revealed. Indeed, the fact that the inventor has taken inspiration from the operation of the sun and imitated it through the use of a vapor lamp should never be a reason for invalidating a patent. Actually, imitating Nature is what many inventions do. Moreover, Dr. Steenbock had not claimed the process only but also the product. If the Court's argument could be accepted, at least the patent should have been retained for the product. But, more significantly, for the first (and, I believe, the last) time, a U.S. Court admitted that, if it was not for the invalidation of the patent on grounds of lack of novelty, it was ready to invalidate as a sanction to the appalling abuse of the licensing rights by the patentee:

> *It is strongly arguable that such a suppression of the patent's use is vastly more against the public interest than its use for a mere control of prices as in* United States v. Masonite Corp., supra, *or the tieing of unpatented with patented material in* Mercoid Corp. v. Mid-Continent Co., supra.

Anyway, the facts around these patents and the Ninth Circuit's opinion have had two major consequences that endure up to today: The Foundation was the first patent licensing office to be created within a major University. Several decades later, that idea was embraced by the Bayh-Dole Act, and most Universities in the United States have created that sort of department. That same idea is also gradually being accepted in other countries. The second enduring consequence is the oligopoly of Vitamin D suppliers that emerged from the Foundation's licensing practices, which soon would license Kellogg's to sell its enriched cornflakes, as well as a few pharmaceutical companies, which soon would collude to control production, distribution, and prices all over the world.

§1.44.1 Dr. Steenbock's First Patent (Excerpts) Concerning the Production of Vitamin D-Rich Products—1928

Patented August 14, 1928—1,680,818

United States Patent Office

Harry Steenbock, of Madison, Wisconsin, Assignor to Wisconsin Alumni Research Foundation, a Corporation

Antirachitic Product and Process

Application filed June 30, 1924. No Drawing.

This invention relates particularly to a method of preparing antirachitic products of edible character, such as foods and medicines, and to the products obtained by such method of treatment.

The process is effected by subjecting edible substances to the action of rays of the region of the ultra violet rays of the spectrum in such manner as to effect the antirachitic activation, care being taken to avoid the destruction of the antirachitic principle after it has been imparted. The sterilization of water by means of ultra violet rays is known. Also, it has been proposed to sterilize milk by means of ultra violet rays, but the treatment given to the milk to effect sterilization has also had the effect of spoiling the taste and otherwise injuring the milk and thus this method of sterilization has failed to come into commercial use. Also, it has been proposed to employ X-rays, or Roentgen rays, to effect sterilization. These rays are not suited to the present purpose, however.

It has not been known prior to the present invention that it is possible to so treat edible products by the use of ultra violet rays as to render them antirachitic. The present invention enables this to be effected with a wide variety of edible substances suited to the needs of mankind and animals. The treatment is understood to impart other favorable properties of the substances treated… .

What I regard as new, and desire to secure by Letters Patent, is:

1. The process of imparting antirachitic properties to organic substances of dietary value (for example carbohydrate foods, fats, oils, protein, foods, or composite foods), which comprises subjecting the same to the action of ultra-violet rays, such as are produced by a quartz mercury vapour lamp, for a period sufficient to effect antirachitic activation but so limited as to avoid subsequent substantial injury of the antirachitic principle.
2. The process set forth in claim 1 as applied to oils and fats containing unsaponifiable lipoids.
3. The process set forth in claim 1 as applied to naturally liquid glycerides.
4. The process set forth in claim 1 as applied to olive oil.
5. Naturally deficient (in the antirachitic factor) food substance antirachitically activated in accordance with the process set forth in claim 1.

6. The naturally deficient (in the antirachitic factor) liquid glycerides containing constituents antirachitically activated in accordance with the process set forth in claim 1.
7. Olive oil antirachitically activated in accordance with the process set forth in claim 1.
8. The process of imparting antirachitic properties of organic substances of dietary value (for example carbohydrate foods, fats, oils, protein foods, or composite foods), which comprises subjecting the same to the action of ultra-violet rays, such as are produced by a quartz mercury vapour lamp, for a period sufficient to effect antirachitic activation but so limited as to avoid subsequent substantial injury to either the antirachitic principle or the palatability.

§1.44.2 Dr. Steenbock's Second Patent (Excerpts)—1932

Patented August 9, 1932—1,871,135

United States Patent Office

Harry Steenbock, of Madison, Wisconsin, Assignor to Wisconsin Alumni Research Foundation, a Corporation of Wisconsin

Antirachitic product and process

No drawing. Application filed December 27, 1926. Serial No. 157, 429.

The present invention or discovery pertains to a method of antirachitically activating cereals and cereal products, such as meals, starches, flours, breakfast foods, etc., and to the products obtained by such method of treatment.

The present application is a continuation-in-part of my application Serial No. 723,171, filed June 30, 1924, issued as Patent No. 1,680,818, and claims are included herein for subject matter originally disclosed in the application here mentioned... .

What I regard as new, and desire to secure by Letters Patent, is:

1. The process of preparing antirachitic food substances which comprises: subjecting cereals, solid cereal products, etc., to the action of ultra violet rays, such as emanate from a quartz mercury vapor lamp, for a period sufficient to effect antirachitic activation but so limited as to avoid subsequent substantial injury to the antirachitic principle and/or palatability.
2. The process set forth in claim 1 as applied to cereal products in broken or comminuted condition.
3. Cereal and cereal products antirachitically activated in the manner set forth in claim 1.
4. Breakfast foods containing an antirachitically activated cereal product, which has been thus activated directly by artificially produced ultra-violet rays.

§1.44.3 Dr. Steenbock's Third Patent (Excerpt)—1936

Patented October 13, 1936—2,057,399

United States Patent Office

Antirachitic Product and Process

Harry Steenbock, of Madison, Wisconsin, assignor to Wisconsin Alumni Research Foundation, a corporation of Wisconsin

No drawing. Application filed May 14, 1932. Serial No. 611, 444.

The present invention or discovery pertains to an antirachitically activated substance and a method of activating the same.

The present application constitutes a continuation-in-part of my application Ser. No. 157,430, filed December 27, 1926, now Patent No. 1,871,136.

The discovery upon which the present application is based is that yeast, which is a fungus, is capable of being antirachitically activated by means of ultra-violet rays.

The activation may be accomplished in any suitable manner. Preferably, the yeast is spread in a thin layer and subjected to the action of light containing ultra-violet rays until activation is accomplished in a sufficient degree to the give to the product the desired degree of antirachitic potency... .

§1.44.4 In the Wake of World War II, the Court of Appeals for the 9th Circuit Vehemently Condemns the Misuse of Dr. Steenbock's Patent Rights—1944

Circuit Court of Appeals, Ninth Circuit.

November 24, 1944.

Vitamin Technologists, Inc., v. Wisconsin Alumni Research Foundation

146 F.2d 941 (1944)

Denman, Circuit Judge.

Appellee Wisconsin Alumni Research Foundation brought its complaint below alleging that appellant Vitamin Technologists, Inc., and H. F. B. Roessler, one of appellant's employees, were making an infringing use of a process of producing vitamin D by activating ergosterol and yeast, claimed to be organic substances of dietary value, with the ultra violet rays of the spectrum, produced by a mercury vapor lamp, a use of the rays claimed to be in violation of one or another of three patents, Nos. 1,680,818, 1,871,136 and 2,057,399. Their filing dates are, respectively, June 30, 1924, December 27, 1926, and May 14, 1932. The patents were granted August 14, 1928, August 9, 1932, and October 13, 1936.

These patents were secured by Dr. Steenbock of the faculty of the University of Wisconsin and assigned to appellee. They are hereafter referred to as the first, second and third patents in the order of their dates of patenting. The second patent is claimed to be an extension in part of the first patent and the third patent such a continuation of the second. Infringements of product claims of the patents were also alleged.

Appellant answered claiming unclean hands, laches, invalidity of the claims on their face, and anticipation. The district court found the challenged claims valid and adjudged infringements by appellant both as to the process and its products and the court's interlocutory judgment ordered a perpetual injunction. This appeal followed. The district court also held that Roessler did not infringe, from which decision Wisconsin Alumni Research Foundation took an appeal. As to the latter appeal, our holding as to the invalidity of the patents requires an affirmance of the judgment.

The application for the first patent specifies the claimed discovery of a new process of producing vitamin D in such dietary substances by exposing them to the ultra violet rays of the spectrum. The process is of great value to mammalian animals, including human beings, and to poultry. Its contribution to the cure or amelioration of rickets is admitted by all the parties and proved by the testimony.

Many plant and animal foods of man and other animals contain no vitamin D, or less than is necessary in the diet composed of them, properly to support the bone forming functions of the body. Mammals whose food has this deficiency suffer from rickets. Many such foods, however, contain constituents called pro-vitamin D which when exposed to the ultra violet rays of the spectrum develop through their radiation the vitamin D in quantities sufficient to increase the body's bone metabolism.

This pro-vitamin, called a lipoid, is contained as a part of the fat-like material of some animal substances. Similarly in green vegetable material and in the oil of the meat of the coconut and certain other vegetable oils there exist such lipoids containing the pro-vitamin of vitamin D. In the ancient process of soap making from fatty materials there is an unsaponifiable part in which the pro-vitamin is mainly, if not entirely, contained....

Several of the infringements found by the district court consist of appellant's use of the patent's claimed process of projecting ultra violet rays produced by a quartz mercury vapor lamp to irradiate and create vitamin D in ergosterol. Ergosterol is a concentrated extract of unsaponifiable lipoids, derived from animal and vegetable food substances. Other infringements held are in so activating such lipoids in yeast. The district court held on sufficient evidence that both ergosterol and yeast are "organic substances of dietary value," as that phrase is used in claim 1 of the first patent. The possession and sale of the products of so processing ergosterol and yeast were also held to infringe.

A. The success of the monopoly of the aid to or cure of the rachitic.

Appellee contends that all the claims obtain support from the commercial success of the monopoly granted. It describes the great number of children suffering from malformation of their bodies due to the defective bone metabolism. The record contains pathetic pictures of such malformations and statistics of the large numbers of such unfortunates. Other maturer sufferers are described, all proving the great numbers of afflicted who, ex necessitate if they are to use such a boon to humanity, have been customers of the licensees of appellee. From the appellee's business manager it appears that it was largely from need of the poor that the business was supported… .

We take notice of the future continuance of the poor and of others afflicted and that such customers are excluded by the patents, if valid, from any unlicensed source of the remedy of foods so irradiated to contain vitamin D.

Dr. Steenbock's continuing interest in the management of appellee's business is apparent from his testimony regarding the refusal of licensing of the irradiation of oleomargarine, one of the foods of the poor, with the antirachitic vitamin D… .

We agree that it has been shown that the monopoly on this aid or cure of the rachitic has been a commercial success which well warrants the consideration of the court. Apart from its legal implications, the large financial returns from such a profit-controlled monopoly barrier between the great numbers of the afflicted and their potent remedy is an interesting episode in the history of the law of patents… .

However, we do not agree that such commercial success overcomes either the unclean hands and laches or the invalidity of the first two patents, later discussed.

B. Appellant's claim that in any event relief should be denied because the Wisconsin corporation uses its property in patents against the public interest.

Herein consideration of the refusal to use the patented process to irradiate oleomargarine against the interest of the public in the health of citizens.

It is now well established that a patentee may not put his property in the patent to a use contra to the public interest. The grant of a patent is the grant of a special privilege "to promote the Progress of Science and useful Arts." … Const. Art. I, § 8. However, as stated in *Mercoid Corp. v. Mid-Continent Inv. Co.*, … it is not the private use but "… the public interest which is dominant in the patent system. *Pennock v. Dialogue*, … *United States v. Masonite Corp.*, … The patent is a privilege. But it is a privilege which is conditioned by a public purpose." …

In a license agreement of August 8, 1928, between the Fleischmann Company and the Wisconsin corporation, the following provision appears:

> The Foundation grants the Company … the following rights and licenses …
> C. The exclusive right and license to make and the *exclusive* right and *license to sell*, but only to other licensees of the Foundation, *yeast and yeast products*, as defined in Paragraphs A and B above, *but unactivated*, for use as a source of antirachitically activatable unsaponifiable lipoids for antirachitic activation … . (Emphasis supplied.).

This contract was assigned to Standard Brands, and many times modified. It does not appear that this provision has ever been changed. Here is a clear violation of the principle established in the Mercoid Corp. and Masonite cases, *supra*… .

The court also notes, *sua sponte*, as a tribunal concerned that equitable processes not be used contra to the public interest, a matter in which the court is not "at the mercy" of the parties, that in a subsequent agreement with Standard Brands it was agreed that the licensee should not incorporate its activated yeast products into oleomargarine. The specific words are that Standard Brands "shall not use or sell such activated yeast products for incorporation in the following products viz. margarine … ."

A similar provision so excepting margarine appears in a license to one Kovacs, "except with the written consent of the licensor." These provisions of the licenses are relevant to Dr. Steenbock's testimony, supra, that none of the licensees had irradiated or fortified oleomargarine under the licenses because the Wisconsin corporation is unsympathetic with those developments.

This raises the question, not argued, whether the effect on the public health of refusing to the users of oleomargarine, the butter of the poor, the right to have such a food irradiated by the patented process is against the public interest. As seen, the general business manager of the Wisconsin corporation testified that it is the poor people suffering with rickets who constitute the principal market for appellee's monopolized processes and products. The evidence and appellee's briefs are replete with well verified statements of the great boon to humanity of Dr. Steenbock's scientific discoveries for the prevention and cure of rickets. The truth of such statements make the stronger the contention that it is a public offense to withhold such processes from any of the principal foods of the rachitic poor, or, indeed, from those of any such sufferers... .

We judicially notice the legislation in Wisconsin and other states of large vested interests in dairying imposing heavy restrictions upon the competition of oleomargarine with butter. Various devices are used such as taxation of oleomargarine itself, on its sale, in license fees of its vendors and the like penalties for violation of the restrictions. We take it, however, that such restrictive legislation does not require us to disregard its value as a food, so attractive and so satisfying to the human palate. Indeed, in these days of war restricted diet, oleomargarine has become the butter of the well-to-do and the rich.

The successful activation of oleomargarine and its fortification by irradiated material are described in the first patent and covered by its claim 1. Such irradiation of oleomargarine or its fortification by irradiated material is made a subject-matter of the second, a continuation in part, patent. That patent specifies that the first patent's "claims are included herein for subject-matter originally disclosed in the application here mentioned." It is also covered by the product claim of the second patent. It is thus seen that none but the licensees of this Wisconsin corporation or the corporation itself may either irradiate vitamin D into oleomargarine or fortify it with vitamin D by compounding it with an extract so irradiated and it appears that none of these is permitted so to do.

Suppression of the use of the property in a patent has often been held the right of the holder of the patent monopoly, but the question has not been raised in connection with the public interest in restoring the health of the afflicted. An early case, reviewing many others, on the question of suppressing the use of a patent against the public interest is *Continental Paper Bag Co. v. Eastern Paper Bag Co.*, ... There it is held that the suppression of the use of a patent for paper bags was not against the public interest, but the Court's opinion, ... concludes with this statement

> ... Whether, however, a case cannot arise where, regarding the situation of the parties in view of the public interest, a court of equity might be justified in withholding relief by injunction, we do not decide.

In the last decade, in the many cases cited above and in others, the relief of a court of equity has been denied because of the conduct of the patentee with reference to his monopoly property, against the public interest. We know of no case in the Supreme

Court since the *Paper Bag* case, *supra*, which has considered the patentee's refusal to license the use of its patent to protect the health of great numbers of the public such as are here shown to be suffering with rickets. It is strongly arguable that such a suppression of the patent's use is vastly more against the public interest than its use for a mere control of prices as in *United States v. Masonite Corp.*, *supra*, or the tieing of unpatented with patented material in *Mercoid Corp. v. Mid-Continent Co.*, *supra*.

Appellant claims that the Wisconsin corporation is shown to have unclean hands, by selecting as typical two of the many license agreements in the record those with the Commander Larrabee Company and with Kovacs. Appellant claims with regard to these (a) that they control resale prices and (b) that they control the potency of vitamin D in the products of vitamin D processing under claim 5 of the second patent, stated *infra*.

While recognizing the duty of the court, *sua sponte*, to protect the public interest, regardless of the contentions of the parties, this also falls within the functions of the Attorney General. *United States v. Masonite Corp.*, *supra*. The matters above considered are suggested to him. In this we follow the practice pursued where a public offense appears to have been disclosed, for instance, perjury in a civil or criminal proceeding. Since our consideration of the record convinces us that the patents are invalid, we have concluded that equity will best be served by disposing of the case on that ground... .

E. The claims of the first two patents are invalid because of indefiniteness of the area of the claimed monopoly.

Assuming that Dr. Steenbock made a novel discovery of process and product, the discoveries, however valuable, do not automatically become patented by the filing of applications disclosing them. In addition to the disclosure, the applicant must "particularly point out and distinctly claim the part, improvement, or combination which he claims as his invention and discovery," as required by 35 U.S.C.A. § 33... .

We hold that Dr. Steenbock's patents No. 1,680,818 and No. 1,871,136 are also invalid because they fail to inform the public of the limits of the area of the claimed monopoly.

§1.45 INDIA AND BRAZIL REVIVE A NINETEENTH-CENTURY TREND OF BANNING PATENTS ON FOOD-RELATED SUBSTANCES AND PROCESSES—1970 AND 1971

We saw above (see §1.34) that in the nineteenth century, a number of countries, following the example of the 1844 French Act on Patents that excluded medicines from patentability, adopted provisions banning patents for foodstuffs and corresponding methods of production. As explained, such a ban was grounded on various reasons, one of them being the association of certain dietary substances with medicines. Although that ban did not last, in the second half of the twentieth century, it was revived by means of the patent laws of India and Brazil—two large developing countries that traditionally have been very reluctant to adopt international standards of patent protection, in search of a national capacity of inventing in certain areas that, in the view of national parliaments, deserved special attention. Medicines corresponded to one of those areas.

And so did foodstuffs. Significantly, the banning of the patenting of food-relating appears in the laws of those two countries, within the same provision that banned the patenting of pharmaceutical products (as well as, in the case of Brazil, the processes of their making). Clearly, in those two countries, lawmakers associated the two types of inventions. Inventors in those areas had to wait for the entry of the TRIPS Agreement into force for such discriminatory treatment to be put aside (in exchange for concessions regarding tariffs and sanitary and phytosanitary measures).

§1.45.1 India Imposes Restrictions on the Patentability of Food-Related Inventions—1970

India

Patent Act 1970

Chapter II Inventions not Patentable

§ 3. What are not inventions.
The following are not inventions within the meaning of this Act,—

...

§ 5. Inventions where only methods or processes of manufacture patentable.
In the case of inventions—

(a) claiming substances intended for use, or capable of being used as food or as medicine or drug, or
(b) relating to substances prepared or produced by chemical processes (including alloys, optical glass, semi-conductors and inter-metallic compounds), no patent shall be granted in respect of claims for the substances themselves, but claims for the methods or processes of manufacture shall be patentable.

§1.45.2 Brazil Excludes Foodstuffs and the Respective Methods of Production from Patentability—1971

Law No. 5,772, of December 21, 1971

Industrial Property Code

Chapter II

On non patentable inventions

Art. 9° The following is not patentable:

...

(c) substances, materials, mixtures or food, chemical-pharmaceutical and medicinal products, of any kind, as well as the respective processes for obtaining or modifying;

§1.46 A COURT IDENTIFIES THE BOUNDARIES OF THE PROTECTION TO BE ACCORDED TO A SECRET RECIPE FOR BAKING CHOCOLATE CHIP COOKIES—1984

The following text is an important opinion clarifying when a secret recipe is to be treated as a trade secret. The simplicity and few formalities required to secure secrecy over a cookie recipe (namely, to take reasonable measures to keep secrecy) make trade secret law the easiest way of appropriating knowledge in the field of cooking. Moreover, for a piece of knowledge to be protected as a trade secret, there is no need for a minimum level of inventiveness. On the other hand, if the trade secret that is discussed in the case does not receive protection against disclosure—as was the case here—the confidentiality is lost, and it loses economic value.

Peggy Lawton Kitchens, Inc. vs. Terence M. Hogan & others.

18 Mass. App. Ct. 937

July 25, 1984

Nothing is sacred. We have before us a case of theft of a recipe for baking chocolate chip cookies. The issue is whether the plaintiff, Peggy Lawton Kitchens, Inc. (Kitchens), possessed a protected trade secret.

A Superior Court judge found that Kitchens first added chocolate chip cookies to its line of prepackaged bakery products in 1960. They were an indifferent success. In 1963, Lawton Wolf, a principal officer of Kitchens, mixed the chaff from Walnuts ("nut dust" he called it) in his chocolate chip cookie batter. This, as the judge found, "produced a distinctive flavor. It was an immediate commercial success." Lawton Wolf, in his testimony, described what nut dust did for his cookies in rhapsodic terms: "Miraculous." Sales, he said "took off immediately. It did to the cookies what butter does to popcorn or salt to a pretzel. It really made the flavor sing."

The judge found that, from the beginning of its use, Kitchens carefully guarded the cookie recipe. One copy of the recipe was locked in an office safe. A duplicate was secured in the desk of William Wolf, Lawton's son. To satisfied customers who asked for the recipe, Kitchens wrote that the formula was a trade secret. For work day use, Kitchens broke down the formula into baking ingredients, small ingredients (e.g., the nut dust), and bulk ingredients. The three components were kept on separate cards which contained gross weights. Even though those cards concealed the true proportions of the ingredients, access to the cards was limited to long-time trusted employees. The defendant Terence Hogan, whose responsibilities at Kitchens were plant and equipment maintenance and safety, was not among those entrusted with the ingredients' cards. Hogan, the judge found, had gained access to the cards through a pretext, and after Hogan left Kitchens' employ, a master key, which could open the vault and the office in which William Wolf's desk was located, was found in Hogan's desk.

Hogan and his wife organized a bakery business to sell prepackaged bakery products under the trade name Hogie Bear. Among the first products Hogie Bear made was a chocolate chip cookie. It had the same recipe, including the miraculous nut dust. The judge found that about forty brands of chocolate chip cookies were sold in New England. Except for those made by Kitchens and Hogie Bear, no two are alike. The judge found Hogie Bear's cookie "similar in appearance, color, cell construction, texture, flavor and taste. They are 'formulated' in a similar fashion. They are the same." ...

As to damages, the judge described the evidence as too vague and speculative to support a finding. A judgment was entered enjoining the defendants from making, baking, and selling chocolate chip cookies which use the plaintiff's formula. On the basis of a finding that the defendants had violated G. L. c. 93A, Sections 2 and 11, the judge assessed against the defendants' legal fees of $14,771.50 and disbursements of $1,740.38. A further judgment adverse to the defendants was entered on their counterclaim, which alleged various unfair practices by the plaintiff Kitchens. We affirm... .

1. Was there a trade secret? No doubt, the basic ingredients, flour, sugar, shortening, chocolate chips, eggs, and salt, would be common to any chocolate chip cookie. The combination in which those ingredients are used, the diameter and thickness of the cookie, and the degree to which it is baked would, however, constitute a formula which its proprietor could protect from infringement by an employee who either gains access to the formula in confidence or by improper means... . In any event, the insertion of the nut dust into the mix served to add that modicum of originality which separates a process from the everyday and so characterizes a trade secret... . Lawton Wolf's testimony that "sales took off immediately" supports a determination that the improved recipe had competitive value so far as Kitchens was concerned.
2. Conduct of the defendants. Once information qualifies as a trade secret, determination of whether the trade secret has been misused steers the inquiry to examining the conduct of the defendant, and the legal character of that conduct, in turn, is much affected by the steps taken by the proprietor of the trade secret to protect it... . Here, as we have seen, the holder of the secret took reasonable steps to maintain its mystery and to narrow the circle of those privy to its essentials... . We do not think that the absence of admonitions about secrecy or the failure to emphasize secrecy in employment contracts (if there were any in this relatively small business) is fatal to the plaintiff. That Hogan brought no experience in volume baking to his employment with Kitchens and that he employed a ruse to examine the ingredients cards and may have helped himself to a look at the formula tucked away in Kitchens' safe or William Wolf's desk are relevant factors... . Listing of nut meal on the plaintiff's label does not constitute publication of the recipe because it discloses nothing about

the proportions in which the ingredients are used, nor does it say what kind of nuts or what part of the nuts imparted special zing to Kitchens' cookies.

3. The length and breadth of the injunction. The injunction against use of the plaintiff's recipe was permanent and without limit as to area. Injunctions of that length and breadth are unusual, but not without precedent... . We do not think the judge was bound to calibrate a more precise area and duration for an injunction as limited as the one imposed. It does not drive Hogan or Hogie Bear Snacks, Inc., out of the cookie business; the injunction forbids only use of Kitchens' precise formula. Other recipes—and the evidence included many—are available to Hogie Bear. There is no limitation on Hogie Bear's packaging or marketing methods... .

Judgments affirmed.

§1.47 A US COURT AFFIRMS KFC'S RIGHT TO CHOOSE THE SUPPLIERS OF ITS SECRET RECIPE AS A FORM OF PROTECTING ITS SECRECY—1985

Part of the reputation and success of KFC's chain of fast-food restaurants is based on the secret recipe of the seasoning used in some elements of the menu. KFC does not make the seasoning. That task has been accorded by KFC to two companies under a scheme that it has devised so as to protect the secret. Under that scheme, neither of the two companies knows the technical specifications of the portion of the seasoning the other makes.

The text that follows consists of excerpts of an important court opinion that rejected the claim by a third-party manufacturer of a chicken seasoning, Marion-Kay Co., who wished to manufacture and supply the product to KFC's franchisees. Marion-Kay, obviously, was not in possession of KFC's recipe but alleged that it was easy to find the formula. Marion-Kay also alleged that KFC's refusal to authorize its franchisees to buy the season from it constituted an antitrust violation.

The Court did not discuss the feasibility of acquiring the knowledge of the secret recipe just by experimenting, i.e., without KFC's communicating it. However, implicitly, the Court did not believe Marion-Kay's allegation, as it rejected its claim on the ground that for KFC to authorize a new supplier to its franchisees, it had to communicate the secret to that supplier. That would destroy the secret, in view of the care exercised by the franchisor in avoiding that the knowledge of the recipe fell into the hands of a single supplier.

In other words, a trade secret may constitute a barrier to entry but, given its nature as private property, is a legitimate one.

US District Court for the Southern District of Indiana

KFC Corp. v. Marion-Kay Co., Inc.

620 F. Supp. 1160 (S.D. Ind. 1985)

October 18, 1985.

Barker, District Judge.

Findings of Fact

1. KFC initiated this action with the filing of its complaint on December 9, 1981, alleging that Marion-Kay violated § 43(a) of the Lanham Act, 15 U.S.C. § 1125(a), through false descriptions and representation of Marion-Kay seasoning products to KFC franchisees of "Kentucky Fried Chicken" restaurants and that Marion-Kay tortiously interfered with KFC's contractual relations with its franchisees. In its amended counterclaim and third-party complaint, Marion-Kay claims that KFC, Sexton, and Stange entered into a contract, combination, and conspiracy to unlawfully restrain trade in violation of § 1 of the Sherman Act, 15 U.S.C. § 1.
2. KFC is a Delaware corporation with its principal place of business at 1441 Gardiner Lane, Louisville, Kentucky, and is the franchisor of "Kentucky Fried Chicken" restaurants.
3. Marion-Kay is an Indiana corporation with its principal place of business at U.S. Highway 50 West, Brownstown, Indiana, and is engaged in the manufacturing of chicken seasoning known variously as "Marion-Kay Seasoning" or "99X Chicken Seasoning."
4. Sexton is a corporation allegedly having a place of business at 222 Riverside Plaza, Chicago, Illinois.
5. Stange is alleged to be a Delaware corporation having a place of business at 342 Northwestern Avenue, Chicago, Illinois.
6. As the franchisor of "Kentucky Fried Chicken" restaurants, KFC has developed and registered certain trademarks and service marks used in connection with its business. KFC's registered service marks and trademarks are as follows: ...

KFC grants each of its franchisees a license to use these trademarks and service marks in connection with the preparation and sale of "Original Recipe Kentucky Fried Chicken."

7. Original Recipe Kentucky Fried Chicken is sold only by KFC and its franchisees, and is prepared by a special cooking process featuring the use of a "secret recipe" seasoning known as "KFC Seasoning." This blend of seasoning was developed by KFC's founder, Colonel Harlan Sanders.
8. KFC Seasoning, its blending system, and the method of preparing Original Recipe Kentucky Fried Chicken are subject to protection as trade secrets.
9. As a condition of each franchise contract, KFC requires that its franchisees use only KFC Seasoning in connection with the preparation and sale of Kentucky Fried Chicken.
10. To protect the secrecy of the composition of KFC Seasoning, KFC has designed a blending system for making the seasoning. With permission from KFC, one part of KFC Seasoning recipe is blended by Sexton and

another part is blended by Stange. Neither company has knowledge of the complete formulation of KFC Seasoning nor of the other's specific activities in the production of the other's part of the product. Both companies have entered into secrecy agreements with KFC, binding them to maintain the confidentiality of that portion of the KFC Seasoning formula to which each is privy. KFC's relationship with both Sexton and Stange has existed for more than 25 years. No other companies are licensed to blend KFC Seasoning.

11. After KFC Seasoning is blended by Sexton and Stange, it is then mixed together and sold directly by Stange to all KFC retail operators and to distributors acting on behalf of KFC retail operators.
12. KFC neither manufactures nor sells KFC Seasoning to its franchisees and does not receive a royalty or other economic benefit from the sale of KFC Seasoning by Sexton and Stange.
13. Marion-Kay has never been licensed by KFC to manufacture or distribute seasoning to be used in preparing Original Recipe Kentucky Fried Chicken.
14. In early 1973, Marion-Kay requested permission to market its seasoning products to KFC franchisees. By letter dated March 15, 1973, Edward E. Ellis, General Counsel for KFC, advised Marion K. Summers ("Summers"), President of Marion-Kay, that KFC would not grant Marion-Kay permission to sell its seasoning to KFC franchisees for use in the preparation of Original Recipe Kentucky Fried Chicken. The letter provides in relevant part as follows:

> We did explore a number of possibilities here for a mutually beneficial relationship of some kind with you, and I am sorry to say that the conclusion was that we should continue with our present arrangements.
>
> Having come to that conclusion, based on the best information available to us, I should perhaps point out again that an essential element of our contractual relationships with our franchisees is that they use in their operations the spice formula, process and recipe which are the exclusive property of Kentucky Fried Chicken Corporation. Using any other spice formula, process or recipe would be a serious violation of their franchise agreements and a matter of grave concern to KFC is our desire to vigorously protect our trademarks, trade secrets and standards of national uniformity and quality in the preparation and sale of Kentucky Fried Chicken. I well understand that it is not your desire to interfere in any way with our contractual relationships with our franchisees and I solicit your continued cooperation in that regard. This is of course well within the boundaries of business ethics which I believe, after my conversation with you, you have practiced these many years… .

15. On February 3, 1977, KFC's General Counsel, Michael J. McGraw ("McGraw"), sent a telegram to Summers advising him that KFC had learned that Marion-Kay was supplying KFC franchisees with a Marion-Kay blend of seasoning. McGraw insisted that Marion-Kay cease supplying KFC franchisees with its seasoning product… .

16. On February 10, 1977, McGraw sent a second telegram to Summers, demanding that Marion-Kay discontinue selling its seasoning product to KFC's franchisees... .
17. In a letter dated February 21, 1977, McGraw again made known KFC's continuing objection to the sale of Marion-Kay seasoning to KFC franchisees and stated that Summers' actions constituted intentional interference with KFC's contractual relationship with its franchisees: ...
18. On February 10, 1977, a KFC franchisee sought KFC's approval of the use of Marion-Kay seasoning in connection with the preparation of Original Recipe Kentucky Fried Chicken. This request was rejected by KFC by letter dated February 22, 1977... .

Conclusions of Law

...

7. The Court finds that the use of the KFC trademarks and service marks by the KFC franchisees is so interrelated with KFC Seasoning, that no reasonable person could find that the franchise (trademarks) and KFC Seasoning are two separate products for tying arrangement purposes. Therefore, the requirement that KFC franchisees purchase KFC Seasoning through Sexton and Stange is not an unlawful tying arrangement in violation of Section 1 of the Sherman Act.
8. The Court further finds as a matter of law that KFC may, in order to protect its trade secrets and quality of its goods, choose any manufacturer it pleases to reproduce and distribute KFC Seasoning to the franchisees. The fact that Marion-Kay is precluded from manufacturing and distributing KFC Seasoning is not a violation of the anti-trust laws.
9. Any finding of fact stated above, to the extent that it constitutes a conclusion of law, is herein incorporated by reference as an additional conclusion of law by the Court.

Memorandum

...

III. Marion-Kay Has No Right To Become A Distributor Of KFC Seasoning

In the counterclaim, Marion-Kay also contends that it is entitled to become a distributor of KFC seasoning. Specifically, Marion-Kay claims that KFC's exclusive arrangement with Sexton and Stange for the production and distribution of KFC seasoning is a restraint of trade in violation of § 1 of the Sherman Act. Marion-Kay maintains that KFC seasoning can be easily duplicated by any competent spice blender and that the rationale of *Kentucky Fried Chicken v. Diversified Packaging Corp.*, 549 F.2d 368 (5th

Cir. 1977), compels a ruling requiring KFC to open the KFC seasoning market and approve such competent seasoning blenders. KFC, on the other hand, argues that because KFC seasoning is a trade secret, central to the success of its business, the Court cannot require it to disclose its recipe secret to any supplier claiming it is worthy to produce seasoning.

In *Kentucky Fried Chicken v. Diversified Packaging, supra,* the case relied on by Marion-Kay, KFC brought an action claiming that the defendants were infringing its trademarks and engaging in unfair competition by selling boxes and other supplies to KFC franchisees. 549 F.2d at 372. Defendants had placed KFC trademarks on the supplies without KFC's consent and had allegedly misled the franchisees as to the source and quality of the supplies. Defendants counterclaimed, alleging that KFC's franchise agreements, which required that all franchisees purchase supplies from sources approved by KFC, constituted an unlawful tying arrangement. Specifically, KFC required that its franchisees purchased various supplies from KFC or from approved sources. The franchise agreements provided that the approval "shall not be unreasonable." *Id.* at 373. KFC had approved nine independent suppliers and had maintained its own subsidiary supplier strictly for purposes of supplying these products. KFC had never refused a request for approval by any independent supplier. *Id.* The District Court ruled in KFC's favor on every issue and the Fifth Circuit Court of Appeals affirmed. *Id.* at 372.

On appeal, the Fifth Circuit Court of Appeals stated that a franchisor who requires its franchisees to purchase

> trademarked supplies does not escape the impact of tying principles to any extent. The franchisor's right to prevent others from selling supplies bearing its trademarks must yield to the anti-trust laws' command to open the tied market to competitors. (citations omitted).

Id. at 376. The Court recognized, however, that as a defense to the tie-in claim a franchisor could demonstrate that the tied product was necessary to maintain the quality of the end product being sold to the consumer. As a part of this defense, the Court held that it was incumbent upon the franchisor to show that the "tie constituted the method of maintaining quality that imposes the least burden on commerce." *Id.* The Court of Appeals also held that KFC's approval system did not constitute a tie, stating that the principal evil associated with tying arrangements, *i.e.*, the foreclosure of competition in the tied market, was not present under this system. *Id.* at 378. In addition, the Court held the approved-source system was not an unlawful tying arrangement because the franchisees had the option of shopping around for the supplies:

> The option is limited to approved suppliers, but there are ten such suppliers of cartons, and franchisees are free to nominate additional suppliers whenever they can be found.... Franchisees might fare better if fifty or a hundred suppliers competed for their business, but a market with ten suppliers and unrestrained entry surely poses a far different problem than a market available to the victim of a traditional tie: one supplier and no entry. *Id.*

Marion-Kay argues that based on *Kentucky Fried Chicken v. Diversified Packaging*, KFC cannot preclude other spice blenders from supplying KFC seasoning to its franchisees as long as the seasoning meets KFC specifications. As mentioned previously, KFC seasoning is manufactured and distributed solely through Sexton and Stange. Unlike the situation in *Diversified Packaging*, KFC has no method of approving other blenders who wish to distribute KFC seasoning.

The facts before the Court in the present case are easily distinguished from the situation in *Diversified Packaging*. KFC seasoning is a trade secret, which this Court has already held constitutes the franchise itself. To require KFC to open up its seasoning market to any spice supplier wanting to supply its franchisees would require KFC to divulge its trade secrets. No Court has ever forced a supplier or manufacturer to disclose a trade secret to a distributor wanting to manufacture and distribute that product .... *Diversified Packaging* did not involve trade secrets. Rather, in that opinion the Court scrutinized the KFC's approval policies for the distribution of commonplace supplies such as cartons, containers, and napkins bearing KFC's trademark, all of which were available from several sources.

Finally, Marion-Kay alleges that the contractual arrangement between KFC and Sexton and Stange for the distribution of KFC seasoning is evidence of a conspiracy to exclude Marion-Kay as a supplier of the seasoning. Marion-Kay also seems to argue, albeit erroneously, that because KFC has disclosed the trade secret to Sexton and Stange it is estopped from denying supplier status to other spice blenders.

Under these contracts, neither Sexton and Stange is given the complete specifications for the production of KFC seasoning. Rather, each supplier is given only a portion of the "recipe," and each has agreed to maintain the secrecy of the formula to which it has privy. Sexton and Stange have no input whatsoever in KFC's exercise of control over the production, sale, and use of the trade secret. In other words, KFC has maintained unilateral and complete control over KFC seasoning. KFC can terminate the contracts with Sexton and Stange with 120 days from the notice of termination and can select another supplier to distribute KFC seasoning without violating the contract. Thus, in effect, KFC has not disclosed its trade secrets to anyone, which fact disputes Marion-Kay's claims and defeats Marion-Kay's argument that KFC should be estopped from denying disclosure of its trade secrets to other suppliers. This Court will not require KFC to disclose its trade secrets to Marion-Kay, and the fact that KFC has entered into an agreement with Sexton and Stange, for the distribution of KFC seasoning, to the exclusion of Marion-Kay, does not constitute a conspiracy to violate the anti-trust laws. KFC has an absolute right to choose who will distribute KFC seasoning without violating section 1 of the Sherman Act.

Accordingly, for all the foregoing reasons, KFC's motion for partial summary judgment on Marion-Kay's counterclaim is *granted*.

§1.48 TWO BRAZILIAN INVENTORS OBTAIN PATENTS FOR CULINARY RECIPES, BUT THEIR BUSINESSES MEET OPPOSITE FATES—2001, 2008

Patents are often taken as synonymous with commercial success. The general (and wrong) view is that they generate monopoly power, which transforms their owners into millionaires. That is not, as a matter of course, what reality shows. Along this first chapter, we have seen, for example, that individual cooks have avoided patenting their creative recipes and have preferred keeping them under secrecy or, indirectly, appropriating the prestige that they could extract from their cooking through copyright, advertisement and the exclusivity of branding. The story that follows concerns two small Brazilian inventors who invented new recipes for popular foodstuffs and patented them—but only to find opposite fates. The first inventor modified a very popular Brazilian sweet, known in Portuguese as paçoca, *made of ground peanuts, sugar and salt, by basically adding a chocolate cover to it. The invention seemed to be aimed at a significant commercial success, for the patent, after being granted, was the subject of no less than three canceling procedures by associations of small entrepreneurs, makers and sellers of* paçoca. *In the end, those three procedures led to nothing because the patent expired in the meantime. But today (November 8, 2023), a search on Google under "paçoca com cobertura de chocolate"* (paçoca *with chocolate coverage) yields 371,00 results. And yet, as a document posted on the website of the civil court of Piracicaba, São Paulo, reveals, the patent owner has had its bankruptcy decreed for payment default.*

The opposite fate has fallen upon an entrepreneur in the State of Paraná (South of Brazil), who improved a recipe for the frozen dough for English cake and obtained a patent for the product and its process. In a few years, the company has expanded its business of selling food ingredients (including the patented paste) to bakeries spread though several States of Brazil and has received accolades from the specialized press and awards in food exhibitions and competitions.

This contrast should give pause for thought to all those who look at the patent system with an attentive eye: patents may be tools for commercial success, given the exclusivity that is associated with them, but real success depends on the consumers' accepting the product, in the first place, and, second, on the owner's business acumen.

§1.48.1 Brazilian Patent for a Sweet and the Method of Its Making (and the Subsequent Bankruptcy of the Patent Owner)—2001

INPI-BR Patent no. PI 10105341-8 A

Paçoca Cork Production Line with Chocolate Coating

Applicant: Indústria e Comércio de Chocolates Scarassati Ltda.

CLAIMS

1) "Paçoca Cork Production Line with Chocolate Coating," characterized [by] consisting [of] a peanut-based confection (1), substantially cylindrical in shape, and completely coated with a chocolate coating (2) that can be hydrogenated, fractionated, with milk, white, etc.
2) "Paçoca Cork Production Line with Chocolate Coating," according to claim 1, characterized in that the paçoca cork production line involves a process in which, in the first stage, the sugar is crushed and reduced to a very fine-grained powder; in the second processing stage, peanuts and salt are added to the sugar; in the next stage, this mixture passes through a grinder, where the result is a homogenized mass; in the fourth stage, this resulting mass is taken to a modeling press, where it takes the shape of a cork, that is, a cylindrical shape; and after shaping, the confection is transported to a covering, where it is completely covered with a layer of chocolate that can be hydrogenated, with milk, white, etc., and, in the final stage, the product passes through a cooling tunnel, where it obtains the necessary consistency.

Figure 1.19 The two drawings that accompany the specifications of Brazilian patent no. PI 10105341-8 A

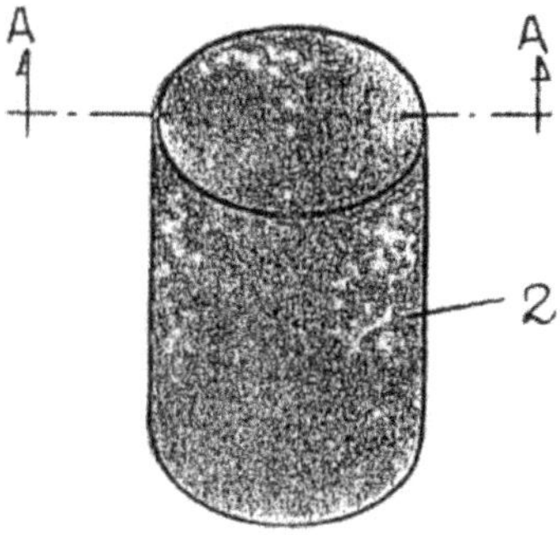

FIG. 1

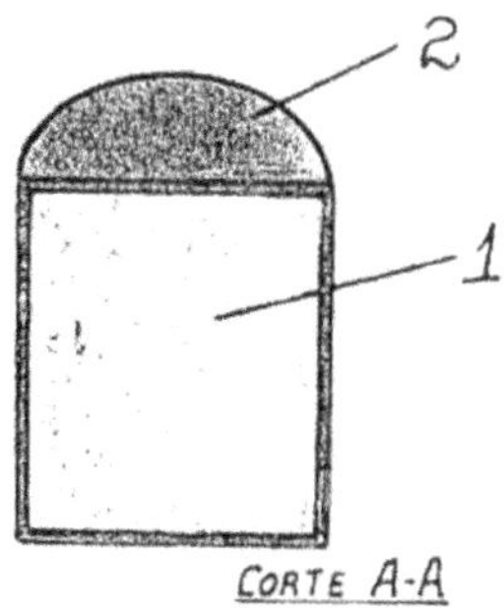

FIG. 2

§1.48.2 A Clerk Submits to the Judge of a Bankruptcy Court His Assessment of the Worth of the Patent Owner's Real Estate Assets That Had Been Seized (Excerpt)

Procedure: 0015587-97.2005.8.26.0451

Marcos Antonio Libardi Ferreira, Master in Production Engineering, Specialist in Environmental Management, Specialist in Environmental Education, Civil Engineer, CREA [Regional Council of Engineering and Agronomy] no. 060119.353-2/D, and Occupational Safety Engineer no. 17,369, Expert designated and duly committed in the file corresponding to Procedure no. 2256/05 "Bankruptcy of Entrepreneurs—Default", Plaintiff Santa Luzia S/A Ind. de Embalagens and Defendant Indústria e Comércio de Chocolates Scarassati Ltda ([bankruptcy] decreed), after due diligence and on-site inspection of the pieces of real estate in question and carried out inspections of the situation found, respectfully presents the results obtained in a simplified report: ...

§1.48.3 Brazilian Patent for a Method of Frozen Cake Dough and Its Recipe (and the Subsequent Success of Its Owner)

INPI-BR Patent no. PI 0802968-7 A2

Process for Obtaining Frozen Cake Dough and Formulating Frozen Cake Dough

Owner: Indústria de Alimentos El Shadai Ltda. (DoceD'Ocê)[49]

CLAIMS

1) Cake dough formulation characterized by comprising a mixture of the following ingredients, in the respective proportions of the final product: Flour 30%, Water 14%, Eggs 25%, Sugar 20%, Corn starch 1.4%, Yeast 1.4%, Volumex 1.4%, Glucose 5.38%, Emustab 1.4%, Calcium propionate 0.01%, Sorbic acid 0.01%.
2) Cake dough formulation characterized by comprising a mixture of the following ingredients, in the respective proportions of the final product: Flour 28%, Sugar 20.8%, Corn starch 3.7%, Margarine, 7.4%, Volumex 2.2 %, Milk 18.58%, Eggs 14.9%, Yeast 2.2%, Glucose 2.2%, Calcium propionate 0.01%.
3) Process for Obtaining Frozen Cake Dough characterized by comprising a step of mixing and homogenizing the dough, consisting of the formulation of claims 1 or 2, for a period of 3 minutes, followed by a packaging step in a paper form or sachet, and finally, a storage stage under the deep-freezing system at a temperature of around -40° C, and for a period of around 60 minutes.
4) Process for obtaining frozen cake dough, according to claim 3, characterized in that a product obtained after the deep-freezing process is packaged and stored for consumption under refrigeration at a temperature of around 0° C.
5) Process for obtaining frozen cake dough, according to claim 3, characterized by additional baking for 30 minutes at a temperature of 197° C.

49. "Doce D'Ocê" is a Brazilian popular expression, abbreviated from "Doce de Você" ("Sweet of You"), which sounds like the accent of those persons born in Minas Gerais. A few years ago, the patent owner adopted that popular expression as a brand, eventually with the purpose of reaching a broader clientele. In the future, however, it may have problems with similar trademarks that have been used for many years by small bakeries and pastry shops in the State of Minas Gerais.

§1.48.4 On Its Website, the Patentee Announces a Number of National Awards It Has Received for Its Innovative Product (Frozen English Cake Dough) and Respective Making Process

We are nationally awarded

Baker Top Award

Doce D'ocê won the Baker Top Award, the most recognized and prestigious in the segment, in the Gold Bakery category in 2009. Recognizing the work well done and compliance with strict quality standards.

CNI [National Industry Confederation] Award

In 2009, Doce D'ocê won the CNI Award as the industry recognition for having created a deep-frozen dough for English cake. The new product has facilitated the cake preparation process, generating savings for the sector and end consumers.

SENAI [National Service for Industrial Education] Award

In 2010, Doce D'ocê was awarded in the first edition of the Senai Award for innovation with Quick-Frozen Dough for English Cake. The homemade recipe product has extended its shelf life 10 times, facilitated distribution logistics and quadrupled the company's productivity.

SESI [Industry Social Service] Award

Doce D'ocê won the SESI Quality at Work Award in 2012 in Paraná, in the innovation category. The award had a record number of entries and highlights the investment in differentiated management practices and employee recognition, with initiatives that increase productivity and market competitiveness.

§1.49 THE SECRETARIAT OF WIPO ENUNCIATES A BASIC TRUTH: CHEFS' COMMERCIAL SUCCESS DOES NOT RELY ON PATENTS; LIKE MEDICAL DOCTORS, THEIR SUCCESS RESULTS FROM INDIVIDUAL SKILLS AND PRESTIGE—2002

In a statement submitted to a discussion on the patentability of methods of human treatment (involving genetic therapies and stem cells) promoted by the European Group on Ethics and Science and New Technologies to the European Commission, in 2002, the WIPO Secretariat explained that there should be no concerns about that topic given that international patent law (namely, the TRIPS Agreement) did not impose it. In a statement submitted in the context of a discussion on the patentability of methods of human treatment (involving genetic therapies and stem cells) promoted by the European Group on Ethics and Science and New Technologies to the European Commission, in 2002, the WIPO Secretariat said that there should be no concerns about that topic given that international patent law (namely, the TRIPS Agreement) did not impose it. The Secretariat added that the absence of patents concerning therapeutic methods did not discourage research and invention in that field because inventive medical doctors could extract revenue from their solutions because of the prestige associated with their names. In a footnote, the Secretariat added that, mutatis mutandis, that was the same case of chefs.

European Group on Ethics and Science and New Technologies to the European Commission

Opinion on Ethical Aspects of Patenting Inventions Involving Human Stem Cells

Opinion No. 16, May 7, 2002 (excerpt)

20. On a different but related issue, recent scientific advances in research on human stem cells have dramatically increased the importance of looking anew to the matter of patenting therapeutic methods. With the exception of one or two countries,[50] therapeutic methods have consistently been held non-patentable subject matter. The reason generally indicated for that legal solution is based on professional ethics—therapeutic methods have traditionally been scrutinized by peer review, not by patent offices, and the inventors' colleagues should naturally be entitled to share the inventions. Actually, the true reason for the lack of patent protection in the field of therapeutic methods (or for the immunity against patent infringement, as established in the United States a few years ago) lies somewhere else. Therapeutic methods, as well as diagnostic and surgical methods, are, with very few exceptions, individual procedures whose success depends much more on the individual skills of doctors or surgeons than on the methods themselves. In other words, therapeutic methods are not to be mass applied (even when they are repeatedly applied), which characteristic confines their economic relevance to the extremely narrow market of the few patients of a given doctor or surgeon. Therefore, it is not necessary to patent those methods in order to appropriate them. Creative doctors and surgeons shall be paid through increased professional prestige and higher fees.[4]

> [4] *Mutatis mutandis* this also explains why patents are [usually] not granted for [culinary] recipes, in spite of the fact that recipes are nothing else than expressions of chemical formula (and that, incidentally, were the subject matter of the first patent law ever adopted, in the Greek colony of Sybaris, in the sixth century BC). Like therapeutic methods, the success of recipes depends on the individual skills of chefs, whose gains will stem from one or two additional stars in some cuisine guide, and expanded clientele, and higher prices, of course. Recipes, like therapeutic methods, do not need patent protection to be privately appropriated.

50. The WIPO Secretariat was referring to the United States and Australia.

§1.50 TODAY, AS FAR AS CULINARY RECIPES ARE CONCERNED, THE PATENT SYSTEM CONTINUES PRIMARILY SERVING INVENTORS WHO CREATE RECIPES DESTINED FOR MASS PRODUCTION—2020

It should now be clear that recipes, as literary expressions for chemical formulae, are patentable subject matter. And it should also be clear that after the patenting habit that inventors of new cooking devices and foodstuffs acquired during the Industrial Revolution, the economic value of patents remained confined to those foods that were conceived as staple foods, or foods or generalized consumption. This is not, of course, the case of individual chefs, whose inventive skills are exercised every day within the confined space of their kitchens, and yet their commercial success is expressed by means of their individual prestige and that of their restaurants and, eventually, by their receiving awards, either occasional, such as in competitions and fairs or regular, such as the well-known Michelin's stars. Just for the sake of example, the following text reproduces the abstract of a patent issued by the USPTO in 2020 for a recipe concerning popcorn.

United States Patent No. US 10,798,956 B2

Date of Patent: October 13, 2020

Food Bases on Popcorn and Cheese and Respective Production Method

Abstract

A method is provided for producing at least one popcorn grain substantially entire and coated, completely or partially, with at least a first layer of a first melted cheese directly in contact with the popcorn grain. The first melted cheese has an initial moisture content of less than 35%, or alternatively, the first melted cheese is cooked too and its moisture after cooking is lower than 8%. A second layer of a second cheese may be applied to the food product.

§1.51 PATENTS FOR HOSPITALITY SERVICES

Even though this book is about the intellectual property of food and hospitality, this first chapter has dealt primarily with food. The reason is objective: hospitality is basically about services, and the abstract nature of services makes them inappropriate for serving as subject matter to patents, in view of the principle of materiality that is subjacent to the whole system—since the Statute of Monopolies, patents are seen as titles granted for inventions concerning manufactures, *which imply the* manual *handling of corporeal objects, of things.*[51] *However, given that some patent offices and, in particular, the USPTO, have been showing some tolerance toward applications concerning abstract inventions (provided they require some sort of handling of devices, such as computers), patents have lately been granted for services of hospitality, such as the management of hotels and the organization of conferences and other events. The five following texts are examples of that trend. Four come from the USPTO, and the other comes from KIPO. The Google Patents database contains similar patents granted in other countries, such as Canada and China, whose applications have been filed through the Patent Cooperation Treaty (PCT) system.*

§1.51.1 First Example: A US Patent Issued in 2009

United States Patent No. US 7.584,110 B2

Date of Patent: Sep. 1, 2009

System and Method for Booking of Hotel Accommodations for Travelers

Inventor: David Robertson, Dubai (AE)
Assignee: Emirates, Dubai (AE)

51. In *Hornblower and Maberley v. Boulton and Watt, in error,* a case (of 1799) that discussed whether the process of operating and using a machine (the steam engine) was patentable under the 1623 Statute, Lord Kenyon, Chief Justice in the Court of King's Bench, accompanied by the other three Judges, confirmed the patent because the invention consisted of the manipulation of corporeal devices. In his reasoning, the Judge said: "But having now heard everything that can be said of the subject, I have no doubt in saying that this is a patent for a manufacture, which I understand to be something made by the hands of man."

ABSTRACT

A method of making a hotel reservation includes receiving a reservation request from a booking Source, wherein the reservation request is based on an allocation to the booking Source from a hotel and wherein the reservation request is price-blind; transmitting the reservation request to the hotel; receiving a confirmation from the hotel; and transmitting the confirmation to the booking source. The booking source can be a consolidator, a travel agent, a tour operator, a Global Distribution System or a wholesaler. The method also includes connecting to the hotel using a web service to transmit the reservation to the hotel. If the reservation request exceeds the allocation, the hotel has an option of accepting the reservation request or declining the reservation request. The method also includes receiving polling inquiries from the booking Source prior to transmitting the hotel's confirmation to the booking source. The confirmation from the hotel can be received using a web service. The confirmation can be transmitted to the booking source using a web service. The reservation request can include a "special request." The method can also include translating parameters of the reservation request from a format of the booking source to a format of the hotel.

§1.51.2 Second Example: A US Patent Issued in 2013

United States Patent No. US 8.620,753 B2

Date of Patent: December 31, 2013

Restaurant Management System and Method

Inventors: James W. Burns, Naperville, IL (US) ; Cathy E. Berenschoft, Wheaton, IL (US); Gerald Calabrese, Wayne, IL (US); Charles D. Kasper, III, Aurora, IL (US); Rosemarie Lovell, Shorewood, IL (US)
Assignee: Restaurant Technology, Inc., Oak Brook, IL (US)

ABSTRACT

A restaurant management system and method interface [are] provided. In accordance with the invention, data from various restaurant operations is collected and stored for processing. The data is processed into useful metrics, such as those indicative of various categories of restaurant staffing, efficiency, performance and quality. The useful metrics can be displayed as a human-readable chart, graph or report. The data can be processed in real time, permitting managers to promptly make adjustments and to alert restaurant workers or crew members of deficiencies so that prompt and effective remedial action can be taken to improve restaurant performance. Reports may be generated that provide the performance of restaurants individually and as a combined group.

Figure 1.20 One of the six drawing sheets that accompany US Patent No. US 8.620,753 B2.

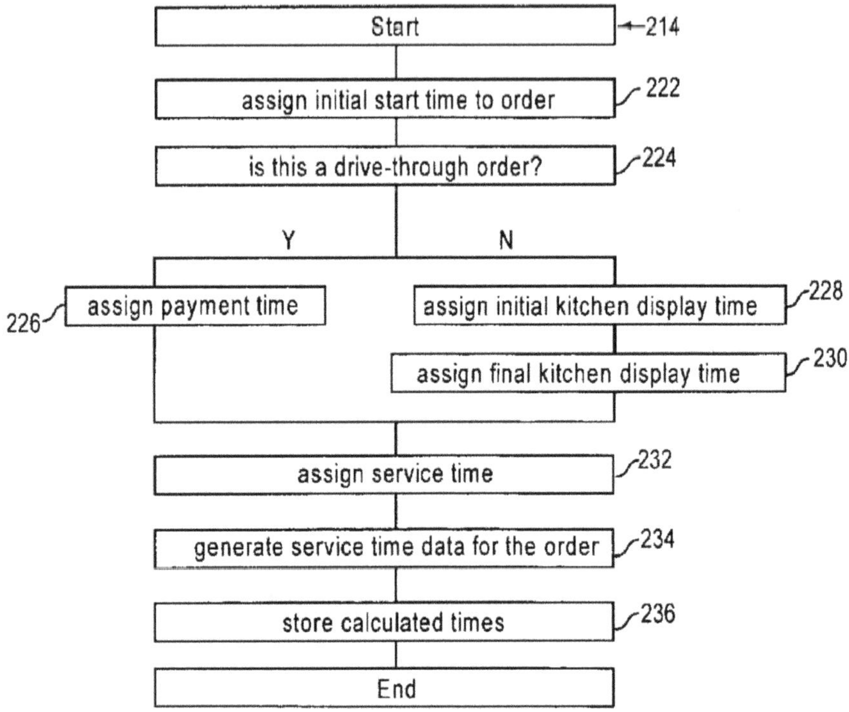

§1.51.3 Third Example: A South Korean Patent Issued in 2018

South Korean Patent KR101843987B1

Server, device, and method for servicing and recommendation of wine information

ABSTRACT

The present invention relates to a wine information service server which comprises: a database configured to store meta information with respect to a plurality of wine; a memory configured to store a wine recommending program; and a processor configured to store a program stored in the memory wherein the processor extracts taste information of a user from a bulletin board message of the user and a profile of the user corresponding to a wine information service terminal, extracts wine matched with the taste information of the user among the plurality of wine and transfers the wine to the wine information service terminal. And, the meta information is defined with respect to each wine and includes at least one of a kind, a production area, a price, a raw material, a production year, a name, and taste information.

Figure 1.21 One of the nineteen drawings that are part of patent KR101843987B1.

§1.51.4 Fourth Example: A US Patent Issued in 2019

United States Patent No. US 10,383,170 B2

Date of Patent: August 13, 2019

Systems and Methods for Customizing Hotel, Timeshare, and Rental Property Guest Experiences, and Conserving Resources and Utilities Using Internet of Things Devices and Location Tracking Augmented with Contextual Awareness

Inventors: Yani Deros, Phoenix, AZ (US); Jodi Deros, Phoenix, AZ (US)
Assignee: Atom, Inc., Scottsdale, AZ (US)

ABSTRACT

A system for customizing a hotel, timeshare, or rental property guest experience includes a layered in-room PaaS System with an IOT network control module configured to control a plurality of IOT connected room devices including a remotely controlled electronic or mechanical devices; a Cloud platform to collect system, property and guest data that will then be processed through analytics and algorithms to improve the guest experience and deliver cost savings for the property, a mobile app running on a guest mobile device, the mobile app configured to remotely control the IOT network control module; an enterprise server configured to communicate with the IOT network control module; and a local computing module configured to communicate with the enterprise server, wherein the enterprise server controls the transmission of data between the IOT network control module and the property.

Figure 1.22 One of the thirteen drawing sheets that accompany US patent no. 10,383,170 B2.

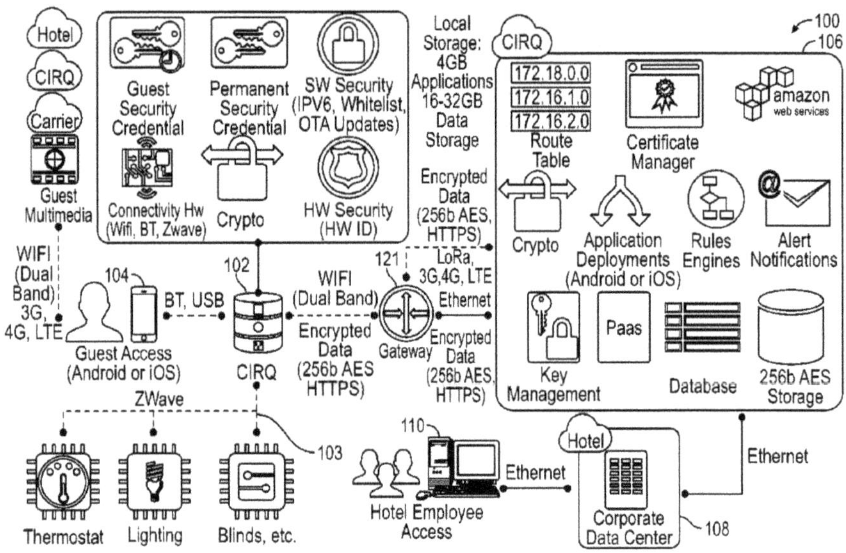

§1.51.5 Fifth Example: A US Patent Issued in 2022

United States Patent No. 11,378,927 B2

Date of Patent: July 5, 2022

Hotel Management System

Inventors: Shan Guan, Fremont, CA (US); Tao Zhao, Shanghai (CN)
Assignee: Qixingtian (Beijing) Consulting Company Ltd., Beijing (CN)

ABSTRACT

The present application provides a hotel management system and method. The system includes at least one control panel; the control panel includes a first sub-panel and a second sub-panel; the first sub-panel is used to verify a first authorization key; and the first authorization key is used for hotel identity verification; the second sub-panel works independently of the first sub-panel, and the second sub-panel includes at least one physical regulator. The physical regulator is used to control sensing module and room equipment; and the first sub-panel controls the physical regulator. The first sub-panel and the second sub-panel are detachably connected. The hotel management system and guests can interact with each other and a smarter, more convenient and more powerful hotel environment control system is integrated in[to] the hotel management system.

§1.52 BACK TO THE FUTURE? DIFFERENTLY, BUT WITH THE SAME GOAL AS THE AUTHORITIES OF SYBARIS, IN THE SIXTH CENTURY BC, NASA (THE US SPACE AGENCY) AND CSA (THE CANADIAN SPACE AGENCY), IN THE TWENTY-FIRST CENTURY, SET FORTH THE DEEP SPACE FOOD CHALLENGE, PROMOTING THE INVENTION OF NUTRITIOUS AND PALATABLE FOOD FOR ASTRONAUTS THROUGH AWARDS—2022

The first episode of knowledge appropriation in the domain of food, as we saw above, took place in Sybaris in the sixth century BC (see §1.1). The idea was to promote the invention of delicious recipes for public banquets. Sybaris, anticipating a capitalistic solution—that of leaving the rewards for inventors in the (invisible) collective hands of consumers—designed a system that was based on something very similar to today's patents. We have also seen that, subsequently, inventive cooks were rewarded with monetary awards, as opposed to the appropriation of their invention. More than twenty centuries later, NASA (USA National Aeronautics and Space Administration) and CSA (Canadian Space Agency) join forces and organize a program that promotes the invention of "nutritious and palatable" recipes for being used by astronauts and future space colonists. NASA's and CSA's programs are more similar to the way Romans envisaged the promotion of invention (through monetary awards) than to Sybaris', but the rationale is the same. In other words, the future has moved backward to twenty-eight centuries ago. Eventually, the proprietary interests resulting from the inventions made under the Deep Space Food Challenge will belong to NASA and CSA, given that those inventions, being made on Earth, are not subject to the Outer Space Treaty of 1967.[52] *However, no patents directly covering foodstuffs and the process of their making are found in NASA's, CSA's, or ESA's patent database.*

Deep Space Food Challenge Phase 2

January 20, 2022

Description of Challenge: The Deep Space Food Challenge seeks to create novel food production technologies or systems that require minimal inputs and maximize safe, nutritious, and palatable food outputs for long-duration space missions, and which has

52. The Outer Space Treaty leaves countries free to apply the principle of territoriality (and sovereignty) over inventions made within their borders or within spacecraft registered under their flags. At some point in the future new negotiations must be realized concerning inventions made by multinational teams in outer space colonies, that is, multinational colonies settled on other planets.

a potential to benefit people on Earth. Phase 1 of the challenge was a design phase, and Phase 2 will be a proto-type and demonstration phase.

The Deep Space Food Challenge will identify food production technologies that:

Help fill food gaps for a crew of four (4) for a three-year round-trip exploration mission with no resupply

Improve the accessibility of food on Earth, in particular, via production directly in urban centers and in remote and harsh environments

Achieve the greatest amount of food output with minimal inputs and minimal waste

Create a variety of palatable, nutritious, and safe foods that requires little processing time for crew members

Phase 2 of this Challenge offers a total prize purse of $1,000,000 and seeks to incentivize Teams to develop novel technologies and/or systems for food production that need not meet the full nutritional requirements of future crews, but can contribute significantly to and be integrated into a comprehensive food system.

Sponsoring/Partner Organizations: NASA coordinated with the Canadian Space Agency (CSA) to develop and launch the Challenge; with CSA providing its own prize purse for Canadian Teams. The Methuselah Foundation is the Allied Organization executing the Challenge for NASA.

For information on the CSA prize competition see https://impact.canada.ca/en/challenges/deep-space-food-challenge.

Benefits of Participation/Awards Available:

NASA Prize Purse for U.S. Teams

Up to 10 top scoring U.S. Teams will be named "finalists" and will receive $20,000 USD each from NASA and will move on to compete in the final on-site demonstration. Up to 5 top scoring U.S. Teams after the final on-site demonstration will each be awarded $150,000 USD and be invited to compete in Phase 3 (should Phase 3 open for competition). Additionally, a total of $50,000 USD will be available for bonus prizes for up to 5 U.S. Teams to be awarded when finalists Teams are announced. U.S. Teams do not need to be named as a finalist to be awarded a bonus prize. U.S. Teams must meet the eligibility requirements for the NASA Prize to receive a prize from NASA.

Recognition for Other International Teams

Up to 5 top scoring International Teams will be recognized as "finalists" and will move on to compete in the final on-site demonstration. Up to 3 top scoring International Teams will be recognized as Phase 2 challenge winners. International Teams are not eligible to be awarded prize money from NASA and must meet the eligibility requirements to participate in the Challenge and be recognized as winners.

Registration Open Date: January 20, 2022; 10:00AM Central Time

Registration Close (U.S. and Other International Teams): February 28, 2022; 5:00PM Central Time

Submission Deadline: May 20, 2022

Frequency: Ongoing

For More Information: www.deepspacefoodchallenge.org.

Figure 1.23 The logo of the Deep Space and Food Challenge, organized by NASA and CSA.

CHAPTER 2
Business Identifiers

SECTION 1 BUSINESS IDENTIFIERS ASSOCIATED WITH FOODSTUFFS IN GENERAL

§2.1 STAMPS, TRADEMARKS, AND SLOGANS FOR FOODSTUFFS IN ANTIQUITY; THE COUNTERFEITING OF WINE

Amphorae were probably the first examples of packaging products for mass consumption. Used between 1,500 BC (initially by the Canaanites, followed by the Phoenicians, with whom the Greeks eventually learned to mark goods) and 500 AD (when they were replaced by barrels made of wooden strips, invented by the Gauls), they were manufactured mostly for storing and transport the most common food commodities of Mediterranean trade in both the Greek and Roman periods: wine, olive oil, cereals and garum *(a sauce made from macerated fish entrails). Their shapes, although different from production center to production center, adjusted to the normal use made of them.*

As Diana Twede explains, the efficiency of any packaging depends on maximizing the ratio of the quantity of liquid to its weight.[53] *Therefore, as far as amphorae are concerned, the larger the volume loaded and the thinner the walls (without breaking), the more efficient they would be. Indeed, the oval shape of the amphorae provided a very resistant structure. Furthermore, amphorae were naturally intended for the maritime transport of goods. Their heavy weight and large volume made them unsuitable for land transport, as Greek roads were almost non-existent and Roman roads were built for the movement of legions, not goods. Therefore, most amphorae were manufactured in coastal cities: the products were brought in from the interior, placed in amphorae, and then taken to the holds of ships, which transported them to all points along the Mediterranean coasts (and even beyond). The shape of the amphorae, with their beaked*

53. Diana Twede, *Commercial Amphoras: The Earliest Consumer Packages?*, 22 Journal of Macromarketing 98 (2002) DOI: 10.1177/027467022001009.

base, made them specially adapted to be stored in the holds of ships, one next to the other, and in several layers.

Amphorae were perhaps the most common ceramic product in Antiquity: archaeological excavations have revealed the existence in Palestine of settlements whose single economic activity was the manufacture of pottery. In Jerash, in ancient Syria (today in Jordan), there was a potters' guild.[54] *In the Agora of Athens alone, the remains of more than 40,000 amphorae with marks were found.*[55] *Amphorae were also manufactured within vertical production integration systems. There are cases of agricultural and industrial complexes involving the production of amphorae in wine- and fish-producing centers. The same family (the Sestii family) that lived near the Roman port of Cosa owned the vineyards, the mills and the fish processing units, as well as the ships and a pier.*

Some amphora-producing centers adopted forms that were slightly different from those of other centers. Some amphorae became easily recognizable due to these different shapes, such as those from Thasos, Rhodes or Phenicia—because Thasos, Rhodes and Kos were known for the superior quality of their wine, the external shapes of the amphorae thus came to also constitute an indication of origin. Therefore, already in the Roman period, when the trade in goods packaged in amphorae had expanded throughout the Mediterranean basin, the imitation (or counterfeiting) of famous and reputed forms of amphorae became a widespread practice. The raw material used in the manufacture of amphorae—clay, generally extracted near the potteries—could also serve as an identification element, and that is why the surface of some amphorae was covered with a colored paste with the purpose of imitating the color and texture of clay of other amphorae, produced in known centers, close to places of production and of dispatch of coveted items. The purpose of this imitation was not to copy the packaging itself, as it was not frequent (although it sometimes occurred) that empty amphorae were sold remotely (they were too heavy to be transported without anything that added value). The intention was to mislead buyers regarding the products contained therein.

The texts and figures that follow give a clear example of this sort of counterfeiting that involved the wine from the Greek island of Kos, which was greatly appreciated by Roman consumers. Pliny has made a special reference to the imitation of wine of Kos in Italy, and indicated that Cato, in his De Agricultura, *explained how to make that sort of wine. It is noteworthy that Cato was aware that he was teaching how to make wine similar to that of Kos with the objective of its counterfeiting. In effect, he starts his teaching with this sentence: "If you want to make wine of Kos with another wine." Italian producers of "wine of Kos" went farther in eluding consumers because they would ship*

54. *Id.*
55. Carolyn G. Koehler e Philippa M. Wallace Matheson, *Knidian Amphora Chronology, Pergamon to Corinth*, in Jonas Eiring e John Lund (eds.), TRANSPORT AMPHORAE AND TRADE IN THE EASTERN MEDITERRANEAN—ACTS OF THE INTERNATIONAL COLLOQUIUM AT THE DANISH INSTITUTE AT ATHENS, SEPTEMBER 26-29, 2002, at 164 (Danish Institute at Athens, Aarhus, 2004). Mount Testaccio, in Rome, was built with broken amphorae destined to carry and store olive oil. It is estimated that in its interior there are remnants of no less than 24 million amphorae. José Nieto, HISTORIA DE ROMA—DÍA A DÍA EN LA ROMA ANTIGUA, at 170 (Libsa, 2000).

it to clients in amphorae whose shape and color created the same impression as amphorae produced in Kos.

Amphorae displayed two types of signs. On the wings (in some cases, on just one wing; in others, on both wings) was printed a set of signs that varied with time and place but which, in their most complete forms, contained: an eponym (the name of the magistrate), the name of the manufacturer, and a figurative mark. These figurative marks took on the most varied forms. For example, in Cyprus, figures of roses (the most common mark), vine leaves, ship anchors, burning flames and stars were found printed on the handles of amphorae originating from Greece. They were not trademarks or trade names like those of today. The printing of the eponym next to the name or sign representing the manufacturer would be a certification of the exactitude of the declared (and taxed) contents. In fact, amphorae had standardized dimensions, but the lack of precision instruments naturally led to greater or lesser variations in those dimensions. Therefore, the magistrate's printed name had two functions: to ensure that the dimensions of the marked jar did not deviate unreasonably from its normal dimensions; and, in addition, it would serve to certify that the due fees had been paid. For example, in Tasso, one of the largest wine-producing and -exporting centers (packaged in amphorae), around 425-412 BC, a law was adopted on the production and commercialization of this drink. A specific rule mentioned the seals and their value, as one of the following texts shows.

The figurative mark was, therefore, an expression of certification. Some of these symbols were possibly dictated by the magistrate, who, through them, might have expressed personal values and idiosyncrasies, such as, for example, the cult of certain gods. Sometimes, the origin of the amphora was confirmed by a stamp with the design of a local coin. Therefore, the figurative symbols on the wings are not evocative of the products contained in the amphorae (except, perhaps, in some cases and indirectly, such as the drawings of Dionysus, grapes and vines, for example, which are found in certain amphorae used to transport wine). On the other hand, the manufacturer's identification, when associated with a certain reputation, was intended to differentiate.

These symbols and marks were printed on the amphorae while the paste was still soft, that is, before the amphorae were placed in the ovens to cook. The marks were not drawn directly. As it happened with Mesopotamian seals, the marks on Greek and Roman amphorae were also placed on seals that served as molds. With these seals, figures and words were printed on the handles of the amphorae. Seals were made by specialized artisans. The details of the use of these distinctive signs are not known. It is possible that the seals were ordered directly by the amphora makers, but printed on them only after the magistrate had given authorization. Furthermore, as the figurative signs were affixed by determination of the magistrate, it was he who determined (or approved) the figure to be printed on the handles of the amphorae. The fact that seals are printed before cooking also explains why signs evocative of the nature of the product are rarely found on the handles of amphorae—after all, that same amphora, in certain regions, could be used to package different products. Evocative or descriptive signs, like the ones mentioned above, were probably only used in production centers whose amphorae were intended to package a single type of merchandise.

*The second type of distinctive sign is found in the painted inscriptions (*dipini *or* tituli picti*) on the neck or the body of the amphorae. The painted inscriptions completed the information on the stamps with the name and origin of the product and the name of the merchant (either the seller or the buyer). It is here that we find the distinctive signs that are closest to those of today, to the point that some authors want to see in them some modern expressions of industrial property, such as geographical indications and well-known marks. These are anachronisms, but the parallels are still catching—indeed, the* tituli picti *were the labels of the past. It is known today that the words painted on the amphorae that transported oil from Spain and destined for Rome were more or less standardized, containing between four and five informative elements: the first was the net weight of the amphora; the second was the gross weight of the amphora with its contents; the third was the name of the shipping carrier; the fourth element was a series of symbols designating the public officials who supervised the export, the type of product, the farm where the product had been manufactured, and the name of the city in which the inspection had taken place. The fifth element, when it appears, seems to refer to notes relating to the port and the loading operation. Twede says that this data would already be sufficient to satisfy the requirements of current US law on packaging and labeling.*[56]

The tituli picti *were placed after cooking the amphorae and, therefore, do not serve, like the signs on the wings, as reliable elements to identify the origin of the amphorae. Furthermore, because they were simply graffiti scrawled on the outer walls of the amphorae, many of them have disappeared. But those that remain give us some important clues as to how traders at the time already used certain marketing practices.*

In the ruins of the house of Aulus Umbricius Saurus, the most famous garum *manufacturer in Pompeii, mosaics were found with the reproduction of some of the amphorae in which he packaged his famous product (exported to the four corners of the Roman Empire). On those amphorae, identical to those found during excavations,* tituli picti *identify the contents (*garum *and other sauces), their manufacturer, and express slogans.*

§2.1.1 Indications of Origin and Trade Name Inscribed on Egyptian Amphorae for Wine—*Circa* Fourteenth Century BC

Year 37: Wine from the Estate Nehmaatra—life!—prosperity!—health!—is the Splendor of the Aton (of) the Western River; the Chief Vintner Ptahmay.

§2.1.2 The Law of Thasos (Greece), on Wine Trade—Fifth Century BC

... When anyone buys wine in wine-jars, the sale will be valid if the wine-jars are sealed.

56. *Supra* note 40.

§2.1.3 Slogan Inscribed on an Amphora Found in London

The best fish sauce Lucianus Tettius Africanus, from Antipolis, made by Africanus.[57]

§2.1.4 Marks and Slogans Inscribed on Amphorae Used to Transport Fish Sauces Made in the Manufacture of Scaurus (Pompei)—First Century AD

G(ari) F(los) SCO [m] (bri) / SCAVRI / EXXOFI [CI] / NA CAV/RI
Flower of *garum*, made of mackerel, according to the recipe of Scaurus, made in the manufacture of Scaurus.[58]
LIQVA(minis) / FLOS
Flower of *liquamen* [sauce]
G(ari) F(los) SCOM(bri) SCAVRI
Flower of *garum*, made of mackerel, according to the recipe of Scaurus
LIQVAMEN / OPTIMVM / EX OFFICI [n] / A. SCAVRI
Excellent *liquamen* made in the manufacture of Scaurus[59]

§2.1.5 A Slogan as Part of the Sign of Euxinus' Inn at Pompeii—First Century AD

PHEONIX FELIX ET TUU
The phoenix is lucky; may you be too.

§2.1.6 Wine from Kos Counterfeited in Italy: Pliny and Cato Give Its Recipe

Pliny the Elder, Natural History

Book XXII, Chapter 10

The people of Cos mix sea-water in large quantities with their wines, an invention which they first learned from a slave, who adopted this method of supplying the deficiency that had been caused by his thievish propensities. When this is mixed with white must, the mixture receives the name of "leucocoum." In other countries again, they follow a similar plan in making a wine called "tethalassomenon." They make a wine also known as "thalassites," by placing vessels full of must in the sea, a method

57. *Id.*
58. The best *garum* was made from mackerel viscera. But there were other cheaper types of fish sauce, and not as popular, made from other types of fish, such as tuna and eel. The first and third inscriptions suggest that Scaurus had some sort of exclusivity in his recipe, which implies that he has kept it secret—perhaps the main reason for the success of his business.
59. The expression "flower of *liquamen*" (a type of *garum*) probably referred to the best quality sauce, prepared according to more rigorous criteria in the selection of raw materials and the manufacturing process. But the word "excellent" does not raise any doubts of interpretation: it is a slogan, a term of recommendation that aims to induce the consumer to purchase it.

which quickly imparts to the wine all the qualities of old age. In our own country too, Cato has shown the method of making Italian wine into Coan, in addition to the modes of preparation above stated, he tells us that it must be left exposed four years to the heat of the sun, in order to bring it to maturity.

M. Porcius Cato, Rural Economy

If you want to make Kos wine with other wine, seventy days before the harvest draw sea water from a place in the open sea where fresh water does not reach, while the sea is calm and that there will be no wind. When you have drawn this water, you will pour it into a barrel without filling it: on the contrary, this barrel must be able to contain more than five quarters of liquor; you will put a lid on it, leaving an opening through which air can enter. One month later, transfer it neatly into another barrel, very gently, in order to leave the deposit at the bottom. Twenty days later, transfer it to another barrel, where it will remain until the harvest. Leave the grapes with which you want to make Kos wine on their vine, so that they have time to ripen properly: and only pick them after it has rained and dried. Place it in the sun for two or three days outdoors, provided it does not rain; if it rains, arrange it on racks at home, and peel off all the grains that may be spoiled: then take the sea water about which we were talking about earlier, and put ten quarters of it in barrels with a capacity of fifty *sextarii:*[60] then take bunches of black grapes from which you will scrape the grains with your hand in these barrels, so that they can soak up the sea water. When you have filled the barrels, cover them, leaving an opening through which air can enter; three days later, remove these grapes from the barrels, and crush them in the press; you will put the wine that it will yield into good, very clean and dry barrels.

Figure 2.1 From top to bottom, first row, left: fragments of Egyptian containers with the name of the owner, of the wine producer, and a greeting that can be understood as a slogan—on display at the Metropolitan Museum of Art, New York, USA; right: an amphora for the transport of garum *produced by Scaurus, depicted in mosaics found at the ruins of his house, in Pompei. Second row, left: neck of a wine amphora from Spain (Azaila, Teruel), with* tituli picti *indicating the owner or the trader, the quantity and the possible date of bottling at origin; right,* tituli picti *on the reverse side of the same amphora, as they appear on the table placed by its side, on display at the Museo Arqueológico Nacional, Madrid, Spain; the symbols, according to the Museum, are probably trademarks. Third row: the signboard of Euxinus' inn, at Pompeii, comprising a slogan. Fourth row: shop signs at Pompeii; left: the shop sign of a wine merchant; right: the sign of a milk shop.*

60. One *sextarius* was a Roman unit of measure, equivalent to about half a liter.

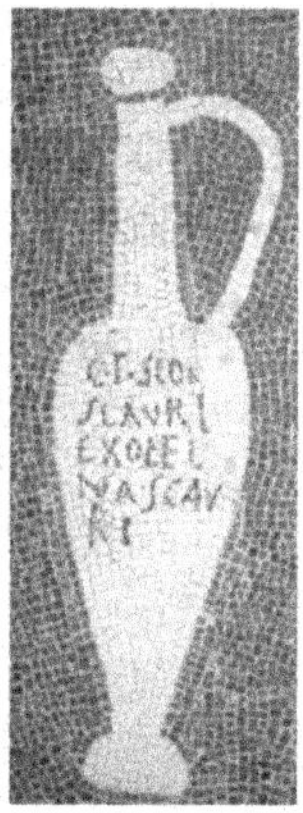

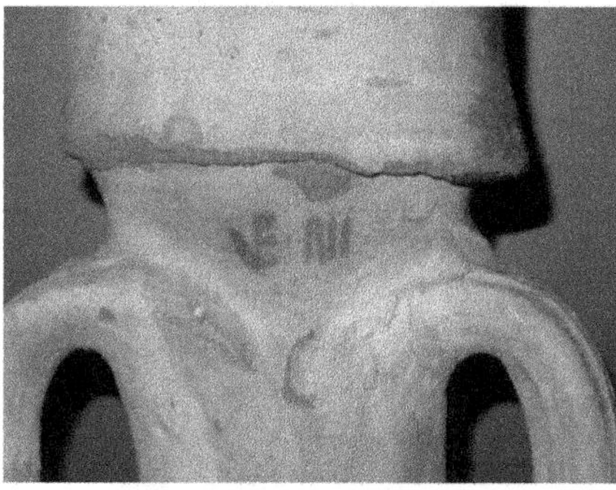

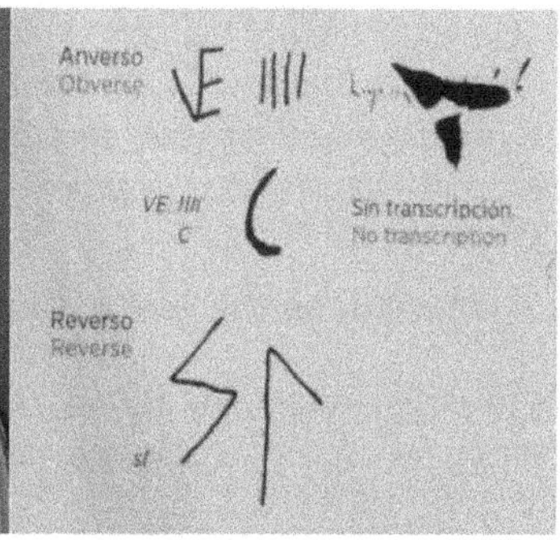
Anverso
Obverse
VE IIII
C
Sin transcripción
No transcription
Reverso
Reverse
st

§2.2 CHEESE FROM LUNA (LIGURIA, ITALY) WAS STAMPED WITH THE DRAWING OF THE CRESCENT MOON, A SORT OF A FIGURATIVE GEOGRAPHICAL INDICATION—FIRST CENTURY AD

The texts that follow illustrate that Romans not only used the names of places as geographical indications of foodstuffs but also figurative symbols with the same purpose. The first text is an Epigram by Marcus Martial, the Roman poet, in which he mocks the size of cheese made at Luna. Every piece of cheese from Luna was marked with the figurative sign of the crescent moon, designating its geographical origin. The second text is a transcription from Pliny's Natural History, reporting that each cheese from Luna could weigh up to 1,000 pounds. It was from a temple dedicated to Luna that the city of Luni or Luna has taken its name. Luna was located in the northwestern region of Italy (currently Liguria). It was founded by the Romans in 177 BC on the shores of the Magra River as an outpost for the army. The colony would later become known for the cheese it produced and exported in large round pieces on which the city's symbol—the crescent moon—was printed as proof of their origin.

§2.2.1 Martial, on the Size of Cheese from Luna

XXX. Cheese, stamped with the crest of Etruscan Luna,
will afford your slaves a thousand lunches.

§2.2.2 Pliny the Elder, on the Same Topic

The pastures of the Alps recommend themselves by two sorts of cheese; the Dalmatic Alps send us the Docleatian cheese, and the Centronian Alps the Vatusican. The kinds produced in the Apennines are more numerous; from Liguria we have the cheese of Ceba, which is mostly made from the milk of sheep; from Timbria we have that of Aesina, and from the frontiers of Etruria and Liguria those of Luna, remarkable for their vast size, a single cheese weighing as much as a thousand pounds.

Figure 2.2 Left: The Roman Goddess of the Moon (Luna), holding the crescent. Engraving by Giulio Bonasoni, 1530-1570. Right: The city of Luna, as depicted in Tabula Peutingeriana, a Roman map elaborated between the first and fourth centuries AD. The map also shows the colonies of Pisa and Lucca, as well as the islands of Corsica and Sardinia.

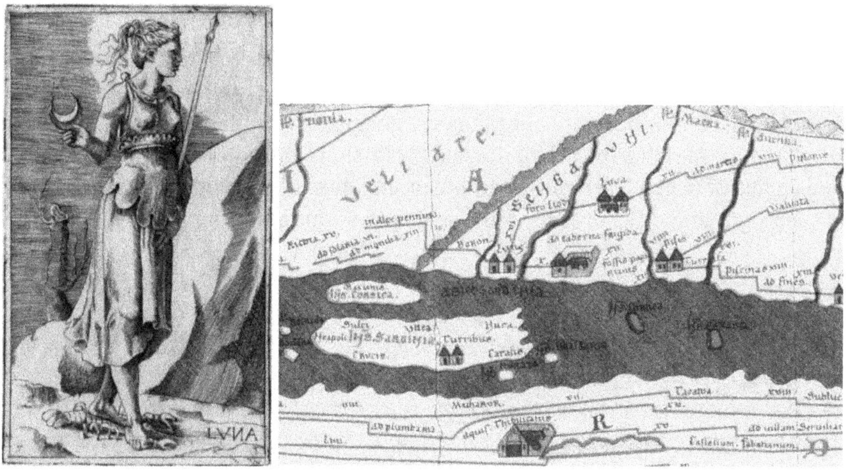

§2.3 THE PREDECESSORS OF COLLECTIVE MARKS: THE ARMS AND EMBLEMS OF MEDIEVAL GUILDS—1467

This is not the first regulation on the organization of the professions in Paris. As seen above (§1.2), various guilds were already established and had their own by-laws at the end of the thirteenth century. The new aspect of this regulation of 1467 was the association of various professions into specific guilds under special banners and the imposition of an obligation for those guilds to adopt collective marks (all with one common element—a white cross—but with differentiating identifiers, which each collectivity could choose as they would see fit).

Ordinance on the organization of the professional bodies of Paris under various banners

Chartres, June 1467

Louis [XI], etc. We make it known for all present and for those to come, for the good and safety of our good city of Paris… .

What follows is what has been decided, done and ordered, by the commissioners, designated and instructed by the king to wear arms and clothes of the residents and inhabitants of all classes of the good town and city of Paris.

First. After the said commissioners have spoken and demonstrated the intention and good pleasure of the King to the inhabitants of all classes, on what it is said, and that they have said and responded that they are ready to obey the King and to serve him with all their power and to wear arms and clothing, to maintain and keep the said city in his good obedience, it has been decided by the said commissioners that, to organize and implement this work, the professionals and merchants from the said city will be separated and divided into sixty-one banners and companies, in the following manner:

Namely, ... bakers, one banner; pastry chefs, millers, one banner; ... butchers of the grand butcher shop [certain butcher shops in Paris], and other butchers, one banner; butchers from the butcher shops of Beauvais, Gloriette, Cimetière-Saint-Jean and Notre-Dame-des-Champs, one banner; ... coopers and wine carriers [those who lower the wines into the cellars], one banner; ... poultry dealers, cooks, roasters and sausage makers, one banner; ... livestock sellers and dealers, sea fish sellers, one banner; freshwater fish merchants and fishermen, one banner; ... winegrowers, one banner; ...

(2) Item. And that in each of the said professions and companies there will be one banner, each of which will be armored and ornamented with a white cross in the middle, and such signs and coats of arms as the said professions and companies will see fit.

...

Figure 2.3 Clockwise, starting on top left, the banners of the guilds of the bakers and pastry chefs of Clément, of the bakers of Brioude, and of the bakers of Clermont. Clearly inspired in the military banners of Antiquity, these collective symbols led the artisans' religious processions celebrating their respective saint patrons. At the same time, the banners represented an association of artisans who worked in the same profession—with hindsight, they were a sort of a collective trademark. Bakers' banners frequently showed the picture of the shovel (with three round indentations) that they used to place into and extract the bread from the oven.

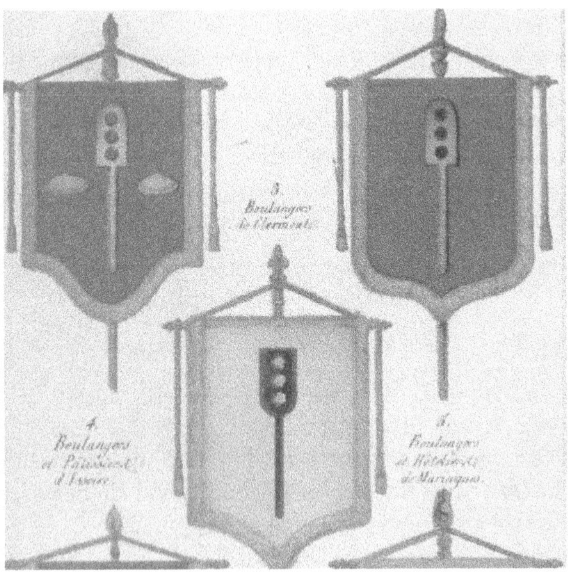

§2.4 THE BY-LAWS OF THE GUILD OF GROCERS AND SPICE SELLERS OF AMIENS PROHIBITED THE LICENSING AND THE ASSIGNMENT OF TRADEMARKS WITHIN THE INDUSTRY—1661

On the one hand, the regulations of the guilds would frequently contain clauses discouraging competition and, on the other hand, suppressing some inconveniences that could result from monopolistic trade. Clauses prohibiting the association of masters and the hoarding of raw materials were frequent. Price controls were also frequent. Those concerns would sometimes have an impact on trademark regulations. In some guilds, the licensing and assignment of trademarks would not be allowed unless in the case of the death of the master. This text, extracted from the by-laws of the haberdashers, candle makers, grocers and spice sellers of Amiens, prohibits the licensing and assignment of trademarks, as well as the use of foreign marks unless that was necessary in times of war.

This makes it even more exceptional the authorization granted by the King of France in 1364 for the assignment of a cutler's trademark (see §2.28.2).

By-laws of the haberdashers, candle makers, grocers and spice sellers of Amiens

September 9, 1661

Louis [XIV], by the grace of God, King of France and Navarre, to all present and future, greetings... .

Given at said Amiens, the ninth day of September one thousand six hundred and sixty-one. Which articles follow... .

44- Item, that no merchant of the mentioned status shall make or contract association with anyone if [the latter] is not merchant and master approved to that status, nor lend their names or marks for the effect of the goods dependent on that status and trade, under the penalty of the loss of the mastership and a fine of sixty sols, and use foreign names and marks, except if that [use] is for passing the strait [the English Channel] and the danger of the enemy, if they are constrained to do so, in which case they will be required to advert the masters in charge, prior to arrival of said goods, under the penalty of [the goods] being declared foreign.

§2.5 PROVISIONS ON THE MARKING OF BARRELS AND OTHER VESSELS FOR THE SALE OF WINES, CIDERS, BEERS, VINEGARS, OILS, AND OTHER BEVERAGES AND LIQUEURS—1608

The marking of the containers of beverages and other food-related liquids, such as vinegars and oils, has been an important issue since the Middle Ages. Both the coopers and the measurers were liable for the making of vessels with the wrong dimensions. Interestingly, in the following regulation approved by the King for the measurers and inspectors of Normandy, the individual trademarks of the coopers were granted by the Measurers.

Henry by the grace of God, King of France and Navarre, to all present and to those to come, Greetings. With the purpose of stopping the abuses that were committed in the sale of wines, ciders, beers, vinegars, oils, and other beverages and liqueurs by the malice or negligence of the Measurers of vessels provided by virtue of the Edicts of the late Kings Henry the Second and the Third, our predecessors, and others introduced for the same reasons by the Communities, Mayors, Consuls, Jurors, Aldermen, and other Magistrates of the cities of our Kingdom, and establishing good order on them.

...

We have also ordered that all Coopers, before beginning to start working on any new or old barrels, would be required to take from those Measurers, by paying them five sols, a sample marked with their mark according to the old Measure of the locality where they would reside, so that they would not, in their work, exceed in height, weight, or volume, on the penalty of confiscation

...

We want all new vessels which will be made and worked by the Coopers, and those which will be bound and sold, both by them and the merchants tavern keepers, innkeepers, and others, to be marked and gauged by the said Measurers at the time of the sales, in particular because it is in the way of making those vessels that the abuses are committed, ...

§2.6 A FRENCH LAW DICTIONARY CITES TWO COURT DISPUTES INVOLVING TRADEMARKS AND SHOP SIGNS RELATED TO CUTLERY AND HOSPITALITY—1610 AND 1647

Pierre Jacques Brillon, in his very popular, often-cited dictionary of case law (entry "Enseigne"), cited a few decisions applying the law on shop signs/trademarks. Of particular interest in the context of food and hospitality are the following two summaries.

... A Cutler from Moulins had the mark of the Heart; another took the same mark of the heart, and put an arrow in the middle to mean the wounded heart; the latter said that, having bought a house where this mark had always been, he could have taken it and changed his own. Judgment of the Parliament of Paris of February 10, 1610, which decides it in this manner: *Plaidoyers de Corbin, chap. 114.*

Two hotel keepers may not have in the same street two similar signboards. Judgment of the same Parliament of February 16, 1647. See the facts of the case in *Soëfve, to. l. Cent. 1. ch. 100.*

§2.7 A FRENCH JURIST STATES THE LAW OF BUSINESS IDENTIFIERS, WITH A SPECIAL FOCUS ON THE SIGNBOARDS OF INNS AND TAVERNS—1698

In this text, a celebrated French jurist and practicing attorney of the sixteenth and seventeenth centuries, Gabriel-François du Pineau, describes the law of business identifiers that prevailed in France at that time. Besides stating the general status of that law, he makes some points implying that, at that time, an understanding had already evolved toward distinguishing trademarks from shop signs or signboards as separate categories of business identifiers. The foundation of the protection of business identifiers in general was—and continues to be—the protection of the consumer. Interestingly, du Pineau sets some parallels between trademarks and coats of arms (as Sassoferrato, whose authority he quotes, did in the fourteenth century[61]*).*

The text, it seems, was prepared as a supporting piece of du Pineau's arguments in the representation of a client in a lawsuit involving the ownership of a hotel's shop sign, which is mentioned at the end. The text says that the judge had dismissed the case on the argument that the prevailing law on shop signs did not apply to hotels and pubs and that an appeal had been filed but not yet judged.

On the shop signs and marks of Merchants and Artisans

This is not where I want to deal with Signs, Arms, Coats of Arms, Escutcheons, Pennons, and Guidons of Princes, Grand Lords, Knights, Gentlemen and other illustrious persons, about whom one must understand the texts... .

I go deeper down, to speak of the shop signs and marks of the Merchants and Artisans, which our Doctors call *signa, insignia*. I said, *shop signs*, meaning the signs that the Merchants and Artisans hang from their houses, and affix on the bags and packages of their goods, or on the chests, vessels, wagons, boats and ships in which they put them for keeping, carrying and transporting them; I said *marks*, to express the signs that the Artisans, and those who work and toil with the hands, print on their works.

The question is whether such kinds of people can take the signs and marks of each other, Ulpian. *m. l. 3. Dig. of solut.* said *"inter artifices longa differentia est, & nature, & ingenii, & doctrina, & institutionis"* ["among artisans, there is a great difference of intelligence, and of nature, and of instruction, and of science"]; so much so that if any Artisan has acquired perfection in his Art, or by inclination or goodness of mind, or by experience, and if a Merchant has decided to sell and distribute good articles only, and at a reasonable price, and both have acquired a reputation in their professions, so that he is sought after even by those who do not know his name, the usual expedient to preserve this reputation, to maintain his commerce, and to give confidence to those who wish to buy their articles or works, is that the Merchant hangs a signboard at his shop, and the Artisan marks his works with a mark of his own. And it is asked whether in the same City, in the same town, very closely established, another Merchant, or another Artisan of his profession can take and usurp the same shop sign or mark.

On which it will be noted that when any of the Doctors has wished to infer that it is permissible to take the shop sign, the mark, or even the coat of arms of another, since it is permitted to take his name, this argument is not acceptable, reasonable or probable, because there is quite a difference between changing the name (which is lawful, provided it is done without fraud, *l. un. Cod. de mutat. nom.*) and take the name

61. Bartolo da Sassoferrato is considered the first jurist who discussed the principles presiding over trademarks. His treatise *De Insigniis et De Armis*, published posthumously in 1358, applies the principles of heraldry to trademarks. *See* Nuno Pires de Carvalho, FROM BABYLON TO THE SILICON VALLEY, *supra* note 10, at 86-87.

of another, which is still tolerated, even ordinary and necessary as far as the first name is concerned. But as for the surname, *cognomen*, which is the name of a family and a race, it is not allowed to take it, because to affirm [falsely] to be part of the family is seen as a usurpation, and a sort of falsehood sanctionable, Paul. *lib. 5. sent. tit. 25. § si quis. l. falsi, Dig. ad L. Cornel. de fals. Benedict. ad cap. Rainutius, verbo, Rainutius, num. 57.* Moreover, the Texts ordinarily cited are not appropriate. In *l. cum filius, §. pater. Dig. of leg. 2* it is an ancestor who charges his daughter to give to his nephew Sempronius more than to his other children in honor of his name; or if these words, *in honorem nominis mei*, mean "because it bears my name," it is not that he has usurped it, nor that *genus, parentesue sinxerit*, as Paul. says in the place above, since he has the name by the consent of his ancestor; and that being of the family, he is well founded to wear it: in *l. facta, § if vero nominis, Dig. ad S.C. Trebell.*, it does not matter that it is the usurpation of another's name, or that, to the contrary, the testator charges the heir to take his name. It follows that this argument *a simili* does not proceed; but the considerations of the Doctors are judicious and relevant, and the conclusion is that one cannot take the mark, or the shop sign of an Artisan or of a Merchant, if this usurpation is prejudicial to the one on which it is carried on, or to the public. As for the mark of the Artisan that he prints on his works, it cannot be taken or usurped by another, says Bartole. *Tract. insignii. § arm. num. 7. & 8.* where he quotes *cap. in nonnullis, de Judais, ap. Greg.*, which in its true intelligence would better apply to the signs of the houses than to the marks of the works: for, on this matter, the Council of Latran, held under Innocent III, not only forbids the Jews to wear clothes similar to those of the Christians, but also enjoins them from wearing such [clothes] that *publice ab aliis populis distinguantur.* Bald. *ad l. 1. Cod. qua res vendi not poss.* deals with the shop signs of the Merchants and the marks of the Artisans, and says that when someone has taken them *pro libito sue voluntatis*, another can also take them, provided that it be without fraud; otherwise he could not [do it], and adds this remarkable decision that this concerns who have them *per usum longi temporis*; after which, for a long time, *alius talia signa accipere non potest, quia jus ea habem di qualitum est primo*; unless it does not harm anybody, on what there is the need for weighing in the first place these words *longi temporis*, from which it follows that the possession for ten years suffices.

In the second place, that is a right, *jus*, and not a simple faculty. The same Balde, *ad cap. quanto. de jurejurando, ap. Gregor. num. 3*, after saying that one cannot carry another's coats of arms, if one does it by deception and circumvention with the intent of deceiving someone; he adds that it is the same for the marks affixed on the Merchants' bags, because by usurping them, it turns to the detriment of others; and gives as a conclusion that in those things that concern the public utility, *Melior is conditio occupantis*; and of whom has the right to have them *ex consuetudine, vel ex privilegio, Panormit. ad cap. dilecta de except Pralat. ap. Gregor. num. 4* says that if a good Artisan or a Merchant has some mark, and another wants to use it *ut habeat concursum, and sic decipere populum*, the Judge can forbid him to do so; but that each individual may take such coats of arms or signs as he sees fit, even those of another, provided that it is not to his detriment nor of the public.

Benedict. *ad cap. Rainutius, verbo, Rainutius, num. 59*, dealing with this matter, and speaking of the injunctions of the Judge against the usurper, says that the Judge can and must order them on his own initiative, in the absence of a party's request, especially since the public good is involved, *ne populis decipiatur*. The author of the Songe du Vergier, chap. 127, is of this opinion, because not only the Artisan or the Merchant would be interested, but the people deceived, because the individuals would buy the works of one for the works of the other.

Of the same opinion are Sains. *in Cons. Turon, tit. des droits de Chastelenie, art. 6.* Ming. *in Cons. Andegav. art. 49. num. 7.* Rat. *in Cons. ictav. art. 1. gl. ult. in fine.* Chassan, *in Catal. glor. mundi, part 1 considerat. 38. conclus. 31 & seqq.* deals extensively with this matter of the marks of the Artisans and the shop signs of the Merchants, and says in *conclusion 32.* that an Artisan cannot take the sign or mark of another Artisan; which he repeats in *conclusion 34.* and extends to the shop sign of a hotel (as Benedict. had done, at the place mentioned above *d. num. 59.*) and to the sign that the Merchant or the Artisan has in front of his house by usucaption, as his predecessors and himself have used, for the usucaption of which the very long period of thirty years is required, although it is based on the excerpt from Balde *ad. l. I. Cod. qua res vendi not poss.* who only speaks of long periods, i.e. of ten years, as I have noted above.

But by our use, especially as these signs are taken *pro libito voluntatis*, says Balde, it is enough to have given notice; for in this case those who wish to take the same sign, could do it only by fraud, envy, and jealousy; which must be understood with this caveat of Chassanée, when the usurpation would occur between neighbors; because if the houses are far from each other, and in different streets, the case for prohibition would cease, especially when the second would add some difference between his shop sign and that of the first; which I believe to be unquestionable as far as the signboards that hotel and tavern keepers hang in their houses; but, as regards the marks of the Artisans, my opinion is that there must be more severity, and that in the same town or village no Artisan must be allowed to take the mark of another Artisan; this has been thus decided by two judgments of the Court that Mornac cites, *ad. l. quod si neque, Dig. of peric. & comm. rei vend.*, because between two grocers the judgment there mentioned is grounded on the neighborhood of the two houses; and it seems to me that as regards the marks of two cutlers (which are in conformity with the shop signs) the fact of the neighborhood has not been accorded such weight, given that the distance and diversity of the places would be of little consideration in cities and boroughs of the Kingdom other than Paris, where the Artisans are all neighbors.

As for the Merchants and Artisans, the doctrine is confident that they cannot take the signs or the marks of each other, even if artificially disguised by some addition, the main body remaining. Thus, it was judged, says Mornac, for the benefit of the one who had the heart as a shop sign against the one who took the wounded heart, having added an arrow. And from this, as far as Merchants and Artisans are concerned, all the Doctors offer this reason—the public interest, so that the people are not deceived by the usurpation of the shop sign or the mark, buying dearly bad articles, instead of the good ones, which are sold by those who had the first shop sign or mark; because this norm is of a political nature and has been introduced for the public good among those who have Masterships, By-laws and Masterpieces, and who make public proof of the Prince's authority and justice, of their ability in their profession.

Doubt remains if the rule is the same for hotel and tavern keepers, as Benedicti and Chassanée say: and it can be said that, in their profession there having no Mastery of seniority, nor Masterpieces or by-laws, our fathers did not consider that their profession concerns the public interest, and did not care whether those people would have good wine and good cooks for passers-by, given moreover that their houses are not supposed to receive those from the Province, as well as foreigners, and eventually many strangers, tramps, vagrants, and some derelicts who are taken care by the places in which they arrive. We can nevertheless say that we must reject all emulation, and that Justice must not accept that an individual does to others what he would not like to be done to him, since in this usurpation there is an obvious presumption of a purpose of doing harm to that of the same profession, having chosen his shop sign in the neighborhood, having been lawful to take that of someone who exercises another trade.

This question was pleaded in our Hearing of Monday, December 13, 1638, between the hotel keeper who holds the old house and hotel of Notre-Dame du Faubourg, through which one goes to Chateau-Gontier, and the new hotel keeper who took a house on the other side of the street, on which he put the same sign of Notre-Dame in a bigger board. The hotel keeper who exploits the house of the old Image called on the keeper of the house so that he took his shop sign out and put another. In this dispute the parties were dismissed from the court and the procedure. The judge did not consider that the opinion of the Doctors concerning the Merchants and Artisans should be extended to the hotel and tavern keepers, notwithstanding the expansion by Benedict. and Chassan. This opinion is under appeal, on which we await the judgment of the Court.

§2.8 AN ADMINISTRATIVE COURT OF PARIS, IN SETTLING TWO DISPUTES CONCERNING NON-COMPETITION BETWEEN MASTER DISTILLERS, ACKNOWLEDGES THE PROTECTION OF TRADE DRESS—1699

The following text reflects an aspect of corporative life that was common to almost all professions: new and old masters competing for the location of their businesses. But this case brings an important and new element: not only should new masters establish their shops at a reasonable distance from the old masters' ones (at least twenty houses, if on the same street, or in another street), but they should also refrain from decorating their shops in a way similar to their former masters. This is an early acknowledgment of trade dress as an element of differentiation of merchants.

Sentence of the Police, of June 6, 1699, by decision of the following July 15. Which prohibits all Companions leaving a Master's shop from establishing themselves in the same street within the distance of twenty houses or in a different street, as well as from having the same displays.

To all those who will see these present Letters: Charles-Denis de Bullion, Knight Marquis de Gallardon, Lord of Bonnelles, Bullion & other places, Counselor of the King in his Councils, Provost of Paris; Greetings. We make it known that a request for a judgment has been made to us, in the Police Chamber of the Châtelet of Paris, by Gilles Savin, Attorney for Toussaint Fouhet, Merchant, Master Distiller in Paris, plaintiff for the complaints he made to the Commissioner Regnault on May 23 last, and request by him to Us presented on the 16th. Discovery carried out by Rousseau Sergeant in Verge, on the 27th of the said month and year, verified in Paris on the same day by Gueriboult, upon which he presented himself to the Court, pleading that prohibitions be made to the defendant hereinafter named to establish himself in the shop that he rented, adjoining that of the plaintiff, and also to continue the establishment and opening of the said shop, with costs, damages and interest, except for him to retire to another neighborhood. Also as a plaintiff, following his responses served on the 30th of the said month of May last by Barangue, Bailiff-Clerk in this Court, pleading that prohibitions be made to the said defendant from establishing himself or performing any function as Master or servant of any Master of the said Trade, in the same street and neighborhood of the plaintiff under whatever pretext, assisted by his Attorney Barbier, against Varnier the younger, Attorney of Martin Dupuis, Master Seller of Lemonade and Distiller, Merchant of Spirits and of all Liqueurs in Paris, defendant, assisted by his Attorney Forestier, the parties having been heard, together with Commissioner Regnault in his report. Reading of the Notice of Opposition submitted by the said Fouhet to the Attorneys of the said Dupuis, served on the Jurors of the said Community on May 18, of the said complaints, request, discovery and evidence and of the Statutes and Regulations of the said Community. We ... order that the Distilling Jurors will be summoned to turn up on the first day; However, we forbid all Masters who have served other Masters as Companions from establishing themselves in the same street except at the distance of twenty houses, or in a different street: and also from having the same ceilings, displays and shop ornaments, so that theirs cannot be mistaken for that of their Master. And after having heard from Commissioner Regnault who reported to us that Forestier runs his shop only five houses from that of Barbier, we ordered him to leave immediately, and to place himself at the aforementioned distance from the shop of Barbier; we order Forestier to pay half the costs, the other half reserved; And this Sentence shall be recorded in the Registry of the Community of Master Distillers, so that no one is unaware of it, which will be executed notwithstanding any oppositions or appellations, and without prejudice to them: As witness to this We have had these presents sealed, which were made and delivered by Messire Marc-René de Voyer de Paulmy Dargenson, Knight Counselor of the King in his Councils, Lieutenant General of Police, in charge, on Tuesday, June 2, one thousand six hundred and ninety-nine.

Signed, Tardiveau.

§2.9 THE PROVINCE OF SOUTH CAROLINA ENACTS A STATUTE ON THE GAUGING OF CONTAINERS FOR BEEF AND PORK, INCLUDING PROVISIONS ON TRADEMARKS—1699

In 1699, the British province of South Carolina enacted a statute that was very similar to that adopted in France, in 1608 (see §2.5) on the marking of barrels and other containers for the transportation of food-related substances. The South Carolina Act was confirmed in 1703.

An Act for the Ascertaining the Gauge of Barrels, and for Avoiding Deceits in Selling and Buying Beef and Pork

Forasmuch as Beef and Pork are two of the principal commodities of the product of this part of this Province, and great quantities thereof are transported beyond the seas, and whereas complaint has been made that the barrels which the said commodities are usually packed up in within this part of this Province are of less number of gallons than barrels which are used for the holding of the said commodities in other countries, and that great frauds and deceits are practiced and used in false packing and in the barreling up bulls flesh, boars flesh, and other unmerchantable and corrupt meat, to the great abuse of traders in the said commodities, and to bringing said commodities into great disrepute abroad; For remedy whereof, ...

And all barrels and half barrels that shall be exposed to sale, to hold beef or pork, shall be made of good seasoned wood; and the said copper or other person, b efore he or they do expose to sale any barrels or half barrels for beef, pork, pitch, or tarr, shall set his or their proper burnt mark upon every such barrel or half barrel, which mark he or they shall cause first to be recorded in the Secretary's office of this Province, upon pain that every cooper or other person or persons offending in making such barrels or half barrels of lesser number of gallons than is aforesaid, or making and exposing to sale any such barrel or half barrel for packing beef or pork, of unseasoned wood, or not putting his or their proper mark upon every such barrel, or not recording his or their mark in the Secretary's office aforesaid, shall for every such offense respectively forfeit the sum of five shillings for every barrel and two shillings and six pence for every such half barrel.

X. And it is further enacted by the authority aforesaid, That the said Packers or their deputies shall not set the said Packer's mark of this part of this Province upon any barrel or half barrel of beef or pork that has not on the said barrel or half barrel the Cooper's mark aforesaid, nor any barrel or half barrel packed up with bulls flesh, boars flesh, or any other unmerchantable or corrupt meat, or that has any of the same mixed among merchantable meat, nor any one barrel or half barrel of beef or pork that is untruly, deceitfully or falsely packed, upon pain of twenty shillings for every barrel and ten shillings for every half barrel for every such offense.

§2.10 THE BY-LAWS OF THE GUILD OF GROCERS OF ABBEVILLE ESTABLISH RULES ON THE MANDATORY MARKING OF GOODS AS A TOKEN OF LIABILITY—1712

Two aspects of this text are of particular interest. First, it is worth noticing that professions apparently so distinct have been reunited under one single banner. The association between grocers and apothecaries is understandable because, in the eighteenth century, the making of medicines was very much dependent on the use of imported spices, which grocers would sell. Moreover, the association of wax makers and candle makers with apothecaries was also common because the latter frequently used wax and candles in treatments. But the association of ironmongers with druggists is not that obvious. Anyway, the second interesting aspect is that these by-laws, although enacted on the verge of the French Revolution and the victory of liberal principles, still mention the purpose of trademarks as elements of designating liability. This was the very first reason of being and origin of the first distinctive signs used in Mesopotamia several thousands of years ago: to ascertain the liability of the merchant who dispatched his articles of trade to distant markets.

Statutes and Regulations of Merchant Haberdashers, Jewelers, Ironmongers, Grocers, Apothecaries, Druggists, Wax Makers and Candlemakers of the City of Abbeville from January 4, 1712.

Letters Patent of King Louis Paris on June 9, 1714. And act of registration of said Statutes and Patent Letters made at the Secretariat of the Court of Parliament, in Paris, on June 9, 1714. All recorded at the Secretariat of the Town Hall of the City of Abbeville, and the civil offices (*Sénéchaussée*) of Ponthieu on July 2 and 5 of the said year 1714.

I.

Firstly, that the said Merchant Haberdashers, Jewelers, Ironmongers, Grocers, Apothecaries, Druggists, Waxers and Candlemakers, are and shall remain in the future, as they were in the past, united and incorporated into one and the same Body of Community, and governed under the same Laws, Statutes and Ordinance, under the same Flag and Banner, and by the same Banner Heads, and Guards, who will be elected by them in the form and manner hereinafter declared, their not being permitted to separate for any cause or occasion whatsoever.

...

XXII.

The said Merchant Haberdashers, Grocers and others of the said Community shall not contract association with any person, if he is not a Merchant and Master accepted into the said Body, nor lend their name and mark in relation to those Goods, on the penalty of a fine of twenty pounds, for the first time, and forfeiture of the Mastership in the event of a repeat offense.

...

XXXVI.

We forbid Artisans and Tradesmen from exhibiting for sale any goods, if they have not been made or manufactured by them, or their servants, domestics, in this City and outskirts, on pain of confiscation, and a fine of ten pounds; which goods they shall be required to mark with their mark, so that one can know from which worker they proceed, so that, in case of defect of the said works, one may contact them, as being responsible, no matter in what hands the said works and goods can be found.

§2.11 THE FRENCH KING'S STATE COUNCIL SETTLES A DISPUTE BETWEEN THE GUILD OF LIQUEUR MAKERS AND ONE INDIVIDUAL WHO, NOT HAVING BEEN RECEIVED AT THE GUILD, OPENED A SHOP—1719

Disputes between guild members and non-incorporated professionals were very common (until the guilds were dissolved and banned with the French Revolution). The text that follows illustrates that fact: a certain Grignon had been designated a privileged merchant of vinegar, replacing another who had ceased his professional activities. A privileged merchant was one who exceptionally received permission to carry out his profession, even though not being a regular member of a guild. That was the case, for example, for some professionals, such as cooks, who were hired to work in the kitchens of the king or of the nobility.[62] *Grignon had not been received by the guild masters, but his right to carry out his profession had been assigned to him by the Grand Council, which had no authority for such a designation. This text is about the claim of the guild, whose masters wished to see Grignon disbarred of his illegal privilege and prohibited from carrying the profession of making and selling vinegar, as well as from using the distinctive signs proper of the trade. One year earlier, in 1718, the King's State Council accepted the guild's claim.*

Decision of the King's State Council.

Rendered in favor of the Community of Master Vinegar Makers, Makers of Green Grapes Juice, Mustard Makers, Distillers, Sellers of Liqueur, and Spirit of Wine of the City, Outskirts and Suburbs of Paris.

Against Charles Grignon, allegedly Privileged by the Grand Council, by whom His Majesty dismissed Grignon's opposition, orders that the Judgment of February 26, 1718 be executed, and he shall close his Shop and remove its exterior signs, prohibits him from continuing the Profession of making vinegar, on the penalty of a fine of three hundred pounds, and all costs, damages and interest.

Orders the said Grignon to pay the costs of this Judgment, set at forty pounds.

February 23, 1719.

Extracted from the Records of the King's Privy Council of State.

Seen at the King's Private Council of State, the Judgment rendered there on February 26, 1718 on the Request of the Trustee and the Community of Master Vinegar Makers of the City of Paris, deciding, overruling the Ruling of the Grand Council of the twenty-third March, notified on the twelfth August 1715, as well as the alleged Privileges provided by that same Ruling, prohibits Charles Grignon from enjoying [the privilege] and carrying the Profession of Vinegar Maker in this City of Paris, and for having done so condemns him to 500 pounds of damages and interest, and to the costs of the Judgment which will result from the mentioned Request, ...

...

62. The same idea of privilege was also associated with the industrial privileges granted during the Middle Ages to lure foreign artisans who hold certain technical knowledge of particular interest to the city or country that accorded them the patent letters. Those artisans were "privileged" in the sense they were authorized to carry their profession even if they were not enrolled with the local guild.

Request of the Community of Vinegar Makers of the City of Paris, in the sense that it please His Majesty to order that notwithstanding and without having regard to the opposition of the said Grignon of March 21 of 1718, shall be executed according to its form and content, in doing so that the Shop of the said Grignon shall be closed, and that the external signs of his Profession shall be removed, as well as making iterative prohibitions for him to continue the Profession of Vinegar, and to sell and distribute the goods under the penalty of a fine of one hundred pounds, ...

...

And all things considered, the King in His Council, dismissing the opposition of the said Grignon against the Ruling of the Council of February 26, 1718, which His Majesty has not accepted, ordered and orders that the said Ruling will be executed according to its form and content, and consequently that the said Grignon shall be required to close his Shop and remove the external signs of his Profession; His Majesty prohibits him from carrying his Profession as a Vinegar Maker, and from selling and distributing the goods, on the penalty of a fine of three hundred pounds, and all costs, damages and interest, and condemns the said Grignon to pay the costs of this Judgment, amounting to forty pounds.

Done at the King's Privy Council of State, held in Paris on February 23, one thousand seven hundred and nineteen. Collated.

Signed, De Mons.

§2.12 THE BY-LAWS OF THE GUILD OF MAKERS AND MERCHANTS OF SPIRITS OF PARIS ORDERS THAT THE NAMES OF THE MASTERS AND WIDOWS BE INCLUDED ON THE SHOP SIGNS AND BOARDS OF THEIR SHOPS—1738

Decision of the Police of May 22, 1738.

Homologating a Deliberation of the Community of Master Distillers, Merchants of Spirits, and all kinds of Liqueurs, which orders that the Masters and Widows of this Community, shall be required within one month to have their names added to their Shop Signs or Sign Boards, on the penalty of a fine of ten pounds for the benefit of the Brotherhood of the said Community.

To all who see these present Letters; Gabriel-Jérôme de Bullion, Lord Count of Eselimont, Lord of Wideville, Crespierres, Mareil, Montainville and other places, Marshal of the Camps and Armies of the King, his Counselor in all his Councils, Provost of Paris; Greetings... .

Seen ... the Request [submitted] to Us by the Jurors/Guards in charge of the Community of Master Distillers, Merchants of Spirits and all kinds of Liqueurs, in Paris, that We would be pleased to homologate the deliberation taken in their Community by the Masters of these, on January twenty-ninth, one thousand seven hundred and thirty-eight, transcribed at the top of the said Request, to be executed according to its form & content, in all its content. In doing so, that the said Masters and widows of their Community would be required within one month at the latest, to have their names inscribed on their signs or on the boards of their Shops, and this, on the penalty of such fine as We would be pleased to impose on their refusing to do so ... ;

We, with the consent of the Royal Prosecutor, say that the above-mentioned deliberation is and has been homologated, to be executed according to its form and content; we order that this Sentence will be, at the behest of the said Jurors present in charge, recorded in the registers of the said Community, printed, read, published & displayed in the Office of the City, and in all the usual places and crossroads of the City, Outskirts and suburbs of Paris, and wherever necessary, so that all the Masters and widows of the said Community do not claim cause of ignorance, and have to comply with it, on the penalty of a fine of ten pounds against each of the offenders, applicable for the benefit of the Community, which will be executed notwithstanding and without prejudice to the appeal; as witness to which We have sealed these Presents. This was done and given by the aforesaid Judge, on the day twenty-two of May one thousand seven hundred and thirty-eight. Collated. Signed, Debeauvais. Sealed, June 7 1738. Signed, Sauvage.

§2.13 PRIVILEGE FOR THE EXCLUSIVE DISTRIBUTION OF MINERAL WATERS, WHICH WERE TO BE DESIGNATED BY A CERTIFICATION MARK, ALONG WITH THEIR TRADEMARKS—1739

For a long period, the borders between food and health were practically inexistent. Treatises on secrets for medicines of the sixteenth and seventeenth century would commonly include food recipes. Mineral water was no exception. Mineral waters have been since early times considered as medicines, and thus their extraction and trade have been regulated with the health of people in the regulators' mind. The following text refers to the mandatory use of a certification mark (the coat of arms of François Chicoyneau, counselor to Louis XV and his first physician), so as to ensure customers of their quality and genuineness.

Exclusive privilege for selling and distributing mineral waters granted to Dr. Nicolas Bise, at Versailles, on April 1, 1739, registered at the offices of the administration (*Sénéchaussée*) of Marseille on April 24, 1739.

François Chicoyneau, counselor to the King in his state and private councils, His Majesty's first physician, Chancellor of the University of Medicine of Montpellier, general superintendent of Waters, baths and mineral and medicinal fountains of France, to all those who this letter will see, greeting. By virtue of the powers granted to our predecessors by letters patent of His Majesty dated September 7, one thousand seven hundred and eighteen, and those given in our favor on September 28, 1783, registered at the Great Council on September 12, 1719, and on December 7, 1783, well and duly sealed, which allow us to designate persons of probity and sufficient capacity, by patent signed by us and countersigned by our ordinary secretary, for carrying out the transport, sale and distribution of all mineral waters in all the cities of the Kingdom.

As we have been recently informed that in the city of Marseille several individuals without our permission have engaged in distributing various mineral Waters [in a manner] that results in abuses and disadvantages detrimental to the public, which would not happen if those mineral Waters were distributed and commercialized in the correct order and the required trust; therefore, we, by virtue of the mentioned powers, following King's orders, and wishing to enable that the Bourgeois and the inhabitants of the city of Marseille and its suburbs receive from the use of those Waters the help they can expect for, and for remedying the abuses that have occurred and which could be committed in the distribution of those Waters in the city of Marseille, and considering that Mr. Nicolas Bize, besides being well and duly embedded with good life, morals, Catholic, apostolic and Roman religion. For these reasons and others that have persuaded us to proceed in this manner, we have appointed and appoint, have provided and provide hereby Mr. Nicolas Bize, [with the authorization] to extract, load and transport the mineral and medicinal waters of Ballaruc, Vais and in general all other mineral Waters of France and foreign Waters as well, and sell and distribute them in the city and suburbs of Marseille and in its outskirts, to the exclusion of any other not provided with similar letters, allowing him to seize, in his name, by reason of these presents and the letters patent of His Majesty, Mineral waters that enter either by land or by sea in the city of Marseille or which will be given without being provided with an express and written permission signed by us and countersigned by our secretary and to impose on the offenders the fine of fifteen hundred pounds and costs, damages, and interest, in accordance with the letters patent of His Majesty, on the condition that Bize delivers to our hands the oath of loyalty of well and faithfully trading and distributing mineral Waters in the way it is below mentioned and has these letters registered along with the oaths at the Seneschalty (*Sénéchaussée*) of the city of Marseille in the event of a contravention and by appeal to the Great Council; we command the privileged to have published and displayed the whole together in the city of Marseille and its suburbs as well as in the various sources of the Kingdom these presents and the Regulation by us given and not to distribute mineral Waters other than in glass bottles and, for greater security with regard to the people who make use of the said Waters; we command the aforementioned privileged and his agents to have affixed the stamp of our arms that we have sent him, by the supervisors and keepers of the various sources from which the Waters will be extracted on the seal of the bottle caps.

We forbid the privileged from distributing any waters that have not been sealed with the appropriate seal for the said waters, the name of which is marked around the coat of arms. We decide that the privileged brings us the receipt of the said seals of the fountain keepers from each source to whom he will have sent them, however the affixing of our arms shall not prevent the owners of those mineral waters, if there is any, from affixing their own, this precaution aiming only at establishing public security and the privileged shall not be obliged to provide the public with bottles of mineral water sealed with our arms before three months after the publication of these presents... .

Today, fourth of April of the present year of 1739, we have received the oath of fidelity from Mr. Nicolas Bize for the exclusive privilege that we have granted him for the transport, sale, distribution, and commercialization of all mineral and medicinal

Waters of France and foreign. Done at Versailles on the day and place aforementioned. Chicoyneau, signed in the original.

Received the letters and Patent registered attached hereto in Marseille on April 25, 1739.

§2.14 A FRENCH COURT SETTLES A DISPUTE BETWEEN TWO MERCHANT GROCERS INVOLVING SIMILAR SIGNBOARDS—1745

We have already seen that in the eighteenth century, the law had already developed and settled on the protection of shop signs or signboards. The following text, an excerpt from a collection of French cases and opinions, has the particularity that the infringer was treated more severely than he might expect because he had been an apprentice of the aggravated party for many years (nearly twelve years). The seriousness of the offense was, therefore, greater, and he was ordered to leave his shop (neighboring that of the defendant, his former master) and move to a (considerable) distance of six streets.

By a judgment rendered on March 17, 1745, based on the conclusions of the attorney general d'Ormesson, the court confirmed a police sentence of September 11, 1744, which condemned Nicolas Guérin, merchant grocer, to change his signboard, which was almost identical to that of Mr. Brouet, also a grocer, his neighbor: Plaidoyeries, fol. 201-202, n° 22, listed 2776.

The same judgment orders that Mr. Guérin shall leave his shop, rue Dauphine, next Saint John's Day, and will withdraw to the distance of six streets. The cause of this last conviction is that Mr. Guérin had lived, as a boy, with Mr. Brouet, for nearly twelve years, and that he had established himself in the neighborhood of his former master, a very short time after leaving his service.

§2.15 THE PARLIAMENT OF NORMANDY OBLIGES FISHERMEN TO IMPRINT THEIR MARKS ON BARRELS USED TO SELL HERRINGS—1765

This is another regulation containing a provision on the marking of food containers. In this case, the obligation is confined to the merchants (fishermen, in the case), but we have seen before that some regulations were also addressed to the coopers, who were expected to make the barrels and other vessels of good quality and in the right dimensions.

Decision of the Parliament [of Normandy], serving as a Regulation for the Curing of Herring.

May 23, 1765

On the exposition made to the Court by the King's Attorney General, showing that the safety of Commerce and the preservation of the health of Citizens oblige him to protest against abuses introduced in the fishing, curing and dressing of Herrings which are done in Dieppe and other Ports of the Province.

...

XX. To facilitate the Buyer's claim against the Fishermen responsible for defective filling, either in terms of quality or quantity, all Boat Masters will be required, before starting their Fishing, to file with the Registrars of the Admiralty and of the Consular Jurisdiction, in the Ports where there is one, free of charge, a duplicate of the Mark with which they intend to print each of the barrels by them used for the said Fishing ...

§2.16 FAIRS AND EXHIBITIONS AND THEIR INTELLECTUAL PROPERTY BY-PRODUCT: INDUSTRIAL AWARDS (FOR PICKLES)—1862

The text that follows concerns industrial awards, which are business identifiers in their own right. Industrial awards are the product of their time. Between the late 1700s and the early 1900s, when the Industrial Revolution was pushing production and invention to unprecedented levels, entrepreneurs had several ways of advertising the excellence of their articles, such as the press, with its limited geographical coverage, and public events, such as theater and circus shows. Another effective means of advertisement was participation in regional, national, and international exhibitions. Exhibitions were organized with great care and expense. The most important ones would be preceded by the adoption of rules on the admission of exhibitors, the granting of awards and the selection of juries.

The medals and awards granted by certain well reputed exhibitions were coveted by entrepreneurs as powerful weapons of advertisement of their articles. Soon, those indications of excellency started being the object of abuses by dishonest competitors, who would falsely claim having received awards for their products. In some cases, those competitors had actually been distinguished, but for products different than those in regard of which they asserted the awards.

The text that follows illustrates the convoluted manner in which the institutions of intellectual property evolve. In spite of Great Britain's leading role in putting the Industrial Revolution in march and the seriousness of the country's efforts in organizing and participating in international exhibitions and fairs, English courts would at first hesitate in acknowledging industrial awards as signs of differentiation that were of protection. In the first case where the abuse of an award was alleged, the court refused to issue an order against the defendant, on the ground that the plaintiff had not been able to show an association by his customers between the designated products and the reference to the award. In other words, in the court's view, the award had not (yet) become a trademark. The court acknowledged the fraudulent intent of the defendant, but in the absence of harm, it would not interfere.

Just one year later the Parliament enacted the Exhibition Medals Act, 1863—26 § 27 Vict. c. 119, *which would overrule the conclusions of* Batty v. Hill.[63]

63. *See* Nuno Pires de Carvalho, FROM BABYLON TO THE SILICON VALLEY, *supra* note 10, at 137.

Batty v. Hill

28 May 1862

This was a motion to restrain the defendant Hill from placing on his goods the words "prize medal, 1862," and from in any manner representing or inducing persons to believe, or endeavouring so to do, that he had gained in respect of his goods a prize medal from the International Exhibition, 1862, and from in any other way infringing the plaintiff's trade mark, or depriving, &c., the plaintiff of the benefit of the grant of the medal to him.

The plaintiff, who was an oil and Italian warehouseman in the city, obtained in July last one of the two prize medals awarded by the jurors of the International Exhibition for "pickles and preserved fruits." The defendant, who had formerly been in the plaintiff's employment, but now carried on business as an "export oilman and confectioner," in Bury-street, Aldgate, had supplied the refreshment department at the exhibition with pickles, but had not exhibited and had not obtained a prize medal. In June last, before the awards were made, the defendant Hill stamped his labels with the words "prize medal, 1862," and also placed these words in a prominent form upon the packing goods, in which he exported pickles, &c., to Australia and elsewhere. Under these circumstances the plaintiff had filed his bill to restrain the use of the words "prize medal, 1862," alleging that the representation contained in these words was altogether false, and calculated and intended by the defendant to obtain for his goods the benefit of the reputation attached to the medal and to the plaintiff's goods, which are extensively known in this country and abroad in connection therewith. The plaintiff also alleged injury to himself from the use by the defendant of these words, and from his inducing persons (especially in the colonies where the facts as to the grant of medals were not so well known) to mistake his goods for those which were known in connection with the medal, and in particular for the plaintiff's goods... .

The plaintiff, in an affidavit in support of the motion, stated that the words "prize medal, 1862," had become his trade mark, and was an important means of identifying his goods, especially in the colonies and abroad; "and I believe that my goods have become and are extensively known and distinguished in the colonies and abroad, and also in this country, by means of and in connection with the said statement of the said medal; and I believe that my goods have acquired and now enjoy a great additional reputation by reason and means of such medal, especially by reason of my being (except Partridge) the only person who received such medal for pickles."

The defendant in his affidavit denied having imitated the plaintiff's label, as he had adopted the words "prize medal, 1862," for at least a month before the plaintiff had done so; showed the difference between the labels and trade marks, and denied that the plaintiff had acquired any greater reputation than himself for the manufacture and sale of mixed pickles. He also stated that his goods commanded higher prices than those of the plaintiff, and were in greater demand; so that any attempt to pass off his goods as those of the plaintiff would be no advantage, but a positive detriment... .

Wood, V.C., regretted that he could not interfere. Upon the balance of convenience and inconvenience, it had been rightly put, that by granting the injunction the defendant would only suffer the inconvenience of having to tell the truth. His principle would seem to have been, as was too often the case,

"Rem facias, rem, Si possis, recte, si non, quocunque modo rem;"

and he was admittedly guilty of a deliberate and bare-faced falsehood. But the case did not rest there. If it had turned upon a deliberate imitation of the plaintiff's trade marks, or there had been any previous attempt to do so, and the defendant had added to his imitation this falsehood, that would have been a very strong ingredient in the consideration of the whole case. But there was no appearance of an attempt to copy, the labels being totally different in shape, colour, and arrangement. The only thing, therefore, was this deliberate falsehood. The pleader had evidently felt the difficulty, and the bill halted between two views. If a person chose to put a false statement upon his goods, provided it did not interfere with the property of the person entitled to that which was falsely asserted by the other to belong to him, this Court could not interfere. Was it alleged that the plaintiff's goods had acquired such a reputation abroad by the term "prize medal," and were so connected with it that anyone asking for prize medal pickles would mean those manufactured by the plaintiff, and those only? If proved, that would have been a very important circumstance. But the averment in the plaintiff's affidavit (to which his Honour referred) did not go to that extent. Further than this, the defendant had taken this very immoral course of affixing the words "prize medal" to his goods, and issuing them under that title, before the plaintiff obtained his medal. Upon this ground it was very difficult for this Court to interfere in favour of the plaintiff. There was this further difficulty, that the plaintiff had erroneously made the other prize medalist, Partridge, a defendant to the suit. If the prize medal had become so identified with the plaintiff's goods as to constitute a trade-mark, then, on that theory, Partridge, or any other person, would have to be enjoined. His Honour, after referring to the case of Dent's business, where the firm became split into two upon the testator's death (see *Dent v. Turpin, Tucker v. Turpin*, 9 W. R. 548), and to the circumstance that for some articles—oil, for instance—no less than thirty or forty prize medals had been awarded, where no such exclusive right as had been claimed by the plaintiff could possibly be asserted, said that no order could be made upon the present motion, and the costs would be costs in the cause.

Figure 2.4 Success at international exhibitions at the end of the nineteenth and beginning of the twentieth centuries was seen as a decisive competitive factor. The figure shows three posters advertising chocolate, a baby feeding bottle and biscuits, with great emphasis on the medals received by the three products at exhibitions. Interestingly, the first poster (top left) says: "The numerous counterfeits of Chocolat-Menier oblige us to present here a drawing of the two sides of a tablet of real Chocolat-Menier (Fine yellow paper quality) the most requested because of its good quality and its low price. The color of the paper changes for other qualities, but the stamp and label are unchanged." In the bottom, on the two sides, the same sentence appears: "Any Chocolat-Menier bar must bear the trademark above."

§2.17 IN A CASE INVOLVING THE SALE OF FOODSTUFFS, THE NEW YORK SUPREME COURT SETS THE FOUNDATIONS FOR MODERN TRADEMARK LAW—1867

The text that follows is a landmark United States trademark case. In this case, the New York Supreme Court drew the line defining the boundaries of exclusivity in a distinctive sign, and the reasons for such boundaries.

Burnett v. Phalon

N. Y. Super. Ct. 22 Monthly L. R. (12 N. 5.) 220, June, 1867.

The plaintiffs being manufacturers of a hair-oil which they sold under the name of "Cocoaine" the defendants began to sell an oil of their own under the name of "Cocaine." Injunction granted to restrain the defendants from selling their oil under that name, or any other name imitated from the name applied by the plaintiffs to their oil, that name being held to be a valid trade-mark and the property of the plaintiff.

Per Pierrepont, J.: "Every man has a right to the reward of his skill, his energy, and his honest enterprise; and when he has appropriated, as his trade-mark, letters combined into a word before unknown, and has used that word, and has long published it to the world as his adopted trade-mark, he has acquired rights in it which the courts will protect."

§2.18 UNITED STATES AND ENGLISH COURTS ENFORCE RIGHTS IN TRADEMARKS AS A WAY OF ENSURING EXCLUSIVITY IN TRADE SECRET FOR FOOD RECIPES—1874, 1878, 1897

In general, trademarks are seen as tools that protect reputation. But in the United States their assignment is not accepted when made in gross, i.e., it is not accepted when the transfer of the sign is not linked to the making and selling of the designated product or service by the assignee. Using that principle, the first text shows a case involving a trademark whose exclusive effects have been asserted to preserve the ownership of a trade secret in the sense that, because the trademark assignee had not been communicated of the formula of the sauce, which had been kept in secrecy, the assignment had not occurred in reality.

The same association between the reputation expressed by a trademark and the possession of a secret recipe has also been acknowledged by British courts, as it will be shown in the second and third texts.

This sort of association can be of great importance for individual chefs and restaurants in protecting their identity against rivals. If we expand the element of the trademark into the notion of trade dress, that association becomes even more significant and gains efficacy. We will come back to this when we present a recent case of unfair competition involving the famous and prestigious restaurant Le Relais de l'Entrecôte, *in Geneva.*

§2.18.1 *Cotton v. Gillard*—1874

November 24, 1874. Jessel, M. R. 4A L. J. Ch. 90.

The defendant having invented a sauce which he called the "Licensed Victuallers' Relish" and placed in bottles labelled with a view of the Licensed Victuallers' Asylum, the sauce was sold at first by the defendant and his partners in business, and after the dissolution of partnership (on which event the recipes and formulas used by the defendant reverted to him) by the defendant's son, who also bought the interest of the defendant's former partners in the sauce. The son becoming bankrupt, his interest in the sauce was bought by the plaintiffs from his trustee in bankruptcy, but the defendant retained the secret recipe, and publicly announced his claim to the title and trade-mark.

Suit for an injunction to restrain the defendant from using the name and trade-mark. Injunction refused, on the ground that a trade-mark could not exist or be transferred in gross, and that the plaintiffs were not entitled to apply to an article of their own invention the name and mark appropriated to an article of the recipe, of which they were ignorant, the result of such a course of proceeding being to pass off a spurious article on the public as the genuine one of the defendant's invention.

§2.18.2 *Dence v. Mason*—1878

Dence v. Mason

Malins, V.C.—W. N. 1877, p. 23; 1878, p. 42; L. J. Notes of Cases, 1877, p. 33.

January 25, 1877; February 12, 1878.

The plaintiffs having recently acquired a provision dealer's business in Little Stanhope Street, Mayfair, carried on under the name of "Brand & Co.," and which name was placed on all the packets of essence of beef and other preparations made by the firm; F. Mason, who had been for many years in the employ of the plaintiff's predecessor in business, and who alleged that during that period he had been the discoverer of the essence of beef, left their service, and began to deal in the same class of goods, in partnership with one Brand as "Brand & Mason." In consequence of proceedings taken by the plaintiff, this name was changed to "Mason & Brand," and shortly afterwards Brand refused to continue in the partnership, or to permit the defendant to make use of his name, but the defendant nevertheless continued to trade under the name of "Mason & Brand," and to represent that he was the original maker of the article.

On motion by the plaintiffs for an injunction to restrain the defendant from infringing their rights, and again at the hearing of the action:

Held, (1) that during the continuance of the partnership between Mason and Brand it was impossible to prohibit entirely the use of the latter's name in the business; (2) but that after the retirement of Brand the defendant was not entitled to continue to use his name for the purpose of imitating the plaintiff's name and marks, although he was at liberty to manufacture the same article as the plaintiffs under his own name;

(3) that in arranging with the proprietor of a small shop in the same street as the plaintiffs for the exhibition on her shop-front of the words "Agent for Mason & Brand's Essence of Beef," the words "Agent for" being in small and the rest in large letters had acted in a manner intended and calculated to deceive; (4) that, supposing the defendant to have discovered the recipe of the essence of beef, which was not established, he was nevertheless not entitled to represent himself as the original maker, since whatever essence of beef he had made had been made by him as the servant of the plaintiffs or their predecessors, but that he might state that he had been in the plaintiffs' service, and had there learnt the recipe; (5) and that an injunction must be granted to restrain the defendant in the particulars above mentioned.

§2.18.3 *Powell v. The Birmingham Vinegar Brewery Company*—1897

In the House of Lords

Before Lord Halsbury, L.C., Lord Watson, Lord Herschell, Lord Shand, and Lord Davey.

July 2, 5, and 6, 1897

Powell v. The Birmingham Vinegar Brewery Company, Ltd.

The Syllabus and excerpts of the opinion follow:

Trade name.—Action for injunction to restrain passing off Defendant's sauce as Plaintiff's by the use of "Yorkshire Relish."—Fancy or descriptive name.—Difference in composition of sauces.—Probability of deception.—Position of owner of secret recipe.

The Plaintiff had for 34 years made a sauce according to a secret recipe, and sold the same in bottles bearing labels with the name "Yorkshire Relish" prominent thereon, and had very largely advertised "Yorkshire Relish." In 1884, the Plaintiff registered the words "Yorkshire Relish" as an old Trade Mark. In 1893, this Trade Mark was struck off the Register on a motion by the Defendant Company, and this decision was affirmed by the Court of Appeal and the House of Lords. In November 1893, the Defendant Company began to sell a sauce under the name of "Yorkshire Relish" in bottles, with a label bearing the words "Yorkshire Relish" in bottles, with a label bearing the words "Yorkshire Relish" prominently thereon, and also manufactured by "The Birmingham Vinegar Brewery Company, Ld.," and other particulars. The Plaintiff thereupon brought this action to restrain the Defendant Company from passing off their sauce as his by the use of the term "Yorkshire Relish." An interlocutory injunction was granted by Stirling, J., and the Court of Appeal. The Defendant Company then ceased using their original label, and sold their sauce with a label bearing the words "Holbrook's" in large letters, then "Yorkshire Relish" in smaller letters, and then "manufactured by the 'Birmingham Vinegar Brewery Company, Ld., successors to Holbrook and Co.," and other particulars. The Plaintiff gave notice of motion for sequestration of the Defendant Company's effects for contempt of Court in using this label, but this motion was arranged to stand over until the trial. At the trial, the Plaintiff adduced evidence to show that his sauce had been known alone as "Yorkshire Relish" for 34 years; that to the trade and the public "Yorkshire Relish" meant his sauce; that all attempts by other persons to use "Yorkshire Relish" had been stopped; that the Defendant Company's sauce was not made from the same recipe, and that it was sold to retail dealers at a less price than the Plaintiff's, and resold by them at the same price as the Plaintiff's; that the defendant Company's use of the name "Yorkshire Relish" was calculated to deceive the public, and that persons had actually been deceived both by the first and second label.

The Defendants adduced evidence that the sauces were almost the same in constitution, the difference, according to their evidence, not amounting to more than a pinch of salt; that the labels could not possibly be mistaken; and they contended that they were entitled to use the name "Yorkshire Relish" as descriptive of the article they sold, so long as their labels were fairly distinguishable from the Plaintiff's.

Held, by Stirling, J., that "Yorkshire Relish" was a fancy name, and not descriptive of the article; that on the Defendant Company's own evidence the sauces differed in composition; that the Defendant Company, by calling their sauce "Yorkshire Relish," were thereby representing it was the same thing as the sauce hitherto procured under that name, which was not the truth; that "Yorkshire Relish" to the trade denoted the Plaintiff's sauce, and that persons ordering "Yorkshire Relish," who knew the Plaintiff to be the manufacturer, would expect to get the Plaintiff's sauce, and persons who did not know the manufacturer's name would expect to get what they had previously had; that it was accordingly incumbent on the Defendant Company to take every precaution to guard against mistake; that the defendant Company's first label was likely to cause mistake, and that the second label, although much less objectionable, was likely to deceive in some cases.

The Defendants appealed.

Held, by the Court of Appeal, that "Yorkshire Relish" was not a descriptive name; that the Defendants, in effect, were, by the use of the name "Yorkshire Relish," passing off and enabling others to pass off the Defendants' goods as and for the Plaintiff's goods; and that the Plaintiff was entitled to an injunction, and not the less so because it might, in effect, give him a monopoly of the words "Yorkshire Relish."

The Defendants appealed to the House of Lords.

Held, that the appeal be dismissed, with costs.

The Lord Chancellor:

Now, my Lords, in this case we have a singular course of argument adopted. The gentleman who is complaining before your Lordships has invented a sauce which he calls by the name "Yorkshire Relish." He has invented it, and he has carried on the business of selling it for a great number of years. It is not denied that, under that name, it has a reputation in the market which has made it a popular thing, and that people buy it freely. Now, it is said, on behalf of the Defendants as a first proposition of fact, that there is no representation that what they sell is the manufacture of the original inventor by calling it "Yorkshire Relish," because it has become a well-known commercial article, and calling it by that name merely means that it is that thing. We have had a very long argument on that subject. My Lords, the first objection that can be advanced against that argument is, that it is not true. As a matter of fact, this is not the well-known article. The composition of the well-known commercial article is a secret. The exclusive manufacture of it is by the person who knows the secret, and nobody else can manufacture it because they do not know how it is made. It is obvious, therefore, that the first proposition of fact which is supposed to encounter the Plaintiff's right is displaced by the existing state of evidence. As to that, there really is no conflict in the evidence in this case. Upon the question of whether or not it is identical, I will not say that "Counsel has been darkened by many words," but, as a matter of fact, we have had a long disquisition as to the difficulties of knowing what exactly is thought of in the mind of a purchaser when he purchases a bottle of this "Yorkshire Relish." But without going into that interesting discussion, it is obviously true that the thing that is bought does not simply consist of something or another which has a particular taste. Its reputation may depend upon whether (as I think it has been suggested more than one in the course of the argument) it is wholesome, and whether it assimilates well with the digestion, and so on.

Without going through all these points, it is sufficient that the thing that the person who buys it desires to have is "Yorkshire Relish." ...

...

Lord Davey.—My Lords, when once the facts of this case are fully grasped, it does not appear to me to present any great difficulties for our decision. The Plaintiff, the Respondent in this appeal, has a secret recipe for making a sauce or relish for food which he and his predecessors in the trade have sold for 34 years under the name of "Yorkshire Relish." The Appellants' contention is, if I understand it rightly, that the Respondent has no monopoly of the manufacture, and that all the world may manufacture these goods if they can, and if they can succeed in manufacturing these goods, they are entitled to call them by the only name by which these goods can be described. Now, my Lords, I do not find it necessary to say much or anything as to the legal validity of the Appellants' argument as I have described it; but it falls in fact. The Appellants do not pretend that they have discovered the Respondent's secret, or that their goods are made according to the same recipe. All they say is that they are substantially identical with the Respondent's, or a "wonderful match." Other words are used indicating a close similarity between the two sauces; but it is not pretended that the Appellants' sauce is made of the same compounds or made in the same way, although it is said that it produces much the same result. The Appellants, therefore, are misrepresenting the character of their goods when they call them "Yorkshire Relish." They are not, in fact, "Yorkshire Relish," though I assume they closely resemble that compound.

...

My Lords, so long as the Respondent can succeed in keeping his secret he is, in fact, the sole manufacturer of "Yorkshire Relish" in the market, and the Appellants' act of selling their goods as "Yorkshire Relish," when they are not "Yorkshire Relish" as a fact, is at once a fraud upon the public, and at the same time amounts, in my opinion, to a representation that the goods are the goods of which the Respondent is the sole manufacturer... .

Figure 2.5 Left, the label used by the Plaintiff, inventor of the secret recipe. In the middle, the first label used by the Defendant, and which he was ordered by the Court, in a preliminary injunction, to stop using. Right, the second label used by the Defendant.

§2.19 A FRENCH COURT IDENTIFIES THE THREE REQUIREMENTS FOR THE PROTECTION OF SHOP SIGNS (SIGNBOARDS)—1901

Industrial property.—Shop sign.—Unfair competition.—Requirements.

In regard of shop signs, for there to be unfair competition, three conditions must be met; 1st whether they are similar industries; 2nd that there is a proximity of the two establishments; 3rd that confusion between them is possible for the public.

Aumelas v. Pacchiodo

Judgment

Whereas Mr. Aumelas operates a grocery store in Marseille, rue de la Darse, 71, bearing the name "Grande Epicerie Française"; that it also uses this name on his letterheads and its current and printed prices;

Whereas Mr. Aumelas, claiming to have an exclusive right to this sign, complains that Mr. Pacchiodo has given to a grocery store that he operates, cours Lieutaud, 176, the title of "Epicerie Française;" he claims that there is an usurpation of a sign likely to produce confusion in the public, and asks the Court to order the deletion of the words "Epicerie Française" from the shop sign and commercial papers of Mr. Pacchiodo, under penalty of a fine per day of delay; he also claims damages for the harm caused;

Whereas in terms of shop signs, for there to be unfair competition, three conditions must be met: 1st that they are similar industries; 2nd that there is a proximity of the two establishments; 3rd possible confusion for the public between the two establishments;

Whereas in this case the two businesses involved are similar, but the distance between them is such that there can be no possible confusion between the two grocery stores; that such confusion is all the more impossible as the sign is not identically the same, and that on the printed matter and headings of the two grocery stores, the term is followed by the name of each owner in the header and in very visible characters;

Whereas in these circumstances, by adopting the sign bearing the words "Epicerie Française", Mr. Pacchiodo did not commit any act of unfair competition; that these two establishments can subsequently continue to exist under the names adopted by their respective owners, without there being any prejudice to Mr. Aumelas;

For these reasons, the court dismisses Mr. Aumelas's allegations and orders him to pay the costs.

January 14, 1901.—Pres., Maître Sauze, judge.

§2.20 A BRITISH COURT SANCTIONS A COMPANY THAT HAD FRAUDULENTLY ADVERTISED IT HAD RECEIVED AWARDS AT EXHIBITIONS—1902

In Batty v. Hill *(supra §2.16), a British court refused to see an act of unfair competition in the fraudulent advertisement of the reception of awards at certain exhibitions. As noted in the text that introduced that opinion, just one year later, in 1863, Parliament enacted a law on the mandatory recognition of awards and business identifiers. The following text, although not mentioning that statute, shows the strong repulse by a court against a dried soup manufacturer who, in spite of winning a case in which he had been accused of counterfeiting a trademark, was not exempted from the corresponding costs, because of his blatant use of a reference to exhibition awards that his product had not earned.*

The Defendant appealed against that Decision and the Court of Appeal, in a judgment of April 3, 4, and 5, 1905, in spite of recognizing the abusive use of the references to untrue awards, decided that the lower court did not have judicial discretion to deprive the Defendant of the costs. This means that the Plaintiff should have complained of the false advertisement by the Defendant instead of invoking trademark counterfeiting.

In the High Court of Justice.—Chancery Division.

Before Mr. Justice Joyce.

December 11, 1903.

Before Mr. Justice Kekewitch.

June 16, 1904.

King & Co., Ld. V. Gilliard & Co., Ld.

Action for passing-off.—"Get-up."—Soup-packets in steel boxes.—Points of resemblance common to the trade.—Injunction refused.—Successful Defendant deprived of costs by reason of false statements as to medals and awards.

The Plaintiffs and their predecessors for upwards of fifteen years had made and sold three varieties of a special preparation of dried materials for soup in packets of certain size, shape, and printing, and these packets were put up in steel boxes of a peculiar kind. They claimed that their goods had become and were known and recognized and distinguished from all other prepared soups by means of their mode of packing and get-up. In 1903 the Defendants, who had been pickle manufacturers for many years, began to make and sell similar preparations of soup which were put up in a series of similar packets and boxes, and their name "Gilliard's" appeared where "Edwards'" appeared on the Plaintiffs' goods. The wrappers of the Defendants contained untrue statements as to medals and awards in the same position as accurate statements of the Plaintiffs.

Held—(1) that the get-up of the Plaintiffs' goods was not distinctive of goods of their manufacture; (2) that the Defendants' goods only resembled the Plaintiffs' in points common to the trade; (3) that no case of actual deception had been proved; (4) that the Defendants' goods were not calculated to deceive even an unwary purchases. The action was dismissed, but judgment was given for the Defendants without costs by reason of the untrue statements as to medals and awards made on their wrappers.

Per Kekewitch, J.—"Deception is not always the deception of the person who purchases, not proceeding from his or her mind, but it is the deception of the person who sells; and where you can see that the person who sells has been enabled by the resemblance of the goods to practice deception, that is quite as conclusive as any deception that is really entertained by the mind of the person buying."

The Plaintiffs in this action, *Frederick King & Co., Ld.*, and their predecessors, were old-established manufacturers of and dealers in provisions, and for upwards of fifteen years had made and sold a special preparation of dried materials for soup, which from the outset they designated "Edwards' Desiccated Soup." This preparation had for many years been made up, advertised, and sold in three varieties ... .- The three varieties were packed in small oblong rectangular packets of uniform size under colored wrappers, ... Each of the packets contained a reference to Exhibition Awards actually gained for the goods... .

...

The Defendants, *Gillard & Co., Ld.*, were sauce and pickle manufacturers, who, in September 1903, began to manufacture and introduced upon the market a dried soup preparation in the same three varieties ... The wrappers of the separate packets corresponded closely in the range of the three varieties with the corresponding preparations of the Plaintiffs, including the longitudinal and vertical printing, but the colorings were not the same, and the name "Gilliard's" appeared instead of the name "Edwards" in clear letters in front of the words "Desiccated Soup." The Defendants' wrappers included reference to Exhibition Awards for the soup preparations. The paper wrappers of the steel boxes were folded in the same way, and in the case of the white soup, were closely similar to those of the Plaintiffs'.

...

Kekewich, *J.*

...

Here I find the name distinct and I do not find any other circumstances calculated to deceive except such as are necessarily common to the trade... .

The result is, taking the broad view appealing to my own eyes, there is no case made out here; the evidence has made no case, and the Plaintiffs fail in my opinion to establish what they came here to establish, and the result is that there will be judgment for the Defendants.

Now I come to the question of costs, and upon that I think I am bound to make some strong observations. On a packet of *Gillard's* Desiccated Soup I find printed "Highest Award at the Coolgardie Exhibition, Western Australia, 1902," and again "Highest Award at another Exhibition," and "10 Gold Medals awarded." The Defendants only started this business last September, and the Coolgardie Exhibition was long before that. They never had these Awards and it is untrue. The answer made is: "It is customary to put upon goods sold by a firm notice of the awards which they have received in the shape of prizes in respect of other goods." Custom of course in the legal sense there cannot be. I suppose it is meant that it is usual to do that, and I am extremely sorry to hear that it is usual to be dishonest, for this is dishonest. There can be no possible object in putting this statement on goods of this kind, except to induce the purchaser to believe that these Awards have been granted for these particular goods, and, therefore, to enhance the value in the purchaser's eyes, and it is intended to be used of course as an advertisement. That seems to me distinct dishonestly, which the Court ought to reprobate. Therefore, in giving judgment for the Defendants I shall give it without costs.

Figure 2.6 Advertisement of Edward's Desiccated Soup, with reference to Exhibition Awards, published on the Belfast Street Directory, 1887.

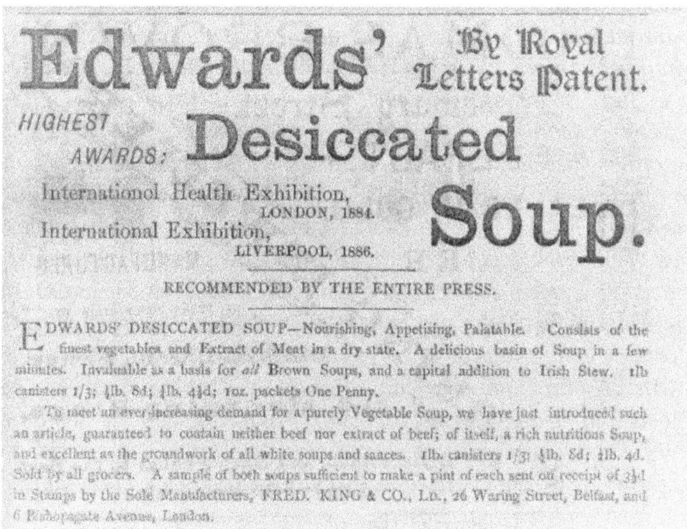

§2.21 THE SHAPE OF THE COCA-COLA BOTTLE: A DESIGN? A TRADEMARK? OR BOTH? OR NEITHER?—1915 ONWARD

The following texts illustrate the struggle of Coca-Cola, makers of one of the most ubiquitous soft drinks of modern times, to secure an important differentiating aspect of its business: the peculiar shape of the bottle that, more than one century ago, the Company had one of its suppliers to design (and patent). On its website (< www.coca-colacompany.com/about-us/history/the-history-of-the-coca-cola-contour-bottle >), the Company describes in detail how the idea appeared for the product to become more differentiated from competing products, whose manufacturers would not hesitate in imitating Coca-Cola's trademark. The Company started by inviting a number of glass bottle makers to create a new and unique bottle contour, which would contribute to identifying the soft drink in consumers' eyes. Once the winning design was chosen, it was patented (in 1915). The patent was extended for several years until it expired. Coca-Cola then needed to keep the design as its exclusive property and consequently applied for the registration of the bottle's contour as a trademark. The application was successful, and the trademark was registered in 1960 by the USPTO. Since then, the registration has been renewed.

But Coca-Cola is a global beverage, and as large as the internal U.S. market can be, the market for the soft drink goes much beyond national borders. So, the struggle for Coca-Cola to have that same contour registered in other countries started with mixed results. The center of the matter is not simply a question of the presence or absence of distinctiveness of the bottle's shape as a trademark (according to Article 6quinquies *of the Paris Convention, Contracting Parties may refuse the registration of trademarks registered in other Parties "when they are devoid of any distinctive character or consist exclusively of signs or indications which may serve, in trade, to designate the kind, quality, quantity, intended purpose, value, place of origin, of the goods, or the time of production, or have become customary in the current language or in the bona fide and established practices of the trade of the country where protection is claimed") but of whether it is acceptable that a certain design that had been previously patented and thus was destined to fall into the public domain after a certain period of exclusivity, can later be "recaptured" and given undetermined protection. This was the argument based on the 1986 decision of the House of Lords to reject the application of Coca-Cola, which wanted to convert its previous design (registered in the UK) into a trademark.*

The General Court of the European Union has also rejected Coca-Cola's application for its bottle as a three-dimensional trademark. Agreeing with the Board of the OHIM (formerly, the European Agency in charge of registering EU trademarks), the Court agreed that the bottle was not in itself sufficiently distinctive and that the applicant had failed to give clear evidence that consumers, across the whole territory of the Union, had learned to identify the shape as an indication of the beverage's source. Excerpts of this decision can be found below.

One could add the notion of functionality to this debate. In general, a container for a beverage is given a shape that makes it particularly adapted to the function it is expected to perform. We saw this at the very beginning of this chapter in relation to the shapes of amphorae in Classical Antiquity. What about the Coca-Cola bottle? Is it purely functional? One can say that the bottle has certain functional features, as it has been designed to improve the holding of it so that one can drink directly from it. But, on the other hand, the bottle has been designed from the beginning with the purpose of making it a distinctive feature of the product. Some—or most—of its features are arbitrary and, therefore, are inherently capable of distinctiveness. Eventually, the Coca-Cola bottle's contour should have been registered as a trademark from the very beginning.

Moreover, what about the consumer? It seems that this question has not been answered by the authorities that have denied the registrability of the Coca-Cola shape as a trademark. Once consumers start looking at the bottle and, through it, identify the product that is inside it, those consumers are facing a trademark. Indeed, Coca-Cola's bottle is not a product itself but an element of differentiation of the product. The fact that the Company eventually changed its mind and ceased to see the bottle shape as a mere design and started looking at it as a symbol that represents and identifies a product is not relevant from the standing point of public policy. After all, when it comes to assessing whether a given sign is a trademark or not, it is the opinion of consumers that matters.

Anyway, if Coca-Cola has had defeats, it has also obtained good results in registering its bottle as a trademark in countries like Japan and Thailand.

§2.21.1 The Shape of the Coca-Cola Bottle Is Patented in the United States—1915

United States Patent Office

Alexander Samuelson, of Terre Haute, Indiana, Assignor to Root Glass Company, of Terre Haute, Indiana

Design for a Bottle or Similar Article

48,160—Specification for Design—Patent November 16, 1915.

Application filed August 18, 1915. Serial No. 46,196—Term of patent 14 years.

To whom it may concern:

Be it known that I, Alexander Samuelson, a citizen of the United States, residing at Terre Haute, in county of Vigo and State of Indiana, have invented a new, original, and ornamental Design for Bottles or Similar Articles, of which the following is a specification, reference being had to the accompanying drawings, forming a part thereof.

Figure 1 is a perspective view of a bottle showing my design. **Figure** 2 is a bottom plan view of the same.

I claim:

The ornamental design for a bottle or similar article, as shown.

Alexander Samuelson.

Figure 2.7 Left: The designs that accompanied the specification of the Design Patent for the shape of the Coca-Cola bottle, in 1915. Right: The shape of the Coca-Cola bottle registered as a trademark in the United States, since 1959.

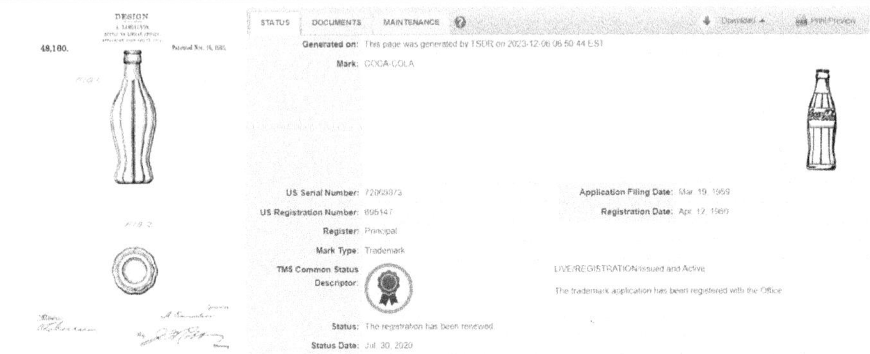

§2.21.2 The EU General Court Refuses the Registration of the Shape of the Coca-Cola Bottle as a Trademark—2016

Judgment of the General Court (Eighth Chamber)

February 24, 2016

(Community trade mark —Application for three-dimensional Community trade mark —Shape of a contour bottle without fluting —Absolute ground for refusal —No distinctive character —Article 7(1)(b) of Regulation (EC) No 207/2009 —No distinctive character acquired through use —Article 7(3) of Regulation No 207/2009)

In Case T-411/14,

***The Coca-Cola Company v. Office for Harmonisation in the Internal Market* (Trade Marks and Designs) (OHIM)**

Action brought against the decision of the Second Board of Appeal of OHIM of 27 March 2014 (Case R 540/2013-2), concerning proceedings for the registration as a Community trade mark of a three-dimensional sign consisting of the shape of a contour bottle,

Judgment

1. On 29 December 2011, the applicant, The Coca-Cola Company, filed an application for registration of a Community trade mark at the Office for Harmonisation in the Internal Market (Trade Marks and Designs) (OHIM), pursuant to Council Regulation (EC) No 207/2009 of 26 February 2009 on the Community trade mark (OJ 2009 L 78, p. 1).

2. Registration as a mark was sought for the three-dimensional sign reproduced below:

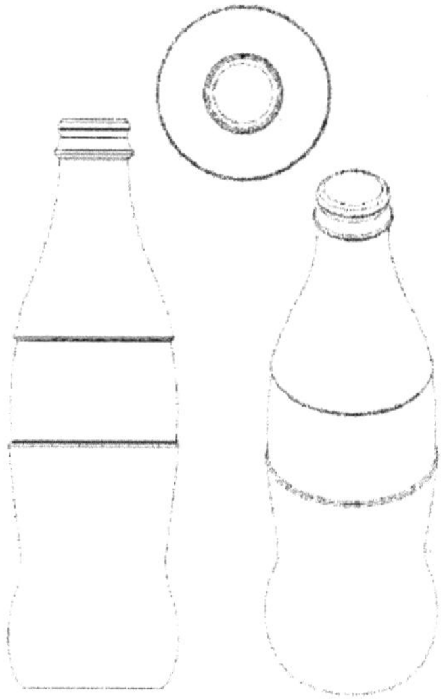

3. The goods in respect of which registration was sought are in Classes 6, 21 and 32 of the Nice Agreement concerning the International Classification of Goods and Services for the Purposes of the Registration of Marks of 15 June 1957, as revised and amended, and correspond, for each of those classes, to the following description:

> Class 6: Common metals and their alloys; metal building materials; ironmongery, small items of metal hardware; goods of common metal not included in other classes; metallic bottles
>
> Class 21: Household or kitchen utensils and containers; unworked or semi-worked glass (except glass used in building); glassware, porcelain and earthenware not included in other classes; glass and plastic bottles;
>
> Class 32: Beers; mineral and aerated waters and other non-alcoholic drinks; fruit drinks and fruit juices; syrups and other preparations for making beverages.

4. On 23 January 2012, the examiner informed the applicant that, on the basis of Article 7(1)(b) of Regulation No 207/2009, he had to refuse registration for some of the goods applied for ...

5. On 23 March 2012, the applicant informed OHIM that it wished to maintain its application for registration in respect of all the goods concerned, claiming that the sign for which registration was sought had acquired a distinctive character under Article 7(3) of Regulation No 207/2009... .

26. The applicant raises two pleas in law in support of its action. The first plea alleges infringement of Article 7(1)(b) of Regulation No 207/2009 and the second plea alleges infringement of Article 7(3) of that regulation.

First plea in law: infringement of Article 7(1)(b) of Regulation No 207/2009

27. The applicant criticizes the Board of Appeal for failing to take into account, in accordance with the case-law of the Court, the norms and customs of the sector. In that regard, the applicant claims that if the market for the goods concerned is crowded and competitive, that may act as a major incentive for some traders to design their product packaging so as to stand out from the crowd, draw the consumer in and enable retention of the particular shape for future purchase.

28. That is the case, according to the applicant, in the beverages sector. The applicant maintains that, whilst it is true that bottles may be simply functional, on account of having a long cylindrical section and a neck, many bottle shapes are sought to be designed so as to catch the eye of the consumer and act as distinctive signifiers of a particular trader. According to the applicant, consumers are therefore used to regarding a shape which departs from the usual shape of bottles as amounting to a trade mark. The applicant claims that such is the situation in the present case.

29. The applicant also submits that the Board of Appeal erred by failing to consider the mark applied for as a whole and the way its various features had been combined, with a view to comparing this with the usual shapes on the market... .

31. The applicant also claims that the Board of Appeal, in paragraph 35 of the contested decision, has made the same mistake as that found by the Court of Justice in the judgment of 20 October 2011 in *Freixenet v. OHIM* ... . It claims that the Board of Appeal was wrong to consider that, since the goods are also sold with a distinctive word mark, in the present case a label, that necessarily results in the shape of the product being devoid of any distinctive character. That approach is tantamount to finding that no shape can be distinctive, since no shape is ever sold without a word mark or other type of branding.

...

33. Under Article 7(1)(b) of Regulation No 207/2009, trade marks which are devoid of any distinctive character are not to be registered.

34. According to settled case-law, for a trade mark to possess distinctive character within the meaning of that provision, it must serve to identify the goods or services in respect of which registration is sought as originating from a particular undertaking, and thus to distinguish those goods from those of other undertakings ... .

35. That distinctive character must be assessed, first, by reference to the goods or services in respect of which registration has been applied for and, secondly, by reference to the perception of them by the relevant public, which consists of the consumers of those goods or services ... .

36. Also according to settled case-law, the criteria for assessing the distinctive character of three-dimensional trademarks consisting of the appearance of the goods themselves are no different from those applicable to other categories of trade mark ... .

37. However, when those criteria are applied, account must be taken of the fact that the perception of the average consumer is not necessarily the same in relation to

a three-dimensional mark consisting of the appearance of the goods themselves as it is in relation to a word or figurative mark consisting of a sign which is independent of the appearance of the goods it designates. Average consumers are not in the habit of making assumptions about the origin of goods on the basis of their shape or the shape of their packaging in the absence of any word or graphic element, and it could therefore prove more difficult to establish distinctive character in relation to such a three-dimensional mark than in relation to a word or figurative mark … .

38. More specifically, since liquid goods must of necessity be packaged for sale, the average consumer will perceive the packaging first and foremost simply as a form of container. A three-dimensional trade mark consisting of such a container is not distinctive unless it permits the average consumer of the goods concerned, who is reasonably well informed and reasonably observant and circumspect, to distinguish those goods from the goods of other undertakings without any detailed examination or comparison and without being required to pay particular attention … . .

39. In those circumstances, only a mark which departs significantly from the norms or customs of the sector and thereby fulfils its essential function of indicating origin is not devoid of any distinctive character for the purposes of Article 7(1)(b) of Regulation No 207/2009 … .

40. In the light of the foregoing, it is necessary to ascertain whether the mark applied for departs significantly from the norms and customs of the relevant sector.

41. First of all, it must be noted that it is not disputed that, as the Board of Appeal correctly found, the goods covered by the mark applied for are everyday consumer goods aimed at the general public. Furthermore, it must be found (and is not disputed, as noted in essence by the Board of Appeal) that, having regard to the fact that the goods at issue are intended for everyday consumption, the level of attention of the relevant public must be considered to be average.

42. According to the applicant's description, the mark applied for consists of a flat base which curves out to give a flared appearance; a tapered section which tapers inwards and extends up to the first horizontal line to form a trapezium-like shape; a bulging centerpiece which is inset slightly and has a vertical appearance, although the sides curve slightly to provide a smooth profile; and a top section which tapers upwards like a funnel and bulges slightly at the neck.

43. It follows that the mark applied for is a composite sign comprised of several features.

44. It is therefore necessary, for the purposes of appraising the distinctive character of the mark applied for, to consider it as a whole. Nevertheless, that is not incompatible with an examination of each of its individual features in turn … .

45. First, as regards the lower section of the mark applied for, it must be considered that that section of the bottle does not possess any characteristics that distinguish it from other bottles available on the market. It is well known that the lower sections of bottles can vary greatly. Nevertheless, such variations do not, generally, enable the average consumer to infer the commercial origin of the goods concerned.

46. Secondly, as regards the middle section of the mark applied for, it must likewise be considered that that section does not display any particular features which stand out from what is available on the market. As the Board of Appeal correctly

pointed out, the purpose, in normal trade practice, of that section of the mark applied for is to house a label stating the brand name, consumer information on ingredients, content volume, and the names of the manufacturer and the distributor. The fact that that section is slightly curved does not render the mark applied for distinctive in such a way as to enable consumers to infer its commercial origin.

47. Lastly, as regards the top section of the mark applied for, which consists in a funnel shape that bulges slightly at the neck, it is well known that the bottles available on the market feature characteristics which are more or less similar to those of the mark applied for. Indeed, the top section of a bottle usually comprises a funnel shape and a neck. It follows that, even though that feature is somewhat original, it cannot be regarded as departing significantly from the norms and customs of the sector.

48. Thus, the mark applied for is made up of a combination of elements, each of which is likely to be commonly used in the trade of the goods covered by the trade mark application and is therefore devoid of distinctive character in relation to those goods … .

49. It is clear from the case-law that the fact that a composite trade mark is made up only of features which are devoid of any distinctive character in relation to the goods concerned generally leads to the conclusion that that trade mark, taken as a whole, is devoid of distinctive character. That would not be the case only if concrete factors, such as the way in which the various features are combined, were to indicate that the composite trade mark, taken as a whole, is greater than the sum of its parts … .

50. There is no indication that such factors exist in the present case. The mark applied for is characterized by its shape which has a curved silhouette. However, that shape represents nothing more than the sum of the parts of the mark applied for, that is to say, a bottle like the majority of bottles on the market. Such a shape is indeed likely to be commonly used in the trade of the goods covered by the trade mark application. It follows that the manner in which the components of the composite trade mark at issue here are combined is not capable of giving it distinctive character either … .

51. The mark applied for is thus a mere variant of the shape and packaging of the goods concerned which will not enable the average consumer to distinguish the goods in question from those of other undertakings … .

52. The Board of Appeal therefore made no error in finding that the average consumer in the European Union would perceive the mark applied for, as a whole, merely as a variant of the shape and packaging of the goods for which registration of that mark is sought.

53. That conclusion cannot be challenged by arguing that the Board of Appeal failed to carry out a global assessment of the mark applied for. It is evident in particular from paragraph 27 of the contested decision that the Board of Appeal assessed the mark applied for having regard to the 'sum of the features displayed by the applicant's container'. The Board of Appeal also stated, in paragraph 35 of the contested decision, that 'an overall view of the characteristics cited by the applicant [did] not create a global impression capable of giving the sign applied for distinctive character'.

54. As regards the argument that the Board of Appeal failed to take into account the fact that the relevant sector is highly competitive and that it is common for players on such a market to try to make their products stand out by means of their packaging, it must be held that those circumstances do not suffice in themselves to render the mark

applied for distinctive. Moreover, the Board of Appeal did indeed consider the market conditions when carrying out the global assessment of the mark applied for. It is evident in particular from paragraph 28 of the contested decision that the Board of Appeal found that, owing to the fact that the degree of freedom when designing bottles is not very high, minimum variations of usual shapes cannot be registered as trademarks because the public will not regard them as an indicator of origin.

55. Lastly, the applicant's criticism of the Board of Appeal for stating in paragraph 35 of the contested decision, for the sake of completeness, that the end user will usually direct his attention more to the label on the goods or on their packaging and the name, image, or graphic design displayed thereon, than simply to the design of the packaging itself, is, in any event, not such as to call into question the findings of the Board of Appeal … . In the course of its assessment of the distinctive character of the mark applied for under Article 7(1)(b) of Regulation No 207/2009, the Board of Appeal examined the mark applied for taking account of all its relevant features, and substantiated its conclusion to the requisite legal standard on the basis of the mark applied for, namely the bare form of the contour bottle … .

56. It follows that the first plea must be dismissed as unfounded.

Second plea in law: infringement of Article 7(3) of Regulation No 207/2009

…

66. Under Article 7(3) of Regulation No 207/2009, the absolute grounds for refusal referred to in Article 7(1)(b), (c) and (d) of that regulation do not preclude the registration of a trade mark if it has become distinctive in relation to the goods or services for which registration is requested in consequence of the use which has been made of it. In the circumstances referred to in Article 7(3) of Regulation No 207/2009, the fact that the sign which constitutes the mark in question is actually perceived by the relevant section of the public as an indication of the commercial origin of goods or services is the result of the economic effort made by the trade mark applicant. That fact justifies putting aside the public-interest considerations underlying Article 7(1)(b), (c) and (d), which require that the marks referred to in those provisions may be freely used by all in order to avoid conceding an unjustified competitive advantage to a single trader … .

67. It is clear from that case-law that, in order to have the registration of a trade mark accepted under Article 7(3) of Regulation No 207/2009, the distinctive character acquired through the use of that trade mark must be demonstrated in the part of the European Union where it was devoid of any such character under Article 7(1)(b), (c) and (d) of that regulation. In addition, a mark must have become distinctive through use before the application for registration was filed … .

68. Furthermore, in the case of non-word marks, such as that under consideration in the present case, it may be assumed that the assessment of distinctiveness of their character will be the same throughout the European Union, unless there is concrete evidence to the contrary. Since, in the present case, the examination of the first plea in law and of the documents before the Court do not show that such evidence exists, it must be held that the absolute ground for refusal under Article 7(1)(b) of Regulation No 207/2009 in relation to the mark applied for applies throughout the European Union.

That mark must therefore have become distinctive through use throughout the European Union in order to be registrable under Article 7(3) of that regulation … .

69. It is also apparent from the case-law that, for a mark to have acquired distinctiveness through use, it is necessary that at least a significant proportion of the relevant public, by virtue of that mark, identifies the goods or services concerned as originating from a particular undertaking. However, the circumstances in which that requirement for acquisition of distinctive character through use may be regarded as satisfied cannot be established solely by reference to general, abstract data such as predetermined percentages … .

70. Furthermore, in assessing, in a particular case, whether a mark has become distinctive through use, account must be taken of factors such as the market share held by the mark; how intensive, geographically widespread and long-standing use of the mark has been; the significance of the investments by the undertaking to promote it; the proportion of the relevant class of persons who, because of the mark, identify the goods as originating from a particular undertaking and statements from chambers of commerce and industry or other trade and professional associations. If, on the basis of those factors, the relevant class of persons, or at least a significant proportion thereof, identifies goods as originating from a particular undertaking because of the mark, it must be concluded that the requirement for registering the mark laid down in Article 7(3) of Regulation No 207/2009 is satisfied … .

71. According to the case-law, the distinctive character of a mark, including distinctive character acquired through use, must also be assessed in relation to the goods or services in respect of which registration is applied for and in the light of the presumed perception of an average consumer of the category of goods or services in question, who is reasonably well informed and reasonably observant and circumspect … .

72. Lastly, it is apparent from the case-law that proof of distinctive character acquired through use cannot be furnished by the mere production of sales volumes and advertising material. Likewise, the mere fact that the sign has been used in the European Union for some time is also not sufficient to show that the public targeted by the goods in question perceives it as an indication of commercial origin … .

76. It must also be pointed out that, as noted by the applicant, a three-dimensional mark may, in certain circumstances, acquire distinctive character through use even if it is used in conjunction with a word mark or a figurative mark. It is sufficient that, in consequence of such use, the relevant class of persons actually perceive the goods or services, designated exclusively by the mark applied for, as originating from a given undertaking … . In that regard, the Court notes that, unlike the mark at issue in the judgment in *Nestlé* … the mark applied for is not clearly distinguishable from the mark it is alleged to be a part of. In the present case, it is not obvious, from the evidence provided by the applicant and particularly from the advertising material, whether the bottle that is shown in them is a representation of the contour bottle with fluting, or a representation of the mark applied for. The same is true as regards the items of evidence showing contour bottles without fluting. The mark applied for is not used in combination with the mark it is alleged to be a part of but absorbs that mark or, inversely, is itself absorbed by it to the extent that the silhouettes of the mark applied for and the mark it is alleged to be part of overlap. In those circumstances, it is necessary to ascertain whether the evidence

proves that, in the eyes of the relevant public, the mark applied for can be perceived as an indicator of origin of the goods at issue.

77. As regards the territory in which use must be demonstrated, it must be borne in mind that, under Article 1(2) of Regulation No 207/2009, the Community trade mark is to have a unitary character, which implies that it must have the same effects throughout the European Union. It follows from the unitary character of the Community trade mark that, in order to be accepted for registration, a sign must have distinctive character throughout the European Union. Accordingly, under Article 7(1)(b) of Regulation No 207/2009, read in conjunction with Article 7(2) thereof, a mark must be refused registration if it is devoid of distinctive character in part of the European Union and the part of the European Union referred to in Article 7(2) may be comprised of a single Member State … .

78. Article 7(3) of Regulation No 207/2009, which permits registration of signs which have acquired distinctive character through use, must be read in the light of that requirement. According to the case-law cited in paragraph 66 above, it must be established that a mark has acquired distinctive character through use throughout the territory in which it initially did not have such character. However, it would be unreasonable to require proof of acquisition of distinctive character through use, in accordance with the case-law cited in paragraphs 66 to 68, with regard to each individual Member State … .

79. It is therefore necessary to ascertain whether, in the light of the case-law referred to in paragraphs 66 to 68 above, the applicant has been able to establish that the sign in question had, before the application for registration was filed, acquired distinctive character through use throughout the European Union in respect of a significant part of the relevant public. To that end, the applicant was given the opportunity to submit before OHIM various types of evidence, including those set out in paragraph 58 above.

80. First, as regards the surveys relied on by the applicant, it must be held that the Board of Appeal was correct to find, in paragraph 51 of the contested decision, that those surveys were not capable of proving that the mark applied for had acquired distinctive character throughout the European Union in respect of a significant part of the relevant public. The surveys were conducted in 10 EU Member States, namely Denmark, Germany, Estonia, Greece, Spain, France, Italy, Poland, Portugal and the United Kingdom, even though the European Union had 27 Member States at the date on which the application for registration was lodged. It is true that the surveys in question concluded that the mark applied for had acquired a distinctive character in the 10 Member States where they were carried out, with the recognition rate being between 48% (Poland) and 79% (Spain); however, they did not establish that that was also the case in the other 17 Member States. The results of those surveys cannot be extrapolated to the 17 Member States in which no surveys were conducted. In that regard, it must be pointed out that, particularly in respect of the countries that became members of the European Union after 2004, the surveys provide almost no information regarding the perception of the relevant public in those Member States. Even though surveys were conducted in Poland and Estonia, there is no justification for extrapolating the conclusions relating to those two countries to the other states which became members

of the European Union after 2004. Furthermore, the applicant has not demonstrated that certain Member State markets covered by the surveys are comparable to others and that the results of those surveys could be extrapolated to them. It is not for the Court to make assumptions in that regard.

81. In the light of the foregoing, it must be concluded that the surveys are not sufficient, in themselves, to prove to the requisite standard that the mark applied for has acquired distinctive character through use, throughout the European Union, in respect of a significant part of the relevant public.

82. Secondly, as regards the investments which have been made in advertising and communication, it is clear from the case-law that the amount invested by the undertaking in promoting a mark may be taken into account for the purposes of considering whether that mark has acquired distinctive character through use. However, in the present case, it should be noted that the figures provided in that regard do not specifically relate to the mark applied for. According to the sworn statement made by the marketing counsel of the applicant's subsidiary in France, the figures provided refer only to the Coca-Cola, Coca-Cola Light and Coca-Cola Zero beverages without specifying which packaging is being referred to. Therefore, it is not possible to draw conclusions from those figures with regard to the relevant public's perception of the mark applied for.

83. Thirdly, as regards the sales figures and the advertising material, it must be pointed out, first of all, that they constitute only secondary evidence which may support, where relevant, direct evidence of distinctive character acquired through use, such as provided by the surveys submitted by the applicant.

84. The sales figures and advertising material as such do not show that the public targeted by the goods in question perceives the mark applied for as an indication of commercial origin. In respect of the Member States for which no survey has been conducted, proof of distinctive character acquired through use cannot, as a rule, be furnished by the mere production of sales figures and advertising material. That particularly applies in the circumstances of the present case since it is apparent that the sales figures provided are not reliable.

85. In that regard, even though there is no doubt that the sales figures prove that the applicant has sold large quantities of beverages throughout the European Union, it must be stated that they are, as the applicant acknowledged at the hearing, marred by inconsistencies. For instance, the sales figures for Belgium and Luxembourg, which together have a population of approximately 12 million, are almost the same as those for Germany, even though that country has a population of almost 80 million. Likewise, the sales figures for Lithuania, which has a population of approximately 3 million, are almost twice those for Poland, even though that country has a population of almost 38 million. Moreover, the sales figures for Latvia doubled between 2009 and 2010. The applicant confirmed those inconsistencies at the hearing but was not able to explain them. To conclude, it must be held that this evidence has no probative value.

...

88. As regards the items of evidence containing photos, articles and website extracts to prove that the mark applied for had been used in business communications, website publications, pop art, third party publications and other media, it must be held

that the Board of Appeal was correct to find that almost all those items did not relate to the mark applied for. It is not obvious, on the basis of those items, whether the bottle that is shown in them is a representation of the contour bottle with fluting, or a representation of the mark applied for. Likewise, the documentation regarding the history of the applicant's non-alcoholic beverages showed only images of the contour bottle with fluting. In addition, the Board of Appeal's finding that, for the most part, those documents contain images taken outside the European Union (particularly in the United States) or in unknown locations, must be upheld. Consequently, those documents also fail to establish that the mark applied for has acquired distinctive character in the European Union.

...

90. In the light of the foregoing, none of the items of evidence, considered in isolation, is sufficient to establish that the mark applied for has acquired distinctive character through use. Likewise, assessing all the items of evidence as a whole also fails to establish that such is the case. In that regard, it should be noted that the surveys covered only a part of the European Union and that the other items of evidence submitted by the applicant during the administrative proceedings before OHIM do not, in view of their imprecisions and inconsistencies, compensate for that deficiency.

91. In consequence, as none of the pleas put forward by the applicant is well-founded, the action must be dismissed in its entirety.

§2.22 FOR THE SAKE OF PUBLIC HEALTH, THE UNICEF AND THE WHO REQUIRE THE REDUCTION OF THE DISTINCTIVENESS OF TRADEMARKS CONCERNING BREAST-MILK SUBSTITUTES—1981

There is a general understanding that the more distinctive trademarks are, the better because distinctiveness ensures the differentiation of products and services by consumers and ensures fair competition. Merchants and manufacturers, grounded on robust trademark rights, are able to capture the reputation they have gained by serving consumers well with care, creativity, and acumen.

But trademarks may become symbols, thus acquiring meanings that go beyond the products or services they designate. Trademarks, especially when accompanied by effective advertisement, may awaken consumers' feelings of happiness, personal success, and well-being. Such symbolic meanings are frequently sought voluntarily by merchants, with the intention of increasing sales or obtaining the loyalty of customers—or both. In general, there is nothing wrong with this practice. But as regards some specific products, those symbolic meanings may be undesirable in the eyes of public authorities, to the extent they may lead to certain patterns of consumption that should be avoided.

One type of product whose trademarks may give rise to that sort of public concern is that of breast milk substitutes. The argument is that no product can replace breast milk completely. The policy of organizations such as the United Nations Children's Fund (UNICEF) and the World Health Organization (WHO) has been to encourage mothers to breastfeed their babies so that they do not fall into the temptation of feeding them with artificial substitutes. By this same token, the two organizations have expressed a special concern with the symbolism of certain trademarks that, when associated with breast milk substitutes, evoke feelings of good health, beauty and well-being for the babies who are fed with them. This concern is particularly strong in the context of poverty. Poor, uneducated mothers may fall more easily prey to the misguiding symbols of certain trademarks, especially those that are figurative, as far as the nutritive qualities of milk-substitutes are concerned.

In the late 1970s and early 1980s, the decision bodies of UNICEF and the WHO adopted rules restricting the ways manufacturers of breast-milk substitutes can brand those products. The main purpose of those rules, codified as the International Code of Marketing of Breast-milk Substitutes, is to avoid breast-milk substitutes being promoted as if they were effective substitutes of the natural product. As far as intellectual property is concerned, Articles 4.2 and 9.2 of the Code reduce the freedom of manufacturers in branding their products to the extent that they prohibit the use of certain nominative and figurative elements that may be understood as promoting the consumption of breast-milk substitutes. Consequently, the photos or designs of infants should not compose the trademarks that are printed on the packages of infant food formulae. The same applies to any other sort of designs that "idealize" the consumption of breast-milk substitutes, namely those that associate the consumption of those products with feelings of happiness, joy and well-being. As said, the idea is that many pregnant women in poor countries are illiterate, and to them, the face of a healthy, smiley baby, as well as figures depicting idealistic scenarios, such as rainbows, unicorns, chirping birds, are persuasive elements as to the effectively nurturing power of the branded substitutes.

A 2022 Status Report of the UNICEF on "Marketing of breast-milk substitutes National implementation of the *International Code*" *informs that:*

> *As of March 2022, a total of 144 (74%) of the 194 WHO Members States (countries) have adopted legal measures to implement at least some of the provisions in the Code. Of these, 32 countries have measures in place that are substantially aligned with the Code. This is seven more countries than reported in the 2020 report, reflecting the fact that most of the new legislation and regulations enacted in 2020-2021 were closely aligned with the Code. A further 41 countries have measures that are moderately aligned and 71 have included some provisions; while 50 have no legal measures at all.*[64]

The implementation of the Code gave rise in the 1990s to a dispute between the United States and the then U.S. company Gerber Products Co., on the one hand, and the government of Guatemala, on the other. Guatemala's Ministry of Health refused to register Gerber's infant formula as a substitute for breast milk because of its trademark, which, in its original configuration, includes the picture of a smiley baby's face (based on a drawing of Ann Cook Turner's face, when she was four months old). In view of the 1986 Guatemalan law and its implementing regulations (see the following texts), such trademark would need to be modified, with the elimination of the baby's picture. The

64. The Report is available at www.unicef.org/media/120071/file/Marketing%20of%20Breast-milk%20Substitutes%20Status%20Report%202022.pdf (accessed on December 6, 2023).

company refused to comply and sued—alleging, among other matters, that the government of Guatemala had expropriated its trademark. The United States' diplomacy intervened in its favor, and, in the end, the Supreme Court of Guatemala decided that Gerber's trademark was acceptable because the 1986 statute and its regulations only applied to formulae nationally manufactured, not to imported products. In the meantime, Gerber Company was acquired by Novartis, and later, Novartis sold it to Nestlé. So, today, Gerber's worldwide well-known trademark is part of the vast line of Nestlé's infant products.

The International Code of Marketing of Breast-milk Substitutes, in fact, inaugurated a movement toward the reduction of the differentiation of trademarks and other business identifiers for the sake of public health. In this particular case, the issue is the fear of promoting the consumption of breast-milk substitutes and, consequently, inducing the reduction of breast feeding.

This is not the place for debating the merits of this relatively new trend in health-related laws vis-à-vis trademark rights and the international treaties that protect them,[65] *but the total elimination of the distinctive features of trademarks seems exaggerated. Health authorities, instead of reducing the distinctive capacity of trademarks and their inducing power, should engage in campaigns of education of future mothers, which would be much more effective than simply attacking the brands, with the attendant effects of destroying product differentiation and reputation and reducing competition, a reduction which usually translates into higher prices.*

§2.22.1 International Code of Marketing of Breast-Milk Substitutes (Excerpts)

World Health Organization Geneva 1981

The Member States of the World Health Organization:

Affirming the right of every child and every pregnant and lactating woman to be adequately nourished, as a means of attaining and maintaining health;

Recognizing that infant malnutrition is part of the wider problems of lack of education, poverty, and social injustice; ...

Conscious that breast-feeding is an unequalled way of providing ideal food for the healthy growth and development of infants; that it forms a unique biological and emotional basis for the health of both mother and child; that the anti-infective properties of breast-milk help to protect infants against disease; and that there is an important relationship between breast-feeding and child-spacing; ...

Considering that, when mothers do not breast-feed, or only do so partially, there is a legitimate market for infant formula and for suitable ingredients from which to prepare it; that all these products should accordingly be made accessible to those who need them through commercial or non-commercial distribution systems; and that they

65. For an extensive discussion of the consistency of this sort of limitations in the acquisition and protection of trademark rights, *see* Nuno Pires de Carvalho, The TRIPS Regime of Trademarks and Designs, at 365 et seq. (4th ed., Wolters Kluwer, 2019).

should not be marketed or distributed in ways that may interfere with the protection and promotion of breast-feeding; …

Recognizing further that inappropriate feeding practices lead to infant malnutrition, morbidity and mortality in all countries, and that improper practices in the marketing of breast-milk substitutes and related products can contribute to these major public health problems; …

Considering that manufacturers and distributors of breast-milk substitutes have an important and constructive role to play in relation to infant feeding, and in the promotion of the aim of this Code and its proper implementation; …

Believing that, in the light of the foregoing considerations, and in view of the vulnerability of infants in the early months of life and the risks involved in inappropriate feeding practices, including the unnecessary and improper use of breast-milk substitutes, the marketing of breast-milk substitutes requires special treatment, which makes usual marketing practices unsuitable for these products;

Therefore:

The Member States hereby agree the following articles which are recommended as a basis for action.

Article 1. Aim of the Code

The aim of this Code is to contribute to the provision of safe and adequate nutrition for infants, by the protection and promotion of breast-feeding, and by ensuring the proper use of breast-milk substitutes, when these are necessary, on the basis of adequate information and through appropriate marketing and distribution.

Article 2. Scope of the Code

The Code applies to the marketing, and practices related thereto, of the following products: breast-milk substitutes, including infant formula; other milk products, foods and beverages, including bottle-fed complementary foods, when marketed or otherwise represented to be suitable, with or without modification, for use as a partial or total replacement of breast milk; feeding bottles and teats. It also applies to their quality and availability, and to information concerning their use.

Article 3. Definitions

For the purposes of this Code:

Breast-milk substitute means any food being marketed or otherwise presented as a partial or total replacement for breast milk, whether or not suitable for that purpose.

Complementary food means any food whether manufactured or locally prepared, suitable as a complement to breast milk or to infant formula, when either become insufficient to satisfy the nutritional requirements of the infant. Such food is also commonly called *weaning food* or *breast-milk supplement*.

Container means any form of packaging of products for sale as a normal retail unit, including wrappers… .

Infant formula means a breast-milk substitute formulated industrially in accordance with applicable Codex Alimentarius standards, to satisfy the normal nutritional requirements of infants up to between four and six months of age, and adapted to their physiological characteristics. Infant formula may also be prepared at home, in which case it is described as *home-prepared*... . *Marketing* means product promotion, distribution, selling, advertising, product public relations, and information services... .

Article 4. Information and education

... 4.2 Informational and educational materials, whether written, audio, or visual, dealing with the feeding of infants and intended to reach pregnant women and mothers of infants and young children, should include clear information on all the following points: ... Such materials should not use any pictures or text which may idealize the use of breast-milk substitutes... .

Article 9. Labelling

9.1 Labels should be designed to provide the necessary information about the appropriate use of the product, and so as not to discourage breast-feeding.

9.2 Manufacturers and distributors of infant formula should ensure that each container [h]as a clear, conspicuous, and easily readable and understandable message printed on it, or on a label which cannot readily become separated from it, in an appropriate language, which includes all the following points: ... Neither the container nor the label should have pictures of infants, nor should they have other pictures or text which may idealize the use of infant formula. They may, however, have graphics for easy identification of the product as a breast-milk substitute and for illustrating methods of preparation... .

§2.22.2 Guatemala's Law on the Marketing of Breast-Milk Substitutes (Excerpt)

Decree Law No. 66-83, of June 7, 1983

Article 1. Objectives and scope. The purpose of this law is to seek the establishment of the necessary measures to protect and promote breastfeeding, ensuring the proper use of breast-milk substitutes, based on appropriate information, when necessary, and the modalities of trade and distribution of the following products: breast milk substitutes, including infant formulae; other dairy products, foods and beverages, including complementary foods administered by baby-bottles, when marketed or when otherwise indicated that they can be used, with or without modification, to partially or totally replace breast-milk. It will also apply to the quality and availability of the related products and to the information on their use... .

§2.22.3 Guatemala's Regulation on the Marketing of Breast-Milk Substitutes (Excerpts)

Ministry of Public Health and Social Assistance

Governmental Agreement No. 841-87, September 30, 1987

Article 5. Informative, didactic, advertising material or any other intended to disseminate the feeding of infants, of children under two years of age, as well as [those addressed to] pregnant women or mothers of children under two years of age, shall include the following: ...

b) It will not carry photos, figures, sounds or messages [relating to] children under two years of age or other images that idealize the product or cause confusion about its properties;

...

Article 12. The label announcing breast milk substitutes or industrialized baby foods shall not contain information that may stimulate the use of the baby bottle. Moreover, it shall not contain messages like the following:

a) Images of infant children or others that may idealize the use of the baby bottle;
b) Legends, drawings or illustrations that directly or indirectly tend to create the conviction that the substitute food is equivalent or superior to breast milk... .

Figure 2.8 The worldwide well-known (and registered) Gerber trademark, which appears on the packages and labels of a large series of products destined for infants and toddlers.

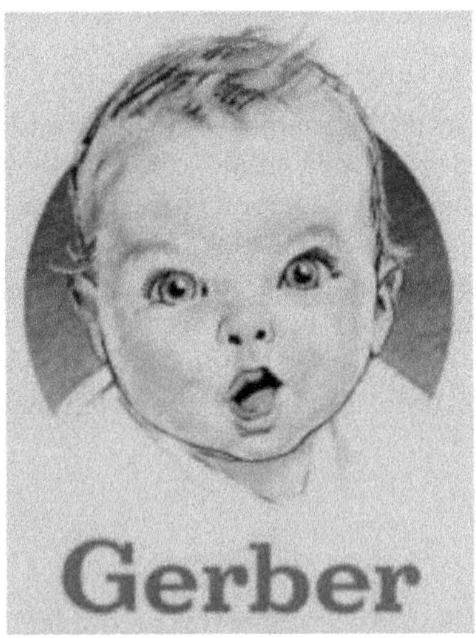

Figure 2.9 Examples of figures that are recurrent in baby milk formula. The teddy bear is perhaps the most recurrent motive, but other friendly animals also appear, as well as rainbows, colorful stars, and fanciful, dreamful figures, such as unicorns.

§2.23 IT IS NOT THE REGISTRATION THAT MAKES A TRADEMARK OUT OF A TERM BUT THE MANNER IT IS USED AND THE WAY CONSUMERS IDENTIFY IT—*MCDONALD'S CORP. V. MCBAGELS*, 1986

The opinion that is transcribed below (excerpts) is of great importance to the extent that it acknowledged that a small part of a nominative mark, such as a name's particle, is entitled to the same protection as the trademark itself, provided the consumers have learned to associate that small part with the mark owner and/or the products (or services) it refers to. In the case, it was the particle Mc that was in question. Even though McDonald's Corp. had never registered Mc as a trademark, the Court recognized the company's right to oppose the use of the particle by a company that did business in a related field (and into which McDonald's could someday extend its operations), given that the particle was associated to a generic name of a foodstuff (Mc + Bagel).

This opinion is remarkable in the sense that it has given preponderance to the sensitiveness of consumers in the field of fast-food restaurants (i.e., mostly unsophisticated consumers), who saw in the particle Mc an association with McDonald's—unless that particle was associated with a word that did not refer to food and/or restaurant services in general. For dilution to occur, Article 16.3 of the TRIPS Agreement requires, among other requirements, the use of a registered trademark by the infringer. Without mentioning that provision, the McDonald's case has introduced a sort of fine-tuning in that language: dilution may also be caused by the use of a portion of a registered trademark when that trademark is so strong that the mere use of that portion leads to the same result (in customers' minds) as if the whole trademark was being used.

This brings us to an interesting conclusion: trademarks may be more decisive in protecting prestige and reputation in some fields than in others because of the characteristics of the consumers involved. Those marks receive, therefore, more protection than those that are used in narrow, technological fields or in fields that involve sophisticated, highly informed customers. Trademarks of fast-food restaurants, foodstuffs for mass consumption, and fast fashion stores are examples of distinctive signs that call for stronger protection, meaning greater care against similarities, even if those similarities are less than plainly obvious, as in McBagel's case.

U.S. District Court for the Southern District of New York

McDonald's Corp. v. McBagel's, Inc.

649 F. Supp. 1268 (S.D.N.Y. 1986)

December 10, 1986

Opinion, Walker, District Judge:

Plaintiff McDonald's Corporation ("McDonald's") brings this action to enjoin the Defendants McBagel's, Inc. ("McBagel's") and its sole shareholder Ken McShea ("McShea") from using the name "McBAGEL'S" in connection with a bagel bakery and restaurant located in Fishkill, New York. McDonald's claims that defendants are violating both statutory and common law, and asserts causes of action for trademark infringement under 15 U.S.C. § 1114(1) (a); unfair competition under 15 U.S.C. § 1125(a); common law unfair competition; and dilution under New York General Business Law § 368-d (McKinney 1984).

...

McDonald's and Its Business

McDonald's, a Delaware Corporation with its principal place of business in Oak Brook, Illinois, is perhaps the largest fast food chain in the United States. Since its founding in the mid-1950s, McDonald's has grown steadily.

In 1955, Ray A. Kroc opened a single restaurant in Des Plaines, Illinois, a suburb of Chicago. Kroc originally licensed the right to use the name and mark "McDonald's" from Richard and Maurice McDonald, who had operated a restaurant under that name in San Bernadino, California. A few years later, Kroc paid the McDonald brothers several million dollars, purchasing rights to use the name McDonald's throughout the United States. During the past 30 years, McDonald's has expanded to include more than 9,000 restaurants throughout the world, 6,800 of which are located in the United States. In 1984, the company's revenues exceeded $2.5 billion.

McDonald's opened its first New York State restaurant in 1958, and since that time has established several hundred restaurants in New York. One of these is located in Fishkill, about one mile from the McBagel's bagel bakery and restaurant. The Fishkill McDonald's, like about 75 percent of McDonald's restaurants, is operated as an independent franchise and staffed by local residents.

In 1955, McDonald's original menu consisted of hamburgers, French fries, and milkshakes. Subsequently, McDonald's has experimented with, tested, and sold a wide variety of products in various stores throughout its system. For instance, in 1968, after market testing in California, McDonald's introduced a breakfast sandwich called the "EGG McMUFFIN" in restaurants across the United States. In 1979, McDonald's first experimented with a chicken dish called "CHICKEN McNUGGETS." These "McNuggets" are now served at most McDonald's restaurants.

Today, McDonald's restaurants offer a substantially uniform menu, including hamburgers, cheeseburgers, special sandwiches, French fried potatoes, chicken nuggets, fried fish sandwiches, shakes, hot pies, sundaes, cookies, soft drinks, and other beverages. Most McDonald's restaurants operating in the United States and Canada are also open during breakfast hours with a breakfast menu that includes the "EGG McMUFFIN" and "McMUFFIN" sandwiches, pancakes, and other breakfast fare. Still interested in expanding the range of food items available in McDonald's stores, the company frequently test markets new items and licensees often participate in or initiate such testing.

McDonald's has made a point of identifying each new product or service with the "Mc" or "Mac" prefix. Although McDonald's holds no trade or service mark registration for the "Mc" prefix standing alone, it has registered some thirty-four marks which contain "Mc" or "Mac". These registered marks represent a variety of food items and services.

McDonald's Advertising Efforts

McDonald's originally advertised only its name "McDonald's" and its well-known "ARCHES" trademark. In recent years, however, it has expanded this advertising to include other distinctive marks, which are derived from "McDonald's" and begin with "Mc" or use "Mac", such as "EGG McMUFFIN", "SAUSAGE McMUFFIN", "McD.L.T.", "BIG MAC", "RONALD McDONALD", and CHICKEN McNUGGETS". Today, all advertisements contain the mark "McDonald's" and the "ARCHES", and most include at least one of these specific products designated by the "Mc" or "Mac" formative.

McDonald's makes substantial investments in advertising and marketing the products designated by its trademarks and service marks. In fiscal year 1984, McDonald's and its licensees spent over $300 million in national and local television, radio, newspaper, magazine, billboard, and other advertising. In 1985, the McDonald's system increased its advertising expenditures to $350 million. In that year, in addition to its general advertising expenses, McDonald's spent $125 million on in-store promotions.

About ninety percent of this large annual advertising budget is used solely for television commercials. The Court received in evidence numerous storyboards proposed for McDonald's local and national television commercials, which usually run for from four to six weeks. As of the trial of this action, McDonald's was the nation's largest advertiser of any single good, service, or establishment, and the nation's fifth largest advertiser overall.

McBagel's, Its Business and Advertising

McBagel's, owned by defendant and sole shareholder Ken McShea, was incorporated in the State of New York in August of 1984. After completing construction in December

1984, McBagel's opened its bagel bakery and restaurant in a Fishkill, New York shopping center under the name "McBagel's".

Since its opening, McBagel's primarily has sold a variety of bagels baked each day on the premises. McBagel's menu includes bagels, salads, sandwich fillers such as egg salad, tuna fish, chicken salad, shrimp salad, as well as a wide variety of hot and cold sandwich meats. The restaurant also serves soft drinks, soup and breakfast items, such as eggs, buttered bagels, egg & ham on a bagel, and traditional breakfast beverages. The name "McBagel's" appears on a neon sign reading "McBagel's Bagel Bakery & Restaurant", which defendants have placed above the entrance to the store, and on cardboard signs serving as menus, which are located inside the restaurant. McBagel's has an advertising budget of between $10,000 and $15,000 a year, and has used "McBagel's" in flyers and coupons, weekly newspaper advertising, telephone directory ads and regularly-broadcast radio commercials. In the year prior to trial, McBagel's also received some free advertising from the coverage by various local newspapers, WCBS-TV in New York and INN News, of the instant dispute between McDonald's and McBagel's.

The Parties' Contentions

Plaintiff McDonald's objects to the defendant's use of the "Mc" prefix in conjunction with a generic food item, the bagel, to denote McBagel's services as a bagel bakery and restaurant. McDonald's first voiced it opposition to the restaurant's name in December 1984, and subsequently filed this action in October 1985. The essence of plaintiff's claim is that defendants' use of the phrase "McBagel's" creates confusion among customers as to whether McDonald's somehow sponsors or is otherwise associated with McBagel's.

McDonald's, however, has limited the scope of the trademark protection it requests in this action. McDonald's expressly stated at trial that it had no complaint with defendants' use of the "Mc" prefix in conjunction with a word unrelated to food products. Thus, plaintiff would not have objected had defendants called the bakery and restaurant "McSheagels," the name selected by the public, but never adopted by defendants, in a name contest run by defendants after they first learned of McDonald's opposition to their use of the name McBagel's.

McBagel's, on the other hand, broadly asserts that McDonald's extensive advertising program actually eliminates any possibility of confusion with McBagel's, since the McDonald's marks and every aspect of its distinctive business, including McDonald's unique restaurants and their golden arches, are so well known.

The Mark Which McDonald's Seeks To Protect

The mark for which McDonald's claims protection is the prefix or formative "Mc" when used with a generic food item, as in the numerous marks already registered by plaintiff ... . While it does not hold a registered mark in "Mc", plaintiff may claim protection for this prefix as a common component of a "family of marks." ... In other words, if McDonald's can demonstrate that it has established a "family of marks", the corporation may obtain trademark protection against one whose mark is thought to emanate from the same source as the plaintiff's family.

The existence *vel non* of a family of marks is a question of fact based on the distinctiveness of the common formative component and other factors, including the extent of the family's use, advertising, promotion, and its inclusion in a number of registered and unregistered marks owned by a single party. In this case, the Court has no hesitation in finding that McDonald's owns a "family of marks", both registered and unregistered, whose common characteristic is the use of "Mc" or "Mac" as a formative. The existence of this family is evidenced by the mark registrations noted above, as well as by credible testimony as to the massive advertising expenditures devoted by McDonald's to create recognition for marks beginning with "Mc" or using "Mac". Such marks include "MAYOR McCHEESE", "EGG McMUFFIN", "McCHICKEN", "McHAPPY DAY", "MINI MAC", "CHICKEN McNUGGETS", "McSNACK", "McMUFFIN" and "McD.L.T." The Court received in evidence more than one hundred McDonald's storyboards of television commercials, run nationally and locally between 1975 and 1986, a majority of which promoted one or more members of the "Mc" family of marks. In 1976, television commercials were aired that created an entire "Mc" language, using words such as "McFriendliest", "McGreatest", "McCleanest", "McClown", "McFavor-ite", in a campaign promoting the clown Ronald McDonald as McDonald's symbol. The Court also received evidence of extensive print advertising in national magazines, such as Time, Newsweek, and Sports billboard advertising, and promotional materials used in MacDonald's 6,800 United States outlets, all of which promoted the "Mc" formative.

In addition, the Court finds that there is substantial news media use of the "Mc" language in independently created articles about McDonald's. For example, a 1982 news article in Chicago describing a wedding held at a McDonald's restaurant is entitled: "Here Comes McBride." A nationally-syndicated political cartoon depicted President Reagan in front of a "McRonald's" sign on plaintiff's golden arches, posting the number 10 next to the words "million unemployed." Indeed, a news article about this very case was entitled "McDonald's McMakes Trouble for McBagel's."

Finally, there is substantial evidence, credited by this Court, that McDonald's has actively policed its rights in the "Mc" formative prior to defendant's use of the mark "McBagel's." Many agreements between McDonald's and other prospective "Mc" users, as well as a number of court or administrative orders, have resulted in prohibitions against the use of "Mc" formative marks, the assignment of marks using this formative to McDonald's, and other limitations on outside use of this formative.

Upon the totality of the record, it is clear that the "Mc" formative has been extensively used, promoted widely at great expense, made the subject of numerous federal registrations, and actively policed. McDonald's is thus able to use the family of marks denoted by the "Mc" formative as a basis for its trademark enforcement action in this case … .

I. Trademark infringement

Under the Lanham Act, section 32(1) (a), 15 U.S.C. § 1114(1) (a); as well as section 43(a), 15 U.S.C. § 1125(a), defendants are liable for infringement if their use of the name McBagel's is likely "to cause confusion, or to cause mistake or to deceive" typical consumers into believing some sponsorship, association, affiliation, connection or endorsement exists between McDonald's and defendants.

There is no precise formula for identifying the circumstances under which a trademark owner may enjoin a defendant's use of a similar mark on different products. The interests, however, which justify trademark protection in situations where plaintiff and defendant advertise non-identical products under similar names provide the framework for analyzing these problems. The three interests which justify this trademark protection are:

[F]irst, the senior user's interest in being able to enter a related field at some future time; second, his interest in protecting the good reputation associated with his mark from the possibility of being tarnished by inferior merchandise of the junior user; and third, the public's interest in not being misled by confusingly similar marks....

In protecting these interests, the consideration which the courts have repeatedly emphasized is "whether there is any likelihood that an appreciable number of ordinarily prudent purchasers are likely to be misled, or indeed simply confused, as to the source of the goods in question." ...

Moreover, it is clearly established in the Second Circuit that likelihood of confusion refers to confusion *of any type*, ... including confusion of source, sponsorship, affiliation, connection, or identification ... . As the Court of Appeals stated in *Dallas Cowboys Cheerleaders, Inc. v. Pussycat Cinema, Ltd.*, 604 F.2d 200, 204 (2d Cir. 1979):

> "In order to be confused a consumer need not believe that the owner of the mark actually produced the item and placed it on the market. The public's belief that the mark's owner sponsored or otherwise approved the use of the trademark satisfies the confusion requirement."

In reaching a conclusion as to whether a likelihood of confusion exists, a court must consider and weigh numerous equitable factors... .

In this case, McDonald's has cited advertising employed by defendants to attract customers to McBagel's as the cause of actual or potential confusion suffered by consumers. Plaintiff contends that the harm to it occurs when the hungry customer seeking a quick meal is drawn to McBagel's after seeing the name in the paper or hearing it on the radio and associating it, however fleetingly, with plaintiff's goods, services, sponsorship, or other support. With the issue thus presented, the Court must also consider whether a likelihood of confusion exists in light of the advertising efforts employed by the two companies.

Strength of the Mark

The first consideration to address is the strength of McDonald's mark "Mc". The strength of a mark is a function of its distinctiveness, or its tendency to identify the goods or services sold under the mark with a particular source ... . Arbitrary and fanciful marks which are non-descriptive and nongeneric are by their nature stronger trademarks because they are easily identified solely with a particular product or service ... . The category of such nongeneric, non-descriptive marks includes marks like "DIAL," "SANKA," and "PEPSI." When these marks are registered, they are accorded the highest degree of protection ... .

The defendants argue that the family of marks for which McDonald's seeks protection is weak because the marks, consisting of the "Mc" formative attached to food items such as pizza, chicken, and muffins, "fall into the category of generic, or at most descriptive" marks … . The Court disagrees. The "Mc" formative, standing alone, is arbitrary and fanciful and describes nothing. It does not lose that characteristic when added to a generic food term.

McDonald's massive advertising efforts and its determined promotion of marks using the "Mc" prefix also has enhanced the distinctiveness of the McDonald's family of marks. As found above, this advertising has resulted in the development of a "Mc" language by which plaintiff has become known. The strength of McDonald's marks is further established by a lengthy record of judgments, consent decrees, and agreements which prevent competitors from using the "Mc" formative. These court orders and agreements evidence a general recognition in the business community that the "Mc" formative stands as a symbol of McDonald's services and products… .

Finally, a survey conducted on plaintiff's behalf, which the Court credits, provides additional evidence of the strength of the "Mc" mark. A number of people who responded to the survey questionnaire believed that McDonald's sponsored or promoted McBagel's. When asked why they made this association 58 percent nationally and 68.8 percent in New York State gave as their reason the use of the "Mc" formative in the name McBagels.

Although the defendants introduced some evidence as proof of the weakness of the "Mc" family of marks, this Court attaches little weight to it. Defendants' evidence consists of the existence of third-party registrations of "Mc" or words prefixed by "Mc." … Although weakness of a family marks might be shown by use or promotion of the same mark by third parties, or by evidence that consumers identify the mark with products other than those of the owner seeking protection, the Court finds that defendants have produced no such evidence here. Mere registrations, by themselves, prove neither actual use of any of the marks registered by competitors, nor the degree of competitors' promotion of their marks through advertising. Finally, and most importantly, there is no evidence before this Court that consumers recognize such marks and identify them with a specific product that is not sponsored by McDonald's … .

In sum, the Court finds that defendant has established the strength of the "Mc" family of marks.

Similarity Between the Two Marks

Although defendants seem to agree that the name "McBagel's", taken in isolation, is similar to plaintiff's family of marks, they argue that similarity must be considered in the context in which the public becomes aware of the marks. Thus, it is argued, McDonald's advertising always uses the "Mc" formative together with other distinctive McDonald's marks, usually the name "McDonald's" together with the "ARCHES" that stand in front of the McDonald's restaurants. According to the defendants, this means that McDonald's advertising is dissimilar from McBagel's because McBagel's does not use any of these distinctive marks in its advertising. Also, defendants argue that they publicize the slogan "McBagel's" in ways that distinguish the two companies. The defendants advertise McBagel's three ways: in print, together with the term "Bagel Bakery and Restaurant"; on the radio, without any allusion to McDonald's; and at the restaurant's premises, which are different in design than McDonald's restaurants. Taken together, defendants assert, the distinctions between the two marks as advertised eliminates any possible similarity arising from the simultaneous use of "Mc" by McDonald's and McBagel's.

While some of these differences do exist, the Court is of the view that the balance on this point tips toward similarity and away from dissimilarity. Contrary to defendants' assertions, any distinctions between defendants' mark and plaintiff's family of marks are, in fact, considerably reduced by the style of defendants' advertising. First, in all of defendants' print advertising, the mark "McBagel's" is featured prominently and in larger print than the word "Bagel Bakery and Restaurant", and nothing printed eliminates the possibility that McDonald's does not sponsor the bagel establishment. Second, defendants' radio advertising features the name "McBagel's" without any emphasis on the bagel bakery. This advertising technique highlights the restaurant services, many of which McDonald's offers as well, and so any possible distinctions between the two marks as advertised become insignificant.

The Court also notes that the advertising mediums used by the parties are similar as are the cross-sections of the public reached by this advertising. Where advertising methods and the market targeted by two parties are different, there is less likelihood of consumer confusion. But in this case, both McDonald's and McBagel's use radio and print advertising, and both reach the same market in the Fishkill area. Neither directs its advertising to a different portion of the Fishkill population. Instead, both look to a market that includes, as one of plaintiff's witnesses testified, "anyone with a stomach."

While there are differences in restaurant trade dress, these differences in physical appearance, atmosphere and style of the restaurant establishments do not dispel any possible association between the two companies. McDonald's has both a history of expanding into new services and products and has restaurants that, like McBagel's, are not independent structures but instead are located in malls or buildings side-by-side with other retail establishments. Nor does the fact that McBagel's does not use other distinctive McDonald's marks, such as the golden arches, detract from the similarity between the two marks. The McBagel's customer could mistakenly believe that McDonald's has just entered the bagel market under a slightly different name and style.

Finally, McBagel's emphasis on trade dress distinctions misses the point that once confusing advertising has drawn the customer to McBagel's restaurant, he is more likely to make a purchase decision at McBagel's, whether or not trade dress distinctions at the restaurant appear, than if he had not been subjected to the advertising in the first place.

The Proximity of the Products

Defendants argue at length that because McBagel's is a bagel bakery as well as a restaurant, and because many of the food items sold at McBagel's are not sold at McDonald's restaurants, the products covered by the parties' marks are different. This argument founders on two separate grounds.

First, the McBagel's mark denotes restaurant services, albeit in addition to the bagel bakery, and it is these services that McDonald's also provides. The fact that these services are not precisely the same is immaterial. Indeed, it is because defendant's services may be somewhat different, and possibly (but not necessarily) inferior to those offered by plaintiff, that protection from likely confusion is available to the plaintiff.

Second, even if the Court were to accept the contention that the defendants' services are different but closely related to services offered by plaintiff, McDonald's is nevertheless entitled to protection... . In *Yale Electric Corp. v. Robertson*, 26 F.2d 972 (2d Cir. 1928), Judge Learned Hand wrote:

> However, it has of recent years been recognized that a merchant may have sufficient economic interest in the use of his mark outside the field of his own exploitation to justify interposition by a court. His mark is his authentic seal; by it he vouches for the goods which bear it; it carries his name for good or ill. If another uses it, he borrows the owner's reputation, whose quality no longer lies within his control. This is an injury, even though the borrower does not tarnish it, or divert any sales by its use; for a reputation, like a face, is the symbol of its possessor and creator, and another can use it only as a mask. And so it has come to be recognized that, unless the borrowers use is so foreign to the owners as to insure against any identification of the two, it is unlawful... . The disparity in quality between such wares and anything the ... [junior user] makes no longer counts... . The ... [senior user] need not permit another to attach to its good will the consequences of trade methods not its own.

More recently, in *King Research, Inc. v. Schulton, Inc.*, ... this Court held that:

> [T]he protection which the law affords to a mark holder is not confined to goods which have a strict functional interchangeability because the zone of protection may reach into the area of noncompeting goods.... [P]rotection extends to products which may be reasonably thought to originate from the same source.

See also Giant Food, Inc. v. Nation's Foodservice, Inc., ... (supermarket and fast food restaurant services sufficiently proximate).

Thus, a trademark owner is entitled to protection against the use of its mark not only on the particular product it markets, but also on a closely related product that consumers could reasonably believe is manufactured or sponsored by the first user. Even if McBagel's services are not exactly the same as McDonald's, the parties' businesses are so closely related, particularly given McDonald's history of expanding the range of its services, that any consumer could reasonably think that McDonald's sponsors McBagel's. The Court, therefore, finds that the products or services sold by McBagel's and McDonald's are sufficiently proximate to weigh heavily in favor of trademark protection for McDonald's and against McBagel's use of the "Mc" mark.

The Likelihood That McDonald's Will Bridge the Gap

As indicated above, there is a substantial common element in the services offered by both parties. Each sells food for take-out and for on-premises consumption. Moreover, to the extent that differences in the services offered do exist, substantial probative evidence established that McDonald's has an ongoing program to test new products, and has even sold bagels under this program. Thus, there is a distinct possibility that McDonald's will expand its product line to include bagels.

Actual Confusion

Although evidence of actual confusion is not essential to proving likelihood of confusion, ... any evidence of actual confusion is, of course, highly persuasive in proving the existence of its likelihood. This Court finds, upon considering the evidence, that substantial actual confusion has occurred.

McDonald's Fishkill area supervisor credibly testified that on several occasions he received inquiries as to whether McDonald's was going into the bagel business. While defendants argue that these inquiries may have been in jest, the fact that they occurred at all strongly suggests that a common association between plaintiff's and defendant's marks was established in the minds of the persons making inquiries.

Plaintiff also presented survey evidence. The survey, conducted over the phone, was in two parts. One obtained a national response and the other obtained a response in New York state. The survey was conducted randomly and included 504 persons nationally and 500 in New York... .

Thus, this Court finds that in this case both direct and survey evidence of actual confusion, while not conclusive on the issue of likelihood of confusion, is substantial and probative.

Defendant's Good Faith

This Court is persuaded by McDonald's showing that defendants have acted in less than good faith in using the "McBagel's" mark... .

The Quality of Defendant's Product

This factor reflects the law's recognition that a prior owner should not be subjected to the risk that the public perception of his product will suffer if it is associated with a product of inferior quality ... . However, product quality is not an essential element of the plaintiff's case, since plaintiff is entitled to the protection of his mark from all infringing users, regardless of the quality of the second user's product or service... .

While the parties dispute the superiority of each other's products and services, the Court need not resolve this question. Even if defendants had achieved superiority, the plaintiff is entitled to prevent them from using its mark, since to conclude otherwise would subject it to the "risk that the public's perception of his product will suffer" by Defendant's suggested comparison.

The Sophistication of Buyers

It is clear that the likelihood of confusion is increased where buyers are unsophisticated or make their purchasing decisions quickly and casually ... . In this case, both McDonald's and McBagel's cater to purchasers of fast food or other inexpensive restaurant services. Consumers in this market do not make sophisticated restaurant choices; they make these decisions quickly and casually. Under such circumstances, there is a greater likelihood of confusion between similar trademarks than would be the case if the goods or services were expensive or required buyer sophistication.

Conclusion as to Likelihood of Confusion

After considering all of the factors in *Polaroid Corp. v. Polarad Electronics Corp.*, ... and after a careful evaluation of all the evidence, this Court concludes that plaintiff has made a clear showing that a sufficient likelihood of confusion exists to warrant the injunction requested.

Balancing of the Hardships

This is not a case where an injunction will unfairly disadvantage a second user who has expended considerable sums to promote his trademark before the first user raised the issue of infringement. Here, McBagel's and McShea were on notice, even before the restaurant opened, and certainly before the expenditure of significant promotional sums, that McDonald's objected to the use of the name "McBagel's." Any subsequent investment was made with knowledge that use of the name "McBagel's" might have to be discontinued. Accordingly, defendants are in no position to complain of any hardship caused by the injunction. *Compare Chandon Champagne Corp. v. San Marino Wine Corp.*, 335 F.2d 531 (2d Cir. 1964).

...

In framing appropriate injunctive relief, the Court thus looks to McDonald's interests in its "Mc" mark and to defendant McShea's interest in the "Mc" part of his name. The Court concludes that McDonald's will be fully protected by prohibiting any use by the defendants of "Mc" solely in combination with a generic food item. This result will encompass the scope of McDonald's rights, while allowing defendant McShea to make a reasonable use of his name, including the name selected in his consumer competition: "McSheagels".

Although this Court finds that defendants have infringed plaintiff's trademark rights, this Court cannot conclude that McDonald's has a boundless monopoly on the "Mc" formative. McDonald's itself has acknowledged that had the defendants changed the name of their restaurant to "McSheagel's," this lawsuit would not have been necessary. The Court, however, recognizes that McDonald's has expended considerable effort and resources to create a public identification between its "Mc" family of marks and the goods and services it offers. The evidence presented in this case, discussed at length above, demonstrates that plaintiff has succeeded in this goal. Yet, this does not entitle McDonald's to rights that bear no relationship to the manner in which it has used the prefix "Mc" to promote its business.

McDonald's has used the "Mc" mark primarily to expand the food services it offers to consumers by presenting the "Mc" phrase in some combination with a generic food item. For instance, the phrase "McVEAL," which like the name "McBagel's" uses the "Mc" formative with a generic food name, would tend to evoke visions of the Golden Arches in the mind of the unsuspecting consumer. Although one can imagine more difficult examples involving the outer boundaries of plaintiff's trademark rights, resolution of such problems are not raised in the instant case. In this case, it is sufficient for the Court to conclude that plaintiff has established the legal right to exclusive use of the "Mc" formative with a generic food item, and defendant's name "McBagel's" violates this right.

Conclusion

Accordingly, McBagel's is enjoined from using the specific name "McBagel's" and any other name utilizing the phrase "Mc" in any combination with a generic food item. The parties are hereby ordered to submit an appropriate order for an injunction consistent with the Court's decision within five days from the date of this opinion.

So ordered.

§2.24 A US COURT HAS AN ENLIGHTENING DISCUSSION ON THE NOTION OF TRADE DRESS FOR A RESTAURANT—1987

In today's business of restauration, the chef's name and the location may be of great importance. But the trade dress is likewise of fundamental significance because it is that element that many times offers patrons the persuading element that makes them return to the restaurant. We will see next, in the case involving Le Relais de l'Entrecôte, *that the imitation of the trade dress was determinant in the court's decision to reinstate the Geneva restaurant in the enjoyment of its exclusive prestige. The text that follows is of great importance as it discusses in detail what may constitute a restaurant's trade dress. In some parts of the opinion, the court, without saying it explicitly, seems to accept the idea that a particular business model of a restaurant may be part of its trade dress. We will see that other courts have followed the same understanding, namely the US court of the Fuddrucker's case (see in the following text the reference to "style of service") and the Geneva Court of* Le Relais de l'Entrecôte *case (see §2.26). This means that, indirectly, trade dress could be called to protect innovative business models.*

U.S. Court of Appeals for the Ninth Circuit

826 F.2d 837 (9th Cir. 1987)

Argued and Submitted July 16, 1986. Decided August 24, 1987

Fuddruckers, Inc. and Freddie Fuddruckers Franchising, Inc., v. Doc's B.R. Others, Inc.

Fletcher, Circuit Judge:

Fuddruckers, Inc., appeals from a jury verdict denying Fuddruckers' claims for trade dress infringement and unfair competition under section 43(a) of the Lanham Act, 15 U.S.C. § 1125(a) (1982). We reverse and remand for a new trial.

Background

Fuddruckers operates a national chain of "upscale" hamburger restaurants. The restaurants serve hamburgers, hot dogs, wurst, steak, French fries, beans and jalapeños. Although its restaurants do not all have precisely the same decor, the majority of them share a great many design elements. Fuddruckers claims these design elements as its trade dress. Fuddruckers alleges that defendants Doc's B.R. Others, Inc., Douglas, Mary, Gerald, and Steven Koppes are using its trade dress wrongfully in their restaurant, Doc's B.R. Others.

The heart of Fuddruckers' design concept is that its food preparation areas are visible to its customers. In particular, the areas in which it bakes its buns, cuts its meat, and grills the food it serves are open to the public. Various food items are presented in glassed-in display cases. Another important facet of Fuddruckers' claimed trade dress is that various food items are kept in bulk in the main part of the establishment in both packaged and unpackaged forms. There are stacked cartons of beer, produce and other items in the patron areas. Iced tea is served out of a light-colored plastic 32-gallon container that looks suspiciously like a garbage can. Patrons can help themselves to melted cheese, melted cheese with jalapenos, and sauerkraut out of large, black, round crocks. Onions, lettuce, and tomatoes are available precut at a large condiment bar that also features cartons and bags of the same items uncut. Salt and pepper are served in institutional-sized containers.

The most important non-food design elements at Fuddruckers are ubiquitous two-by-four white tiles found on the walls, the bar, and the counters. Fuddruckers also uses neon signs, many mirrors, brown and white checked flooring and tablecloths, brown director's chairs, and exterior yellow awnings.

In addition to these visual items, Fuddruckers uses a number of devices that it considers part of its trade dress. Its bakery area is labeled "Mother Fuddruckers." It uses its ceiling music system to call patrons when their orders are ready. It offers a restaurant "newspaper" to patrons at each table. Customers are allowed to buy bones for their dogs, with the proceeds going to animal shelters. There are several other less important design elements and devices that Fuddruckers also claims to be part of its trade dress.

In late 1982 or early 1983, Gerald and Doug Koppes became interested in operating a Fuddruckers franchise in Los Angeles, Denver, or Phoenix. At that time, Fuddruckers owned two restaurants in Texas and had several franchises operating outside Texas. For reasons that are disputed, the Koppes did not obtain a franchise. They then became interested in opening a restaurant of their own.

Fuddruckers announced in mid-June of 1983 that it had found a franchisee for New Mexico, Arizona and Colorado, and that it planned to have the first restaurant opened in Phoenix in December of that year. About the same time, with knowledge of Fuddruckers' intentions, the Koppes began plans for their own restaurant in Phoenix. There was evidence presented from which the jury could conclude that they developed the plan for their restaurant with Fuddruckers as a model. The Koppes opened Doc's B.R. Others restaurant near Phoenix in early December, 1983. The Phoenix Fuddruckers opened a short time later.

Doc's has many interior features like those of Fuddruckers... . The major food preparation areas are exposed and look similar to Fuddruckers'. The same shape and brand of ubiquitous white tile can be found around Doc's. Doc's also uses neon, mirrors, and director's chairs. Doc's has a newspaper like Fuddruckers, calls its bakery, "Mother Other's," and sold dog bones for a time. A number of witnesses testified that they thought the restaurants looked very much alike and the photographs in evidence support this conclusion.

Pointing to the similarities between the restaurants and the Koppes' awareness of and interest in Fuddruckers during the planning stages of Doc's, Fuddruckers claims that the Koppes intentionally copied its design, concept and style. On the other hand, the Koppes denied that they copied Fuddruckers, and there is corroborating evidence to back them up.

Doc's witnesses pointed out that there are differences between the restaurants. Doc's name is prominently displayed on its directors' chairs and elsewhere in the restaurant. Its checked floor is black and white rather than brown and white, and the checks are a different size. There is a very large mural and a large screen TV at Doc's which have no equivalent at Fuddruckers. Doc's' expert testified that the overall look of the restaurant was different from a Fuddruckers and that there is "more going on at eye level" in Doc's.

There was evidence at trial that after Fuddruckers opened, consumers were confused by the similarity between the restaurants. For example, a Fuddruckers employee testified that Fuddruckers personnel received more than one hundred questions a week about whether Doc's and Fuddruckers had common owners. Doc's' witnesses claimed to have heard a few similar questions or comments, although they believed that more people thought Doc's was like a different restaurant altogether, Flakey Jake's.

About six months after Fuddruckers opened in Phoenix, Fuddruckers brought this suit alleging infringement of its trade dress and seeking damages and injunctive relief. The jury rendered a verdict for Doc's, finding specifically that there was no likelihood of confusion between the two establishments and that Fuddruckers' trade dress had not acquired secondary meaning in the Phoenix area at the time Doc's opened. The district court awarded attorney's fees to Doc's, on the theory that Fuddruckers' suit was merely an anti-competitive ploy .... Fuddruckers timely appeals.

The parties make a variety of claims on appeal relating to the sufficiency of the evidence to support the verdict, the adequacy of the jury instructions, and specific evidentiary rulings. As will become apparent, the case turns on the adequacy and correctness of the instructions that the court gave to the jury to define the elements of Fuddruckers' trade dress infringement action. We therefore must examine those elements in some detail.

Discussion

Section 43(a) of the Lanham Act provides a remedy for a broad range of deceptive marking, packaging and marketing of goods or services in commerce... . A plaintiff seeking to recover for trade dress infringement under section 43(a) must show that its trade dress is protectable and that defendant's use of the same or similar trade dress is likely to confuse consumers... . .

Prior trade dress infringement cases in this circuit have involved the copying of products' packages and displays... . The test we have articulated for trade dress infringement "is whether there is a likelihood of confusion resulting from the total effect of the defendant's package on the eye and mind of an ordinary purchaser." ... This case expands the boundaries of trade dress infringement, seeking protection for a combination of elements employed in the marketing of restaurant services. Fuddruckers' suit seeks protection for more than the visual elements of a package or restaurant exterior. Fuddruckers claims that it is entitled to protection of the total visual image of its restaurant services under the rubric of trade dress protection. Other courts have adopted expansive definitions of trade dress, ... We agree with Fuddruckers that a restaurant's decor, menu, layout and style of service may acquire the source-distinguishing aspects of protectable trade dress such that their imitation is likely to cause consumer confusion... . .

We also conclude that the elements of a claim for this variety of trade dress infringement should be the same elements we have required for protection in our prior cases. Other courts that have analyzed trade dress infringement claims involving claimed similarities between restaurant decor and image have used the analysis developed in more typical trade dress cases... . Under this analysis, trade dress may be protected if it is nonfunctional and has acquired secondary meaning and if its imitation creates a likelihood of consumer confusion... . We have applied this trade dress analysis in cases involving imitation of packaging, and overall product configuration, ... and we agree with the other courts that have confronted the issue that it is the appropriate analysis to apply to a case such as this one. We must, thus, examine the trial court's instructions on the issues of functionality, secondary meaning, and likelihood of confusion.

A product feature is functional if it is essential to the product's use or if it affects the cost or quality of the article... .

The trial court did not instruct the jury on functionality. Both Fuddruckers and Doc's argue that the trial court's omission of an instruction on functionality was error. Doc's asserts that the absence of such an instruction effectively directed a verdict that Fuddruckers' trade dress was nonfunctional. Fuddruckers claims that there was so much discussion of functionality at trial that the jury might have assumed that its trade dress was functional.

Fuddruckers does not dispute that its trade dress includes functional elements. That, however, does not end the inquiry. We examine trade dress as a whole to determine its functionality, ... functional elements that are separately unprotectable can be protected together as part of a trade dress... . In other words, our inquiry is not addressed to whether individual elements of the trade dress fall within the definition of functional, but to whether the whole collection of elements taken together are functional. A restaurant claiming protection for its trade dress "claims as its mark the particular combination and arrangement of design elements" that distinguish it from others using the same concept. Id. at 76. A restaurateur cannot prevent others from using any particular color or feature, but can protect a combination of visual elements "that, taken together, ... may create a distinctive visual impression." ...

It is not sufficient that Fuddruckers' trade dress be nonfunctional. In order to qualify for protection under section 43(a) it must also have acquired secondary meaning. The trade dress of a product or service attains secondary meaning when the purchasing public associates the dress with a particular source... . The court instructed the jury that for its trade dress to be protectable, Fuddruckers had to prove that it had secondary meaning in the Phoenix area at the time Doc's opened. The jury found that it did not.

Fuddruckers claims that it did not have to prove secondary meaning because its trade dress is inherently distinctive and because Doc's intentionally jumped into its zone of expansion. It also claims that the secondary meaning instruction did not allow the jury to give enough weight to intentional copying.

Fuddruckers' argument that a showing of secondary meaning should be unnecessary in connection with an inherently distinctive trade dress has some intuitive appeal. Secondary meaning is, after all, probative of whether claimed trade dress is distinctive, in the trade mark sense of signifying the source of a product or service to an appreciable portion of the purchasing public... . If, as Fuddruckers argues, its claimed trade dress is inherently distinctive, the further requirement of a showing of secondary meaning should be superfluous. Fuddruckers cites cases from other courts that have held that an inherently distinctive trade dress may be protected without proof of secondary meaning... . Furnishing apparent support for Fuddruckers position is the fact that inherently distinctive service marks may be registered without evidence of secondary meaning. See 15 U.S.C. §§ 1052, 1053.

Fuddruckers has not registered its "inherently distinctive" trade dress as a service mark, as the statute may permit. It nonetheless seeks to avail itself of the benefits, including nationwide priority, see 15 U.S.C. § 1115, that registration would have secured to it.

Fuddruckers, moreover, has not offered this court a definition of what "inherently distinctive" in the trademark sense might mean in the absence of secondary meaning. If purchasers do not, in fact, associate Fuddruckers's trade dress with a source of restaurant services, then it is difficult to see how that trade dress distinguishes Fuddruckers' service from the services of others... . We need not, in any event, decide whether it is ever appropriate to protect an inherently distinctive trade dress without proof of secondary meaning. It is clear to us that such an approach is not called for here. We have reviewed the record carefully, and conclude that the evidence Fuddruckers presented would not have supported a finding that its trade dress is inherently distinctive. Fuddruckers claims trade dress protection for the impression created by a collection of common or functional elements of restaurant decor. Such an overall impression may receive protection, but it is simply not the sort of arbitrary or uncommon trade dress that might qualify as inherently distinctive... .

Fuddruckers' second concern with the secondary meaning instructions is that the court required that it show secondary meaning in Phoenix, prior to Doc's opening its restaurant. We agree with Fuddruckers that the instruction was unduly narrow. The source of the geographical and time limitations the court included in its instructions is a line of cases defining rights in unregistered trademarks between geographically remote users who adopted similar marks in good faith and without knowledge of each other's use... . The rule that developed in those cases permits junior users to continue to use a mark adopted in good faith in the geographical area of the junior user's actual use. The rule has only limited applicability to services such as hotels or restaurants, because their customers "are ambulatory and on the move back and forth across the nation." ...

Doc's concedes that it was aware of Fuddruckers' operations, and familiar with its trade dress, so the good faith junior user line of cases does not apply here. Under these circumstances, we see no justification for requiring Fuddruckers to prove that secondary meaning developed in the Phoenix area before Doc's opened its restaurant. Fuddruckers is a national restaurant chain, and restaurant customers travel. Fuddruckers should be permitted to show that its trade dress had acquired secondary meaning among some substantial portion of consumers nationally... .

The court instructed the jury that it could "consider" a finding that Doc's had copied Fuddruckers' trade dress on the issue whether the dress had acquired secondary meaning. Fuddruckers claims that the instruction did not go far enough. We disagree.

Our cases recognize that evidence of deliberate copying is relevant to a determination of secondary meaning... . Indeed, in appropriate circumstances, deliberate copying may suffice to support an inference of secondary meaning... . The trial court's instruction permitted, but did not require, the jury to infer the existence of secondary meaning from a finding of intentional copying. Fuddruckers would have us go further, and hold that evidence of deliberate copying shifts the burden of proof on the issue of secondary meaning. We decline to so hold. Competitors may intentionally copy product features for a variety of reasons. They may, for example, choose to copy wholly functional features that they perceive as lacking any secondary meaning because of those features' intrinsic economic benefits... .

Even if Fuddruckers trade dress is protectable, in order to constitute an infringement, Doc's use may be likely to confuse consumers. The trial court asked the jury to determine whether there was "a likelihood that consumers would believe that Doc's was owned and franchised by Fuddruckers." Fuddruckers claims this instruction was too narrow, and argues that the likelihood of any mistaken consumer belief that the two operations had the same source constitutes infringement. We agree.

Likelihood of confusion " 'exists when customers viewing the mark would probably assume that the product or service it represents is associated with the source of a different product or service identified by a similar mark.' " ... Lindy Pen Co. v. Bic Pen Corp., 725 F.2d 1240, 1243 (9th Cir. 1984) (Lindy Pen I) ... ; see also *id.* at 1246 (test for likelihood of confusion embraces "confusion between the goods or sponsorship of the allegedly infringing goods"). Nothing in the Lindy Pen I definition suggests that actionable likelihood of confusion should be limited to consumer belief that the infringer is being operated by the original user. The potential for harm is equally great if the consumers believe that the infringer runs the original user. For example, if consumers believe that Doc's runs Fuddruckers, and they are disappointed with the quality of Doc's food or service, they may be deterred from patronizing Fuddruckers. Doc's points to no cases that hold that one type of confusion is more actionable than the other. The court's instruction was error.

Doc's asserts that the error is harmless. We disagree. There was considerable evidence of actual confusion as to source. Fuddruckers' primary witness on the issue testified that perhaps one hundred times a week, consumers asked if Fuddruckers was owned by the same people who own Doc's. Another witness testified that people asked if Fuddruckers is associated with Doc's and if they are "the same restaurant or not." Doc's witnesses testified that consumers occasionally asked if Doc's was affiliated with Fuddruckers. There was little or no evidence presented, however, that consumers asked specifically whether Doc's was owned or franchised by Fuddruckers. The jury might well have discounted the evidence of actual confusion because it did not precisely fit what the court instructed them to look for.

The factual elements that make up likelihood of confusion include evidence of actual confusion, the defendant's intent in adopting the mark, similarity of marks, similarity of goods and marketing channels, and the strength of the mark... .

Evidence of actual confusion is persuasive proof that future confusion is likely.... A showing that the defendant intended to adopt the plaintiff's trade dress is also "entitled to great weight because a defendant is presumed able to accomplish this purpose." .... Fuddruckers presented credible evidence of both actual confusion and intent to copy.

In addition, the products and marketing channels of the parties were nearly identical, so a finding by the jury that the marks were very similar would have been sufficient to support a verdict for Fuddruckers on this issue... .

Despite the strength of Fuddruckers case on this issue, the evidence of intent to copy was not conclusive, and the jury was entitled to disbelieve the evidence of actual confusion because it was presented primarily through Fuddruckers' employees... . Moreover, the jury was in a better position than a reviewing court to determine the similarity of the two trade dresses; it viewed many photographs and visited the restaurants... . Doc's presented evidence of a number of differences between the two establishments, and given the level of detail involved in Fuddruckers' trade dress, slight variations in color or design might be sufficient to eliminate confusion... . In short, Fuddruckers' evidence, although strong, does not compel a finding of likelihood of confusion and a reasonable jury, even with proper instructions, might have reached the same conclusion the original jury reached... .

Conclusion

Trade dress infringement under the Lanham Act is a complicated area of the law made more difficult by a heavy overlay of case law that seems at least facially inconsistent. Moreover, the trial court's task in this case was made more difficult because most of our rulings on the subject have been made in the context of review of bench trials and little guidance was available to the parties or the court in respect to jury instructions. This is a difficult and close case, and a jury on retrial may again find that Fuddruckers' trade dress is unprotectable or that there was no likelihood of confusion. However, Fuddruckers is entitled to a verdict that is based on instructions that correctly present the law to the jury.

Reversed and Remanded.

§2.25 THE SUPREME COURT OF THE UNITED STATES DEFINES THE SCOPE OF THE PROTECTION OF TRADE DRESS, WITHOUT THE NEED FOR THE FINDING OF SECONDARY MEANING—1992

Two Pesos Inc. v. Taco Cabana, Inc.

505 U.S. 763 (1992)

Argued April 21, 1992, Decided June 26, 1992

Respondent, the operator of a chain of Mexican restaurants, sued petitioner, a similar chain, for trade dress infringement under § 43(a) of the Trademark Act of 1946 (Lanham Act), which provides that "[a]ny person who ... use[s] in connection with any goods or services ... any false description or representation ... shall be liable to ... any person ... damaged by [such] use." The District Court instructed the jury, *inter alia*, that respondent's trade dress was protected if it either was inherently distinctive—*i.e.*, was not merely descriptive-or had acquired a secondary meaning—*i.e.*, had come through use to be uniquely associated with a specific source. The court entered judgment for respondent after the jury found, among other things, that respondent's trade dress is inherently distinctive but has not acquired a secondary meaning. In affirming, the Court of Appeals ruled that the instructions adequately stated the applicable law, held that the evidence supported the jury's findings, and rejected petitioner's argument that a finding of no secondary meaning contradicted a finding of inherent distinctiveness.

Held: Trade that is inherently distinctive is protectable under § 43(a) without a showing that it has acquired secondary meaning, since such trade dress itself is capable of identifying products or services as coming from a specific source. This is the rule generally applicable to trademarks, ..., and the protection of trademarks and of trade dress under § 43(a) serves the same statutory purpose of preventing deception and unfair competition. There is no textual basis for applying different analysis to the two. Section 43(a) mentions neither and does not contain the concept of secondary meaning, and that concept, where it does appear in the Lanham Act, is a requirement that applies only to merely descriptive marks and not to inherently distinctive ones. Engrafting a secondary meaning requirement onto § 43(a) also would make more difficult the identification of a producer with its product and thereby undermine the Lanham Act's purposes of securing to a mark's owner the goodwill of his business and protecting consumers' ability to distinguish among competing producers. Moreover, it could have anticompetitive effects by creating burdens on the startup of small businesses. Petitioner's suggestion that such businesses be protected by briefly dispensing with the secondary meaning requirement at the outset of the trade dress' use is rejected, since there is no basis for such requirement in § 43(a). pp. 767-776.

Justice White delivered the opinion of the Court.

The issue in this case is whether the trade dress 1 of a restaurant may be protected under § 43(a) of the Trademark Act of 1946 (Lanham Act), 60 Stat. 441, 15 U. S. C. § 1125(a)... .

I

Respondent Taco Cabana, Inc., operates a chain of fast-food restaurants in Texas. The restaurants serve Mexican food. The first Taco Cabana restaurant was opened in San Antonio in September 1978, and five more restaurants had been opened in San Antonio by 1985. Taco Cabana describes its Mexican trade dress as

> a festive eating atmosphere having interior dining and patio areas decorated with artifacts, bright colors, paintings and murals. The patio includes interior and exterior areas with the interior patio capable of being sealed off from the outside patio by overhead garage doors. The stepped exterior of the building is a festive and vivid color scheme using top border paint and neon stripes. Bright awnings and umbrellas continue the theme. ...

In December 1985, a Two Pesos, Inc., restaurant was opened in Houston. Two Pesos adopted a motif very similar to the foregoing description of Taco Cabana's trade dress. Two Pesos restaurants expanded rapidly in Houston and other markets, but did not enter San Antonio. In 1986, Taco Cabana entered the Houston and Austin markets and expanded into other Texas cities, including Dallas and El Paso where Two Pesos was also doing business.

In 1987, Taco Cabana sued Two Pesos in the United States District Court for the Southern District of Texas for trade dress infringement under § 43(a) of the Lanham Act, 15 U. S. C. § 1125(a) (1982 ed.),2 and for theft of trade secrets under Texas common law... .

Engrafting onto § 43(a) a requirement of secondary meaning for inherently distinctive trade dress also would undermine the purposes of the Lanham Act. Protection of trade dress, no less than of trademarks, serves the Act's purpose to "secure to the owner of the mark the goodwill of his business and to protect the ability of consumers to distinguish among competing producers. National protection of trademarks is desirable, Congress concluded, because trademarks foster competition and the maintenance of quality by securing to the producer the benefits of good reputation." ... By making more difficult the identification of a producer with its product, a secondary meaning requirement for a nondescriptive trade dress would hinder improving or maintaining the producer's competitive position... .

On the other hand, adding a secondary meaning requirement could have anticompetitive effects, creating particular burdens on the startup of small companies. It would present special difficulties for a business, such as respondent, that seeks to start a new product in a limited area and then expand into new markets. Denying protection for inherently distinctive nonfunctional trade dress until after secondary meaning has been established would allow a competitor, which has not adopted a distinctive trade dress of its own, to appropriate the originator's dress in other markets and to deter the originator from expanding into and competing in these areas.

As noted above, petitioner concedes that protecting an inherently distinctive trade dress from its inception may be critical to new entrants to the market and that withholding protection until secondary meaning has been established would be contrary to the goals of the Lanham Act... .

III

We agree with the Court of Appeals that proof of secondary meaning is not required to prevail on a claim under § 43(a) of the Lanham Act, where the trade dress at issue is inherently distinctive, and accordingly the judgment of that court is affirmed.

It is so ordered.

§2.26 THE PROTECTION OF A COMBINATION OF TRADE DRESS, A BUSINESS MODEL AND A TRADE SECRET—*LE RELAIS DE L'ENTRECÔTE*, GENEVA—2015

Any reader who visits Geneva, Switzerland, and appreciates eating meat should not fail to visit the restaurant that has been at the center of the IP-related dispute that is the topic of this paragraph. At Le Relais de l'Enrecôte, *the customer will find him/herself in an elegant atmosphere and will be attended by efficient and polite waitresses, who will serve him/her a tasty beef entrecote cooked to his/her liking, accompanied by thinly cut, well done French fries, and seasoned with a unique sauce, the recipe of which has been kept secret for a couple of generations. Besides the friendly, elegant atmosphere, the entirely adequate service, the excellent quality of the meat and the accompanying fries at* Le Relais de l'Entrecôte *in Geneva, the customer is introduced to a peculiar business model, the elements of which are described in the opinion that follows.*

Frequenting Le Relais de l'Entrecôte *of Geneva is an expression of culture, a token of a way of living, and a moment of great gustatory pleasure for families, friends, and businesses. But the success of the restaurant—that of Geneva as well as of the whole of the chain of restaurants in which it is inserted, as it will be briefly described below—lies not only on its trade dress or on the business model it follows, or on the food ingredients it serves: at the core of* Le Relais de l'Entrecôte*'s success, patrons find the sauce that seasons the entrecote in a unique, delicious fashion. One can say that* Le Relais de l'Entrecôte *is a restaurant built around a trade secret.*

Great success, unfortunately, usually invites attacks by dishonest competitors, particularly in an overpopulated business area like that of restaurants. The story goes as follows: the premises that Le Relais the l'Entrecôte *occupied on Rue de Rhône in Geneva were part of a building that was acquired by Zurich, an insurance company. Intending to have those premises occupied by a more lucrative business, such as a luxury boutique or jewelry, the owner of the building, once the rent contract expired, evicted* Le Relais de l'Entrecôte. *While the owner of the Paris-based chain of restaurants was looking for a new place to continue her business in Geneva, she learned that the premises that she had occupied for many years were about to receive another restaurant, which would open under a signboard that invoked her culinary specialty—entrecote—and would imitate her business model. Clearly, the owner of the new restaurant was looking to deviate from the clientele of* Le Relais de l'Entrecôte, *formed by a crowd of loyal customers and tourists who visit Geneva. Those tourists come to Geneva lured by the massive building of the former siege of the Society of Nations (today, the headquarters of the United Nations in Europe) and the city's elegant shops. Those who are lucky to be informed about* Le Relais de l'Entrecôte *have also the opportunity to have a great gastronomic experience.*

According to Wikipedia, Le Relais de l'Entrecôte *is one of three chains of restaurants that are spinoffs of a restaurant originally created in Paris by Gineste de Saurs. The other two branches are* Le Relais de Venise *(run by a daughter of Gineste de Saurs, with locations in New York, London, and other cities around the world) and* L'Entrecôte *(run by a son of Gineste de Saurs, with locations in Toulouse, Lyon, Bordeaux, and other cities).* Le Relais de l'Entrecôte *is owned by another daughter of Gineste de Saurs, Marie-Paule Burrus. This chain has two restaurants in Paris, one in Geneva and one in Zurich.*

Additional details of the dispute involving the trade dress of Le Relais de l'Entrecôte *in Geneva will be shown in the footnotes to the explanation of the facts in the opinion that follows.*

This dispute is, indeed, one of a trade dress. To a large extent, it is parallel to the English court opinions that admitted that the exclusivity in the trademark be used as a tool to protect a trade secret—or the reputation that stemmed from its possession.

Moreover, one cannot put aside that the fact that Le Relais de l'Entrecôte *pursues a peculiar business model—a fact that was noted by the Court—may have been a persuasive factor that helped the restaurant win the dispute. In the case of* Le Relais de l'Entrecôte, *a dishonest competitor attempted to capture the same prestige that resulted from the unique (and secret) recipe for the sauce that accompanies the entrecote served at the restaurant by imitating its trade dress and business model (including resorting to the* débauchage *of a number of employees of that restaurant).*

In the end, Justice has been made, and the owner of Le Relais de l'Entrecôte *has prevailed (as well as the restaurant's loyal patrons). Interestingly, it seems that not only the dishonest rival has learned a lesson, but the owner of the premises where the original restaurant had operated for many years has also received a message—this time not from the Court, but from customers. Indeed, as noted above, the other sad story behind this case was that Zurich, the insurance company that had bought the building, had seen in the leasing of the restaurant's premises to some luxury boutique or jewelry an opportunity to easily increase its earnings. That is why Zurich decided not to renew the lease with* Le Relais de l'Entrecôte. *However, it had difficulties in leasing the same premises to another sort of business, as in the meantime, the State Council of the Canton of Geneva declared those premises a historical heritage. Accordingly, any new lessee could not destroy the wooden panels in the walls or remove the sconces holding the old chandeliers and the furniture, which means that, at least in the short term, those premises could only be used by another restaurant. That was when someone saw a good opportunity to cash easy money on the reputation of* Le Relais de l'Entrecôte *and open a restaurant that, using the same physical environment and imitating its well-known trade dress, could lure its clientele. That attempt failed, and due to the Court decision that follows, a new attempt was made to open there an Italian restaurant. Its opening was even announced in a banner placed outside the premises for some time. But that initiative has also failed. A quick look from Google's Street View, dated October 14, 2023, shows the empty premises. Figure 10 shows the same desolated scenario through a photo taken by the author in September 2023. This means that, nine years later, the old premises occupied by Le Relais de l'Entrecôte remain as a monument erected to greed and unfair competition.*

Republic and Canton of Geneva

Judicial authority

C/288/2015 ACJC/24/2015

Decision of the Court of Justice

Civil Chamber of January 12, 2015

Between [The names of the Parties have been redacted in the publication of the following opinion]

Whereas, in fact, that A______ SA (the plaintiff) aims, in particular, to operate any hotel, café, brasserie and restaurant;

That since 1912, a restaurant has operated on the ground floor of the building located on Rue du Rhône in Geneva;

That the firm acquired, in 1982, the restaurant *Brasserie Bavaria*, which was located at the aforementioned address and has since operated a restaurant there under the brand *Le Relais de l'Entrecôte*;

That the restaurant is characterized, in particular, by the fact that it offers a unique dish composed of a green salad, entrecote accompanied by fried potatoes and a sauce, the recipe of which is kept secret, as well as desserts à la carte;[66]

That, moreover, (the plaintiff) sets out, with supporting photos, other characteristics of his establishment, namely that the waiters wear black clothes and white aprons, that the tablecloths are made of paper, that "retro" posters adorn the wooden walls, to which wall lights are hung and that customers cannot reserve their table;[67]

That, by decision of the State Council of May 25, 2011, the premises housing the restaurant under the signboard *Le Relais de l'Entrecôte* were declared classified monuments, this protection covering both the exterior appearance of the premises (three arcades with metal locks, including an old guillotine, exterior woodwork, special eight-pointed star screws, lower boxes of wooden display cases, etc.) as well as on the interior aspects (crossing space of three rooms in a row, wooded ceilings, benches with wooden files, wooden counter, furniture, original chairs, table feet, etc.);

That this decision was finally confirmed by the Federal Court, which noted that the classification did not oblige the owner of the premises to maintain the activity of *Le Relais de l'Entrecôte*, but only to guarantee the preservation of an architectural heritage;[68]

That the lease of the plaintiff having been terminated, the restaurant operated by it was established, at the end of a long procedure, on July 18, 2014, at *rue Pierre-Fatio*, 6, in Geneva, near its former address;

That the plaintiff states that she had recently learned that a new restaurant was preparing to open its doors in the premises it occupied on rue du Rhône;

That the following announcement appears on the window of these former premises: "Restaurant since 1912, listed as a Geneva heritage site. We look forward to welcoming you soon;"

That the sign of the new restaurant is *L'Entrecôte du Rhône*;

That, according to an article published in the magazine "Bilan," which the plaintiff claims to have taken notice on January 7, 2015, the operator of the new

66. This business model includes two additional features: once the patrons are seated (in tables they cannot reserve in advance), a waitress comes and asks how they wish the entrecote to be cooked. She will write with the initial letter the customer's preference on the white paper tablecloth ("S," for *saignant*, i.e., rare, for example). She will bring a salad, followed by two servings of the meat and fries. There is no possibility of ordering additional sauce.
67. The retro posters advertising beverages of the nineteenth and early twentieth centuries are common to all restaurants that are part of the chain *Le Relais de d'Entrecôte*.
68. The specific nature of the furniture and the appliances would not oblige the owner to rent the premises to a restaurant only, but the special layout does not leave many other options open. And the result is seen in Figure 10: since the attempts to open a new restaurant have failed, the premises remain empty.

restaurant indicates that he will "resume the winning formula of entrecote with sauce and fries,"

That the new restaurant will be operated by the defendant...

That, according to the plaintiff, five of her former employees were hired by B_____ SA, including the former director F_____, the former cook J_____ and two waitresses, K_____ and L_____;

That when questioned by the plaintiff, who reminded them of their obligations in terms of maintaining trade secrets, J_____, K_____ and F_____ responded by similar letters that they had no knowledge of manufacturing or business secrets and could work for a restaurant offering entrecotes;[69]

That according to an affidavit submitted by the Plaintiff, her usual ice cream supplier was contacted by the defendant in December 2014, with a view to ordering the same flavors of ice cream as those delivered to the Plaintiff;[70]

That the same is true according to an affidavit by an employee of the butcher's shop _____, usual supplier of meat to the Plaintiff, contacted by the Defendant in December 2014, with a view to ordering the same quality of meat as the aforementioned firm;

That a letter dated December 15, 2014 addressed to the defendant by WMF relating to the delivery of cups and saucers was sent—by mistake—to the Plaintiff;

That, following the publication of the aforementioned article in "Bilan", the Plaintiff gave the defendant a deadline of January 9, 2015 at noon to give up the opening of her restaurant;

That the Plaintiff alleges that it was by receiving people at *rue Pierre-Fatio*, 6, on January 8, 2015, for the inauguration cocktail that she learned of the imminence of the opening of the restaurant;

That, her formal notice having remained unanswered, the Plaintiff seized, on Friday January 9, 2015, at the end of the afternoon, the Court of Justice of a request for exceptional and provisional measures, based on arts. 2 and 3(1)(d) of the Unfair Competition Act, aiming, as regards the exceptional measures, at prohibiting the defendant, D_____, C_____, E_____ and F_____ and any third party from exploiting, having exploited or participating in any manner whatsoever to the operation of the establishment *L'Entrecôte du Rhône* in the premises located at 49 *rue du Rhône*, that the aforementioned measures are ordered to proceed with the immediate closure of the said establishment and to immediately cease all forms of exploitation and that the order is accompanied by the threat of penalties and sanctions ... ;

That the Plaintiff maintains, on provisional measures, these conclusions and requests, moreover, that the required measures remain in force as long as they have not been revoked by the Court of Justice in a ruling to the contrary; imposes on the

69. The former employees did not have knowledge of the secret recipe for the famous sauce, but they knew the details of how the business was run and who were the suppliers of their former employer. In particular, they knew the cut of the salad and the fries, which is not a secret, but contributes to the overall success of the formula.

70. Here there is no indication whether the newcomer had the intention to present to customers a handwritten list of desserts, as the various branches of the restaurants owned by the Saurs family do.

defendants that they provide proof that the operation of their establishment in a modified version would no longer constitute an act of unfair competition, which implies in particular a waiver from the use of the signboard containing the word "Entrecôte," the omission of any reference to a prior existing establishment (since 1912 in particular) in the same premises; the waiver from any specific reference to beef entrecote in its signboards and communication media; the definitive abandonment of the concept highlighting a dish composed of beef entrecote (with or without fries and/or "café de Paris" sauce), as well as the definitive abandonment of any similarity with the visual and commercial identity of the Plaintiff, in particular the table settings and the clothing of the waitresses characterizing the image of *Le Relais de l'Entrecôte*;

That she argues, in particular, that the resuming, in its former premises, of the same restaurant activity than that which she carried out there, with a signboard including also the term "Entrecôte" with a stylized "e" close to the applicant's "RE" logo,[71] the inscription on the window of the fact that the restaurant has existed since 1912 and is classified as a Geneva heritage site, the hiring of old employees and current suppliers of the Plaintiff, constitute all elements which create a risk of confusion with the restaurant that she;

That this unfair, deceptive and deliberate behavior harms the image and reputation of the Plaintiff and aims at obtaining an illegitimate profit from the reputation, the fame and the products and manufacturing secrets of the Plaintiff;

That on Monday morning January 12, 2015, the defendant filed a preventive brief, in which she explains that the Plaintiff having given publicity to the proceedings which opposed her to her former lessor, the Geneva public knows that the restaurant *Le Relais de l'Entrecôte*, is located now at *rue Pierre-Fatio*, in Geneva;

That the Defendant also refers to her letter of January 9, 2015 to the Plaintiff, by which she notes that the furniture being classified, she cannot be blamed for using it; that the employees targeted by the Plaintiff separated from her several years ago; that the Plaintiff correctly does not contest the Defendant's right to use the term "entrecôte" in her signboard, this not constituting a particularly distinctive sign; that the Defendant has made the choice, "for the moment," not to contact the same butcher as the Plaintiff; that, that being said, "an entrecote remains an entrecote and a fries a fries;" that the same went for the outfit of the waitresses; that the Plaintiff, who had taken away the sconces of origin was ordered to return them, in order to comply with the decision of the State Council;

That, moreover, the recipe used by the Plaintiff was hardly original, since to grill an entrecote according to the cooking desired by the customer and to accompany it with a salad and fries was a "recipe" offered by many establishments in the canton of Geneva, such as the *Café de Paris* in Geneva, the *Restaurant de l'Aviation*, in Vernier and *Mont-Salève*, in Veyrier;

That moreover, the Plaintiff having, in 1959, taken up the concept already existing in Geneva of the *Café de Paris*, she was ill-advised to complain about the Defendant's behavior, who would open the restaurant's doors on January 19, 2015;

71. *See* Figure 10.

Considering, in law, … ;

That the judge orders the necessary provisional measures when the Plaintiff shows it is likely that the right she holds is the subject of an infringement or risks of being so, and that that offense risks causing harm that is difficult to repair … ;

That in the event of a particular emergency, particularly if there is a risk of hindering their execution, the judge can order provisional measures immediately, without hearing the parties … ;

That it is up to the Plaintiff to make the facts she alleges credible, as well as the merits, from the angle of a summary examination, of the claim that she invokes… ;

That the judge must also weigh the interests involved, that is to say, the assessment of the respective disadvantages for each of the parties depending on whether the measure required is or is not ordered… ;

That the measure ordered must be proportionate to the risk of harm… ;

That the person who that takes measures which are likely to give rise to confusion with the goods, works, services or belongings of others, acts unfairly within the meaning of art. 3(1)(d) of the Unfair Competition Act;

That in this case the facts alleged by the Plaintiff, as summarized above, are made sufficiently credible by the elements of proof produced;

That in particular, it is made likely that the Defendant intends to open a restaurant on *rue du Rhône*, whose shop sign is *Le Relais de l'Entrecôte* and which will offer the same menu as the Plaintiff;

That, although the classification decision of the State Council seems to force the owner of the premises to continue to operate a restaurant on *rue du Rhône*, it does not appear at all likely that the public establishment must take on all the characteristics of the services provided by the Plaintiff;

That in this regard, the new sign *L'Entrecôte du Rhône* is not only part of that of the applicant, namely the term "Entrecôte," but also the stylized element of the letter "E," similar to the stylized element that appears in the beginning of the sign *Le Relais de l'Entrecôte*;

That, moreover, it appears from the Defendant's letter of January 9, 2015 that she will propose the same cuisine as the applicant, in particular the same menu, unique, including a beef entrecôte, accompanied by a salad and fried potatoes, with a homemade sauce;

That the affidavit from the Plaintiff's ice cream supplier also makes it likely that the Defendant intends to offer its customers the same ice creams as the Plaintiff;

That in view of these elements, the Plaintiff has made it likely that there is a risk of confusion between the establishment she operates and the one the Defendant intends to open shortly;

That, contrary to what the Defendant suggests, the use of colored tablecloths different from those used by the Plaintiff does not constitute a distinctive element sufficient to eliminate the risk of confusion;

That, moreover, it is certainly well known that the restaurant under the sign *Relais de l'Entrecôte*, operated for many years on rue du Rhône, has been forced to move;

However, it cannot be assumed from this that it would be obvious that the new restaurant would be unrelated to the former;

That such a hypothesis seems all the less likely as the new restaurant invokes the fact that a restaurant has been operating since 1912 in the premises located *rue du Rhône* and that this element, combined with the using of the term "entrecôte" in the sign and of the same menu, suggests the resuming of the activity that the Plaintiff has carried out there or, at the very least, a link between the two restaurants;

That the existence of an emergency situation must also be admitted, the Defendant having indicated that she intended to open her establishment on January 19;

That the Defendant and her managers will thus be prohibited from operating or participating in any way whatsoever in the operation of the establishment "Entrecôte du Rhône" in the premises located at rue du Rhône, the measure being accompanied by the threat of the sanction ... ;

That the threat of sanctions ... appears sufficient to guarantee the execution hereof and that nothing indicates that the Defendant will not comply with the prohibition made, so that it would be disproportionate to provide, in addition, a fine in the amount of 5,000 [Swiss francs] and a daily fine of 1,000 francs, for every day of non-compliance;

That, as the restaurant has not yet opened its doors, there is no reason to order the immediate closure of the said establishment and to immediately cease all forms of operating; ...

For these reasons,

The Civil Chamber:

Ruling on exceptional measures:

Prohibits the defendants from operating or participating in in any way whatsoever to the operation of the *Entrecôte du Rhône* establishment in the premises located on rue du Rhône, in Geneva... .

Sitting:

Mrs. Florence Krauskopf, chair; Mrs. Slvie Droin, Mr. Ivo Buetti, judges; Mrs. Nathalie Deschamps, clerk.

Figure 2.10 On the top left, the entrance to Le Relais de l'Entrecôte, *in its new premises, on* Rue Pierre-Fatio, *6, Geneva, Switzerland. Right, the façade of the same restaurant, side of* Rue d'Aosta. *Below, the façade of the old premises on Rue du Rhône. The destiny may be ironic: while* Le Relais de l'Entrecôte *today thrives in its better, larger premises, just two blocks away from its original location, the old premises, shown below, almost one decade later, were still shut down, as a silent witness to unfair competition and greed.*

§2.27 A CASE OF PUFFING IN BRAZIL—2016

This section started with references to slogans used in Rome, and one of them—"Excellent liquamen *made in the manufacture of Scaurus" (see* §2.1.4)*—constitutes what today we designate as "puffing." Two centuries later, the techniques of advertising have not changed much. The text that follows is an excerpt of an opinion of the Court of Justice of São Paulo, settling a dispute between two giants of the manipulated food industry, Heinz and Unilever, which disagreed on the limits that could be imposed on the freedom of a company's praising its own products. The decision of the Court of São Paulo was confirmed by the 4th Chamber of the Superior Court of Justice in March 2023 (Special Appeal no. 1,759,745).*

Unfair Competition. Comparative advertising. Non-occurrence. Appellant HEINZ, which has limited itself to using the resource called "puffing," advertising exaggeration accepted in current legal system. Phrases like "best in everything what it does" and "the most consumed ketchup in the world", which do not result in demerit to competing trademarks. Impossibility that these claims, on the other hand, will influence the critical sense of consumers, which is why there is no need to talk about undue deviation of customers. UNILEVER, Appellee, holder of the Hellmann's trademark, which also uses the resource questioned in the case, when promoting its products. Unlawful practice attributed to HEINZ, therefore, that is not verified, which makes it unnecessary, for reasons of coherence, to insert a survey confirming that it has the best-selling ketchup in the world. Daily fine undue. Sentence reformed only for rejecting the counterclaim, maintaining in part the acceptance of the grounds of the main action. Heinz appeal granted, that of Unilever rejected.

Having seen, reported and discussed the file of this Appeal no. 1004301-65.2013.8.26.0309, from the District of Jundiaí, in which Heinz is the appellant/appellee Brasil S.A., and Unilever Brasil Ltda. is the appelle/appellant. [The Judges] agree, [sitting] in the 1st Reserved Chamber of Business Law of the Court of Justice of São Paulo, to deliver the following decision: "By majority of votes, they have partially accepted the Plaintiff's appeal and rejected the Defendant's appeal, the chosen declaring rapporteur having been defeated. Judgment with the reviewer, in accordance with the vote of the Rapporteur, which is part of this opinion." São Paulo, February 3, 2016.

[...] One of the ways to ensure the regularity of propaganda, putting aside its characterization as comparative or misleading, consists of demonstrating the veracity of the information conveyed, hence why the Judge did well when he ordered the company Heinz to prove that its ketchup is the "best-selling in the world", inserting, when publishing this claim by any means, the source of the survey that attests such leadership.

This evidence was sufficiently produced in the docket, after all, Heinz ketchup has been present on the world market since the end of the nineteenth century, entering the Brazilian scene only recently, in the face of the old national restriction to the product. [...] It should be emphasized that Unilever itself largely uses the same advertising resources that it seeks to question in the case, by use the expression "true" in its ketchup product, evidently because of the success of a well-known campaign developed for another product, also yours, called "the true mayonnaise." Therefore, in the concrete case, there is no nothing more than an invitation to consumers of one ketchup or another, to, in making their choice, express an opinion based on their preference, even because it is not appropriate to consider that either statement contains an absolute truth.

§2.28 FOOD AND HOSPITALITY, ART AND FASHION—WHERE DIFFERENT FIELDS OF IP MEET

We have already made reference to Braudel and to the linkage he established between food and fashion. Indeed, the world of the high culinary and the chefs awarded with Michelin stars coincide very frequently with that of movie stars, fashion designers and, in general, the world of the affluent. Some TV broadcasts showing cooking competitions have also helped transform competitors and jurors into TV stars. Artists have also been called to lend their talent to the differentiating assets of restaurants and foodstuffs. Figures 11 and 12 are examples of these new interfaces, which may give rise to new intellectual property-related questions. Indeed, art used for commercial purposes and fashion, in general, as discussed elsewhere,[72] *is covered by IP through a multifaceted approach—and, in the case of fashion, an utterly insufficient one. Will the interfaces between food and art and between food and fashion also call for a new approach to IP, such as, for example, a* sui generis *regime that, somehow, can accord the various subject matters a holistic treatment?*

The same can be said of the recent trend of fashion houses to open hotels and restaurants, to which they inevitably lend the prestige of their names: Armani hotels and Versace hotels, for example.

Only time will tell how intellectual property will respond to the challenges eventually created by counterfeiters and imitators of artistic and fashionable signs. We opened this book, in the Preamble, mentioning the impact of social change on the protection of intellectual property—as the ways of people doing business change, intellectual property also changes. Eventually, these new interfaces may mean that intellectual property also has to change in the particular field of food and hospitality.

72. *See* Nuno Pires de Carvalho, The Intellectual Property of Textiles and Fashion, *supra* note 1, in general, but especially at 135, 154.

Figure 2.11 Art meets food. The signboard of a bar and restaurant called "Notorious" located in Chora, the capital of Mykonos, Greece, was painted by Luis Orozco, a remarkable Mexican painter who resided in Mykonos between 1960 and 2021 when he passed away.

*Figure 2.12 Fashion joins food. Italian pasta in packages designed by Dolce & Gabbana, a well-known Italian fashion house, on sale at the delicatessen department of a high-end Italian department store (*Rinascenti, *in Milan).*

SECTION 2 BUSINESS IDENTIFIERS ASSOCIATED WITH SPECIAL SECTORS

§2.29 BUSINESS IDENTIFIERS IN BAKERY: CERTIFICATION MARKS, TRADEMARKS, SIGNBOARDS—1266 ONWARD

Bakers' trademarks are one of the earliest sorts of brands. Originally, they were used primarily for the certification of breads as to their quality and weight. Bread, being a foodstuff of crucial importance for feeding the people, governments were naturally concerned with ensuring respect for those two values. As Figure 13 shows, bakers' marks were already adopted in Antiquity. In the Middle Ages, in England, the sanctions for the failure to observe the statute of the assize, i.e., the statute that set rules on prices and weights, were strict: "the baker to the pillory, the brewer to the tumbler."[73]

The first regulation that imposed the use of trademarks by bakers was the English statute of the assize of ale and bread of 1266. The Statute required that both bakers and brewers had their own marks and made them visible, the bakers by printing their names "upon every Measure, Bushel, Weight, and also upon every Loaf, … distinctly written," and the brewers "shall present their Names distinctly and openly."

Some years later (the precise date is unknown), those provisions concerning the stamping of the brand were repeated.

73. "Tumbler" (derived from the French medieval word "tomberel") means cage. The offending brewer was condemned to be put in a cage and exposed to public scorn, whereas the offending baker was destined to the pillory.

In France, the mandatory use of trademarks by bakers started much later, in the sixteenth century (in 1546). However, once regulation started, a significant number of statutes and guild by-laws were enacted with the same purpose as in England.

The purpose of provisions on bakers' trademarks was primarily one of certification of compliance with strict technical standards as to quality, weight, and composition. In the Middle Ages, bakers were seen with suspicion not only by consumers but also by authorities, and thus, there was no interest in giving them much freedom. Trademarks also had the objective of helping authorities to exact taxes, as in other fields of business. And, of course, subsidiarily, trademarks could also fulfill the main purpose they have today: to ensure the differentiation of entrepreneurs and their products. Such differentiation was not desired within the guild because masters were not supposed to compete with other masters—on the contrary, in accordance with the spirit of brotherhood, they were expected to cooperate. But they would compete with bakers from other cities, and later in this section, we will see special references to "foreign bakers" who established themselves on the outskirts of Paris so as to supply bread to the growing population of that city. Those foreign bakers were required to mark their bread so as to distinguish it from the bread made by Parisian bakers.

Some regulations permitted bakers to choose their own marks, but others would attribute the Jurors of the guild the incumbency of allocating the signs to individual masters. Increasingly, after the sixteenth century, the notion of legal security imposed the obligation to register the marks with a central office, either in the guild itself or in the town hall.

§2.29.1 Statute of the Assise of Bread and Ale required Bakers and Brewers to Clearly and Openly Affix Their Names to Their Products—1266

The Judgment of the Pillory

A Statute of the Assize of Bread and Ale

Anno 51 Henry III, Stat. 6 and 1266 AD

If a Baker or a Brewer be convicted, because he hath not observed the Assize of Bread and Ale, the first, second, and third time, he shall be amerced according to his Offense, if it be not over grievous;

(2) but if the Offense be grievous and often, and will not be corrected, then he shall suffer Punishment of the Body, that is to wit, a Baker to the Pillory, and a Brewer to the Tumbrel, or some other Correction.
(3) First, fix lawful men shall be sworn truly to gather all Measures of the Town, that is to wit, Bushels, half and quarter, Gallons, Pottles, and Quarts, as well of Taverns as of other Places; Measures and Weights, that is to wit, Pounds, half Pounds, and other little Weights, wherewith Bread of the Town or of the Court is weighed, that is to say, one Loaf for every sort of Bread.

(4) And upon every Measure, Bushel, Weight, and also upon every Loaf, the Name of the Owner distinctly written; ...

II. Also if they have in the Town a Pillory of convenient Strength, as appertaineth to the Liberty of their Market, which they may use (if need be) without body Peril either of Man or Woman.

(2) After, they shall inquire of the Assise and Price of Wine, after the Departure of the Justices in Eyre, or of them that were last in Office of the Market of the Town; that is to say, of the Vintners Names, and how they sell a Gallon of Wine; and if any corrupted Wine be in Town, or such as is not wholesome for Man's Body.

(3) Also of the Assise of Ale in the Court of the Town how it is, and whether it is observed; and if not, how much Brewers have sold contrary to the Assise; (4) and they shall present their Names distinctly and openly, and that they be amerced for every Default, or be judged to the Tumbrel, if they sell contrary to the Assise.

Figure 2.13 Bakers' stamps are some of the oldest regulated marks. Mold of a baker's stamp found in Spain (Albacete), first century AD. On display at the National Archeological Museum of Spain, in Madrid.

§2.29.2 Another British Statute Requiring Bakers to Designate Breads with Their Marks—Between 1216 and 1301 (Date Uncertain)

An Ordinance for Bakers, Brewers, and for other Victuallers; and for Ells, Bushels, and Forestallers.

CAP. II.

For what Offense a Baker shall be amerced, and for what set on the Pillory

A Baker, if his Bread be found a Farthing Weight lacking in Two shillings six pence, or under, shall be amerced;

(2) and if it passes the same Number, he shall suffer Punishment of the Pillory, which shall not be remitted to the Offender either for Gold or Silver.
(3) And every Baker shall have a Mark of his own for his Bread.

§2.29.3 In Settling a Dispute Between Bakers and Millers of Bordeaux, the Parliament (Acting as a Court) Approves Rules on the Mandatory Use of Trademarks by the Bakers—1570

In Bordeaux, the settlement of a dispute between bakers and millers (concerning the boundaries of each profession's exclusive line of work) has eliminated the freedom of bakers to choose their marks: these marks were decided and assigned to them by the Jurors of their guild. Next, we will see that this rule also applied to several guilds of cutlers.

The dispute between the suppliers and millers is settled by the judgment of April 6, 1570.

...

And therefore, whoever will be accepted [in the guild], before being allowed to make bread, shall go to Messrs. Deputy mayor and Jurors, to ask for a mark, to mark his bread. Those shall grant and decide the form of such mark, which will be imprinted on the lead board, which is in the Town Hall of the said city [Bordeaux].

And the bakers shall not sell any bread, unless it is marked with their mark, different from the marks of the other bakers, under the penalty of forfeiting the bread that is found not to be marked with his mark. Which bread will be destined to feed the poor in the Hospital of the city, and in addition, whoever contravenes this statute shall pay a fine of sixty-five sols of Bordeaux.

§2.29.4 Certification Marks of the Bakers' Guild of Aberdeen, Scotland—1634

November 6, 1634

Anent [concerning] the weight and stamping of bread.

Sixth November, 1634. The said day it is ordained that ilk twelf penny quheat loaf sail contain ten ounces of sufficient weall bakin bread and the twa shilling loaf to be conform, and in the meantime ordains every neighbour of the calling to have his stamp on his bread, and that the sufficiency or insufficiency of the said bread or lacking of the stamp be tried by the deacon or any of his masters whom he pleases with him until Candlemas next 1635, and who contravenes this present ordnance sail pay six shillings money toties quoties to the craft.

§2.29.5 An Ordinance Establishes That Paris Bakers' Marks Are Reserved for Bread of a Certain Quality—1635

Ordinance of the civil lieutenant on the general administration of Paris

Paris, March 30, 1635

The master bakers of the small bread of this city of Paris are enjoined to bake daily, keep their houses, or workshops and windows always stocked with three kinds of bread, of the quality, whiteness and weight determined by the old ordinances... ; and those bakers shall mark the breads with their special mark: they will have weights and balances in their shops, all on the pain of being deprived of their mastership, and on a greater pain if necessary. They shall nevertheless be authorized to make soft bread, in the fashion of Gonesse,[74] and other kinds for the convenience of those who want to use it: which they shall not display on their shelves; thus, they shall put them in the back of their shop, or in such a place that the bread cannot be seen, on the pain of a fine of 400 Parisis pounds, and greater pain, if necessary.

§2.29.6 A French Historian Mentions the Mandatory Use of Trademarks by the Bakers of Dijon, France—1646, 1709

In France, the mandatory printing on the bread of a reference to the weight was not a common provision. In general, the determination of the weight was part of the regulations, and the presence of the baker's mark imprinted on the bread was an implicit guarantee of compliance with mandatory technical standards. But in the seventeenth century, the city of Dijon decided otherwise. Moreover, the administrative regulations that obliged the bakers to mark the weight of the bread on each loaf also gave precise indications of how the trademarks should look.

By an administrative regulation of 1646, the bakers of Dijon will be called each year to the Chamber [of the guild] on the day which will be decided to bring their mark so that it be placed on a board of copper or of pewter, and that mark shall be visible [on the breads], with the first letters of their name and surname [imprinted in a manner]

74. Gonesse is a city located in the suburbs of Paris. In the seventeenth century, Gonesse became notorious for the concentration of bakers who came from all regions of France to make bread and sell it to the inhabitants of Paris. They were designated as "forains" (literally, foreigners) because they were not members of the guild of bakers of Paris and thus were not bound by corporative rules.

that the baking of the bread they will make cannot erase it. Those bakers will be inspected every week to see if their bread will be of weight and made as it should be.

...

Additional regulations were issued in 1667 and 1669; then a judgment by the Interim Chamber [of the guild] opens the series of those decisions which were held in the eighteenth century. By this judgment of 1709, bakers are once again ordered to mark their bread with a particular mark, the "imprint" of which would be deposited at the registry of the Townhall, plus, as an innovation, they would have to mark on each loaf the "weight of it per as many circles as there are pounds" without an increase of "a single ounce or gram"; and if they make half-pound loaves, they will mark it "by half a circle."

§2.29.7 A Statute of Pennsylvania Requires Bakers to Mark the Bread They Make—1700

The British imposed the regulation of price, weight and quality of bread in several of its provinces in North America, closely following the traditions by then acquired in the mainland. Marking the bread with the baker's name became, therefore, mandatory. It seems that American colonists were not very happy with those regulations and resisted their application.[75]

November 27, 1700

An Act for the Assize of Bread

For the better regulation of bakers, and the assize of bread:

...

And for the more effectual prevention of fraud herein:

[Section III.] Be it further enacted by the authority aforesaid, That all persons within this province and territories who bake any bread for sale, shall at all times hereafter have all their bread that they shall bake, either for sale or to spend in their families, made of the due assize, marked, and yielded to trial of the said officer, as is directed in this law, under the penalty of forfeiting all such bread whatsoever as aforesaid.

75. *See* Karen Anne Balor, *Cooking up a Nation: Food, Culture, and Identity in the Early American Republic*, Master's Thesis, Central Washington University, Summer 2011, available at digitalcommons.cwu.edu (accessed on November 20, 2023).

§2.29.8 In the Eighteenth Century, England Had Not Yet Got Rid of the Suspicion Against Bakers, and a New Assize of Bread Repeated the Same Provisions That Had Been in Force for Several Centuries—1709

CHAPTER XIX

An Act to Regulate the Price and Assize of Bread

...

III. And to the Intent that the good Design of this Act may be effectually complied with be it further enacted by the Authority aforesaid, That every common Baker and every Person who shall make or hake for Sale or any ways expose to Sale any Sort of Bread whatsoever shall from and after the said First Day of May fairly imprint or mark or cause to be fairly imprinted on every Loaf so by him made or exposed to Sale the Sort Price and Weight of such Loaf or any other Mark as shall be appointed by the said Court of Lord Mayor and Aldermen or by the said other Chief Magistrates and Justices of the Peace within the Bounds of their said several Jurisdictions and the said Court of Lord Mayor and Aldermen within the City of London and the Liberties thereof and the said other Chief Magistrates or Justices of the Peace within the Bounds of their several Jurisdictions shall have full Power and Authority from time to time to limit direct and appoint how and in what Manner each Sort of Bread shall be marked for knowing the Baker or Maker Price Weight and Sort thereof and to make and set down any other reasonable Rules and Orders for the better regulating the Mystery of baking Bread and the Sorts Assize Price and Weight thereof and all Things concerning the same as in their Judgments they shall find necessary and convenient.

And if any Baker or other Person or Persons baking or making Bread for Sale or exposing Bread to Sale shall not observe the Assize to be ascertained by virtue of this Act or shall bake or make for Sale or sell or expose to Sale any Bread wanting the due Weight or that shall not be marked according to the Direction of this Act or shall break such Regulations and Orders as shall from time to time be made by virtue of this Act or that shall in any Sort or Way break or infringe any of the Matters or Things before appointed by this Act he or they so doing being thereof convicted by the Confession of the Party or by Oath of One or more credible Witness or Witnesses before the said Lord Mayor or any One or more of the said Aldermen or before the said Chief Magistrate or Magistrates or One of them or in such Town and Places where there are not any such Magistrate or Magistrates before One or more Justices of the Peace of the Country wherein the Offence shall be committed or the Party offending apprehended shall for every such Offence forfeit the Sum of Forty Shillings to be levied by Way of Distress upon the Goods and Chattels of every such Offender by Warrant from the said Lord Mayor Alderman or Aldermen or Chief Magistrate or Magistrates Justice or Justices before whom such Conviction shall be made the said Forfeitures to be given to the Informer or Informers.

§2.29.9 The Restrictions to the Acquisition of Bread from Outside Paris Bakers Are Reinforced—1757

Statutes and Regulations of the Community of Master Bakers of the city and suburbs of Paris

September 6, 1757 (reprinted in 1766)

...

XLIII. The said Jurors are also enjoined to make their visits to the houses of cabaret owners, inn keepers and wine sellers, in the city and suburbs of Paris, to see and find out whether they are selling any bread other than that permitted; ... without them being able to sell large bread, either cut into pieces, coming from the Bakers of Gonesse and other Foreign bakers, to those who go to their shops, on the penalty of confiscation [and] a fine of five hundred pounds: and they will be allowed to buy them only for their family and servants, in the markets, provided that the said breads are marked with the name of the foreign baker who has sold them.

...

Judgment of the Court of Parliament, Providing Regulations for the Community of Master Bakers of the City and Faubourgs of Paris: And Foreign Bakers. (1760)

Louis, by the grace of God, King of France and Navarre, to the first Bailiff of our Court of Parliament or other Bailiff or Sergeant on this required, we make it known that between Pierre Ducastel, François Houy and other Foreign Baker merchants for the provision of Paris, residing in the suburbs of Saint Antoine, plaintiffs in a motion inserted in the judgment of our Court of September 20, 1757, on the one hand, and the Community of Master Bakers of Paris, defendants, on the other hand, ...

Everything seen and considered, together with the conclusions of our Attorney General, our Court ruling on everything... in that under article XLIII, which allows innkeepers, tavern owners, and wine sellers, to buy bread from foreign bakers for their families and servants only, it is said that it will be marked with the name of the foreign baker who will have sold it; ... similarly it prohibits innkeepers, and wine sellers from selling bread from the Foreign bakers and from the Faubourg Saint Antoine, allows them to buy it only for their family and servants, without it being necessary for the said bread to be marked; ...

§2.29.10 In Normandy, Bakers Were Prohibited from Selling Bread by Unit: They Were Required to Sell It by Weight—1769

The generalized suspicion of bakers has already been mentioned several times. The texts that follow bring the measures against bakers' commercial freedom a step higher and prohibited them from selling loaves by unit ("vendre à la marque"); instead, they had to sell the bread by weight.

Judgment of the Parliament of Normandy, which renews the provisions of the Judgments of the Court, of January 13, 1725, November 21, 1740, May 18, June 14, 1752 & March 6, 1754, concerning the obligations of Bakers towards the Public, in the sale of Bread, both in the Cities and in the Towns and Villages of the Province.

October 23, 1769.

As regards the brief submitted to the Interim Chamber established by the King, by the King's Attorney General, exposing that some measures that have been taken to protect the Public from the frauds of the Bakers, in the delivery of Bread, have been usually disobeyed, and will continue to be so as long as we do not subject the Bakers to not being allowed to deliver [the bread] unless than by weight.

...

The provisions of these two decisions were renewed by another ruling of May 18, 1752, prohibiting the bakers of the City, suburbs and Franches-Aires from selling their bread as per the mark;[76] they are enjoined to sell it by weight, of whatever kind it may be, under the penalties expressed therein, which will be incurred by the Bakers who will have delivered their Bread without having weighed it, even if they were not required to do so, in the event that the Bread that they have delivered to Individuals is found, after delivery, to not be of the weight it should have; to the effect of which the said Bakers have been ordered to put on their Breads a distinctive mark of the Baker who made it... .

§2.29.11 The Prohibition of the Sale of Bread by Unit Is Extended to All of France—1771

Decision of Parliament, which orders that the Decisions and Regulations of the Court of January 13, 1725, November 21, 1740, May 18 and June 14, 1752, March 6, 1754, and October 23, 1769, shall be executed; in doing so, it enjoins all Bakers, both in this City and in other Cities within the jurisdiction of the Court, to sufficiently stock their Stalls and Shops with Bread of the quality required by the Ordinances, and of the right weight, to deliver it to the weight to all those who ask for it, etc.; prohibitions against its selling as per the mark, in accordance with the Decision of 1725.

It is the same with the Ruling of 1740—it has been ordered that the shelves of the Bakers' Shops should always be sufficiently stocked with bread of a fair weight and of good quality, and that those who failed to comply in more than an ounce, would be condemned to make up for it and in addition to pay a fine. The Decision of May 18, 1752 had renewed the same provisions, with the injunction to sell the Bread by weight, and not as per the mark, as well as that each [baker] should have on their bread personal trademarks, distinctive from each other, so as to make the fraud known, and punish it even after delivery.

76. "Vendre à la marque" (literally, selling as per the mark) means the sale of unitary loafs (which were marked with the baker's mark).

Likewise to enjoin all Bakers to weigh the Bread even when they are not required to do so, and to have a personal and distinctive mark on their Bread; because in the event of delivery without the correct weight, and even under the pretext that there is not more than one ounce missing per pound, they will be condemned as above in one hundred pounds of alms for the Hospitals, and in addition in fifty pounds for the benefit of the whistleblower, without the said penalties and alms being susceptible to be reduced.

§2.29.12 The Bew By-Laws of the Bakers of Paris and Their Particular Focus on Sideboards and Competition—1783

The year was 1783, on the eve of the French Revolution and the rising of its liberal spirit that would profoundly change the lives and the businesses of European citizens. The concern with quality control and respect for technical standards had not disappeared, but it had lost strength, as the idea of corporativism was vanishing (the Revolution would extinguish all guilds). The by-laws of the bakers of Paris of 1783 reflected this change, and instead of regulating in detail the use and registration of marks by bakers, have put emphasis on the distinctiveness of shops—rather than on the distinctiveness of the bakers—through the imposition of the use of distinctive and visible signboards, and the requirement of distancing between the shops of masters and those of their former apprentices. Interestingly, these regulations quantify the distance between shops: there must be at least four other shops belonging to other bakers between the shops of the former master and that of the former apprentice.

Patent Letters comprising the statutes of bakers of Paris.

Versailles, April 1, 1783

...

9. Masters will be required to have their names printed in large letters outside and in the most visible place in their shop. They will be similarly required, when they change residence, to declare it, within eight days, to the office of the community, and to indicate their new address, which declaration will be recorded free of charge in a register set for purpose... . ; all on penalty of a fine of 10 pounds and greater penalty if necessary.

10. All apprentices and boys of the said profession, when they wish to be accepted as masters and establish themselves within three years following their leaving with a master, are prohibited from renting the shop occupied by the master at which they will remain or have remained; and also from establishing themselves before the end of those three years, near the houses which they have left, from which they will be required to move away so that there are at least four shops of the [same] profession between the houses in which they will have resided and that of their establishment, unless it is with the consent of the master concerned, or to take the establishment of a widow or daughter of a master whom they have married; all under penalty of the closure of the store ... and the payment of a fine.

§2.29.13 In the Nineteenth Century, the Concern of Authorities Focused on the Signboards of Bakeries—1824

In the nineteenth century, Paris had become a very large city, and commerce was thriving. Merchants and shop keepers, eager to lure customers, exaggerated in using signboards not only as differentiating devices but also as advertising devices. Signboards have become too heavy and prominent, and accidents started happening to the point that the authorities of the city, following the example of London, had to intervene and impose conditions on the size and placement of those signs. Later, in 1784, those same rules would be extended to all of France, by a decision of the Cabinet of Finance.[77] *The following text reflects those same rules as applied to bakeries' signboards and adds a few particularities.*

Ordinance Concerning the Mark of the Bread.

Paris, April 8, 1824

We, Counselor of the State, Mayor of the Police,
Given

1st the Ordinance of the Provost of Paris, of November 25, 1546, concerning the bakery;
2nd The Ordinance of the King, of February 4, 1567;
3rd The Patent Letters of June 21, 1577;
4th Articles 2, 26 and 32 of the Decision of the Government of July 1st, 1800; and
5th The letter from His Excellency the Minister of Interior, of June 9 last;

Order the following:
Article I. Within one month, from the day of publication of this Ordinance, the Bakers of Paris will be required to affix on the Breads they make and which are subject to the tax, a particular mark intended to permit the recognition of the establishment in which the Breads will have been made.

Article II. These marks will be distinguished by a number which will be assigned to each bakery, in accordance with the table annexed to this Ordinance.[78]

Art. III. This number will be painted black on a metal plate covered in a light-yellow color. The digit(s) of the number shall be six inches high, by at least one inch width in full. The plaque will be nailed in the most lit and visible place in the Baker's shop, and at his expense.

Art. IV. Each Baker will also provide at his own expense a mark bearing the number of his establishment.

77. *See Ordonnance du bureau des finances concernant la suppression des enseignes et étalages en saillie dans les villes et bourgs de la généralité*, Paris, December 10, 1784. Jourdan, Isambert and Decrusy, RECUEIL GENERAL DES ANCIENNES LOIS FRANÇAISES, DEPUIS L'AN 420, JUSQU'A LA REVOLUTION DE 1789, March 3, 1781-January 1, 1785, at 544-546 (Belin-Leprieur, 1827).
78. The Table comprises a list of names and addresses of 600 hundred bakers.

Art. V. This mark will be composed of a tin plate to which will be welded, on one side and in the middle, a ring or necklace of suitable size to pass the finger through, and on the other the number(s) forming the number of the bakery. These figures, which will not be thicker than the tinplate, will be placed directly on the plate. They will have eight lines of width and eighteen lines of height, in accordance with the model filed with the Prefecture.

Art. VI. The Bakers will apply this mark deeply on the upper part of the Bread in dough in the basket and which makes the floor of the Bread when it is inverted on the shovel loading.

Art. VII. In the event that the Bakers do not comply with the provisions of this ordinance, a report will be drawn up, which will be transmitted to us.

Art. VIII. The appropriate administrative measure shall be taken against offenders, without prejudice to the proceedings to be taken against them before the Courts, in accordance with to Laws and Regulations.

Art. IX. This Order will be subject to the approval of His Ex. the Minister of the Interior.

Art. X. It will be printed and displayed with the Bakeries Table.

§2.30 BUSINESS IDENTIFIERS IN THE INDUSTRY OF CUTLERY—1318 ONWARD

Food as a cultural phenomenon is a vast domain in itself, and digressing on it would require an extensive discussion, which goes beyond the objective of this book. Here, the purpose is not to engage in such a complex topic but rather to look at the ways in which intellectual property has evolved over the centuries in the context of food and hospitality. In such context, making a special reference, although briefly, to the industry of cutlery is of great value for the reason that, until the Renaissance, with the exception of Italy, the fork was not used (even though it was known). Indeed, illuminations of medieval manuscripts (see Figure 14) invariably depict diners around a table, sharing a meal, using knives, using their hands, and, eventually (not always), handling spoons—but no forks are seen. Knives, therefore, acquired a central role in meals.

Of course, cutlers also played an important role in the industry of the Middle Ages because, besides silverware, they also made weapons, like swords and daggers, and, in that context, their profession was heavily regulated. This specialty, however, is outside this book's subject matter.

§2.30.1 By-Laws of the Corporation of Cutlers of Amiens—1318

The Ordinance of 1381 for the corporation of the cutlers of Amiens banned the making of knives and blades during the night. The reason was, on the one hand, to ensure that all work could be verified by the jurors of the profession at any time of the day. Second, there was also a concern with the quality of the work because deficiencies in illumination could lead to defective products. The prohibition of the use of another's trademark had the same purpose of ensuring that the true manufacturer of a defective product could be identified and sanctioned.

February 7, 1381

Ordinance of the Aldermen of Amiens for the Corporation of Cutlers

1. Know all those who will see or have what is written here that it is ordained, for the common benefit of the trade of the cutlers of Amiens, at the request of those of the said trade and their common agreement, that nobody of the said trade, whatever they are, masters, servants, or assistants, and others who are involved in or make a living from the said trade, cannot forge knives, blades, forks or other types of cutlery, in Amiens or in the suburbs, beyond the clock that chimes in the morning at the tower and until the clock that chimes at vesper... .

6. And that no one of the said profession may stamp on his work or in his blades the sign of others, without any ignorance.

Figure 2.14 This illumination of a French manuscript of the fifteenth century shows five men sharing a meal. On the table, only knives can be seen. No forks are shown. Diners used knives to cut the food and their hands to hold it. Extracted from Heures à l'Usage de Troyes, *fifteenth century (third quarter), Champagne, France.*

§2.30.2 The King of France Authorizes the Assignment of a Cutler's Trademark—1364

The importance of the cutlery industry in Medieval Europe has already been emphasized. The following text confirms that at a time in which trademarks still served mostly as tools of quality certification in the corporatist economy, as opposed to an element of differentiation of rival masters (that sort of competition being strongly discouraged), the idea of using business identifiers as objective elements of differentiation for the capture of prestige and reputation was not yet born. Trademarks were linked to individual masters, and their role was to secure liability in the case of defective products. The possibility of assigning a trademark was then a strange concept. And yet, the following text shows a major exception to that rule. The text concerns the king's approval of the transfer of ownership of a trademark that belonged to a merchant who had passed away without heirs or successors. The text does not say it, but it is not impossible that the assignee of the trademark had been an associate of the deceased because reference is made to the fact that the assignee, Evard de Boessay, "is long accustomed to make knife blades under the sign of the stag horn [which is owned] by the heirs of Jean de Saint Denis."

January 1364

Charles ... we inform all present and those to come that, as Evrard de Boessay, knife merchant, is long accustomed to make knife blades under the sign of the stag horn [which is owned] by the heirs of Jean de Saint Denis, otherwise Saint Germain in our city of Paris, for the time that he lived, which sign no one else [could use], other than his people or by his command, under the penalty of a fine of XL Parisian pounds, to be paid for our profit, and to have forfeited his commodities in the case someone dared to counterfeit it, and now has remained no heir or successor of the said Jean who must or may use the mentioned sign, as it is said, and for this Evrard, who has always accustomed to make knife blades under the sign of the stag horn, as it is said, has begged us that we graciously please to grant him and his heirs that he may have forged by any good worker in our kingdom knife blades under the sign of the stag horn in the way Jean and his predecessors did and had done at the time they lived. We incline to the supplication of Evrard, and to Evrard, to him and to his heirs born and to be born from his body in loyal marriage, and who, like him, will seem to become merchants of knife blades, [We] gave and granted to inheritance and by these present [letters] of our certain science, special grace, and royal authority, give and grant the sign of the stag horn, in the event that there would be no heirs from Jean, to whom that sign should belong by reason, and We please and wish that Evrard and his heirs can have forged under that sign by any good worker in our kingdom, so as that other workers or cutlers cannot forge under that sign nor contradict him or forge in any way, except those to whom he will command, under the penalty above said. Thus We determine, in accordance with the content of the present [letters] to the Provost of Paris and all our other justices, officers, and subjects ... that by Our present grace and grant they make and let Evrard and his heirs and successors enjoy and use perpetually and under heritage ... . And that this be firm and stable thing ... . Given in Paris on the year of grace of one thousand CCC sixty-four in the month of January.

§2.30.3 A Dispute over a Cutler's Trademark and Shop Sign Reaches the Court—1402

Shop signs (or signboards) are signs that are placed at the entrance of commercial and industrial establishments with the purpose of designating the places where businesses are conducted. As shown above, they have been used since Antiquity. But it was in the Middle Ages, with the Commercial Revolution and the consequent growth of cities, that the use of shop signs increased as artisans and traders began to concentrate in urban conglomerates. To better monitor compliance with mandatory technical standards and thus make the job of inspectors easier, guilds and municipalities required artisans to open their shops in the same neighborhood or on the same street. Numbers had not yet been introduced to help locate houses and commercial businesses. This fact made signboards even more important.

Later, as we shall see, a minimum distance was imposed between those artisans who used similar signs on their signboards.

The text that follows is a somewhat truncated description of a court dispute that occurred in 1402 between members of the same family involving a cutler's trademark and shop sign—the crescent moon—in Auxerre, France, and the attempts to secure rights in it through its registration with the municipality of Paris (the Châtelet). We have already emphasized the importance of cutlery in the Middle Ages. Cutlers not only made weapons, like swords and daggers but also made the most important piece of silverware at that time: knives.

April 3, 1402. National Archives, Parliament Registry. Between J. Chantepinot, defendant, and J. Coulon, appellant ... from the bailiff of Auxerre. The appellant says that Renaud Chantepinot was a cutler in Auxerre and took the shop sign of the crescent, died, left two sons and one daughter, the two sons were cutlers and took the crescent, the mother married a man who was not of the profession at all. J. Coulon, who was her son, joined the profession of cutlery and took the crescent, adding a dot for a difference and kept this for seven years; and because his uncle Pierre was old and had no male son, he assigned him his crescent shop sign without a difference, and Enault, Pierre's brother, also gave it to Coulon ..., and thereby he has possessed and used it. Notwithstanding J. Chantepinot, who is Pierre's son, obtained letters by which he ordered Coulon to cease [the use of] the said crescent. He opposed and submitted to the bailiff that he possessed the crescent upon his uncles' advice, and that they came from the Chantepinot, and that in Auxerre the enforcement of every right is limited to a period of ten years inter presents, but he had possessed the crescent for thirteen years, in the presence of his uncles ... . The opposing party says ... that he casted his sign at the Châtelet, and therefore no one could take that sign ... notwithstanding Coulon took the crescent and has used it with several differences ... sometimes printing a comma, other times adding three dots ... . Held that the parties shall appear before the provost of Paris .... [It has been] decided that the Court will examine what the parties will show to the Council.

§2.30.4 Provisions on the Mandatory Use and Registration of Trademarks by the Cutlers and Sheath Makers of Abbeville—1494

At the end of the fifteenth century, the mandatory use of trademarks by incorporated professions had become a common administrative practice. The major difference as compared to the rules that applied in the thirteenth century, when trademark law started developing, was the existence of a central registry of trademarks, either in the office of the guilds or in the town hall, with the purpose of ensuring publicity, so as to facilitate the prosecution of those masters who failed to follow the technical standards imposed by the guild's by-laws. In the case of Abbeville, it seems that the master cutlers had the freedom to choose their own marks—as opposed to other cases (see, e.g., §§2.5.5, 6, and 7) when masters would receive the trademarks from the Jurors or, as seen above, where the regulations stipulated the sign's appearance (see §2.4.6)—but they were still required to register them with the office of the aldermen. The statutes that follow do not mention it, but in some other cases, as we will see, the Jurors had the incumbence of carrying out some sort of examination of the trademarks in order to ensure their distinctiveness. It is here that we can see the roots of the modern system of trademarks.

Statutes of the Cutlers and Sheath Makers

June 17, 1494

To all those who will see or have these present [letters], the mayor and aldermen of the city of Abbeville, greetings. We make it known that, upon what the masters, eswards and companions of the said trade of cutlers and sheath makers who are in the said town of Abbeville have presented us, with a certain request regarding our aldermanship, by which they requested that it please us, by extending the old ordinances and statutes of this city, and also to avoid the frauds and deceits that occur daily in their profession, grant them, for the good of this profession, all points and articles hereinafter declared, which request, by the advice and deliberation of several notable advisors being in the said city, both of the king and of our aldermen, we have granted them and hereby grant them in the manner that follows.

...

8. *Item* similarly, no master of the said trade of cutlers shall mark the work that they will make with any other mark than that which they use and are accustomed to marking, which mark will be imprinted in lead, and delivered to and left with the office of the aldermen of the said city, and if they are found making any new work having a mark other than that which they use, they will incur in a fine of xx sols, whenever they are found doing the opposite, to be applied as above.

In witness whereof, etc. On the 17th day of June 1494.

§2.30.5 Statutes of the Cutlers of Paris with Detailed Rules on Trademarks—1565

The following text presents two interesting particularities: the cutlers who worked outside Paris did not have the right to use trademarks, which means that only the articles made by the cutlers of Paris were certified to their quality; and, second, the protection of the trademarks of the cutlers of Paris as to their distinctiveness extended beyond the limits of the city, which put them in a better position in the market for cutlery.

Statutes and Ordinances of the Cutlers of the City of Paris

December 17, 1565

Charles by the grace of God, king of France, To all present and to those to come, greetings. We have received the humble supplication from our dear and beloved Master Goldsmiths, Cutlers, Gilders and Engravers on iron and tempered and untempered steel of our good city of Paris, stating that our predecessors, Kings of happy and laudable memory, whom God absolve, have conceded and granted several beautiful Statutes and Ordinances to the said profession, as appropriate, and is contained and declared more at length in the Letters of Charter of our said predecessors: however, by the negligence and poor care of their predecessors in this profession, to the great detriment and damage to our Kingdom and public affairs, it remained for a long time almost without control; and therefore, the profession is now vitiated and corrupted by people completely inexpert and inexperienced in the art; for that reason, and to obviate it, the supplicants, following the permission granted by our Ordinances made at the General Assembly held in Orléans, to all Merchants, Artisans, and professional people of our Kingdom, have rewritten in intelligible language their old statutes and privileges, with certain new Articles, the contents of which follow.

...

14. *Item*, that no [master] can counterfeit each other's mark, either by printing a hallmark or by engraving it: and that no Master will take a mark, if it is not granted to him by the four Master Jurors of the said profession of Cutler: and that no Cutlers outside the suburbs will be able to mark with any marks similar to those of the Cutlers of the city of Paris, nor any other marks such as they may be, and these Cutlers, moreover, shall not keep servants or apprentices, on the penalty of a fine of forty sols Parisis, applicable to the King, where they fail to comply with the rules above.

15. *Item*, that if any knives or other blades are made without making a mark, and without being marked, as is customary, [the Cutler] must pay a fine towards the King.

§2.30.6 Statutes of the Cutlers of Yorkshire—1623-1624

1623-1624 AD. 1245 21° Jac. I. c. 31, 32. CHAPTER XXXI.

An Act for the good Order and Government of the Makers of Knives and other Cutlery Wares.

Inhabitants of the Lordship of Hallamshire in Yorkshire chiefly Cutlers;

Whereas the greatest part of the Inhabitants of the Lordship and Liberty of Hallamshire in the said County of Yorke doe consist of Cutlers and those that make Knives and other Cutlery Wares, and other Wares made and wrought of Iron and Steele, as Sickles Scissors and Sheers, and by their Industry and Labour in the same Art and Trades have not only gained the reputation of great Skill and Dexterity in the said Faculty, but have relived and maintained their Families, and have been enabled to set on work many poor Men inhabiting thereabout who have very small Means or Maintenance of Living other than by their hard and daily Labour as Workmen to the said Cutlers, and have made Knives of the best Edge wherewith they served the most part of this Kingdom and other foreign Countries, until now of late that divers persons using the same professions in and about the same Lordship and Liberty, and within six Miles compass of the same, not being subject to any Rule, Government or Search of any others of Skill in those Manufactures, have refused to submit themselves to any Order Ordinance or Search ; but every Workman in the said Lordship and Liberty, and within eight Miles compass thereof, have taken liberty to themselves to receive, entertain, and take as many Apprentices, and for what term of years, more Their Trade intruded on by irregular Workmen, &c. without Control.

...

VIII. And be it further enacted by the Authority aforesaid, That no person or persons using the said Art or Handicraft All Knives, Sickles, &c. shall have Steel or any of them within the said Liberty of Hallamshire or six miles Compass of the same as aforesaid shall at any in their Edges, time hereafter make or cause to be made any Knives or Knife blade Sheers Scissors or Sickles except he or they do put Steel into the Edges of them, upon pain to lose for every such Offence Ten Shillings, and the Wares so deceitfully made to be seized and recovered by the Master and Wardens of the said Company for the time being, and to be levied distributed and employed as aforesaid.

IX. And also be it enacted by the Authority aforesaid, That no person using the said Mystery or Craft or any of them put one prescribed within the said Lordship or Libertie or six miles Compass thereof, shall at any time hereafter strike grave or Mark on his Wares, use upon his Knives or the Wares before mentioned, any more marks than one, and that to be such as shall be first appointed or assigned unto him by the said Master Wardens and Searchers of the said Company for the time being or the greater number of them, upon pain to forfeit and lose for every time that he shall offend therein contrary to the true meaning of this Article or any Branch or Clause of the same, all such Goods not so marked, and the sum of Forty Shillings to the Master and Wardens of the said Company for the time being, to be employed as aforesaid.

§2.30.7 Statutes of the Cutlers of Rouen—1734

The particularity of the following statutes was that they added an indication of origin to the mandatory trademark of the cutlers.

Statutes of Cutlers, Engravers, Gilders on iron and steel [of Rouen], in 1734

...

Art. XIV.—No master shall counterfeit the mark of another, neither printing a hallmark or by engraving it, and no master shall take a mark, if it is not attributed to him by the inspectors and imprinted on the board of the profession.

Art. XV.—If unmarked goods are found with a master, they will be subject to fine.

...

Art. XVIII.—No one other than the cutlers of Rouen shall mark the works with the word: "Rouen," and the masters shall not give their works to be made to false workers.

§2.30.8 A French Historian Explains the Procedure for the Registration of the Trademarks of the Cutlers of Chatellerault and Describes How a Conflict Involving a Cutler's Trademark Was Settled—1766

The following text, besides confirming what we have already seen on the procedure leading to the registration of cutlers' trademarks, explains with some level of detail a conflict involving the counterfeiting of a trademark. It seems that the infringer, although having registered a different and distinctive mark, used a mark identical to the plaintiff's. The magistrate resorted to the advice of two experts. Interestingly, a heavy fine was imposed on the Jurors and Clerks of the guild. The reason may have been that they were negligent in their duty to supervise the registration and use of trademarks by masters.

"Today, the fourth of December one thousand seven hundred, Georges Blanchard, master cutler in this town, appeared in person at the Town Hall of Chatellerault, who declared that he had submitted the mark of the crowned P to be used to mark the works of his profession of cutler, which he had affixed to the [board of] copper of the community of master cutlers of this city. Registered at the Hall so that no one is unaware of it and which mark we have seen to be printed to our view with Spanish wax. Certified by this act." (Register XLI.—Municipal archives.)

The marks had to be inscribed on a board of copper in order to confirm the filing and be able to keep its imprint. In most cases, the files concerning the registration of trademarks bear the imprint of the registered hallmark in red wax in the margin; sometimes it is a piece of paper stuck to the register using a sealing block which has been imprinted.

We find, in the archives, a curious demand motivated by the similarity of two marks, similarity which may seem extraordinary when we learn that one of the marks represented the *rose tail* and the other the *cutlass*.

On August 16, 1766, Pierre Fleury, master engraver, and Denis Nivert, master cutler, appeared before the Lieutenant General at the request of the master jurors (Register XLII.230).

Pierre Fleury says that the hallmark which had been seized at Nivert's [shop] is indeed the rose tail, which was crushed by having been inscribed by Nivert on his merchandise, while the hallmark of the cutlass which is presented to him is completely new.

"You have to be blind to claim otherwise," Nivert judiciously adds.

This has been submitted to the examination by experts Michel Lecoq, former goldsmith, and François Treuil, who, who after examining the hallmarks, the scissors and blades of scissors, recognized that the hallmark seized at Nivert's [shop] indeed has the shape of a rose tail.

Subsequently the scissors and scissor blades were returned to Nivert and the engraver Fleury was ordered not to engrave any hallmarks in the future without notifying the first judge of police, on the penalty of a fine of twenty pounds; finally, the Jurors and Clerks were ordered to pay costs to all parties, which amounted to 414 pounds.

The inscription of the marks on the copper board was very irregularly observed, because on May 4, 1769, the Lieutenant General, Gabriel Louis Duchilleau, summoned the Master Jurors of the profession and community of cutlers to order them to inscribe their marks on the copper board of the community and provide another sheet of copper, which would remain at the office [of the Town Hall] to have a duplicate copy of the prints.

§2.31 THE FIRST RULES ON THE PROTECTION OF GEOGRAPHICAL INDICATIONS FOR WINE—1350 ONWARD

Given the close association of the quality of wine with the place where it is produced, not only because of the natural adaptation of the grapes to the soil from which they grow but also because of the techniques developed by local winemakers along generations, geographical indications have naturally been the preferred identifier chosen by merchants and customers to differentiate wines from the different regions they originate from. The same applies to cheese, liquors, etc., and for the same reasons: being natural products, Nature has a unique impact on their characteristics. As we have seen, the Romans had already used a geographical indication—the name of a city through its figurative symbol, the crescent moon—to identify the cheese produced in the city of Luna. It is, therefore, not a surprise that geographical indications started being the subject of legal regulations very early, in the course of the Middle Ages. As it happened with trademarks, such regulations aimed at ensuring the proper payment of taxes. However, the care for quality of products and their certification was also behind the first legal norms that set the standards for geographical indications. Indeed, behind geographical indications lies a sort of a paradox: whereas they are primarily expressions of a special localization of centers of production or of extraction of natural products, their relevance results from the perception of their origin by consumers located outside those centers. In this regard, speaking of food and cooking, Alberto Capatti and Massimo Montanari make this interesting point:

> *In the specific case of gastronomy this [paradox] appears clearly: the 'local' identity is born as a function of exchange, when (and to the extent that) a product or a harvest is confronted with different cultures and rules... . The exclusively 'local'*

> *product is devoid of a geographical identity because it arises from its 'delocalization.' The 'mortadella di Bologna' (or 'Bologna' tout court) is defined as such only when it leaves its production area. The 'all' ascolana' olives take on this name only when they cross the borders of their hometown—except if they return there due to a sort of boomerang effect.*[79]

§2.31.1 The General Rules on Commercial and Industrial Policy of France, Approved by Jean II, Included the Order for Wine Merchants to Respect Wine's Geographical Indications—1350

In 1350, Jean II, of France, approved what today we would call a "Commercial Code," comprising a large number of rules dealing with all sorts of trade and industry professions in the city. As far as the intellectual property of food is concerned, the "Code" included two relevant provisions: one that prohibited tavern keepers from selling wine under false geographical names (which is perhaps the first explicit norm providing for the protection of geographical indications), and another that required that the jaugeurs *(i.e., the measurers) of wine had their own trademarks, which should be registered at the City Hall. Although the reference here concerns marks of certification, two elements are important, which are still valid for today's trademarks: distinctiveness ("provided that they are different from each other and that they can and shall be known") and publicity ("their marks shall be registered and marked [verified] at the [City] Hall"). The idea of a central registry of trademarks was then gaining shape, but it took a few centuries to become an administrative practice applied to all sorts of trade and industry.*

Jean II, Ordinance concerning the [commercial and industrial] policy of the Kingdom.

Paris, January 30, 1350.

Title VI.—About Wine Merchants, Tavern Keepers, Sellers and Wine Brokers.

(1) It is ordered that no wholesale wine merchants can mix two wines together, on pain of losing the wine, and paying a fine... .
(4) The tavern keepers shall not sell all the best red wine made in the kingdom for more than ten *deniers* per pint; [they shall sell] all the best white [wine], for six *deniers parisis*, and no more; and the other [wines] for less. And if they do the opposite, they will lose the wine, and pay a fine.
(5) Those tavern keepers shall not give a name to or designate the wine from any region but by the [name] of the region in which it is made, on pain of losing the wine, and of the fine.
(6) Those tavern keepers shall not mix the wines with others, for selling in the taverns, on the penalties above said.

79. Alberto Capatti and Massimo Montanari, LA CUCINA ITALIANA—STORIA DI UMA CULTURA, at viii-ix (Latterza, 1999).

Title XXII—On the measurement of wines in the city of Paris

8. All measurers shall have their marks, and such as they please, provided that they are different from each other, and that they can and shall be known: so that if they commit any fraud or fault in their mentioned measurements, it can be clearly known who has done it, so as he be punished as appropriate. And their marks shall be registered and marked [verified] at the Hall of the said city [of Paris].

§2.31.2 Paris Adopts Rules on the Trade of Wines, Including Merchants' Obligation of Using the Correct Geographical Indication and Surveyors' Mandatory Adoption of Personal Marks—1415

The trade of wine in medieval Europe was almost as much important as that of bread, and thus it is not a surprise that rules on the intellectual property aspects of such trade were adopted very early, with a double purpose: to ensure that the wrongful use of geographical indications led consumers (and tax collectors) to error and that those in charge of measuring and certifying the quality of wines (the jaugeurs, *literally, those clerks in charge of measuring the wine, hereinafter designated as "measurers") would not commit frauds.*

General administrative regulations for the jurisdiction of the provost of merchants and aldermen of Paris, and establishment of several offices for the surveillance of the ports and markets of the same city.

Paris, February 1415

On the trade of wines

...

(45) *Item.* And if those wines brought to the said town downstream were brought to be sold there, they will be brought to the port of Grève; and if it is Burgundy wine, it will be kept in the *palée*[80] at the port of Burgundy; if it is French wine, it will be kept in the *palée* of the French port, and if it is wine from the Loire river, such as Montereul-Bellay, Orléans, Ris, Saint-Poursain, or others, it will be kept in the *palée* of the Moulins du Temple, if possible; otherwise in the *palée* of the lands of the port of Burgundy, and not otherwise, upon penalty of an arbitrary fine.

(46) Item. And to know the difference between French wine and Burgundy wine, all kinds of wines which will be produced above the Pont de Sens, as well as those from the Auxerrois region, and those from the Beaunois region and elsewhere in those parts, and which will arrive by the Yonne river, will be called Burgundy wines, and will be measured by the Burgundy gauge; and likewise all kinds of wines which will be produced below the said bridge of Sens, coming downstream the water, and also wines produced in the Seine, the town of Marne, and elsewhere in surrounding parts, and

80. "Palée" was a row of piles driven into the ground so as to form a dike or a structure of support.

likewise the wine produced around Paris and below, going downstream the water and the river Oise and parts around it, will be called French wines, and not otherwise, on penalty of a fine of ten pounds Parisis.

...

(49) Item. Those who sell wine, both wholesale and retail, shall not mix two wines together, such as white and red wine, either by *remplage*[81] or otherwise; and they shall not replace their wines with any wine, if it is not good, loyal and marketable; nor shall they give the name to the wine from any country other than that in which it is produced, on the penalty of losing the wine and [paying] an arbitrary fine.

...

About wine surveyors

...

(135) Item. Each measurer will have his mark and such as he pleases, provided that the marks will be different from each other, and that they can and will be known, so that if they commit any fraud or fault in the surveys they do, it is clearly possible to know who has done it, in order to be punished accordingly; and their marks will be registered and marked in the town hall of the said city.

§2.31.3 For the Sake of Certification and the Exaction of Taxes, the Territory of the Production of Bordeaux Wine Was Precisely Identified—1560

The text that follows is a compilation of excerpts of a number of ordinances and regulations adopted by the Parliament of Bordeaux, confirmed by Charles, King of France, in 1560, and by judgments of the Court of Parliament. Among other topics, these texts deal with the certification of the origin of the wine from the region of Bordeaux through the use of marks, with the purpose of certifying quality and ensuring the collection of taxes. The text presents two aspects of particular importance. One is the precise identification of the terroir *where wines produced were to receive and be identified with the mark of the city of Bordeaux. The second was the recognition of another certified origin of wine—wine from Gensac—as a result of the old and continued use of that designation by the winemakers of the zone of Gensac. According to a decision from the Court, those winemakers were also entitled to have their wines sealed and certified with the seal of Bordeaux.*

To the extent the regions allowed to designate the wine they produced as "Bordeaux" were precisely and exhaustively identified, we may see in these Regulations a first initiative aiming at "demarcating" a wine production region.

Prohibited and forbidden wines entering the town and city of Bordeaux: and which cannot be sold at retail and in taverns: and of the mark of those wines.

81. *Remplage* is an old French term that means the completing of a container (of wine) that is not completely full.

All the contents of this chapter were deemed necessary, as confirmed by the patents of King Charles, of January 9, 1560, and authorized by several judgments of the Court.

Since all times and antiquity, the wines that are brought and introduced in the city of Bordeaux, from Castillon, Périgord, de la Mothe Montravel, Saint Antoine, Sainte Foi, Saint Pey de Castets, Sainte Radegonde, Duras, Gensac, Rauzan, Pujols, Cirac, Blaignac, up to the middle of Lengrane: jointly with the wines produced in the region, lands, and lordships of Balie, from the channel of Boglon, on the one hand, and the channel of Freneau on the other, so as to know the difference of the wines, they will be marked with the half mark of the said city, at both ends of each barrel.

And the said wines after having been marked, can be put in and taken out only in the suburbs of the said city, and not within it; as well as other places, outside the walls and walkway of that city, by bearing sufficient and authentic certification, signed by the Judges of the places, or their deputies, and by certifying that the said wines are from the above-mentioned lands and lordships.

...

Agreement made with those of Gensac

Know all present and future, that as a plea and trial had been moved and pending before Monsieur the great Seneschal, or Monsieur my deputy, between the high and powerful Lord Messire Jena d'Albret, Count of Nevers and Rethel, Sieur d'Orval and of Gensac in Bazadois, and the residents and inhabitants in the said jurisdiction and Lordship of Gensac, on the one hand appellants or plaintiffs against Messrs. deputy mayor and Jurors, and Prosecutor of the town and city of Bordeaux on the other hand, on the grounds that the said people of Gensac, and inhabitants of the said lordship alleged to be in possession and enjoyment, and had the right to carry and to have carried wines produced in the said land and lordship of Gensac to Bordeaux, and to put and remove those wines from the ancient outskirts of the said town and city of Bordeaux: and that this they had enjoyed by such a time, that there was no memory of the contrary, except since the last year... .

Item moreover, so that the said Lords of the said city of Bordeaux are and can be better certified, that the said wines are from the territory and Châtelanie de Gensac, they shall have a mark with which the said wines will be marked at the said place of Gensac. And it shall belong to the said Mayors, deputy Mayors and Jurors of Bordeaux, to verify if the said wines are from the said Lordship, to prevent the frauds and deceptions, which each year are committed. And in addition, those, who will bring the said wines, with the certification signed and sealed with the seal of the said city and of the Consuls of Gensac to the said deputy mayors and Jurors, will inform the quantity of the said wines.

Item it has been decided, that after the said feast of Saint Martin, the wines of the city and Lordship of Gensac can be taken and placed within the fences and walls of the ancient outskirts of the said city, until they are by Messrs. Mayors and Jurors of Bordeaux, and not elsewhere in the city. And the said wines or vessels shall be marked with the mark of Bordeaux, before the wines enter the mentioned fence, under the same penalties and condemnation as above.

...

Wines that must be marked with the double mark of the said city, other than those from the high country, and where they are to be collected.

The wines produced in S. Seurin de Montaigne, Tallemont, Royal Berne, Moncuq, Bellot, and other places above the town of Saint Foy le Grand, which will be taken and driven to the said town of Bordeaux, those from Charreux excluded, and which could previously be sold, will be marked on each end of the barrel with the double mark of the city. And they cannot be placed or removed in any other place than Chartreux, on pain of the loss of the said wines.

And before being sold, they will pay to the said city for the right of the said double mark, five sols of Bordeaux for each barrel.

Of the barrels and vessels to hold the wine

...

And the carpenters, who do not make the barrels and other vessels well and duly ... will be punished, according to what is contained in the established customs of the said city and country of Bourdelois, article fifteenth: and each Carpenter will be required, following said custom, to mark its vessels with a known mark and different from other marks.

§2.31.4 Administrative Provisions Putting an End to the Counterfeiting of Trademarks in the Commerce of Bordeaux Wine—1614

This text, extracted from a commentary elaborated by the famous French jurist Antoine de Mornac, is about the counterfeiting of French wine and pastel (blue dye). It is worth noticing that, as far as wine is concerned, the reference to trademarks is only indirect—the prohibition is against copying the same methods of placing the hoops on barrels of Bordeaux wine. It seems, therefore, that the visual appearance of barrels used to load and transport wine from Bordeaux was characteristic of that region. Therefore, we are here in the presence of a measure of protection of the wine through the prohibition of the copy of its containers—a sort of counterfeiting that, as we have seen, had been practiced in Classical Rome.

On the 5th of August 1614, prohibitions were imposed on certain residents in the north of Orleans, to have their barrels hooped like those of the said city of Orleans; which is likewise followed at Bordeaux, for it is not possible to hoop the barrels in the manner of Bordeaux... .

The reason for all this is that one does not sell under such disguises wine as if it were from Orleans or Bordeaux, and yet they are not; ...

§2.31.5 Upper Douro Region, Portugal: For the Second (or First?) Time, a Particular, Specific Geographical Area Is Demarcated for the Purposes of the Protection of a Geographical Indication—1756

The text that follows is an excerpt from a Decree signed by José I of Portugal in September 1756, formally recognizing the Company created for the production and distribution of wine from Douro, known as Port wine (this designation resulting from the name of the city through which it was exported—Porto). The Decree was a response to the initiative of the "main wine makers of the Upper Douro and Good Men of the City of Porto," who, disgusted with the terrible quality of the wine that was produced in that region and whose exports to England were significantly reduced in spite of the increase in the population of that country,[82] *"agreed, with the Royal approval of His Majesty, to create a Company, which, competently sustaining the culture of the vines, at the same time preserves their productions in their natural purity, for the benefit of National and Foreign Trade, and the health of Your Majesty's Vassals." From an intellectual property perspective, the importance of the Decree lies in that it required the demarcation of the territory in which the wine designated as Port wine was produced. Such demarcation would be realized by a group of officers of the Company in the years that followed the approval of the Decree. We have seen that a precise definition of a territory for the production of a specific wine had appeared already in 1560, in association with the region where Bordeaux wine was produced. But the Portuguese initiative was original to the extent it was accompanied by a limitation to the quantity of wine to be produced, which corresponded to the major concern that presided over the Decree: to ensure the quality of Port wine to be exported by Portuguese winemakers to other countries and other Portuguese territories.*

September 1756

...

XXIX

The wines of the Coasts of the Upper Douro and of their territory to be shipped to America and the Foreign Kingdoms shall be separated completely and absolutely from all other wines of the places that only produce them capable of being consumed locally, so that the inferiority of these wines will not ruin the reputation that those deserve for their natural goodness. His Majesty is served that as soon as possible a Map and general record be made of the two Northern and Southern Coasts of the Douro River, that demarcates the whole territory that produces the true wines to be loaded, which are able to leave by the bar of the same River: and specifying each large and small farm of this sort, and declaring through a common estimate, or average calculated upon the productions of the five years that each of those farms usually delivers, so that their

82. This remark appears in a report of September of 1754 on the extremely low levels of quality that Port wine had reached, which caused its exports to England to be drastically reduced (more than two thirds). The report was presented by the "Feitoria Ingleza" (English Factory), an association of the British entrepreneurs and merchants that did business in the city of Porto.

owners cannot sell without disclosing to the Company what they sell, nor a greater number of kites be admitted to be sold to the Company, or to Foreigners, than the number that in said registration is attributed to them, under the penalty that, if they sell in excess of the said quantities, they will pay the excess nine fold, and will be prohibited to sell wines outside the Kingdom.

XXX

From the lands that remain outside the said demarcation no wine can be transported into its territory without bringing letters of guide issued by the whole body of the Town Halls of the places from which the such wines depart, ...

And this so that it does not happen that bad wines are bundled with the good ones in order to increase their quantity to the detriment of their reputation and the Company's, and of Foreigners who will buy them... .

Decree through which Your Majesty manifests his pleasure with the fifty-three chapters and conditions contained in the thirty-six half leaves above written, that the main farmers of High Douro, and Good Men of the City of Porto, have made and ordered, with the Royal consent of Your Majesty, so as to form a Company, which, sustaining the culture of vineyards, maintains their production in its natural purity, to the benefit of agriculture, of trade, and of public health.

§2.32 THE APPELLATION OF ORIGIN "ROQUEFORT"—AN EIGHT-CENTURY-LONG STRUGGLE AROUND ITS PROTECTION INVOLVING GEOGRAPHICAL INDICATIONS, TRADEMARKS, AND EVEN PATENTS—1411 ONWARD UP TO TODAY

It seems that the history of the geographical indication for the Roquefort cheese as a legal asset started in 1411, when the King of France accorded its makers a privilege (against creditors), thus making it one of the oldest protected geographical indications that have survived up to today. It was not a history without hurdles and incidents, however—as it happens with most business identifiers of great success. On the other hand, it has taken not only business identifiers (geographical indications and trademarks) to protect Roquefort. In a period of enthusiasm for patents—the end of the nineteenth and the beginning of the twentieth centuries, when the Industrial Revolution was at its apex—a few Roquefort producers did not hesitate to file for patent protection for some methods of its manufacture. Those patents had the additional advantage of introducing a certain degree of consistency and uniformity to the making of cheese, which, in the previous centuries, could vary significantly in color and taste and which reached today's uniformity in the first decades of the twentieth century. In the following excerpts, we will take stock of some of the incidents that involved the building of the appellation of origin "Roquefort" and the associated business, being of particular interest the struggle for the protection of the common term "Société" as a trademark and the antitrust inquiry by the French government into some business practices of the company that responds for about 40% of the sales of Roquefort. Significantly, the national antitrust agency of France noted that the mere ownership of the caves where, as a requirement for the use of the geographical indication, the cheese is manufactured and matured constitutes a barrier to entry. Also worth noticing is the opinion of the Civil Court of Saint-Affrique that the protection of an appellation of origin is not subject to the statute of limitations or to laches, in view of the principle that "criminal possession cannot furnish title to the person who has committed the offense."

§2.32.1 A French Historian Mentions the Origins of Roquefort as a Protected Geographical Indication

One of the historical proofs of this [the origins of the designation "Roquefort"] is provided by the old and curious documents concerning "Roquefort" which, in the opinion of gastronomes, is the "king of cheeses."

Pliny the Elder speaks of it laudably in his ANCIENT HISTORY.

In 1411 "last of April" letters patent granted by Charles VI prohibit the seizure of the cheeses which are in the cellars of Roquefort, due to debts, except in the absence of other movable property. In those letters, it is explained that in Roquefort, there are cellars:

> very cold in the summer of which the people of the country around who have cheese bring them there to arrange them and better season them and take the trouble and diligence, in exchange of certain money and other profits which they have and take from those to whom the cheeses belong from which the said supplicants earn their bread and support their poor lives.

In 1550, the inhabitants of Roquefort requested and obtained from the Parliament of Toulouse, a decree that assured them the privilege of making cheese and prohibited all individuals, peasants or others, from engaging in this manufacture outside the village of Roquefort, under penalty of a fine of six pounds per quintal [100 kg].

The parliament of Toulouse has prohibited several times the putting on sale under the name of Roquefort, cheeses of different origin, as witnessed by this judgment of August 31, 1661: "which very expressly prohibits and inhibits all merchants, valets and other persons of whatever quality and condition who will have taken and accepted cheese in the cabins and places in the vicinity of the said Roquefort, to sell it, distribute it, or to sell it in bulk or in detail as if it were the real Roquefort cheese, on the penalty of a fine of one thousand pounds."

§2.32.2 Patents Are Issued in France for the Process of Making Roquefort Cheese—1888, 1903

Fifteen-year patent, March 31, 1888; Rigal, represented by Chassevent, in Paris, Magenta Boulevard, no. 11.—Improvement in the manufacturing processes of the so-called *Roquefort* or *Roquefort-style* cheeses.

Fifteen-year patent, May 29, 1903; Société des Caves et des Producteurs Réunis de Roquefort, represented by the society Ch. Thirion and J. Bonnet, à Paris, Beaumarchais Boulevard, no. 95—Improvements in the manufacture of Roquefort cheese.

Figure 2.15 Advertisement of one of the manufacturers of Roquefort Cheese at the beginning of the twentieth century, announcing a new process for "the good manufacture" of the product and informing that it had been awarded gold medals at the Universal Exhibition in St. Louis, MO, USA, of 1904, and in Liège, in 1905. The advertiser, Grande Société P. Lebrou & Cie. was a spin-off of the Société des Caves. It was created by Paul Lebrou, who invented the use of artificial refrigeration in the making of Roquefort and—against the majority of the other producers—proposed that this new method permitted that the cheese be manufactured outside the caves of Combalou (name of the mountains around the village of Roquefort). The opinion whose syllabus is reproduced below (Société des Caves v. Société Nouvelle) reflects that discussion, agreeing with the position of those other producers who sustained that the term Roquefort could only be used in association with cheese manufactured and matured in those caves.

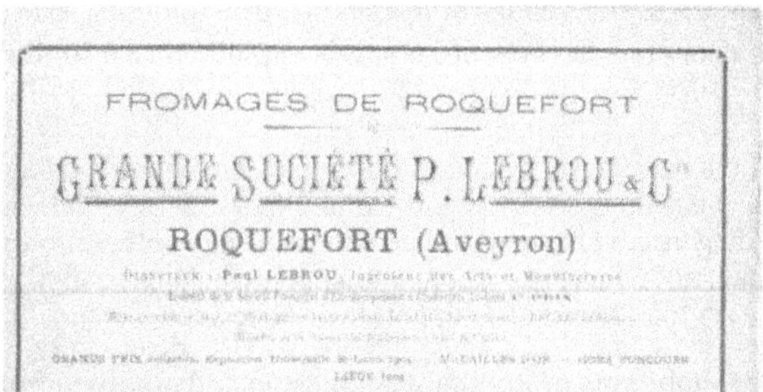

§2.32.3 French Courts Set the Conditions for the Exclusive Right to the Use of the Name Roquefort as an Appellation of Origin—1892 Onward

Court of Aix, October 21, 1892.

Soc. de Roquefort v. Rigaud Bardel

Product, Name of the locality where it is manufactured, Notoriety, Unfair competition.—There is unfair competition in usurping the name of a product which draws its reputation from the locality where it is manufactured, and in offering to the public, as manufactured in that place, a product that does not come from there.—And the same applies even in the case where this reputation comes from a purely natural circumstance, such as the quality of the soil or the caves where the product stays and is worked.—This circumstance in no way prevents the name of the product from being susceptible to appropriation by all those who manufacture in the locality.

Roquefort Caves, Appropriation of the name for the benefit of their owners, Usurpation.—Specifically, the Roquefort cheese industry is characterized by the stay of its products in the caves of this locality and by the handling they are subject to.—The name Roquefort applied to the cheeses that are made there, therefore constitutes exclusive industrial property in favor of those who own those caves, and no one else can take it to designate similar products, without practicing an act unfair competition. *Ibid.*

Invoices, References.—That is the case even if no mark or stamp reproducing the usurped name has been placed on the goods or on the packaging, if this name appears printed and handwritten on the sales invoices.—And even though instead of the word Roquefort alone, it would have been printed: "Roquefort fashion," especially where the word "Fashion," added to the printed mention, is no longer [added] to the written references. *Ibid.*

Civil Court of the Seine, July 21, 1904

Société des Caves et Producteurs Réunis de Roquefort, Rigal, Grimal et autres v. Société Nouvelle de Roquefort

Trademark.—Roquefort cheese.—Natural product.—Influence of the *terroir.*[83]

Roquefort cheese owes its essential qualities to the virtues and influence of a specific territory and constitutes a natural product comparable to wine in the production of which the virtue of the *terroir* and the handling of the worker contribute. The *terroir* where the natural phenomena necessary for the perfection of the cheese occur does not cover the entire extent of the commune of Roquefort but only a limited portion of this commune "the scree of Combalou." The constant, indisputable use, evidenced by authentic documents dating back several centuries, has always attributed the name

83. "Terroir" is a French term that has no literal translation into other languages. It means a specific geographical area where a certain product is made and to which it owes its particular characteristics.

Roquefort to the only cheese matured in the caves crossed by the natural air current emanating from the "cracks of Combalou."

Any cheese which has not been brought to its perfection under the influence of this natural force specific to the *terroir*, is not the same natural product as Roquefort and the fact of delivering a cheese to the trade under the name of Roquefort, because it would have spent a more or less long time in the *terroir* of the commune of Roquefort, in a location where the virtues specific to the *terroir* are not manifested, constitutes a usurpation of name practiced in favor of an ambiguity.

Civil Court of Saint-Affrique, December 22, 1921

Société aveyronnaise des fabricants de Roquefort c. Labadié.

Appellation of origin.—"Roquefort cheese".—Question of quality.—Origin.—Personal right.—Statute of limitation.—Negligence.—Voluntary abandonment.—Long sequence of successive offenses.

Determining the right to use the name Roquefort, as a generic name used to designate the nature of the product, the Court does not have to examine the question of the quality of the cheeses, nor that of the excellence of the caves where they are kept, nor to investigate whether the manufacture of cheeses should be limited to the exclusive use of milk collected in neighboring regions and whether this could result in a product of superior quality, but it is sufficient to note that the cheeses sold under the name of Roquefort were not matured in the caves of this locality;

To be able to inaccurately apply to a product a name of origin which is not its own, this original name would have to have fallen into the public domain and become an indication of the type and the unique and necessary name of the product, the name of the locality no longer reveals the origin of the product, but only its nature, whereas the application of the statute of limitations to this matter can only result from very long negligence or voluntary abandonment by the legitimate owners of this type of collective trademark;

It is to no avail that a usurper would try to sustain that he has the personal right to use the name of Roquefort having acquired it through possession for more than thirty years by selling by himself or his authors under the name of Roquefort cheeses coming from other caves, because assuming it were established, this extended possession would be unable to create for the benefit of the usurper any right to extend by a day or an hour a usurpation and the fact of selling each day, for thirty years or more, foreign cheeses under the false indication of origin "Roquefort" constitutes nothing other than a long series of successive offenses provided for and punished by the law of July 25, 1824, the law of August 1, 1905 and criminal possession cannot furnish title to the person who has committed the offense;

Referring to local, loyal and constant customs, only the cheese made exclusively with sheep's milk and matured in caves crossed by natural, cold and humid air currents coming from the Combalou mountain in Roquefort (Aveyron) is entitled to the appellation "Roquefort."

Court of Montpellier, November 29, 1899

Société Anonyme des propriétaires de Roquefort v. Société des Caves et Producteurs réunis de Roquefort

Trademark.—Trade name.—Partners' rights.—New Society.—Right to the trademark.—Name "Société".—Cheese industry.—Fancy name.—Similar company.—Right to reveal the society's nature.—Measures to avoid any confusion.

The trademark, exploited jointly by partners united in a Society, constitutes a social mark whose notoriety and reputation are increased thanks to the efforts of all; each partner acquires rights to this mark, which, in the absence of any stipulation contained in the Society's by-laws, must be the same for everyone, and the partner assigning his rights to successors, places them in all his rights of ownership and therefore of co-owners of the mark.

However, the plaintiffs, creating a new Society, cannot confer on this new Society the rights that they had in the mark of the old Society, whereas at least in the liquidation of the said Society, they gave to the liquidators, final receipt and discharge without any protest of reservation.

The word "Société" is a generic expression necessary to designate any association of persons or of assets, but it is not an expression necessary to understand the nature of a product such as cheese, and nothing being more arbitrary than giving such a product the name "Société", this purely fanciful name can be the subject of a valid trademark.

The right that a manufacturer has to have the name "Société" to mark [products] can be perfectly reconciled with the undisputed right that a similar limited company has to indicate on its prospectuses and on its brand by the word "Société", its status of commercial association and the trade name it has taken, as long as with the word "Société" it does not seek to create confusion.

Figure 2.16 Package of Roquefort cheese, branded with the trademark "Société." The WIPO Global Brand Database shows (on November 15, 2023) that this trademark is nationally registered in several countries and, under the Madrid System, in 20 countries. Top, left, the seal certifying protection of a European Union appellation of origin. On the right, a seal certifying the quality and the origin of the cheese. Below, in French, English, and Spanish, the sentence: "Matured in our natural caves."

§2.32.4 The Appellation "Roquefort" as Defined by a Statute of 1925

Act of July 26, 1925

Art. 1— It is prohibited to manufacture, exhibit, transport, offer for sale or sell, hold, import, export, under the name of Roquefort, with or without nominal or qualifying addition, a cheese other than that which has been:

a) Prepared and manufactured exclusively with sheep's milk;
b) Manufactured and matured in accordance with local, loyal and constant customs, with regard to both the place of such maturation and the method used.

Art. 2.—The production area of sheep's milk used in the composition of Roquefort is limited to the current French production areas and to areas of metropolitan France with the same characteristics of sheep breeds, pasture and climate.

Art. 3.—Any manufacturer who intends to give his products the name "Roquefort" is required to make a declaration to the town hall of the municipality of the place of maturation.

Art. 4.—The following are prohibited:

> The entry, reception or presence of any milk other than sheep's milk, of any cheese product originating from milk other than sheep's milk, in cheese factories, dairies and maturing premises where Roquefort cheese is prepared, manufactured and matured.

Art. 5.—Except as far as the needs of local consumption are concerned, the entry, transformation, maturing, sale of any dairy or cheese made of milk other than that of sheep are prohibited throughout the territory of the municipality of the place of maturation.

Art. 6.—The offenses against this law will be punished by the penalties provided for by the arts. 8 and 22 of the law of May 6, 1919 on the protection of appellations of origin, without prejudice to the application to the facts noted of the penalties of the law of August 1, 1905 and all other legislative provisions. Art. 463 of the Penal Code is applicable to these offenses.

§2.32.5 The Largest Producer of Roquefort Cheese Is Fined in 5 Million Euros for Collusion with Its Major Distributors—2004

Decision No. 04-D-13 of April 8, 2004 relating to practices by the Société des Caves et Producteurs Réunis de Roquefort in the blue-veined cheese sector.

The Competition Council (Section IV),

Considering the letter registered on December 14, 2000, under number F 1278, by which the Minister of the Economy, Finance and Industry referred to the Competition Council practices implemented by the Société des Caves et des Producteurs Unis de Roquefort;

Considering Book IV of the Commercial Code relating to freedom of prices and competition and Decree No. 2002-689 of April 30, 2002, setting the conditions of its application;

Concerning the observations presented by the Société des Caves et Producteurs Réunis de Roquefort and by the Government Commissioner;

Considering the other documents in the file,

The rapporteur, the general rapporteur, the Government commissioner and the representatives of the Société des Caves et des Producteurs Réunis de Roquefort, heard during the session of January 21, 2004,

Adopt the following decision:

Findings

> 1. On December 14, 2000, the Minister of the Economy, Finance and Industry, acting in accordance with the provisions of Article L. 462-5 of the Commercial Code, referred to the Competition Council a file relating to the "status of competition in the blue-veined cheese sector, comprising two segments, Roquefort and blue cheeses". This referral targeted, in particular, the practices of the group Société (understood as the Société des Caves et des Producteurs Réunis de Roquefort and its subsidiaries, SNC Roquefort Société and SNC Fromagerie Louis Rigal), itself owned by the Besnier group, which became

Lactalis in 1999, and which, as per the referral, had concluded commercial agreements with seven of the main retail companies providing for the exclusive supply of these companies by the group Société in return for global discounts on the total turnover, the said agreements having had the effect of ousting competing producers or restraining access to the market.

...

8. The practices in question concern commercial agreements concluded by the Société des caves with Casino, Francap, Carrefour, Comptoirs Modernes, Système U, Promodès and Loceda. These supply contracts for products from the group Société des Caves were signed by the distributors in return for remuneration in the form of global discounts ranging from 2.25% to 8.6% of the total invoiced turnover.

...

31. The Société des Caves, moreover, benefits from a regulatory barrier to entry due to the obligation imposed on producers to use, for the manufacture of Roquefort, only sheep's milk coming exclusively from "the Roquefort region" and mature it in the caves of the village of Roquefort of which it is the main owner.

32. It is therefore established that the Société des Caves et Producteurs Réunis de Roquefort is in a dominant position in the Roquefort market.

...

68. The various elements noted constitute a body of serious, precise and consistent evidence highlighting practices aimed, on the part of the group Société des Caves, at restricting the access to or the preservation of competing companies on the Roquefort market, particularly for distribution in LMS [large and medium-sized stores]. These practices, which had the purpose and effect of limiting competitors' access to the market, are prohibited by Article L. 420-2 of the Commercial Code.

...

Decision:

Article 1: It is established that the Société des Caves et des Producteurs Réunis de Roquefort has violated the provisions of Article L. 420-2 of the Commercial Code.

Article 2: A financial penalty of 5 million euros is imposed on the Société des Caves et des Producteurs Réunis de Roquefort; ...

§2.33 THE BUSINESS IDENTIFIERS OF BREWERS

Like other artisans, brewers were also compelled to have their own trademarks and register them with the magistrates of their guilds. But in the case of beer, particular emphasis was also given to the trademarks of the makers of barrels because these should correspond to the volume determined by the regulations, with a view to the proper exaction of taxes. According to several local regulations, those barrels determined to be adequate would also be marked with the stamp of the city where they were made.

§2.33.1 The By-Laws of the Corporation of Brewers of Rouen Included Rules on the Mandatory Use and Registration of Trademarks—1456

Statutes of the Brewers of Rouen in 1456

...

Art. X.—No brewer shall put their beers in non-surveyed barrels and their barrels shall be marked with their trademark, under the penalty of a fine of thirty sols, applicable as above [that is, 10 sols for the king, 10 sols to the corporation, and 10 sols to the inspectors of the trade].

...

Art. XIV—All masters before beginning their work will bring to the bailiff or his deputy their mark to be imprinted on a skin leather so that those to whom the containers will belong will be known.

§2.33.2 As in Rouen, in 1456, the Statute of the Brewers of Paris of 1489 Included Provisions on the Mandatory Use of Trademarks

Interestingly, this regulation refers to a central registry of trademarks of the various professions of Paris located at the Grand Châtelet, which, until the eighteenth center, hosted the central court services of the French Kingdom and served as the registry of public acts. We may see here a precedent of today's trademark office, not in the sense of a central service that examined trademark applications but in the sense of a central registry that served the purpose of giving publicity to trademarks.

October 6, 1489

Letters from the provost of Paris, approving the statutes of the brewers in 15 articles.

...

3. *Item* each master of the said profession will have a mark to mark the vases, barrels and other containers in which he will put and deliver the beers and ales that he will make and sell, so that one can easily know and recognize to whom those vases and barrels belong; which mark will be printed, in the presence of the said jurors, on a piece of a lead, which, for this [purpose] will be placed in the chamber of the King's attorney, jointly with the leads where the marks of the other professions of this city are printed, and this fact, registered on the records of the said Châtelet; and who will do the

opposite, he will pay a fine of ten sols Parisis, to be applied as above [one third for the King; one third for the guild; and one third for the inspectors].[84]

§2.33.3 Statutes of the Master Brewers of the City of Paris—1630

The statutes of the brewers of Paris were adopted as early as 1514, and, along the years, they were reenacted with few changes. Interestingly, the statutes provided for the prohibition of débauchage, *which prohibition, as we have seen in Chapter 1, has applied to cooks since the thirteenth century. The reason is that masters of both professions owed their success to the possession of trade secrets, which, to some extent, they could not avoid sharing with apprentices. The* débauchage *of apprentices by rival cooks could, therefore, represent a major loss.*

Articles Containing the Statutes and Ordinances of the Master Jurors Brewers of Beer in the City of Paris.

March 16, 1630

Item. Each Master of the Trade will have a mark to mark the vases, barrels and other vessels in which he will put and deliver Beers and Ales which he will sell, so that one can easily know and recognize to whom the said vases and vessels will belong, which mark will be imprinted in the presence of the Jurors, after they have seen if the said vessels will be of good measure, on a [board of] lead which for this [purpose] will be placed in the Chamber of the King's Attorney, together with the leads that are the marks of the other Professions of this city, and this fact recorded in the Registry of Châtelet, and whoever does the contrary, he will pay a fine of twenty pounds Parisis, to be applied as above.

Item. That the Masters of the said trade cannot subtract the apprentices or servants of the other Masters of this trade, and whoever is found doing the contrary, he will pay twenty pounds Parisis fine to be applied as above.

§2.34 THE BUSINESS IDENTIFIERS (SIGNBOARDS) OF HOSTELS, INNS, AND TAVERNS—1577 ONWARD

The businesses of hospitality have resorted to elements of identification and differentiation since Antiquity. But with the Commercial Revolution, the need for professional traveling has gradually and constantly increased, and the adoption of corresponding regulations on the opening and functioning of inns has accompanied that trend. The objectives of the regulations had to do with hygiene, security of guests, and compliance with rules on the supply of food to guests. Some regulations also had a religious motivation, when the followers of some sects would be prohibited from staying at inns (see §2.32.2). And, as a matter of course, regulations also had to do with the business identifiers of the lodges—namely, signboards—that could help the inspectors assess

84. This same provision appears in the statutes for the profession of brewers of Paris of 1519 and 1687.

compliance with administrative and tax obligations. But there was also a concern with commercial differentiation, given that it is by resorting to signboards that guesthouses can capture prestige and reputation. As we will see below, conflicts involving the unauthorized use of similar signboards by innkeepers reached the courts as early as the sixteenth century.

§2.34.1 A General Regulation on Guesthouses with a Provision on Signboards—1577

Edict on Hotels, Cabarets and Taverns

Blois, Mars 1577; registered with the parliament on July 4.

...

(6) Those provided with our permission will put up, so that no one claims cause of ignorance, in the most visible places of their houses a board with such sign as they please, below which will be written in large letters, *Hotel, Cabaret, or Tavern by permission of the king.* We very expressly forbid all others from running inns, cabarets or taverns, nor receiving anyone in their houses in exchange of money, without that permission, as is said above, on the penalty of a fine of one hundred free Parisis for the first time, which will double the second time, and per bodily punition.

Figure 2.17 Since Antiquity, inns have been identified with signboards, with the double purpose of providing guidance to travelers and capturing the reputation of their owners vis-à-vis competitors. Illumination of the Comedies, of Terence (Publius Terencius Afer) (1190-1159 BC), in a manuscript published between 1400-1500, folio 86.

§2.34.2 The Magistrates of Dijon Rule on a Dispute over the Ownership of an Inn Signboard—1587

The text that follows is an excerpt from reports collected by Joseph Garnier on several court disputes that took place in France from the second half of the sixteenth century onward concerning ownership and imitation of signboards—whose importance for retail commerce in that period should not be underestimated. Of particular interest is a letter that the magistrates of Dijon, Bourgogne, France, have sent to their feudal lord, requesting his advice on a legal dispute involving the ownership of an inn signboard, the Pan. The issue also involved the religion of choice of one of the parties involved (probably, he was a Huguenot), which was possibly the reason for the aldermen of Dijon to seek their supervisor's advice.

(ii) The Aldermen of Dijon to the Earl of Chabot-Charny

Dijon, 1587, 27 mars.

... We have an innkeeper in this city named Antoine Bergier, who formerly held the whole inn of Pan. Since the death of his wife the inn has been shared between him and the children of her first marriage. It was necessary to know who would hold the name and sign of the Pan. This difficulty having been brought to us, it seemed to us for several reasons that the sign was to remain with the inn which had come to the children, because more than thirty years had passed since the sign and entrance of the Pan had been there. In addition, Bergier has always been of the party contrary to the Catholic religion, and if there is a suspect man who comes to this city, he retires to his inn. Furthermore, he made a door in his [wine] press to enter his neighbor's garden, from which he can access the walls of the city, on which the said garden ends. In the same garden there is a view so high that it overlooks the said wall and discovers very far in the countryside. He was the appellant of our judgment, the lieutenant of the bailiff reversed it and ordered that the sign would remain in the inn of Bergier, instead of him and her wife being expelled from the city or detained during these disorders. This, Monseigneur, and many other things, take away from us the means of doing what we would like for the safety of the city, of which we are obliged to alert you. We confide in the subject of your letters, because all men of judgment will consider it to be very perilous, especially as there are enough people in this city who favor the party of those of bad opinion. We beg you very humbly, Monseigneur, to order us what pleases you that we do as regards such perplexity, and want to interest your authority if you find the best thing, so that you are obeyed and the city ensured under the obedience of His Majesty, so much that afterwards we cannot be blamed of anything. Kissing your hands very humbly. We will pray to God, Monseigneur, that it please Him to keep you in happy prosperity and health.

§2.34.3 Inn Signboards in Three Villages in Provence, France—1639

The following text is an excerpt of a summarized list of documents concerning hostels and inns in Provence, France, in 1639. It is curious to note that in two villages, there were inns with the same sign: the Cheval-Blanc. At that time the doctrine had already been accepted that signboards can be conflicting only when there is geographical proximity between the commercial venues. This, of course, was not the case between Apt and Solliès-Pont, both villages located in Provence, at a distance of about 150 km.

1639.—Inn and Cabaret keepers.—... Survey of hotel and cabaret keepers of the city of Apt, the latter "with the branch," they were in the number of 15 and the hostel keepers, in the number of 11. Here are the names in their signboards: l'Ange, le Lion d'Or, Saint-Crépin, la Fleur-de-Lys, les Trois-Maries, Sainte-Marthe, Saint-Éloi, le Double-Écu, l'Écu d'Or, la Croix d'Or, les Trois-Faucons, le Cheval-Blanc, la Cloche,

Saint-Jacques.—At Solliès, the hostel keepers had as signboards: l'Écu-de-France, la Clef d'Argent, le Soleil, le Cheval-Blanc, la Croix-Blanche ; at Castellane there were the following lodges: des Trois-Rois, du Chaperon-Rouge, de la Fonteyne, etc… .

§2.34.4 A French Historian Describes a Curious Dispute Involving the Signboard of a Hotel in Paris—1647

Besides the curiosity of the (true) story that follows, its most significant element lies in the evidence of the importance hotel keepers gave to the differentiating role of their signboards. It was—and it still is today— that role that explained the level of unfairness of the newcomer, who, moved by resentment, tried to harm the business of the innkeeper who had established himself first.

Towards the end of the reign of Louis XIII, the owner of a house or inn, located in the *grande rue Saint-Denis*, near the church of Saint-Leu and Saint-Gilles, and where the signboard *Croix de Fer* ("Iron Cross") hung, was forced to evict a tenant who did not pay the rent for this house. This tenant rented another house in the *rue Bourg-l'Abbé* and, maliciously, also put in it the *Croix de Fer* as a signboard. The building was formed by two large hotel aisles, one located and having its exit on *rue Bourg-Labbé*, and the other in the *rue Saint-Denis*.

These two aisles were separated only by a thick wall, built in the middle of the two courtyards that accompanied those houses. Five or six years later, the vindictive tenant rented the two courtyards, which belonged to a single owner and obtained permission from him, not only to demolish the wall which formed the separation of the two courtyards, but also to have a carriage gate built on rue Saint-Denis, and above this door he also placed the signboard of the *Croix de Fer*. Then, the owner of the house on rue Saint-Denis, "where at all times and antiquity he had had the *Croix de Fer* as a Signboard," had his former tenant summoned before the Provost of Paris, in order to obtain the removal of the competing signboard and its replacement by another.

The defendant answered that the two inns were far from each other and that the signboard placed on *rue Saint-Denis* was a consequence of the one placed at the house which was located on *rue Bourg-Labbé*; the two hotel aisles being nothing else than one single and same house, which had two exits into the aforementioned streets, and, consequently, it would have been ridiculous to require that the same inn had two different signboards. And, on the other hand, as the defendant had been using the signboard of the *Croix de Fer* for more than eight years, without the plaintiff having complained about it, the claim was obviously ill-founded.

The aggrieved homeowner responded that the distance between the houses was not as great as the defendant claimed and that there were no more than twenty houses between the two that were in question. That on the other hand, its former tenant had only rented the new building on *rue Saint-Denis* out of resentment; that, moreover, this last dwelling, according to the old leases, always had as its signboard the *Image Saint-Roch*, "which the defendant had only removed to put there that of the *Croix de Fer*, and by this means divert passers-by, coach drivers and messengers who come from outside and who were since a long time accustomed to come and check-in in the house or hostel of the plaintiff, because the house of the defendant being located closest to the gate of Saint-Denis with the Signboard of the *Croix de Fer*, those who will arrive in Paris, and whose address would be that of the plaintiff, which is known in all towns in France, will instead enter that of the defendant..."[85]

The case had, it seems, already presented itself and the conflict had been settled between two merchants, concerning "the two Pavilions above the Pont Notre-Dame"[86] However, the cause was of greater importance for two inn keepers and the owner of the old hotel on rue Saint- Denis did not claim anything about the sign on rue Bourg-Labbé, but he maintained that the one placed on rue Saint-Denis, for two or three years, was illegal and contrary to the rules of the Police.

Three centuries later, we will no doubt believe that this request was well-founded. Nevertheless, the Provost of Paris put "the parties out of court and from trial" and the case having come to appeal, the sentence was confirmed, despite the pleadings of the attorneys Bataille and Le Vasseur, on February 16, 1647.[87]

According to the indications provided by the seventeenth century document, it is obvious that the ancient *Croix de Fer* inn was near *rue aux Ours*, while the new *Croix de fer* was closer to *rue du Petit Huleu (or Hurleur).*

The case of 1647 is therefore not only curious and amusing; it is also very useful for the little history of an old corner of Paris.

---

85. Note by Adrien Blanchet: "(1) The Iron Cross was obviously a fairly common signboard. In 1577, a house on *rue de la Grande-Truanderie*, opposite to the *Puiys d'Amour*, led to the house on *rue Saint-Denis*, "on which the *Croix de Fer* hangs as a sign" (E. Caron, THROUGH THE MINUTES OF PARISIAN NOTARIES, 1900, at 222, no. 951). It is also known that, toward the middle of the sixteenth century, houses located on *rue Saint-Antoine, grand rue de Saint-Marcel* and *rue de la Harpe* displayed the *Croix de Fer* as a signboard (Ernesl Coyecque, COLLECTION OF NOTARIAL ACTS, RELATING TO THE HISTORY OF PARIS, IN THE SIXTEENTH CENTURY, vol. 1, 1905, nos. 1970, 2761 and 1770). The Commission's zealous collaborator, Mr. Grimault, kindly communicated to me the names of the signs noted in the *Terrier du Roy* [...] for the block of houses in question here. The *Croix de Fer* is no longer there. Houses are often referred to only by the owner's name. However, we find, at no. 64 of *rue Bourg-l'Abbé*, the *Écu Dauphin* (Dolphin Shield); on *rue Saint-Denis*, at the corner of *Porte-aux-Peintres*, the *Ville de Rome* (City of Rome), belonging to Mr. Hélissant [...]; the other corner of Porte-aux-Peintres was occupied by the *Maison du Faisan* (House of the Pheasant), belonging to Marguerite Poisson.
86. Note by Adrien Blanchet: "A similar dispute arose in 1618 between two merchant grocers, initially associated and who separated. The one most guilty of the breakup set himself in a house at just two doors of distance to exercise the same business, with similar-looking signboards, but with a different name (*La Grosse Tête [The Big head]* instead of *La Barbe d'or [The Gold Beard]*). The Provost pronounced a ridiculous judgment which was overturned by the Parliament of Paris. The offender was ordered to completely modify the sign's appearance of the head, which took the name of *Chef Saint Denis* (*rue de la Harpe*)."
87. Note by Adrien Blanchet: "I have summarized the dispute according to the following work: NOUVEAU RECUEIL DE PLUSIEURS QUESTIONS NOTABLES, TANT DE DROIT QUE DE COUTUMES, JUGEES PAR ARRESTS D'AUDIANCES DU PARLEMENT DE PARIS DEPUIS 1640 JUSQUES A PRESENT, DIVISE PAR CENTURIES, *par Maître Lucien Soefoe, ancien avocat audit Parlement*. A Paris, chez Charles de Sercy, au sixième Pilier de la Grand'Salle du Palais, vis-à-vis l'escalier de la Cour des Aydes, à la Bonne-Foy couronnée, 1682, in-f, vol. 1, at 107-108. (*Première centurie, chapitre* C: *Si deux Hosteliers voisins peuvent avoir dans une même Rue deux enseignes semblables*)." This same commentary is summarized in §2.32.5.

§2.34.5 Another Report about the Same Dispute

Parliament, Book I

Chapter D. XXXI

Whether two neighboring hotel keepers can have two similar signboards on the same street.

By Judgment of February 16, 1647, attorneys Bataille for the Appellant, and Le Vasseur for the Respondent, the Court confirmed the decision of the Châtelet, which had dismissed the request made by one of those Hotel keepers who had for signboard the *Croix de Fer* on *rue S. Denys*, near *S. Leu Saint Gilles*, against another hotel keeper, who had placed a similar signboard on an inn on the aforementioned *rue S. Denys*, that the latter be required to remove its signboard and put another one there. The particular circumstances, and the allegations by the parties, are found in the Recueil by Maître Lucien Söefve, Tom. 1, Cent. I, ch. 100.

§2.34.6 Another Conflict Involving Identical Signboards—Havre, 1698

The central archives of the city of Havre are rich in decisions by the municipality concerning the use of signboards by inns and taverns. Of special interest is the report of a decision settling a dispute between one haberdasher, as plaintiff, and two tavern keepers, as defendants. Although the parties were not competitors, the municipality agreed with the plaintiff. Also interestingly, the same archives show that, three months later, on the Grande-Rue, *at the Havre, there was an inn keeper who used the same signboard "Le Pilier Vert." Eventually the distance between the plaintiff's shop and the inn on* Grande-Rue *was considerable enough not to raise worries.*

Dispute concerning a signboard *Au Pilier Vert* affixed by Rousselin and Canu to the detriment of Nicolas Le Roy, haberdasher, in whose house this sign has appeared "from time immemorial." The latter will keep it, Rousselin will put *Au Grand Pilier Vert* and the widow Canu will only put an inscription *Good wine, good cider at the widow Canu*. (May 3).

Jacques Aubourg, master of the *Pilier Vert*, in the Grande-Rue, prosecuted for having accommodated bear "drivers" without having warned them that they needed to obtain permission for their public performances. (July 6)

§2.34.7 A French Jurist Explains the Rules That Preside over the Choice and Placement of Signboards—Seventeenth Century

We have already mentioned that one of the major concerns of French authorities with the signboards of inns and shops in general was with the security of the passers-by because of the numerous accidents caused by signboards that were too big and too heavy. But in that period, a doctrine on the distinctiveness of signboards was also developed. The boundaries of the territorial protection of the signboard are defined: if it is a large city, two similar signboards cannot coexist if the shops or hotels are on the same street; but if it is a village or a suburban neighborhood, the signboard of the merchant who established himself first is protected through the entire locality.

Signboards of cabarets or of merchants

Signs and façade projections can only be placed on the streets with the permission of the officers of the municipality; but in the case of Cabarets, Inns and Merchants, there are two reasons why this cannot be done; if he is a cabaret keeper or an innkeeper, not only he shall not place a signboard or a false cork showing the site and the place where he will place it, so that it does not harm anyone and is installed in such a way that such Signboard must be solid and cannot fall on passers-by in the street. Secondly, it is necessary for that who establishes himself for the first time, if he is a cabaret keeper or an innkeeper, that he shows the Fiscal Attorney the vases, bottles and measures which he intends to use in his inn or cabaret, so that they be inspected and sampled; likewise, if he is a Merchant, he must show to the officers of the municipality his measurements, ells, half-ells, weights, pounds, half-pounds, scales, hooks, and all the instruments which he decides to use in his trade, of which these Officers draw up a report, based on which they grant permission to the citizen to carry out his business and commerce. Without these formalities, the Fiscal Attorney can make them take down their signboards and corks, and have them fined.

It must be observed that a cabaret keeper, innkeeper, or merchant, cannot take as signboard the same figure that is in another signboard established before him in the same street, if it is a large city, or in the same city or neighborhood: anyone who had a similar one placed before the latter would have the right to oppose it and make it take another one. This is what was decided by Judgment of Wednesday, August 12, 1648, based on the Conclusions of Attorney General Bignon, [in a dispute] between Grelant and Aumont, Merchant Grocers of the City of Paris, rue de la Harpe, as reported by Soefve, Chap. 92.

§2.35 THE EARLY BUSINESS IDENTIFIERS OF COOKS—1599 ONWARD

Cooks have been reunited under guilds since very early, as we saw in Chapter 1 (see §1.2), but in the Middle Ages, they did not enjoy the same prestige as in Antiquity. They were considered a professional group like any other and were treated as such. Consequently, we will not find expressions of the capture of individual reputation through business identifiers. That would happen only after culinary-related activities became fashionable, and certain chefs acquired great prestige in the seventeenth and eighteenth centuries. Thus, it is not surprising that until recently—say, until the nineteenth century—the business identifiers of cooks were dealt with in association with the collective interests of the guild in order to secure the exclusivity of their profession against the workers of related activities, such as innkeepers and wine merchants.

§2.35.1 Regulations for the Cooks of Paris, Protecting Them from the Interference of Other Professions in Their Exclusive Business—1599

The following text is an extract of the regulations of the cooks' guild of Paris of 1599 and reiterated several times subsequently. Its provisions dealt primarily with the protection of cooks against interference by other professionals in the area of food, such as inn and tavern keepers, securing cooks' exclusivity in cooking and serving certain sorts of festivities. Of significant interest from an intellectual property standing is the obligation of cooks to use signs (i.e., signboards) in their shops in a way that does not create confusion with other cooks. The essence of that requirement was not yet that of imposing distinctiveness for the purposes of promoting commercial rivalry but had the intent of facilitating the inspection by the Jurors and the "Farmers," i.e., the tax collectors. Nevertheless, there was here already a seed of an intellectual property asset.

Articles, Statutes, Ordinances and Regulations by the Jurors, Master Cooks [Queux, Porte-Chappes] & Caterers of the City, outskirts, Suburbs, Prévôté and Viscounty of Paris.

Extracted from the By-laws accorded to them by the late King Henry the Great according to the Letters Patent of the month of March 1599, registered before the Provost of Paris, or his deputy, based on the Conclusions of the Prosecutor of His Majesty at the Châtelet, on the 29th of the said month, confirmed by the late King Louis XIII, of glorious memory, in the month of December 1612, & by His Majesty now reigning [Louis XIV], in June 1645.

...

XXXIX.

None of those Masters shall take a sign similar to that of his Brother, nor similar to it, in order to avoid all the disorders that could arise, on the penalty of being deprived of the honors of the said Community, and a fine of two hundred pounds, half applicable in favor of the Community, and the rest to the Brotherhood, and of all costs, damages & interest.

§2.35.2 The Provision of the 1599 By-Laws of the Cooks on Distinctive Signs Is Repeated in 1663

August 1663

Statutes of master chefs, cooks, roasters and caterers of the city of Paris, in 45 articles, with confirmatory letters patent from Louis XIV.

...

39. No one among the masters will take a sign similar to that of his colleague, nor similar to it, in order to avoid all the disorders that could arise, on the penalty of being deprived of the honors of the said Community, and a fine of two hundred pounds, half

applicable in favor of the Community, and the rest to the Brotherhood, and of all costs, damages & interest.

40. They are also forbidden to undertake on each other for the market of weddings, feasts, banquets and other things associated with their art, under similar penalty.

§2.35.3 The Same Provisions Are Reiterated in the By-Laws of the Guild of Cooks of 1664, with an Additional Restraint on Competition

Articles, Statutes, Ordinances and Regulations of the Jurors, Masters Cooks and Roasters and Caterers of the City, Outskirts, Suburbs, Prévoté & Viscounty of Paris, extracted from the Statutes granted to them by the late King Henry the Great, following the Letters Patent of the month of March 1599, registered before the Provost of Paris, or his Deputy, based on the Conclusions of the prosecutor of His Majesty at the Chatelêt, on the twenty-ninth of the said month: Confirmed by the late King Louis XIII, of glorious memory, in the month of December 1612, and by his now reigning Majesty, in the month of June 1645.

...

XXXIX.

No one among the masters will take a sign identical to that of his colleague, nor similar to it, in order to avoid all the disorders that could arise, on the penalty of being deprived of the honors of the said Community, and a fine of two hundred pounds, half applicable in favor of the Community, and the rest to the Brotherhood, and of all costs, damages & interests.

XL.

They are also forbidden to undertake on each other for the market of weddings, feasts, banquets and other things associated with their art, under similar penalties.

XLI.

Similarly, they shall not use any Companions unless they see the consent of the Masters under whom they have remained, and are satisfied with [such use], on the penalty of being blamed in their General Assembly, which the said Jurors shall convene for this purpose, with the permission that they will seek to obtain in the usual manner, from the Prosecutor of His Majesty at the Châtelet.

§2.35.4 A Few Decades Later, Cooks and Caterers Lost Some of Their Privileges in Favor of Wine Merchants, but the Requirement to Keep Distinctive Signs Remained—1708

The advance of the ideas of economic liberalism started, hesitantly, to gain strength in the eighteenth century as a sort of an announcement of the upcoming French Revolution and its rationale of liberté *and* égalité. *Consequently, wine merchants were, albeit with limitations, to encroach on the business that until then was exclusive to cooks and caterers. Those merchants, nevertheless, could not adopt signs that might lead customers to identify them as cooks and caterers. The prestige of the profession was also starting to gain a certain dimension as the art and technique of cooking became items of fashion.*

Patent Letters for the Cooks and Caterers of the City of Paris

Confirming the Statutes of that Community

May 19, 1708

Louis, by the grace of God, King of France and Navarre. To all who see these present Letters, Greetings. The Wine Merchants of our good City and Suburbs of Paris, having shown us that the prohibitions which were made to them by the Statutes of the Master Cooks and Caterers of our City of Paris, from undertaking any weddings, feasts, banquets, meals and other things dependent on their Art, caused them considerable harm, and even hampered public freedom; We would have ordered by our Declaration of July 12, 1707, that the said Wine Merchants could provide drinks in their houses and cellars, provide tables, seats, tablecloths, napkins and meats, which they could roast on grills and on spits, in accordance with to the decision of our Parliament of Paris, of August 1, 1705, for those who come to take their meals in their houses, including to receive all wedding parties and all kinds of people indiscriminately, without nevertheless being allowed to have any signs of Caterers or of Cooks at their shops, meat windows, lodges or keep guest, and be considered as Cabaret keepers; ...

§2.35.5 The Guild of Caterers Defends in Court the Exclusivity of Their Profession (and of Their Signs) Against Those That Are Not Members of the Corporation—1730

The following text is a late expression of the corporatist regime, which granted the exclusivity of some professional activities to the members of the respective guilds. The exclusivity included the prohibition of the association of a member of the guild with non-members. The Revolution of 1789 would put an end to such a system, by extinguishing all corporations, as contrary to the ideal of economic and political freedom. Nevertheless, the acknowledgment of business identifiers as elements of differentiation would survive.

Judgment of the Court of Parliament, Rendered in favor of the Community of Master Caterers, against Antoine Jean, François Francois, Martin Caillou, Antoine de Larme, Leger de Ligny, Claude Robillard, Jacques Petit, Jean Jacquesson, & Michel Mesnard, all Master Roasters in Paris. Prohibiting these Master Roasters from associating and remaining in the same house with any Master Caterer.

June 21, 1730.

Our court, settling all matters, has rejected and rejects the appeals, orders that [the decision that has been appealed] will have its full and complete effect; condemns the mentioned Antoine-Jean, Jean-Baptiste Jacquesson, François, Georges Bataille,

Martin Caillou, & Simon Couteux, to a fine of twelve pounds; orders that the Statutes of the Community of the Master Caterers, the Letters Patent confirming the said Statutes, our Declaration of December twenty-fifth, one thousand seven hundred and four, registered in our Court, & the Decisions & Regulations concerning the Community of the Master Caterers, will be executed according to their form & content: Consequently, the mentioned de Larme, de Ligny, Robillard, Petit, Jacquesson & Mesnard are prohibited from contravening them and from associating with any master caterer, including from remaining in the same shop with any of the master caterers, from undertaking on the profession of the Master Caterers, and to put in their boards and signs any name or indication that relates to the profession of Caterer, on the penalty of a fine of three hundred pounds; [and] orders that those [boars and signs] that have been installed shall will be removed & destroyed; ...

§2.36 PERU AND CHILE DISPUTE THE RIGHT TO THE USE OF PISCO AS AN APPELLATION OF ORIGIN—1709 ONWARD

In respect of the protection of the word Roquefort *as an appellation of origin for cheese produced in a very specific place, we have seen that this type of business identifier is the only one that directly and immediately accords distinctiveness to a certain type of product, whose production and characteristics depend on the association between its making (or extraction) and its place of origin. The term* "Roquefort" *has, through the ages, acquired a certain reputation, particularly among its lovers, but even for those who do not appreciate it or do not know about it, it unequivocally indicates a place of origin. That term distinguishes all the cheeses that are produced in that particular place and in accordance with the rules set in the respective regulation, regardless of the individual persons or entities that make them. Individually, those persons and entities will be differentiated through trade names and trademarks, but the product that is common to all will be distinguished from other cheeses through its appellation (which can also be captured, although not as much effectively, through a certification mark).*

Things become more complicated when similar products come from different regions that have received the same geographical designation,[88] *referred to as "homonymous geographical indications." A few of those coincidences are notoriously linked to the migration of the producers of a certain article, who brought with them not only their traditional techniques and their knowledge but also the names of the places they have left. Several European appellations of origin can be found in countries where European*

88. In strict terms, appellations of origin and geographical indications are not the same. The main difference, according to Article 2(1) of the Geneva Act of the Lisbon Agreement on Appellations of Origin and Geographical Indications of 2015 is that geographical indications do not necessarily consist of the names of places, provided the terms in question express a geographical meaning (as a sort of a "secondary meaning" that has been acquired through continued use). Thus, the concept of geographical indication is broader than that of appellation of origin, which consists necessarily of the name of a place.

colons have found refuge decades, if not centuries, ago. This is the case for Rioja, which is shared by Spanish and Argentinian winemakers.[89] *Examples can also be found of two countries, like India and Pakistan, that share the same region, with the same characteristics of soil, sun, and rain, as is the case of Basmati rice (Basmati not being a geographical name, but having acquired a geographical dimension as a secondary meaning). So, sharing a geographical indication is not necessarily a matter of unfair competition.*

But the example of a geographical indication that follows—Pisco—may be a different story, depending on the reader's perspective. Pisco is unequivocally of Peruvian origin. Spanish migrants a few centuries ago took to a region in the South of Peru certain grapes and their know-how of making wine, and started producing wine and spirits. The beverage, as a matter of course, has been designated since the seventeenth century through the name of the port city from which it has been exported—Pisco.

However, in the second half of the nineteenth century, a Spanish entrepreneur who lived in neighboring Chile learned the techniques used by Peruvian producers of spirits designated as Pisco, imported those techniques to his own winery in Chile, and adopted the same designation. Soon, due to the introduction of a French variety of grapes, Chilean Pisco acquired great prestige and several winemakers in the North of that country started producing and commercializing it under the designation "Pisco" in association with individual trademarks (see Figure 16).

By contrast with Europe, in the nineteenth century, South American countries century had not yet realized the importance of geographical indications' legal dimension, and that explains why neither Peru nor Chile thought until recently of securing some legal means to assert property rights in the name Pisco. It is significant in this context the candid intervention of the Chilean delegate at the 1897 Diplomatic Conference for the Revision of the Paris Convention, admitting that Chilean winemakers were using the Pisco designation as if it were a generic name for some spirits they produced and that "There have never been any complaints against this use."

However, the matter has become more complex because Chile today does not challenge the distinctive properties of the term Pisco. On the contrary, Chile also claims its right to the use of the appellation Pisco and has adopted rules that define its use. So, instead of having two countries that dispute whether a geographical indication has fallen to genericism—as it happens with certain claims against the appellation Champagne (understood in some jurisdictions as a name for a technique of making wine[90]*)—we have two countries that claim its validity and, instead of accepting to share it, fight for their exclusive right to its use.*

89. But it is the Spanish appellation that appears on the database of WIPO's Lisbon System.
90. That is the case of Brazil, where a decision of the Supreme Federal Court of 1974 confirmed the opinion of a lower court in the sense that "For us, however, the word Champagne currently does not even constitute a designation of origin, but designates a characteristic type of wine, resulting from a special manufacturing process." Special Appeal no. 78,835/GB, unanimous opinion of the second branch of the Court, delivered by Minister Cordeiro Guerra. Given that this decision is final, the subsequent accession of Brazil to the WTO does not affect its validity within the country.

§2.36.1 A French Geographer Mentions the Geographical Origins of Pisco—1709

This text is an excerpt of a report on the Southern coast of South America, written in 1709 by a French geographer, Louis Feuillée, under the auspices of the King of France.

The countryside of *Pisco* is almost all filled with vines, which bear grapes in abundance, from which excellent wine is made. This city alone supplies Lima, and several other places. All the ships which leave from Callao, either for the North or for the South coast, take their provisions, wine and spirits from *Pisco*; some ships load it for Panama, which is then transported by land to Porto Bello, and from there to Cartagena. The air of *Pisco* is one of the best on the entire coast; the harvest is done there in the months of March and April; there all the species of fruits that we have in Europe are found, which have a wonderful taste; those which are specific to the country are in abundance; and we can safely say that *Pisco* is one of the most beautiful places on the entire coast of Peru.

§2.36.2 A Historical Dictionary of Chile Describes the Origins of the Chilean Pisco—1875

Alba pisco.—The industrialist from Paihuano, Elqui, Don Olegario Alba Rivera, who bought in 1868 the property that today bears the name of Bella Sombra, and which was the industrial cradle of Pisco Alba, went there, in 1875, to study the production of pisco.

That land was previously a mountain full of potholes and stones, which had to be leveled, cleaned and planted with vines. Once this work was done, at the cost of all kinds of sacrifices, ten years later, in 1878, the first production of Chilean pisco came onto the market, at least from that origin.

The product first began to be sold in the Coquimbo market, in 1882 it went to the Valparaíso market, from there it spread throughout all the towns of Chile and then along the Pacific coast until it appeared in the main wine stores in Europe.

In 1884 it was presented at the National Exhibition of Santiago and the jury awarded it the first prize; and then similar rewards followed in Liverpool (1889), in Barcelona (1882) and in Paris (1889).

Subsequently, Pisco Alba invaded the universal market and won honorary rewards in all the competitions it has entered.

...

The industry employs hundreds of workers, it has its own establishments and machinery in Elqui and Coquimbo and represents the joint effort and capital of three generations of progressive and farsighted men.

The founder of the Alba family in Elqui was the Spanish industrialist and merchant, Don Lucio Alba de Ochoa.

Figure 2.18 Top left: although Pisco Alba was the first to reach the Chilean market, the first trademark registered for Pisco in Chile (in 1882) corresponded to the spirit produced by a competitor. Top right: Chilean (left) and Peruvian (right) pisco side by side. The label of Chilean Pisco reads (below): "The authentic pisco of Chile," whereas the label of the Peruvian pisco claims "Pisco Puro" (pure pisco). An interesting difference between the two labels is that the word "pisco" is integrated into the Chilean trademark, as if it were an integral part of it, whereas the Peruvian label distinguishes clearly between the trademark (Biondi) and the geographical indication. And yet, in 1999, Chile passed a law establishing Pisco as a geographical indication (see §2.34.7).

§2.36.3 A Report Prepared by the Organization of the Universal Exhibition of Paris Speaks of Chilean Pisco and Commends Its Quality—1889

Viticulture

Wines.—Spirits.—Liqueurs.

Vines have been cultivated in the country for a long time. It was introduced by the Spaniards immediately after their arrival in this country; but Chilean viticulture has only gained real importance over the last quarter of a century, following the introduction of French grape varieties and modern cultivation methods.

Chile presents exceptionally favorable conditions for the wine industry, and this country is expected to quickly become a major producer of excellent wines of all kinds.

...

In the wine-growing regions of the North and the South, musky wines are distilled, which produces a special spirit called *Pisco*, which enjoys a certain reputation.

Ordinary wines are also distilled; but, in general, too imperfect processes are used to obtain the result that one could hope for. Chilean wines are quite rich in alcohol, and the white wine variety called Folle-Blanche (from which cognac is produced) is particularly remarkable. By extending the cultivation of this grape variety, which has great productivity, to Chile, we would soon have a serious basis for the manufacture of good quality spirits.

§2.36.4 At the Conference for the Revision of the Paris Convention, the Chilean Delegate Mentions the Use of the Designation Pisco by Winemakers in His Country as a Generic Rerm—1897

Mr. Waddington [delegate from Chile] explains that, in his country, the names of certain wine products are used in a generic sense... . Mr. Waddington cites a case which is of particular interest to his country. There is a region in Peru called Pisco, which produces an excellent spirit to which it has given its name. This spirit is also made in Chile, and we then generally add to the name of Pisco that of the Chilean locality where it was produced: we will say, for example, Pisco de Elqui, if the spirit comes from the place of this name. There have never been any complaints against this use. No word could replace the generic term Pisco. (9th session, 13th December 1897)

§2.36.5 A French Newspaper Reports on the Participation of Pisco Alba at the International Food and Hygiene Exhibition (Paris)—1906

The interesting aspect in this piece of news is that the reporter rightly mentions the name of the city—Pisco—that is considered to be the place of origin of the spirit, but does not precise that such city is located in Peru. This could lead to some confusion, readers being led to believe that either the town of Pisco is located in Chile or that Pisco Alba is produced in Peru.

At the International Food and Hygiene Exhibition (Paris, 1906)

Visit of the President of the Republic—South American Exhibitors—Distribution of rewards

...

Great success for the Olegario Alba house, one of the most important distillers in Chile, whose Pisco is expertly presented. Pisco is a kind of South American milestone and it has taken its name from a small village where it is produced in large quantities. Since we are talking about the Alba house, let us note this fact, which a cablegram pointed out to us a few days ago. It was announced that a counterfeiting of Pisco-Alba had been discovered in America. This counterfeiting had been practiced on a large scale for a long time and there has never been success in preventing it. It may have caused great harm to the Alba house, but it constitutes a most eloquent plea in favor of *Pisco*. Indeed, there is no counterfeiting of bad products or of those that are unknown to the public. Incidentally, Mr. Alba should be congratulated for the spirit of initiative that he has never stopped to demonstrate. He must be congratulated all the more since Mr. Alba, who could live on his income, due to his financial situation, has preferred to invest his capital in a large industrial company. He had already appeared at the food exhibition two years ago and won a gold medal.

§2.36.6 Peru Passes Legislation Concerning the Pisco Appellation—1932

Peru began to take legislative measures regarding Pisco and its denomination in 1932, but it was the Supreme Decree No. 001-91-ICTI/IND of January 16, 1991 that officially recognized Pisco as a Peruvian denomination of origin, designating the products obtained by the distillation of wines derived from the fermentation of fresh grapes, on the coast of the departments of Lima, Ica, Arequipa, Moquegua and the valleys of Locumba, Sama, and Caplina in the Department of Tacna. The website of the Parliament of Peru (< www2.congreso.gob.pe >) affirms that "the term 'Pisco' qualifies as an exclusively Peruvian appellation of origin."

Reminding what was said in the introductory note to the text concerning the early protection of geographical indications (see §2.5), the relevance of that sort of business identifier only appears, as a sort of paradox, when the article leaves its original local of production, and is sold in another region of the same country or is exported to other countries. Therefore, the effects of national laws dealing with the geographical definition and the requirements of a given geographical indication are limited to give evidence that the indication is protected by the country of origin. Under Article 24.9 of the TRIPS Agreement, that sort of proof may be required by another country.

[The following statute] contains provisions regarding the production and marketing of national alcoholic beverages.

Law No. 26426 of January 3, 1995

The President of the Republic

Whereas: The Democratic Constituent Congress has passed the following Law:

Article 1.- That the Supreme Decrees Nos. 100 of September 26, 1932 and 001-91-ICTI/IND of January 16, 1991, be enforceable as Laws.

Article 2.- The Executive Branch is charged with ensuring that, through all the means provided by International Law, it obtains the prevalence and definitive recognition of what is stipulated in the preceding article, coordinating for this purpose the actions to be carried out with the entities representing the producers and with the Peruvian Wine Institute.

Article 3.- It is established that the Executive Branch shall enact within 60 days from the publication of this law, all the measures that are required to achieve the recovery and development of national wine production, including the affiliation of the Peruvian State to the International Organization of Vine and Wine—OIV, and prohibiting the entry into the country of beverages manufactured abroad that have the name Pisco or another that includes that word and providing for the other measures required to encourage the dissemination and consumption of that drink, especially in official and diplomatic uses.

...

§2.36.7 Chile Also Passes a Statute Regulating the Use of the Appellation Pisco—1999

Establishes the Regulation for the Appellation of Origin PISCO

Decree no. 521 of December 30, 1999

Article 1.—This regulation regulates the use of the appellation of origin pisco and the conditions, characteristics and modalities that must be met with respect to the raw material to be used, and the preparation and bottling of this product.

...

Article 3.—The protection granted by the appellation of origin pisco includes the right to the exclusive use of such designation to identify, distinguish and recognize said product, to the extent that the legal and regulatory provisions established in this regard are entirely and fully complied with. The protection, in accordance with the Marrakesh Agreement and article 10 bis of the Paris Convention (1967), also includes the right of interested parties to: (a) Oppose, in accordance with the rules of Law No. 19,039, the use of any name of a city, town, locality or village of the Regions of Atacama and Coquimbo, as a trademark or part of it, as a slogan or as an integral part of a label corresponding to Class 33 of the Trademark Classification, to distinguish any distilled alcoholic beverage derived from grapes other than pisco. (b) Prevent the use of other geographical indications that identify distilled alcoholic beverages derived from grapes or any of the distinctive signs of pisco in those beverages, which may lead the public to confuse them with the appellation of origin pisco, even when true origin of the product or the geographical indication is indicated or the geographical indication translated or accompanied by expressions such as "kind", "type", "style", "imitation" or other analogous ones is used. (c) Report, to the corresponding authority, as an act of unfair competition any indications or assertions whose use may mislead the public about the nature, method of production, characteristics or suitability for use of pisco.

...

Article 5.- In the production of pisco, only wine alcohol from the following grape varieties of the species Vitis vinifera L., planted in the pisco area, hereinafter, "pisco grapes", may be used:

...

Article 9.- The wine distillation process for the production of alcohol for Pisco must be done in discontinuous cycle stills.

Article 10.- Piscos must have a total volatile acid content of no more than 1.5 grams per liter and a minimum of impurities of 2.0 grams per liter at 100° Gay-Lussac at 20° C temperature and its content in sugars may not exceed 5 grams per liter. Its minimum alcohol contents will be as indicated below:

...

§2.36.8 Peru Registers the Appellation Pisco for Spirits (Liquors) under the Lisbon System—2005

As a Contracting Party to the Lisbon Agreement of 1956, Peru has registered Pisco. Following the Agreement, some countries have denied protection, generally as a result of bilateral agreements signed with Chile. Some other countries, after refusing protection, have changed their opinion and withdrew the refusal—eventually, after bilateral negotiations with Peru. The conclusion that one can extract from this imbroglio is that, ultimately, Pisco cannot count on protection other than a bilaterally acknowledged one.

(AO 865) PISCO

Basic Information

Number 865 Date19.05.2005 Publication N° 35 : 01/2006
Contracting Party of Origin PE (Peru)
Appellation of Origin PISCO
Good(s) Alcoholic beverage, Pisco is a liquor of grape, obtained by distilling fresh must of recently fermented grapes in accordance with traditional methods established in the production areas previously recognized and classified as such in the normative rules contained in the Peruvian Technical Standard 211-011:2002

Geographical Area The geographical area recognized for the production of Pisco is located in the coast of the Departments of Lima, Ica, Arequipa, Moquegua and the valleys of Locumba, Sama and Caplina in the Department of Tacna, all in Peru

Legal Basis National or regional registration. (Directorial Resolution No. 072087-DIPI of December 12, 1990, Register No. 1)

Beneficiaries, Natural Person or Legal Entity The titleholder of the appellation of origin is the Peruvian State. The Peruvian State is represented in this case by INDECOPI

Transaction History

Refusal of Protection CZ (Czech Republic)—03.07.2006 (PDF), FR (France)—07.07.2006 (PDF), IT (Italy)—07.07.2006 (PDF), HU (Hungary)—10.07.2006 (PDF), SK (Slovakia)—10.07.2006 (PDF), PT (Portugal)—13.07.2006 (PDF), IR (Iran (Islamic Republic of))—10.12.2007 (PDF)

Withdrawal of Refusal MX (Mexico)—24.10.2006 (Date of Refusal) 19.06.2006 (PDF), BG (Bulgaria)—02.05.2007 (Date of Refusal) 14.07.2006 (PDF), CR (Costa Rica)—31.05.2007 (Date of Refusal) 13.07.2006 (PDF)

Credits of Texts and Figures

Texts

Chapter One

§1.1. A.A.J. Liez, N.A. Dubois, and V. Verger (transl.), Histoire Romaine de Tite Live, vol. 15, Livre XXXIX, Ch. VI, at 223 (C.L.F. Panckoucke, 1832). Source : <gallica.bnf.fr>. Athenaeus of Naucratis (end of the 2nd, beginning of the 3rd century AD), The Deipnosophists, or Banquet of the Learned, Book XII, chapters 17 and 20 (excerpts), [Transl. C.D. Yonge]. Source: <archive.org>. Almanach Astrologique, 39th year, 1886, at 123-124. Source: <gallica.bnf.fr>. John Bostock and H.T. Riley (transl.), The Natural History of Pliny, vol. 2, at 403, 468, 499 (Henry G. Bohn, 1855). Source: Google Books, 9–13

§1.2. G.B. Depping, Règlements sur les Arts et Métiers de Paris, Rédigés au XIIIe Siècle, et Connus sous le Nom du Libre des Métiers d'Etienne Boileau, at 175, 176, 177-178 (Imprimerie de Crapelet, 1837). Source: <gallica.BnF.fr>, 13–14

§1.3. A.E. Bland *et alii*, English Economic History—Select Documents, at 147-148 (G. Bell & Sons, Ltd, 1921). Source: <archive.org>, 14–15

§1.4. Nicolás García Tapía, *Pedro Azlor, Médico de Isabel la Católica, y su Patente de Invención*. Source: <asclepio.revistas.csic.es>, 15–16

§1.5. Isambert, Decrusy et Armet, Recueil Général des Anciennes Lois Françaises, depuis l'an 420 jusqu'à la Révolution de 1789, vol. 11, 1483—1514, at 557, 559 (Belin-Leprieur, 1827). Source: <gallica.BnF.fr>, 17

§1.6. Giulio Mandich, *Venetian Patents (1450-1550)*, 30 Journal of the Patent Office Society 166, 219 (March 1948). Roberto Beveglieri, Inventori Stranieri a Venezia (1474-1788)—Importazione di Tecnologia e Circolazione di Tecnici Artigiani Inventorio—Repertorio, at 86-87 (IVSLA, 1995), 17–18

§1.7. Nicolás García Tapía, Patentes de Invención Españolas en el Siglo de Oro, at 41 (Oficina Española de Patentes y Marcas, 1991), 18–19

§1.8. Calendar of the Patent Rolls, Philip and Mary, vol. 4, 1557-1558, at 132-133 (H.M.'s Stationery Office, 1939). Source: <babel.hathitrust.org>). Calendar of the Patent Rolls, Elizabeth, vol. 1, 1558-1560, at 39 (H.M.'s Stationery Office, 1939). Source: < babel.hathitrust.org >), 19–20

§1.9. Rev. Joseph Stevenson (edit.), Calendar of State Papers, Foreign Series, of the Reign of Elizabeth, 1559-1560, at 132 (Longman, Green, Longman, Roberts, & Green, 1865). Source: Google Books, 20

§1.10. Source: Google Books, 21–23

§1.11. Recueil d'Arrêts, Ordonnances, Statuts et Reglemens, Concernant la Communauté des Maîtres Queulx, Cuisniers, Traiteurs de la Ville, Faubourgs et Banlieue de Paris ; Fait en Octobre 1761, par les soins, la diligence & pendant la Comptabilité du Sieur Marcille & des Sieurs Rourad, LePretre & Coquin, Jurés en Charge, at 11 (Imprimerie Le Breton, 1761). Source: < gallica.BnF.fr > , 24

§1.12. Isambert, Taillandier and Decrusy, Recueil Général des Anciennes Lois Françaises, depuis l'an 420 jusqu'à la Révolution de 1789, vol. 16, mai 1610—mai 1643, at 223, 264-5 (Belin-Leprieur, 1829). Source: < gallica.BnF.fr > , 24–26

§1.13. Patents for Inventions—Abridgements of Specifications relating to Cooking, Bread-Making, and the Preparation of Confectionery, at 3-4, 9, 15-16, 47, 56-57, 237 (George E. Eyre and William Spottiswoode, 1873); Abridgements of Specifications relating to Preservation of Food, at 1, 2 (George E. Eyre and William Spottiswoode, 1857), 26–28

§1.14. House of Commons Journal Volume 6: 4 February 1650, in *Journal of the House of Commons: Volume 6, 1648-1651*, at 357 (London, 1802), Source: British History Online, < www.british-history.ac.uk/commons-jrnl/vol6/p357 > [accessed 27 April 2023]. C.H. Forth and R.S. Rait (colls. and edits.), Acts and Ordinances of the Interregnum, 1642-1660, vol. 2, at 357, 389, 492-494 (His Majesty's Stationery Office, 1911). Source: < babel.hathitrust.org > , 29–31

§1.15. Source: < gallica.bnf.fr > , 31–33

§1.16. Alfred Franklin, La Vie Privée d'Autrefois—Arts et Métiers—Modes, Mœurs, Usages des Parisiens du XIIIe au XVIIIe Siècle—Le Café, le Thé & le Chocolat, at 164-166 (Plon, 1893). Source : < gallica.bnf.fr > , 33–34

§1.17. G.B. Depping, Correspondance Administrative sous le Règne de Louis XIV, vol. 3, at 548-9 (Imprimerie Nationale, 1852). Source: < gallica.bnf.fr > , 34–35

§1.18. Alfred Franklin, La Vie Privée d'Autrefois—Arts et Métiers—Modes, Moeurs, Usages des Parisiens du XIIe au XVIIIe Siècle—Le Café, Le Thé & Le Chocolat, at 299, 300 (E. Plon, Nourrit et Cie., 1893). Source: < gallica.bnf.fr > , 36

§1.19. Pierre Clément, Lettres, Instructions et Mémoires de Colbert, vol. 2, at 694-695 (Imprimerie Impériale, 1863). Source: < gallica.bnf.fr > , 36

§1.20. Denys Papin, A New Digester or New Engine for Softning Bones, Containing the Description of its Make and life in these Particulars: Viz. Cookery, Voyages at Sea, Confectionary, Making of Drinks, Chymistry, and Dying. With An Account of the Price a good big Engine will cost, and of the Profit it will afford, at 1-2, 51-52 (J.M., 1681). Source: Google Books. Michel Lévy, Traité d'Hygiène Publique et Privée, vol. 2, at 89-90 (2nd ed., J.-B. Baillière, 1850). Source: < gallica.bnf.fr > , 37–40

§1.21. Source: < digitarq.arquivos.pt > , 40–41

§1.22. Statuts, Ordonnances et Règlements de la Communauté des Maîtres Rôtisseurs de la Ville, Fauxbourgs et Banlieue de Paris, du mois de Juin de 1744, at 20 (Veuve Delatour, 1747). Source: < gallica.bnf.fr >, 41–42

§1.23. William Carpmael, Law Reports of Patent Cases, vol. 1, at 664 et seqs. (A. Macintosh, 1843). Source: < archive.org >, 42–44

§1.24. Nicolas Appert, Le Livre de tous les ménages ou L'Art de Conserver, pendant plusieurs années, toutes les substances animales et végétales (Patris & Cie., 1810). Source: < gallica.bnf.fr >. The English translation of the 2nd edition of Appert's book was published in 1812. Source: < gutenberg.org >. Patents for Inventions—Abridgments of Specifications relating to Preservation of Food, at 4 (George E. Eyre and William Spottiswoode, 1857). Specifications of Augustus de Heine. Preserving Animal and Vegetable Food. (George E. Eyre and William Spottiswoode, 1855). Source: < archive.org >, 44–50

§1.25. Patents for Inventions—Abridgments of Specifications relating to Cooking, Bread-making, and the Preparation of Confectionery, AD 1634-1866, at 47, 56, 229, 237 (George E. Eyre and William Spottiswoode, 1873), 50–52

§1.26. L'Art de la Cuisine Française au dix-neuvième siècle (author's edition, 1833). Le Patissier National Parisien ou Traité Élémentaire et Pratique de la Patisserie Ancienne et Moderne, Suivi d'Observations Utiles au Progrès de cet Art, vol. 2 (2nd ed., Garnier Frères, w.d.), 52–54

§1.27. Collecção das Leis do Império do Brazil, 1833, Parte Segunda, at 108 (Typographia Nacional, 1873). Collecção das Leis do Império do Brazil, 1852, Parte Segunda, at 42 (Typographia Nacional, 1853). Collecção das Leis do Império do Brazil, 1857, Parte Segunda, at 2 (Typographia Nacional, 1857). Collecção das Leis do Império do Brazil, 1855, Parte Segunda, at 35 (Typographia Nacional, 1856). Collecção das Leis do Império do Brazil, 1864, Parte II, at 99 (Typographia Nacional, 1864). Source: < www2.camara.leg.br >. O Auxiliador da Indústria Nacional: ou Colecção de Memórias e Notícias Interessantes (1833 a 1896), ano 1854, 2nd ed., at 254, 375. Source: < memoria.bn.br >, 54–60

§1.28. William Carpmael, Law Reports of Patent Cases, vol. 1, at 180 *et seqs.* (A. Macintosh, 1843). Source: < archive.org >, 60–62

§1.29. Holland Thompson, The Age of Invention—A Chronicle of Mechanical Conquest, at 115-117 (Yale University Press, 1921). Journal of the Franklin Institute, vol. 8, no. 3, September 1831, at 195. Source: < archive.org >. Source: < uspto.gov >. Journal of the Franklin Institute, vol. 14, no. 1, July 1834, at 37-38. Source: < archive.org >. Great Exhibition of the Works of Industry of all Nations, 1851—Official Descriptive and Illustrated Catalogue, Supplementary Volume, at 1530, 1531 (W. Clowes and Sons, 1851). Source: < archive.org >. Source: www.justia.com, 63–69

§1.30. James Manning and T.C. Granger, Cases Argued and Determined in the Court of Common Pleas, vol. 3, at 709 *et seq.* (Saunders and Benning, 1843). Source: Google Books, 69–73

§1.31. The English Reports, vol. CXVI, King's Bench Division, at 35 (William Green & Sons, 1911), 73–74

§1.32. Source: Google Patents. Library of Congress, www.loc.gov/item/2018645040/, 74–75

§1.33. Source: <bases-brevets19e.inpi.fr/>. Jules Claretie, *Échos de Paris*, FIGARO, at 6, November 25, 1865. PRESSE SCIENTIFIQUE DES DEUX MONDES, REVUE UNIVERSELLE DU MOUVEMENT DES SCIENCES, DE LA PHILOSOPHIE, DES BEAUX-ARTS, ET DE L'INDUSTRIE, year 865, vol. 2, July-December, at 628-629 (1865). Source : <gallica.bnf.fr>, 75–78

§1.34. Benjamin Vaughan Abbott, THE PATENT LAWS OF ALL NATIONS, vol. 1, at 15-16, 205, 347, 427 (Charles R. Brodix, 1886) Source: <archive.org>. DIÁRIO DO GOVERNO, January 3, 1853, at 18. Source: <digigov.cepese.pt>, 78–82

§1.35. EXHIBITION OF THE WORKS OF INDUSTRY OF ALL NATIONS, 1851—REPORTS BY THE JURIES ON THE SUBJECTS IN THE THIRTY CLASSES INTO WHICH THE EXHIBITION WAS DIVIDED, at 65 (William Clowes & Sons, 1852). Source: <archive.org>. Bennett Woodcroft, CHRONOLOGICAL INDEX OF PATENTS APPLIED FOR AND PATENTS GRANTED, FROM OCTOBER 1, 1852 TO DECEMBER 31, 1853, at 106 (Great Seal Patent Office, 1860). ABRIDGEMENTS OF SPECIFICATIONS RELATING TO PRESERVATION OF FOOD, at 30-31 (George E. Eyre and William Spottiswoode, 1857). Source: <archive.org>, 82–83

§1.36. BULLETIN DES LOIS DE L'EMPIRE FRANÇAIS, 11TH SERIES, vol. 23, at 590, 603, 605, 611, 642 (Imprimerie Impériale, 1864). Source : <archive.org>, 84–85

§1.37. Baron Brisse, LES 366 RECETTES DU BARON BRISSE, AVEC 1200 RECETTES, at XI (E. Donnaud, 1868). Source: <gallica.bnf.fr>, 85–86

§1.38. Proceedings of the American Academy of Arts and Sciences, New Series, Vol. XX, Whole Series, VOL. XXVIII, From May, 1892, to May, 1893, at 343 (Univ. Press, John Wilson & Son, 1893). Source: Google Books. Google Patents. R.M. Clapp, THE LAW IN PATENTS AND DECISIONS OF THE COURTS IN PATENT CASES, at 19-22 (publ. by the author, 1885) Source: <babel.hathitrust.org>. William Edgar Simonds, A DIGEST OF PATENT CASES: EMBRACING ALL PATENT CASES, DECIDED IN THE FEDERAL AND STATE COURTS FROM THE FOUNDATION OF THE GOVERNMENT, FROM 1789 TO 1888, at 342 (1888). Source: <babel.hathitrust.org>, 86–90

§1.39. Source: <worldwide.espacenet.com>. CULINARY REVIEW—THE CHEF'S NATIONAL MAGAZINE, August 1942, at 10. Source: <gallica.bnf.fr>, 90–92

§1.40. Source: <uspto.gov>. THE TRADE-MARK REPORTER, January 1921, No. 1, vol. 11, at 19, 33, 92–96

§1.41. Source: <uspto.gov>, 97–98

§1.42. LES BELLES IMAGES, no. 1140, 23rd year, July 22, 1926, Paris. Source: <gallica-.bnf.fr>, 98–100

§1.43. LA PROPRIÉTE INDUSTRIELLE, Organe Mensuel du Bureau International pour la Protection de la Propriété Industrielle, à Berne, May 31, 1922, at 70-71, March 31, 1923, at 28-29, June 30, 1923, at 92. Source : <gallica.bnf.fr>. LYON-HORTICOLE, REVUE MENSUELLE D'HORTICULTURE, Juillet 1921, at 83-84. HEARINGS BEFORE THE SUBCOMMITTEE ON PATENTS, TRADEMARKS, AND COPYRIGHTS OF THE COMMITTEE ON THE JUDICIARY, UNITED STATES SENATE, Ninetieth Congress, First Session, May 17 and 18, 1967, at 648 et seq. (U.S. Government Printing Office, 1968). LA COOPÉRATION INTERNATIONALE, publication of the International Committee for International Cooperation, League of Nations, 1930, at 316-317. Source: <gallica.bnf.fr>. ACTES DES CONFÉRENCES INTERNATIONALES POUR LA PROTECTION DES OBTENTIONS

Végétales, at 13-14 (UPOV, 1974). Source : < www.upov.int >. Source: < supreme.justia.com >. Source : < casetext.com >, 100–124

§1.44. Source: < uspto.gov. > Source: < law.justia.com >, 124–132

§1.45. Source: < www.commonlii.org/in/legis/cen/num_act/pa1970109/ >. Source: < www.planalto.gov.br >, 132–134

§1.46. Source: < www.justia.com >, 134–136

§1.47. Source: < www.justia.com >, 136–141

§1.48. Source: < www.inpi.gov.br >. Source: < < www2.canaljudicial.com.br/home/products_pdf_descs/desc_1567015713000_443615.pdf > (accessed on October 31, 2023). >. Source: < grupodocedoce.com.br/quem-somos > (accessed on October, 31, 2023), 142–145

§1.49. European Group on Ethics and Science and New Technologies to the European Commission, Opinion on Ethical Aspects of Patenting Inventions Involving Human Stem Cells—Opinion No. 16, 7 May 2002, at 105 (Office for Official Publications of the European Communities, 2002). Source: < op.europa.eu >, 145–146

§1.50. Source: < www.uspto.gov >, 147–148

§1.51. Source: Google Patents, 148–153

§1.52. Source: < www.nasa.gov/feature/deep-space-food-challenge/ and < www.nasa.gov/solve/deep_space_food_challenge_phase2 >, 153–155

Chapter 2

Section 1

§2.1. William J. Murname, Texts from the Amarna Period in Egypt, at 95 (Scholars Press, 1995). Ilias Arnaoutoglou, Ancient Greek Laws—A Sourcebook, at 38-9 (Rutledge, 1998). Robert Étienne, Pompéi, at 428 (Hachette, 1998). John Bostock and H. T. Riley (transl.), The Natural History of Pliny, vol. 3, at 247-248 (Henry G. Bohn, 1855). Source: < archive.org >. Saboureux de la Bonnetrie, Traduction d'Anciens Ouvrages Latins relatifs à l'Agriculture et à la Médicine Vétérinaire, vol. 1 Contenant l'Economie Rurale de Caton, at 133-134 (P. Fr. Didot, le jeune, 1771). Source: < gallica.bnf.fr >., 157–163

§2.2. Walter C.A. Ker, Martial Epigrams, vol. II, at 403 (William Heinemann, 1920). John Bostock and H.T. Riley (transl.), The Natural History of Pliny, vol. 3, at 255 (Henry G. Bohn, 1855). Source: < archive.org >, 164

§2.3. Jourdan, Decrusy and Isambert, Recueil Général des Anciennes Lois Françaises, depuis l'an 420, jusqu'à la Révolution de 1789, 1438-1483, at 529 *et seq.* (Belin-Leprieur, 1825). Source: < gallica.bnf.fr >, 165–166

§2.4. Augustin Thierry, Recueil des Monuments Inédits de l'Histoire du Tiers État, vol. 3, at 118, 126 (Firmin Didot Frères, 1856). Source: < gallica.BnF.fr >, 167

§2.5. *Edict et Declaration du Roy, pour la Vente en Heredité, des Officiers de Jaulgeurs, Mesureurs, & Visiteurs de tonneaux, bariques, & autres vaisseaux à mettre vin, cidre, bière, verjus, vinaigre, huille, & autres bruvages & autres liqueurs de la province de Normandie* (Martin le Mesgissier, 1608). Source : < gallica.BnF.fr >, 167–168

§2.6. Pierre Jacques Brillon, Dictionnaire des Arrêts ou Jurisprudence Universelle des Parlements de France et Autres Tribunaux, vol. 2, at 71 (Guillaume Cavelier, 1711). Source: <archive.org.>, 168

§2.7. Gabriel Du Pineau, *Diverses Questions, Consultations et Dissertations, in* Coûtumes du Pays et Duché d'Anjou, at 143-144 (Charles Osmont, 1698). Source : <gallica.bnf.fr>, 168–172

§2.8. Recueil des Statuts, Arrêts, Sentences et Règlements de la Communauté des Maîtres Distillateurs, Marchands d'Eau-Vive & de toutes Sortes de Liqueurs, de la Ville & Fauxbourgs de Paris, at 62-64 (J. Chardon, 1740). Source: <gallica.BnF.fr>, 172–173

§2.9. Thomas Cooper, The Statutes at Large of South Carolina, vol. 2, at 157-9 (A.S. Johnston, 1837). Source: Google Books, 173–174

§2.10. Statuts et Reglements des Marchands Merciers-Grossiers, Jouailliers, Quincailliers, Epiciers, Apotiquaires Droguistes, Ciriers & Chandeliers de la Ville d'Abbeville du 4 Janvier 1711. Source: <gallica.BnF.fr>, 174–175

§2.11. Recueil des Statuts, Déclarations du Roi, Arrêts du Conseil, du Parlement, Cour des Aides, Sentences de Police, Election, et du Prévôt des Marchands de la Communauté des Maîtres Vinaigriers, Verjutiers, Moutardiers, Premiers Inventeurs, Distillateurs et Vendeurs d'Eau-de-Vie, et Esprit-de-Vin, en gros et en détail, de la Ville, Fauxbourgs et Banlieue de Paris, at 167 et seq. (Gissey, 1749). Source: <gallica.BnF.fr>, 176–177

§2.12. Recueil des Statuts, Arrêts, Sentences et Règlements de la Communauté des Maîtres Distillateurs, Marchands d'Eau-de-Vie & de toutes sortes de Liqueurs, de la Ville & Fauxbourgs de Paris, at 162-163 (J. Chardon, 1740). Source: <gallica-.bnf.fr>, 177–178

§2.13. Bulletin de la Société Française de l'Histoire de la Médecine, vol. 3, at 346 *et seq.* (Alphonse Picard et Fils, 1904). Source: <archive.org>, 178–180

§2.14. Denisart, Collection de Décisions Nouvelles et de Notions Relatives à la Jurisprudence, vol. 7, at 681 (Veuve Desaint, 1788). Source: <gallica.BnF.fr>, 180

§2.15. Recueil des Edits, Déclarations, Lettres-Patents, Arrêts et Règlements du Roi, Registrés en la Cour du Parlement de Normandie, depuis l'année 1754, jusqu'en l'année 1771, 2nd part, at 708, 714 (Richard Lallemant, 1774), 180–181

§2.16. The Weekly Reporter 1862-1863 (Eleventh Year), Containing Cases Decided in the Superior Courts of Equity and Law, vol. XI, at 745-746 (Ware and Grove, 1863). Public domain. Source: Google Books, 181–184

§2.17. Rowland Cox, Trade-Mark Cases, at 157-158 (The Riverside Press, 1881). Source: <archive.org>, 185

§2.18. Rowland Cox, A Manual of Trade-Mark Cases, Covering All the Cases Reported until the Year 1879; Together with Those of a Leading Character Decided since that Time, at 251-252, 298-9 (Houghton, Mifflin and Co., 1881). Source: <archive.org>. John Cutler (ed.), Reports of Patent, Designs, and Trade Mark Cases, vol. 14, at 720 et seq. (Darling and Son, §1897). Source: <archive.org>, 185–190

§2.19. Journal de Jurisprudence Commerciale et Maritime, vol. 78, 1901, at 166-167 (Bureau du Journal de Jurisprudence Commerciale et Maritime, 1901). Source : <gallica.bnf.fr>, 190–191

§2.20. John Cutler and Frank G. Underhay (edits.), Reports of Patent, Design, Trade Mark, and Other Cases, vol. 21, at 720 *et seq.*, and vol. 22, at 327 *et seq.* (Darling & Son, 1904, and 1905), 191–193

§2.21. Source: Google Patents. Source: <curia.europa.eu>, 193–205

§2.22. Source: <www.who.int/nutrition/publications/code_english.pdf>. Source: <extranet.who.int>, 205–211

§2.23. Source: www.justia.com, 211–222

§2.24. Source: www.justia.com, 222–228

§2.25. Source: <www.supreme.justia.com>, 228–230

§2.26. Source: <justice.ge.ch/apps/decis/fr/acjc/show/1631119>, 230–238

§2.27. Source: <www. app.darts-ip.com/darts-web/client/case-results.jsf>, 238–239

§2.29. The Statutes at Large from Magna Charta to the End of the Reign of King Henry the Sixth, vol. 1, at 28, 29, 186 (Mark Basket, 1783). Source: <archive.org>. Anciens et Nouveaux Statuts de la Ville et Cité de Bordeaus, at 170-171 (S. Millanges, 1612). Source: <selene.bordeaux.fr>. Bain, Ebenezer, Merchant and Craft Guilds—A History of the Aberdeen Incorporated Trades, at 224 (J.&J.P. Edmond & Spark, 1887). Source: <archive.org>. Isambert, Taillandier and Decrusy, Recueil Général des Anciennes Lois Françaises, depuis l'an 420, jusqu'à la Révolution de 1789, vol. 16, at 424, 427-428 (Belin-Leprieur, 1829). A.-V. Chapuis, Les Anciennes Corporations Dijonnaises—Règlements, Statuts et Ordonnances, at 48, 49, 50, 53 (J. Nourry, 1906). Source: <gallica.bnf.fr>. The Statutes at Large of Pennsylvania from 1682 to 1801, vol. 2, at 61 et seq. (Clarence M. Busch, 1896). Source: Google Books. Danby Pickering, The Statutes of the Realm from the Eighth to the Twelveth Year of Queen Anne, vol. 12, at 77-79 (Joseph Bentham, 1764). Source: Google Books. Statuts, Privilèges, Ordonnances et Règlements de la Communauté des Maistres Boulangers de la ville, fauxbourgs & banlieue de Paris, at 39-40, 83-84, 94, 100, 103 (Moreau, 1766). Source : <gallica.bnf.fr>. Recueil des Edits, Déclarations, Lettres-Patents, Arrêts et Règlements du Roi, Registrés en la Cour du Parlement de Normandie, depuis l'année 1754, jusqu'en l'année 1771, 2nd part, at 1224, 1225, 1315, 1317, 1319, 1321 (Richard Lallemant, 1774). Source : <gallica.bnf.fr>. Jourdan, Isambert, Decrusy, Recueil Général des Anciennes Lois Françaises, depuis l'an 420, jusqu'à la Révolution de 1789, du 3 Mars 1781 jusqu'au 1er Janvier 1785, at 269-270 (Belin-Leprieur, 1821-1833). Source: <gallica.BnF.fr>. Tableau des Boulangers de Paris pour l'exercice de l'an 1831, précédé des arrêtés. Ordonnances, décisions, délibérations et instructions conc ernant le commerce de la boulangerie de Paris, at 165-169 (Imprimerie de Lebègue, 1831). Source : <gallica.bnf.fr>, 242–253

§2.30. Augustin Thierry, Recueil des Monuments Inédits de l'Histoire du Tiers État, Région du Nord, vol. 1, at 377-78 (Imprimerie Impériale, 1870). Source: <gallica.bnf.fr>. Pierre Guenois *et alii*, La Nouvelle Conférence des Ordonnances et Edicts Royaux, vol. 2, at 1114, 1237, 1239 (Estienne Richer, 1642). Source: Google

Books. Gustave Fagniez, Etudes sur l'Industrie et la Classe Industrielle à Paris au XIIIème et XIVème Siècles, at 387-388 (Slatkine Reprints, 1975). Source: <gallica.Bn.fr>. Fagniez, Gustave, Documents relatifs à l'histoire de l'industrie du commerce en France, vol. 2, 14th and 15th centuries, at 181 (Alphonse Picard et Fils, 1900). Source: <gallica.BnF. fr>. The statutes of the realm: Printed by command of his majesty King George the Third [Edited by Alexander Luders and others]., v.4 pt.2, at 1242, 1244-5. Source, <babel.hathitrust.org>. Ch. Ouin-Lacroix, Histoires des anciennes corporations d'arts et métiers et des Confréries Religieuses de la Capitale de la Normandie, at 607, 610 (Lecointe Frères, 1850). Source: <gallica.BnF.fr>. Camille Pagé, La Coutellerie depuis l'Origine jusqu'à nos Jours, vol. 1, at 117, 119 (Imprimerie Rivière, 1896). Source: <gallica.BnF.fr>, 253–261

§2.31. Jourdan, Decrusy and Isambert, Recueil Général des Anciennes Lois Françaises, depuis l'an 420, jusqu'à la Révolution de 1789, 1401-1457, at 427, 438, 439, 440, 454, 456 (Belin-Leprieur, 1825). Source: <gallica.bnf.fr>. Decrusy, Isambert, and Jourdan, Recueil Général des Anciennes Lois Françaises, depuis l'an 420, jusqu'à la Révolution de 1789, 1327-1357, at 574, 585 (Belin-Leprieur, 1821-1833). Source: <gallica.BnF.fr>. Anciens et Nouveaux Statuts de la Ville et Cité de Bordeaus, at 190-193, 196-197, 199 (S. Millanges, 1612). Source: <selene.bordeaux.fr>. Antoine Mornac, In Senatu Parisiensi Patroni Observaciones, vol. 4, at 384 (Montalant, 1721). Source: <gallica.BnF.fr>. Colecção das Leis, Decretos, e Alvarás, Que Comprehende o Feliz Reinado DelRei Fidelíssimo D. José I Nosso Senhor, vol. I (A.R. Galhardo, 1797). Source: <purl.pt/33988/2/>, 261–268

§2.32. Jean Loup, *L'industrie lainière en Languedoc, in* Recueil de l'Académie de Législation, fondée à Toulouse en 1851, vol. 27, at 23 (Imprimerie F. Boisseau, 1943). Source : <gallica.bnf.fr>. Bulletin des Lois de la République Française, vols. 37 and 70, at 621 and at 356 (Imprimerie Nationale, 1889, 1905). Source : <gallica.bnf.fr>. Félix Delobre, Table Décenniale du Journal de Jurisprudence Commerciale et Maritime, 1891-1900, 254 (Imprimerie Marseillaise, 1901). Georges Maillard *et alii*, Annales de la Propriété Industrielle, Artistique et Littéraire, vol. 48, at 344 *et seq.*, vol. 51, at 88, vol. 65, at 193-195 (Arthur Rousseau, 1902, 1905, 1923). Source : <gallica.bnf.fr> Annales de la Propriété Industrielle, Artistique et Littéraire, vol. 51, at 88 (M. Arthur Rousseau, 1905). Source : <gallica.bnf.fr>. Georges Maillard *et alii*, Annales de la Propriété Industrielle, Artistique et Littéraire, vol. 65, at 193-195 (1923). Source : <gallica.bnf.fr>. Dalloz, Jurisprudence Générale, Table des Matières des Trois Premières et Cinquième Parties du Recueil Périodique, Année 1922, at 48 (Jurisprudence Générale Dalloz, 1922). Source : <gallica.bnf.fr>. Albert Rens, Lois et Décrets d'Interêt Général, vol. 15, nrs. 8-9, Aug-Sept 1925, at 280-281 (1925). Source : <gallica.bnf.fr>. République Française, Bulletin Officiel, Concurrence, Consommation, Répression des Fraudes, 15 Sept 2008, at 678 et seq. Source : <gallica.bnf.fr>, 268–276

§2.33. Ch. Ouin-Lacroix, Histoire des Anciennes Corporations d'Arts et Métiers et des Confréries Religieuses de la Capitale de la Normandie, at 579, 580 (Lecointe

Frères, 1850). René de Lespinasse, Les Métiers et Corporations de la Ville de Paris, I, XIVe-XVIIIe Siècle, Ordonnances Générales—Métiers de l'Alimentation, at 620, 622 (Imprimerie Nationale, 1886). Source: <gallica.bnf.fr>. Articles Contenant les Statuts et Ordonnances des Maîtres Jurés Brasseurs de Bière de la Ville de Paris. Source: <gallica.bnf.fr>, 276–278

§2.34. Isambert, Decrusy, and Taillandier, Recueil Général des Anciennes Lois Françaises, depuis l'an 420, jusqu'à la Révolution de 1789, vol. 14, 1st Part—July 1559-May 1574, at 320, 323 (Belin-Leprieur, 1829). Source: <gallica.BnF.fr>. Joseph Garnier, Analecta Divionensia—Documents Inédits pour Servir à l'Histoire de France et Particulièrement a Celle de Bourgogne, Correspondance de la Mairie de Dijon, vol. 2, at 113-115 (J.-E. Rabutot, 1870). Source: <gallica-.BnF.fr>. Louis Blancard (org.), Inventaire-Sommaire des Archives Départementales antérieures à 1790—Archives Civiles, Série C (nos. 986 à 2175)—États de Provence, vol. 2, at 334 (J. Cayer, 1892). Source: <gallica.bnf.fr>. *Communication de M. Adrien Blanchet sur un point d'histoire concernant le passage des Peintres*, Ville de Paris, 1925, Commission du Vieux Paris, Séance du samedi 38 février 1925, no 2, at 23-25 (Imprimerie municipale, Hôtel de Ville, 1925). Michel du Chemin, Journal des Principales Audiences du Parlement, vol. 7, supplem., at 107 (Legras, 1754). Source: Google Books. Archives Municipales du Havre BB21. <avenio.lehavre.fr/4DCGI/Web_VoirLaNotice/03_06/BB21/ILUMP28962>. Edme de la Poix de Freminville, Dictionnaire ou Traité de la Police Générale des Villes, Bourgs, Paroisses, et Seigneuries de la Campagne, at 289-290 (Associés au Privilège des Ouvrages de l'Auteur, 1778), 278–285

§2.35. Recueil d'Arrêts, Ordonnances, Statuts et Règlements, concernant la Communauté des Maîtres Queulx Cuisiniers-Traiteurs de la Ville, Fauxbourgs et Banlieue de Paris, Fait en Octobre 1761, par les soins, la diligence & pendant la Comptabilité du Sieur Marcille, & des Sieurs Rouard, Lepretre et Coquin, Jurés en Charge, at 11 (Imprimerie Le Breton, 1761). Source: <gallica.BnF.fr>. René de Lespinasse, Les Métiers et Corporations de la Ville de Paris, I, XIVe-XVIIIe Siècle, Ordonnances Générales—Métiers de l'Alimentation, at 312 (Imprimerie Nationale, 1886). Source: <gallica.BnF.fr>, 285–289

§2.36. Louis Feuillée, Journal des Observations Physiques, Mathématiques et Botaniques, faites par l'Ordre du Roy sur les Côtes Orientales de l'Amérique Méridionale, & dans les Indes Occidentales, depuis l'année 1707 jusques en 1712, vol. 1, at 394 (Pierre Giffart, 1714). Source: <gallica.bnf.fr>. Virgilio Figueroa, Dicionário Histórico y Biográfico de Chile—1800-1925, at 250 (La Ilustracion, 1925). Source: <www.memoriachilena.gob.cl>. Alfred Picard (org.), Louis Grandeau (rapp.), Exposition Universelle Internationale de 1889 à Paris, Rapports du Jury International at 199, 200-201 (Imprimerie Nationale, 1892). Source : <gallica.bnf.fr>. Union Internationale pour la Protection de la Propriété Industrielle, Actes de la Conférence Réunie à Bruxelles du 1er au 14 Décembre 1897 et du 11 au 14 Décembre 1900, at 300, 301 (Bureau International de l'Union, 1901). Source : <gallica.bnf.fr>. La Petite Presse—Journal du Soir, Politique, Quotidien, April 30, 1906, at 2. Source : <gallica.bnf.fr>. Source : <www.gob

.pe>. Source: <www.leychile.cl/N?i=169561&f=2009-04-13&p=>. Source: www.wipo.int, 289–297

Figures

Chapter One

Figure 1. © NPdC, 2022, 13
Figure 2. Source: <gallica.bnf.fr>, 23
Figure 3. Source: <gallica.BnF.fr>, 33
Figure 4. Denys Papin, A New Digester or New Engine for Softning Bones, Containing the Description of its Make and life in these Particulars: Viz. Cookery, Voyages at Sea, Confectionary, Making of Drinks, Chymistry, and Dying. With An Account of the Price a good big Engine will cost, and of the Profit it will afford, at 1-2, 51-52 (J.M., 1681). Source: Google Books, 40
Figure 5. Source: <breweryhistory.com/wiki> (accessed on July 9, 2023), 44
Figure 6. Appert, Le Livre de Tous les Ménages, ou l'Art de Conserver, Pendant Plusieurs Années touts les Substances Animales et Végétales (Patris & Cie., 1820). Source: <gallica.bnf.fr>, 47
Figure 7. *Source*: <archive.org>, 50
Figure 8. *Source*: <gallica.bnf.fr>, 53
Figure 9. *Source*: <gallica.bnf.fr>, 54
Figure 10. Exhibition of the Works of Industry of all Nations, 1851—Reports by the Juries on the Subjects in the Thirty Classes into which the Exhibition was Divided, plate 437 (William Clowes & Sons, 1852). Source: <archive.org>, 69
Figure 11. Left: source: <uspto.gov>. Right: source: Library of Congress, 75
Figure 12. Source: <gallica.bnf.fr>, 78
Figure 13. Alexis Soyer, The Modern Housewife or Ménagère, Comprising nearly One Thousand Receipts for the Economic and Judicious Preparation for Every Meal of the Day, and Those for the Sick and Nursery Room, with Minute Directions for Family Management in all its Branches, at 445, 447 (Simpkin & Marshall, & Co., 1849). Source: Google Books. (September 9, 2023), 83
Figure 14. Good Housekeeping, *For the Homes of the World*, a semi-monthly magazine published in New York, NY, Vol. 1, no. 2, May 30, 1885, at ii. Source: <archive.org>. Rhode Island Picture Post Cards. Source: <thesaltysailor.com/rhodeisland-philatelic/rhodeisland/postcard180.htm>. (September 10, 2023), 90
Figure 15. Source: Canadian Patent Office. Culinary Review—The Chef's National Magazine, August 1942, at 10 (New York, NY, 1942), 92
Figure 16. Source: www.firstversions.com, 96
Figure 17. Source: <uspto.gov.>, 98
Figure 18. *Histoire d'Assoub, le Pâtissier*, par Asy, Les Belles Images, 22 July 1926, Paris. Source: <gallica.bnf.fr>, 100
Figure 19. Source: www.inpi.gov.br, 143
Figure 20. Source: Google Patents, 150
Figure 21. Source: Google Patents, 151

Figure 22. Source: Google Patents., 152
Figure 23. Source: < www.deepspacefoodchallenge.org > , 155

Chapter Two

Figure 1. © NPdC 2018 and 2023. Source: < commons.wikimedia.org > . Source: < www.pompeiiinpictures.com/pompeiiinpictures/R1/1%2011%2011 > . Thomas H. Dyer, Pompeii—Its History, Buildings, and Antiquities, at 84, 85 (2nd ed., Scribner, Welford, & Co., 1870). Source: < archive.org > , 162–163
Figure 2. © Trustees of the British Museum. From a facsimile edition by Konrad Miller, 1887/1888. Source: < commons.wikimedia.org > , 165
Figure 3. J.-B. Bouillet, Histoire des Communautés des Arts et Métiers de l'Auvergne, plate no. 7 (Paul Hubler, 1857). Source : < gallica.bnf.fr > , 166
Figure 4. Source: < gallica.bnf.fr > , 184
Figure 5. John Cutler (ed.), Reports of Patent, Designs, and Trade Mark Cases, vol. 14, at 720 et seq. (Darling and Son, 1897). Source: < archive.org > , 190
Figure 6. Source: www.belfastentries.com/stories/edwards-desiccated-foods/, 193
Figure 7. Source: Google Patents. Source: www.uspto.gov, 196
Figures 8 and 9. Source: < www.wipo.int > and Google Images, 210, 211
Figure 10. © NPdC 2023, 238
Figures 11 and 12. (c) NPdC 2017 and 2023, 241, 242
Figure 13. © NPdC 2023, 244
Figure 14. Source: POP: la base ouverte du patrimoine, www.pop.culture.gouv.fr, 254
Figure 15. Extracted from E. Marre, Le Roquefort, at 216 (E. Carrère, 1906). Source : < gallica.bnf.fr > , 270
Figure 16. © NPdC 2023, 274
Figure 17. The Comedies of Terence, 1400-1500. Source: < gallica.bnf.fr > , 280
Figure 18. INAPI, Historia Gráfica de la Propiedad Industrial em Chile—2010, at 33 (INAPI, 2010). © NPdC 2023, 292

Index

www.ingramcontent.com/pod-product-compliance
Lightning Source LLC
Chambersburg PA
CBHW071239230926
51849CB00001B/163
* 9 7 8 9 4 0 3 5 1 1 3 7 5 *